Thy Kingdom Come

Psychoanalytic Perspectives on the Messiah and the Millennium

W.W. Meissner, S.J., M.D.

Sheed & Ward
Kansas City

Sheed & Ward™ is a service of The National Catholic Reporter Publishing Company.

———————————————◆———————————————

Library of Congress Cataloguing-in-Publication Data

Meissner, W. W. (William W.), 1931-
    Thy kingdom come: psychoanalytic perspectives on the Messiah and the millennium / W.W. Meissner.
      p. cm.
    Includes bibliographical references and index.
    ISBN: 1-55612-750-2 (alk. paper)
    1. Psychoanalysis and religion. 2. Messianism—Psychology.
3. Millennium—Psychology. 4. Millennialism—Psychology.
I. Title
BF1'75'.4.R44M45   1995
200 .1 9—dc20   94-45192
                                                 CIP

———————————————◆———————————————

Published by: Sheed & Ward
               115 E. Armour Blvd.
               P.O. Box 419492
               Kansas City, MO 64141

To order, call: (800) 333-7373

Cover design by John Murello.

Contents

Section III
Christian Messianism

Section IV
Medieval Messianism and Mysticism

Section V
Millennarianism

Section VI
Psychoanalytic Perspectives

Preface

This is a book about psychoanalysis and religion. It is part of a process that over the course of several decades has tried to thoughtfully utilize psychoanalytic approaches and concepts in the effort to enrich and deepen the understanding of man's religious experience. I would see this effort as part of the modern context of psychoanalytic methodology that approaches its subject matter with respect and humility — whether the subject of investigation be another human being on the analytic couch, a historical personality, group phenomena, political movements, or religious experience.

I see this development as a new phase in the psychoanalytic enterprise, in which the analytic effort is not directed to reducing or encapsulating the object within the constraining categories of its Procrustean bed of theory and praxis, but rather one in which the psychoanalyst disciplines himself to enter into the inner life and meaning of that which he studies in a way that respects the integrity of the object and comes to understand its inner workings, as it were, from the inside out rather than from the outside in. My approach to the understanding of religious phenomena is restrictively psychoanalytic, but it is an understanding tempered by faith yet striving constantly to preserve both the coherency of the belief systems in question and the integrity of the psychoanalytic perspective and method.

Religious belief systems maintain a certain constancy and consistency throughout the long course of their history. Two such themes, distinguishable yet intimately linked throughout their course, have to do with the beliefs concerning eschatology — the convictions regarding the last things (death, the afterlife, heaven, hell) — and apocalypticism — the dogmatic perspectives that proclaim the vision of the last days, the coming of the Messiah in glory to judge the world and establish his glorious reign, whether in terrestrial or heavenly terms. These beliefs have played a crucial role in human religious motivation and in the shaping of religious beliefs in many cultural contexts extending over many centuries, even millennia. They have found expression for the most part in beliefs having to do with the Messiah and the conditions of his return in glory. My purpose is to trace the origins and patterns of evolution of these enduring beliefs, and to try to trace the underlying motivations and fantasy systems, more unconscious than conscious, they embody and to some degree derive from.

The enquiry carries us into the dark recesses of primitive and fundamental human motivation and brings us into contact with profoundly meaningful themes touching the quick of human existence and experience — themes of life vs. death, finite vs. infinite, time vs. eternity, world vs. heaven, impotence vs. omnipotence, suffering vs. bliss, reality vs. fantasy, wish vs. frustration, fulfillment vs. disappointment, illusion vs. disillusion, and so on. The psychoanalytic probe seeks to reach beneath the shifting currents of history, theology, and belief in order to bring into sharper relief underlying dynamic forces that drive and motivate these manifest events. Beyond the recurrent themes of apocalyptic and eschatological belief and the kaleidoscopic expressions of their historical variants, there runs a current of basic human desires and unconscious fantasies that give the myths and symbols of these fundamental beliefs a renewed vitality and power. It is this level of deeply seated, unconscious and latent desire that determines the focus and scope of the psychoanalytic method and interest. It was my hope when I began this effort that the psychoanalytic perspective would bring an added dimension to our understanding of these powerful themes; having reached this way-station on the journey, I am more persuaded than ever that such is the case. I hope it will prove to be so for others who will follow the path.

I would like to express my gratitude to those who have contributed in so many and varied ways to what has been distilled into these pages — my theological mentors, my spiritual guides, my psychoanalytic teachers and supervisors, my colleagues who have through the years enriched and deepened my understanding of human motivation, and particularly my patients who provided me with the raw material that taught me by dint of endless repetition how profoundly the sources of motivation run and how insistently they clamor for satisfaction — a dynamic that underlies the full spectrum of the messianic and millennarian themes in this volume. The motivations that underlie these religious themes are the very same as play themselves out on the analytic couch — there is no one better prepared to understand these dynamic forces than the psychoanalyst who encounters them every day in his consulting room, not merely on the pages of history.

A special word of thanks is due to Dr. L. Bryce Boyer, editor of *The Psychoanalytic Study of Society*, who has been generous with his time and interest, and has encouraged my pursuit of these questions. Some of the material in these pages has previous appeared in the *Study* and is utilized with permission. Previously published sections include:

(1988) The cult phenomenon and the paranoid process. *Psychoanalytic Study of Society*, 12: 69-95, part of chapter XV.

(1990) Jewish messianism and the cultic process. *Psychoanalytic Study of Society*, 15: 347-370, incorporated in section II.

Some portions of the material have also appeared in:

(1990) The role of transitional conceptualization in religious thought. In Smith, J.H., and Handelman, S.A. (eds.) *Psychoanalysis and Religion*. Baltimore: Johns Hopkins University Press, pp. 95-116, parts of which have been incorporated in Chapter XX.

(1992) The pathology of belief systems. *Psychoanalysis and Contemporary Thought*, 15: 99-128, parts of which are included in Chapter XVI.

W. W. Meissner, S.J., M.D.
St. Mary's Hall
Boston College

Section I

Introduction

Dreams and Visions

Peter's Sermon

When Peter arose on the day of Pentecost, after the apparition of the mighty wind and the tongues of fire (Acts 2: 2-4), and in the face of the bewilderment of those who heard the apostles preaching and each man hearing their words in his own tongue (Acts 2: 5-13), he spoke the following words:

> Men of Judea and all who dwell in Jerusalem, let this be known to you and give ear to my words. For these men are not drunk, as you suppose, since it is only the third hour of the day; but this is what was spoken by the prophet Joel:
>
> > And in the last days it shall be, God declares, that I will pour out my Spirit upon all flesh, and your sons and daughters shall prophesy, and your young men shall see visions, and your old men shall dream dreams;
> >
> > yea, and on my menservants and my maidservants in those days I will pour out my Spirit; and they shall prophesy.
> >
> > And I will show wonders in the heaven above and signs on the earth beneath, blood, and fire, and vapor of smoke;
> >
> > the sun shall be turned into darkness and the moon into blood, before the day of the Lord comes, the great and manifest day.
> >
> > And it shall be that whoever calls on the name of the Lord shall be saved. (Acts 2: 14-21)

Preaching in the white heat of the pentecostal inspiration, Peter begins his sermon by an appeal to one of the most ancient, enduring, and profoundly meaningful of human desires — the wish for final beatitude, salvation, the release from all worldly cares and sorrows, and the dawn of a new era of peace, joy, and well-being. The "day of the Lord," which the prophet Joel proclaims and which the Prince of the Apostles preaches, is one of the dominant expectations and hopes that inhabited the hearts and minds of his listeners. The "day of the Lord" called to mind images of the promised messiah, the "anointed one," who would bring with him the defeat of the enemies of God's people and the fulfillment of all the promises of glorious satisfaction and peace that had echoed down through the centuries as the ultimate blessing bestowed by a loving and protecting God on His chosen people.

These powerful desires were rooted in the traditional religion of the Jewish people and reflected deep-seated and largely unconscious fantasy systems that touched the primitive wellsprings of human motivation. The task before us is to try to plumb the depths of these pregnant and enduring fantasies and to trace their derivation from the fundamental sources of human motivation and meaning. We can find the details of these fantasy systems in the doctrines of future times and salvation that contained the substance of these beliefs. These beliefs were articulated under two separate but intertwined subject areas — eschatology and apocalyptic.

Eschatology

Eschatology is literally the "doctrine of the last things" — usually referring to the events that will intrude on man, history, and creation at the end of time — questions of life beyond death, salvation, the destiny of individual souls, the final divine judgment of the world, the ultimate fate of humanity as a whole, the existence of heaven and hell, the final return of the risen Christ in glory, the resurrection of the dead, the nature of man's final beatitude, and so on. As Moltmann (1967) says, "These end events were to break into this world from somewhere beyond history, and to put an end to the history in which all things here live and move." (p. 15) There is question whether there was any eschatological belief in the Old Testament prior to the exile. Certainly there was no systematically developed belief with regard to the last things in the sense that we find it in later Christian times. We can find passages in the Old Testament that have an eschatological cast. They contain more or less standard themes — references to a final cosmic struggle between God and the powers of evil; predictions of a cosmic catastrophe resulting in the destruction of the known world and all human institutions; predictions of God's ultimate victory and judgment over all the forces of the world opposing Him; and the beginning of a new age and a new world under the guidance and protection of God. But the themes are merely hinted at or sketched broadly; the fuller, deeper, and more imaginative elaboration of these ideas had to wait for a later time and the development of an apocalyptic literature.

The origins of an explicit eschatology are to be found in Deutero-Isaiah (Is 40-55). The destruction of Jerusalem, the extinction of the kingdom of Judah, and the Babylonian exile were divine punishments that were to be followed by a new covenant and redemption through the power of Yahweh. It was to be the dawn of a new era that was to be introduced by the prodigious feats of Yahweh: the destruction of Babylon by Cyrus (Is 41: 24) or Israel (Is 41: 14-16) or even by Yahweh himself (Is 43: 14-15); the redemption of Israel including the freeing of the captives and their return to Jerusalem and the gathering together of the diaspora (Is 41: 8-9); the renewal and transformation of the land of Israel; and the repudiation of other gods and conversion to Yahweh by the nations (Is 51: 4-5). Thus were laid down the rudiments of the messianic program that was to pervade Jewish history and eschatological expectations ever after.

Apocalyptic

Although they frequently overlap and intermingle, eschatology and apocalyptic can be distinguished. Eschatology concerns itself with the truths concerning the end of time and the disposition of creation that are contained in the revelation of scripture. It speaks not of a present reality, but of a future and hoped-for reality, a final transformation that is promised by God and will be wrought by His intervention. In contrast, apocalyptic reaches beyond reality to a realm of the imagination, to cosmic fantasies and visions that echo dreams and wishes more than realities — either present or future.[1]

---

1. The apocalyptic viewpoint is loosely associated with the doctrine of apocatastasis commonly attributed to Origen. This teaching maintained that the whole of creation — including sinners, the damned, the devil — would in the final times be restored to salvation and eternal bliss. The theme played an important role in Christian eschatology, but was not unknown in pre-Christian times. In early Eastern religions, the cyclical view of time and history, in which the end always returns to the perfection of the beginning, found profound expression. Parsiism propounded the final beatification of all creatures, and finally gave way

A distinction can be drawn between the eschatology of the classical prophets and the apocalypticism that arose in the pre-Christian era. Moltmann (1967) points out that the classical prophets

> . . . stand in the midst of the history of their people and in the transition from the breakdown of the old to the breaking in of the new. History for them does not stand still as in the apocalyptic visions of the end. They do not, like the apocalyptic sects, stand in unworldly detachment over against the "world," the nations and the people of Israel, so that they could give themselves over to contemplating the worldliness of the world and its future fate. On the contrary, here everything is still in flux and the history whose future they announce is still mobile. They know that they themselves and their message are a factor in the movement of the history of God. Thus they certainly speak of "history" as the "work of Yahweh" or the "plan of Yahweh" (Is 28: 29), and also of the "whole work of Yahweh" (Is 10: 12). Yet that is not a history surveyed apocalyptically from the standpoint of the end at which all things stand still, but it is a future announced from the midst of the process of history. (pp. 132-133)

And Schnackenburg (1963) adds a further comment on the apocalyptic impulse:

> A mood of melancholy descends upon devout people without, of course, stifling their hope. But for all that, the apocalyptic literature is a flight into a realm of visions and dreams, a flight away from a steady faith, because men were calling for portents and calculating when the hour would come; they wanted, so to speak, to take a peep at the cards in God's hands. The clamour for divine vengeance upon the godless and sinners, on persecutors and oppressors is at least as emphatic as the yearning appeal for salvation and future glory. (p. 87)

To specify the distinction a bit further, we can say that both the eschatology of the prophets and the apocalyptic literature look to the

---

to the dualism of good and evil of Persian philosophy. This dualism would finally yield to a final victory of the good by way of a fiery renewal of the world, making it perfect and eternal. Similar notions occurred in Stoic philosophy regarding a final cosmic conflagration in which the imperfect world would be destroyed and replaced by a more perfect one. Origen was influenced by these ideas. The same themes emerged in gnostic doctrines of the second century — a cyclic pattern of original spiritual plenitude, followed by a fall resulting in the creation of an imperfect world, and then the appearance of the redeemer who leads the fallen world back to its true divine perfection. See Meissner (in process) and Sachs (1991).

future, but the apocalyptic view of history is deterministic in the sense that it records the unfolding of Yahweh's cosmic plan; for the prophets there is no sense that the final times have been dictated for all time. The great struggle in apocalyptic is between God and the powers of evil that rule the world; in the prophetic perspective, the struggle takes place between Israel and the nations. Apocalyptic looks not just for the final overthrow of evil by good, but toward the final separation of good and evil and replacement of the powers of evil and the world they rule by a world of justice and righteousness — the cosmic dualism of apocalyptic is alien to the prophets. The divine judgment in the final times is not seen as operating in the realm of human freedom so that final condemnation can be averted by repentance and holiness of life, but it is more an immutable fate, a form of inexorable predetermination. While the prophets spoke out of the matrix of history and the people of God, the apocalyptists took their stand in the post-exilic assembly of the saints of Yahweh. Moltmann (1967) sums up these differential strains:

> In short, the question arises whether apocalyptic thinking does not ultimately show signs of non-historic thinking. Does the apocalyptic division of world history into periods according to the plan of Yahweh not merely interpret in terms of universal history earlier, foreign schemata of a cosmological kind? Apocalyptic as the "science of the highest" has such an encyclopedic character, just like the esoteric apocalyptic of the pietistic theology of saving history in the seventeenth and eighteenth Christian centuries. On the other hand, it has been pointed out with good reason how firmly the apocalyptic picture of history is rooted in the historic thinking of Israel and bound up with the prophetic eschatology. In this context Daniel becomes the executor of the testament of the prophets with his first "sketch of world history in terms of universal history." (p. 134)

Old Testament

The eschatological emphasis in earlier writings is muted at best. In the pre-exilic period, the saving and judging acts of Yahweh are articulated and defined within restrictive historical contexts and in terms of specific historical processes. The enemies of Yahweh are specific nations and peoples — His enemies are the enemies of His people. Judgment is cast in terms of specific historical outcomes — the fall of Israel, the defeat of the Assyrians, and so on. Salvation is defined in terms of victory and peaceful prosperity. It is only when the hopes of Israel have been crushed and in the bitter throes of defeat and oppression that eschatological hopes take root. The victory and supremacy of Yahweh must come from outside, beyond any historical hope. The imagery here probably harkens back to more primitive beliefs that associated divine theophanies with storms, earthquakes, and volcanic eruptions. Yahweh was originally the god of the storm or the volcano. The confession of the power of Yahweh in nature laid the foundation for a belief in Yahweh as the savior of His people from their enemies. At Sinai, Yahweh comes as the deliverer of His people with whom He establishes a covenant — His power over nature is the warrant of His power to save Israel and later to exercise the power of judgment over all evildoers and enemies.

If such pre-exilic utterances are not eschatological in a more developed sense, they certainly enunciate a hope for the future. The Israelite belief was that Yahweh would actively intervene in the course of history to bring salvation to His people through his judgments and saving acts. And if Yahweh were truly divine and all-powerful, the struggle against evil would not last forever, but would have to culminate in Yahweh's ultimate and definitive victory. This called for a final act of triumph that would defeat the enemies of God and Israel once and for all and would bring with it the end of history — so that the hope for a future time beyond history becomes eschatological. In the pre-exilic prophets, the ideas of judgment and salvation do not seem to reach beyond the world of human experience; but the sense that Yahweh's intervention will change this world as we know it brings the world to a state that cannot be produced by historical forces.

The consistent theme that runs through the prophetic literature is that history must lead inevitably to the universal reign of Yahweh. In its early expression, as in the oracle of Nathan (2 Sam 7), it looks forward to a worldwide reign of the king-messiah of Israel without any further elaboration. The form and content of the eschatological dreams required further development. If there was to be a promised future reign of Yahweh, it remained to be seen what it entailed and how it would take shape. This early form of Israelite eschatology was in no sense a transcendent eschatology — that development had to await the coming of Christ and Christianity.

Life After Death

Much of Hebrew eschatological thinking was conditioned by attitudes toward death and the question of survival after death. The accepted view is that there is no hint of belief in an afterlife in the Old Testament before the second century BC. This is curious in view of the fact that resurrection of the body played such a significant part in Pharisaic Judaism and Christianity. Apparently the beliefs of the ancient Israelites in this regard lay closer to Canaan and Mesopotamia than Egypt. (Jacobson 1976)

Even the Egyptian concept of the afterlife was little more than a return to a similar state of existence as before — nothing new was added. The satisfactions of life beyond the grave were the familiar joys of life in this world — carnal and otherwise. The *Book of the Dead* requires that the applicant pass an examination of his moral conduct in life in order to gain admittance to the blissful realm, but the results depend more on moral knowledge than on conduct or character. There is no suggestion that anyone would be excluded from such bliss, any more than they were excluded from their present life. Human life was good and there did not seem to be any desire for a changed or new state of existence after death.

All this is very different from basic Israelite beliefs about Yahweh and the existence of man. The Egyptian conception of the afterlife is a secularized version; the afterlife is not dominated by a personal divine presence. There is no sense of personal destiny here, but neither is there any such in early Israelite sources. But the implicit faith in the conditions of man's worldly existence was intolerable to the Israelite mind.

In the Mesopotamian world, there was no survival on any terms. The bodies of the dead lie in the underworld lifeless and silent — without movement or consciousness. The view of death is deeply pessimistic. Only the gods enjoy life; death is the allotted portion of man. One should enjoy life while he had it. Death is, like birth, without moral or religious significance. If man could reach the food and water of the afterlife, he would be like the gods — immortal. But the gods do not grant him this privilege. In Genesis, the food of life is withheld not out of possessiveness or jealousy, but because Adam and Eve had committed a moral fault. Otherwise, the Israelite beliefs did not differ significantly from the Mesopotamian. Death is no more than the termination of life. There is no soul or spirit to survive after the death of the body. Sheol is mentioned often enough, but it is no more than a gigantic tomb where the bodies of the dead are retained in lifeless form (Job 10: 21; 17: 13-16). Sheol is a denial of survival — the place where all life comes to an end, both good and evil. The outlook is less pessimistic than in the Mesopotamian sources. For the Israelites, death was the natural end of life. An untimely death might be the punishment for a wicked life; except for the account in the J narrative of Gen 3, the idea of death as punishment does not occur in the Old Testament.

These beliefs provide the background for Israelite views of the meaning of human existence. Immortality was found in the sons who bore a man's name and in the people of Israel of which he was part. As long as Israel lives, its members live on in and through it. The hope of immortality, then, often took the form of a collective immortality, so that hopes for an eschatological future often took a correspondingly collective form. In the face of a lack of any vitalizing principle that could survive death, the vague and disparate wishes for some form of survival, when it finally came into focus, took the only form possible, resurrection of the body. The hope of resurrection in the vision of the dry bones (Ez 37) is really an expression of the hope that Israel will survive the extinction of 587 BC. The first clear expression of wish for immortality comes in the Maccabean period, in Dn 12: 2. The idea seems to have no significant pre-history; it includes an eschatological view of a new life in a new world — very different from the Egyptian resumption of a continued terrestrial existence. As Stanley (1968a) observed:

> When finally the Old Testament writers became aware of some kind of salvation after death, they did so thanks to revelation of a bodily resurrection, not through the alien idea of the soul's immortality. Despite fundamental differences, it is one of the most notable characteristics of New Testament soteriology that throughout the course of its development it appears to have remained within the Hebraic frame of reference in this regard. (p. 23)

From Old Testament to New

There is little doubt that the Christian dispensation, taking root within the rich soil of Palestinian religious life, carried with it many of the traditions, beliefs, and desires that found expression in the Old Testament. The New Testament depends on and in large measure derives from the Old. The gospels will present Christ as the fulfillment of the hopes and destiny of Israel. The New Testament proclaims Christ as the messiah,[2] implying that the God of the Old Testament is also God of the New, so that the Christian dispensation is part of God's unified plan of salvation. Christ is pictured as perhaps the greatest of the eschatological prophets, one like Moses who has come to proclaim the final times and whose mission was centered on the message that the kingdom of God was at hand (Borg 1987).

---

2. See the development of these themes in section III below.

The Christian claim is that in Jesus the Old Testament idea of history and the hope of salvation are realized. There is no further destiny to which Israel can turn. In Christ, God's saving acts are fulfilled. The Old Testament is thus the record of God's revelation of Himself to men in history. The connection between that record and the new dispensation is one of continuity and development. There is scarcely a single Old Testament theme which does not find its corresponding expression and development in the New Testament. The Father of whom Jesus spoke and to whom he prayed is none other than the God of the Old Testament, Yahweh, whose loving intervention in the history of Israel was well known to every Jewish believer. The radical difference between the Testaments is that the New Testament centers on the person of Jesus Christ and his saving mission as Son of Man, indeed as Son of God.

Eschatology in the New Testament

The eschatological themes take on greater definition in the New Testament. The "last things" take on the meaning of God's definitive intervention in history through Jesus Christ, defined in terms of the first and second comings of Christ. Eschatology becomes more specifically personal (the destiny of the individual soul), collective (now in terms of the destiny of the church rather than the nation), and cosmic (the destiny of the universe).

There is disagreement as to the meaning of *eschaton* in the New Testament texts. One view would hold that the term should be applied narrowly to indicate an act of God coming from outside sacred history and bringing an end to the present historical order. A broader conception would see the *eschaton* as the culmination of the present order bringing to a close events of Christian salvation history already at work in the world. The concept of time is relevant here. The linear sense of time would imply a teleological concept of history — the history of Israel, the church, the universe, have a definable beginning and a purposeful endpoint determined by divine power and providence. But the biblical view implies a more evolutionary process. As Stanley and Brown (1968) have written:

> The dialectic of sacred history, particularly for NT [New Testament] authors, and especially for Paul, moves forward by a series of crises postulating an indefinite number of relatively new beginnings. The NT expectation of "the end" is based upon a set of occurrences in the past by which salvation has been essentially

accomplished in the death and resurrection of Jesus Christ. Accordingly, the *eschaton* — at least the phase that still lies in the future — has been prepared for, determined, and even begun by these crucial events of NT sacred history. (p. 778)

One of the problems that plagued New Testament eschatology was the question of the timing of the *parousia*, the second coming of Christ. The gospels make it seem that the expectations in the early church were that the parousia was near at hand, that the end times were imminent, and that repentance and holiness of life were required as urgent preparations for the great event. But time brought with it disillusionment and the dimming of hopes and expectations. More current views would suggest that the texts declaring the coming of the Son of Man, so basic to the emphasis upon an imminent parousia, cannot be authentically traced to Jesus himself, but were accretions added by the early church (Borg 1987). One theological answer to this dilemma came in the form of "realized eschatology" (Dodd 1935). In this view, Jesus' message boiled down to the fact that in him the *eschaton* had entered history, that the messiah had arrived, that the kingdom of God is now a reality in the world. Because of their traditional mind-set, Christ's disciples would have misunderstood him, taking him to mean that the kingdom of God was only partial or incomplete in the present and only to be fully realized in the future. The literal interpretation of Christ's symbolic implication was corrected only when Paul and John came to appreciate the implications of a realized eschatology.

The eschatology of Christ's mission in the gospel accounts is centered around the notion of the kingdom[3] — an idea that was to occupy a paramount position in New Testament eschatology. The Old Testament emphasis on the "day of Yahweh" shifts to considerations of the kingdom of God in the New. Entrance to the kingdom involves a judgment (Mt 5:20; 13: 41-43) that borrows elements from the apocalyptic tradition. The judgment involves triumph of the divine plan of salvation over God's enemies, particularly over the kingdom of Satan (Mt 8: 29; Lk 4: 34; 10: 18; 13: 16). The parousia of the Son of Man, coming in clouds, power and glory, is cast in terms of conquest and victory (Mk 13: 26). The great apocalyptic battle seems muted, and individual merit plays a greater role — as in Matthew's account of the Last Judgment (Mt 25: 31-46). The extravagances of Jewish apocalyptic are restrained. The judgment is based on merit (Mt 12: 41-42; 18:

---

3. See the further discussion of the kingdom in chapter XII below.

23-35) and leads to the adoption of a new state of beatitude following the "birth pangs" (Mt 24: 8; Jn 16: 21). The judge is sometimes God the Father (Mt 6: 4; 10: 32-33), sometimes Jesus himself (Mt 25: 31-46; Lk 17: 24). All men without distinction are subject to this judgment, and the outcome will be determined on the basis of their attitude toward the kingdom, faith, and repentance (Mt 8: 10-11; 11: 20-21).

The early preaching of the nascent church was basically eschatological, as is evident in Peter's pentecostal sermon. The last days foretold by the prophets were at hand, and the day of Yahweh was a reality. The apostles believed that the spirit of Yahweh had been given them and that they formed the new people of God, the faithful remnant of the prophets (Is 10: 20-21). This meant that the messianic era had been inaugurated by the outpouring of the Spirit and that they could look forward to the promised second coming of Christ in the parousia. The bestowal of the Spirit and the remission of sins in baptism made the initiates members of the new church, but also connected them with the final judgment and the eschatological ingathering of the faithful. In Acts, the call to repentance was also cast in eschatological terms — then Christ, the universal judge, would determine who was to be saved and who not (Acts 10: 42; 2: 47; 4: 12; 5: 31). The apostolic kerygma proclaimed Jesus as the universal ruler at God's right hand (Acts 2: 34) who would come to judge the living and the dead (Acts 17: 31). Even the persecution experienced by the primitive community was viewed as part of the hostility of the world toward the messianic people (Acts 4: 24-30).

Pauline Eschatology

In Paul, the eschatological perspective, as with so much else in Pauline and early Christian preaching, centered around the person of Christ and the meaning of his mission, particularly of his resurrection. The continuity of Paul's teaching with Old Testament themes is clear, but it is also clear that the savior who was to come at the end of time was not some unknown and mysterious figure, but Christ himself. Also the dimension of realized eschatology put a definitive stamp on Paul's eschatology.

Paul's perspective is stamped with apocalyptic perspectives. The dualistic emphasis casts the lot of his opponents with Satan, the "god of this world" who blinds the eyes of men to the truth (2 Cor 11: 13-15). His understanding in mystical and apocalyptic terms views the endtime not as an event in the distant future, but as having already begun. The transformation by the Spirit is a continual process directed toward the final consummation. The pledge of final salvation is found in baptism, guaranteed by the activity of the Holy Spirit.

Apocalyptic and mystical themes were intertwined in first-century Judaism, and Paul is a prime example of this trend. His vision is of an apocalyptic Gentile Christian community. For him, the final days announced in the preaching of Jesus had already begun. The church in his eyes was equivalent to the community of those who had already been saved by their faith in Jesus Christ and in his promised kingdom. The faith of the church was ordered to this apocalyptic vision — the same as Paul had himself received in his conversion experience. This special and privileged knowledge he called an *apokalypsis* or revelation (Gal 1: 2), but it is no more than the harbinger of the revelation to come in the final resolution. The coming of Christ, as well as his appearance to Paul himself on the road to Damascus, were precursors of the final consummation when Christ would return in all his apocalyptic glory. The Son of Man of Daniel and the Enoch literature was none other than Christ himself (Segal 1990).

The tension and uncertainty between the realized and future eschatological views plagued the whole of the apostolic age, particularly in terms of the meaning of the period of history between the first and second comings of Christ. Paul is not immune from this concern. In the early phase of his mission (AD 51-62), Paul seems to have shared the common expectation of his contemporaries that the parousia was imminent. But several factors may have conspired to modify his views as time went on. One factor was the difficulty he experienced in trying to convert diaspora Jews. He met continual opposition and factious debate from the Judaizing element in the communities where he preached. One prominent belief was that the second coming was contingent on the conversion of Israel. Paul's practice was to preach first to the Jews and only when that effort had proven fruitless did he turn to the pagans. By the time of Romans (11: 25-26), however, his attitude had changed. The conversion of the Gentiles had assumed priority. The conversion of Israel had seemed possible in a reasonably short time, but not the Gentiles. The promised return of the Lord began to recede toward the horizon of history.

Paul was not alone in his apocalyptic fervor. He may, in fact, have had to temper the apocalyptic and millenarian tendencies of some of his followers — the Thessalonians being a case in point. But the apocalyptic traits in his preaching were clear enough. His view of the body — the distinction is not between flesh and spirit, but between those who have rejected the gospel (flesh) and those who have accepted it (spirit) — his division of history into two opposed stages, the distinction of law and grace, law and spirit, death and life, sin and love, are all apocalyptic in inspiration (Segal 1990).

Much of Paul's early eschatological preaching drew on apocalyptic imagery, as did the synoptics. He speaks of "the wrath to come" (1 Thess 1: 10), the parousia is described in Old Testament language (1 Thess 4: 13-18; 2 Thess 2: 1-10), and he envisions an eschatological battle between the risen Lord and his enemies (1 Cor 15: 23-28). While the apocalyptic strain is not missing from later letters, he gradually comes to view the eschatological victory as already attained through Christ's redemptive death and resurrection (Col 2: 14; Eph 1: 22). The early views of salvation are linked, in good pharisaic style, with the resurrection of the body in futurist terms (1 Thess 5: 8; 2 Thess 2: 13; Phil 2: 12). Later (2 Cor 6: 2) the present moment becomes the "day of salvation," and he can tell his listeners that they have already been saved (Eph 2: 5, 8; 2 Tim 1: 9; 4: 18; Tit 3: 5). Thus the early letters are dominated by the expectation of the parousia: Christians are to live in the hope and expectation of the glorious return of the Lord.

Much the same story is reflected in Paul's usage regarding judgment and justification. The Old Testament "day of Yahweh" becomes the "day of the Lord" (1 Thess 5: 2; 2 Thess 2: 2; 1 Cor 1: 8; 5: 5; 2 Cor 1: 14). They reflect Paul's earlier viewpoint that the divine judgment takes place in the context of an apocalyptic victory of God and Christ over the powers of evil. Justification has an eschatological dimension, since, even though Christians are justified through faith in Christ's resurrection, it remains an anticipation of a future eschatological salvation. If God the Father is the supreme judge (Rom 2: 2), it is through Christ that He will judge (Rom 2: 16) those who appear before the tribunal of Christ (2 Cor 5: 10). Christians, who believe in Christ and are so justified, have every reason to look forward to this judgment with confidence (Rom 5: 9; 8: 1; 1 Cor 11: 32), since they have Christ himself as their advocate (1 Cor 4: 4) and intercessor (Rom 8: 34). The Qumran documents reveal the extent to which this form of thinking was characteristic of Jewish mystical and apocalyptic lore (Segal 1990).

Johannine Eschatology

The eschatological themes in John's gospel center on the doctrine of the Spirit, who is the guarantor of eschatological promises. The Spirit emerges in John as a divine figure who assumes the mission of continuing and completing the work of Jesus in the world. He is the sanctifier and the principle of life in Christian believers — the new life that Jesus came to give mankind. It is through the presence and action of the Spirit that Christians became sons of the heavenly Father. The life He brings is a share in the divine existence itself.

In John's usage the Spirit is uniquely the "Paraclete" (Jn 14: 16, 26; 15: 26; 16: 7) — the helper and advocate with the Father who will remain until the end of time. The view of the Spirit as present and active in the church and in the lives of Christians made John's eschatology even more "realized" than that found in Paul. Despite the continued expectation of the parousia, John's emphasis is on salvation in the present rather than in some unknown future time. In this he is more akin to the later Paul. Even the heavily eschatological Book of the Apocalypse — also possibly originating from the apostle — addresses the possession of the Spirit as a present reality. It may have been the primitive church's experience of the presence of the Spirit rather than simply the postponement of the parousia that contributed to the development of the realized eschatology (Vawter 1968).

Stanley and Brown (1968) summarize the eschatology of the New Testament in the following terms:

> What gives the NT [New Testament] eschatology its characteristic cachet and originality is the unflagging awareness of its inspired authors that he who comes, the judge who exercises cosmic judgment, is not only already victor and Savior of mankind, but a person familiarly known from the Gospel record of his earthly life of humiliation and suffering. The OT [Old Testament] Day of Yahweh, in consequence, has been transformed into the Day of Christ; and its nature has been essentially revealed to men by Jesus' life, death, and resurrection. Indeed this Day is not so much something ordained to be the termination of this world, but rather a reality already dynamically present in history. And thus history becomes fundamentally salvation history; for the value of the present time, as also the significance of the future, has been created and revealed to us by Jesus Christ. (p. 782)

Apocalyptic Literature

If the writers of the New Testament and the prophets of the Old Testament were men of dreams, the apocalyptic writers were men of visions. The prophets were essentially men of action who proclaimed their message in the face of the evils of the world around them. The apocalyptic writers were men of the word, who communicated their thinking in studied form. If the prophets were immersed in the politics and struggles of their time, the apocalyptists proclaimed a cosmic vision that extended to the whole of human history and beyond. The prophets and evangelists were the champions of the rule of Yahweh over His people and of Christ over his church. The prophets were propagandists for the return of the davidic monarchy, while the apocalyptists envisioned the worldwide domain of Yahweh. They tended to pay less and less attention to the claims of davidic messianism. They were convinced that only the direct action of Yahweh in the world could transform present reality into apocalyptic fulfillment. Their visions were expressed in a symbolic language even they did not fully understand and which was even more confusing to their listeners.

Symbolism was in fact the strong suite of apocalyptic. Everything in the experience of this world could be turned to symbolic use. Parts of the body, animals, clothing, colors could all be transformed through symbolic alchemy to mean something different and more significant. Numbers yielded most readily to the lure of symbolification. As Stuhlmueller (1968) observes:

> Continuing the parallel study of prophet and apocalyptist, we notice that the prophets insisted upon a day of the Lord, sweeping darkness upon the wicked, bringing victory to the elect. The apocalyptists saw the darkness still deeper and the light still more blinding; goodness and evil were interlocked in mortal struggle. For the prophets, this struggle was mostly between the good and the wicked within Israel, but for the apocalyptists it was a world convulsion. The prophets saw the present, sorrowful moment leading to future victory; the apocalyptists watched the heavens open and the future crash into the present. (p. 343)

The evolution of prophecy into apocalyptic was abetted by two primary figures — Ezekiel and Daniel. In Ezekiel's hands, the prophetic took a somewhat different direction. Prophetic moralizing was muted in deference to liturgical renewal. God became more majestic and transcendent, and His worship more permeated with symbolism, angelic ministers, and concerns over eschatological fulfillment. If the apocalyptic impulse owed its resurgence to liturgical developments, Daniel reflected the freeing of apocalyptic from priestly influence. In this period (167-164 BC), the temple worship retained its central position in Jewish religious life, but the temple priests had become rigid and conservative, rejecting any new developments and especially resisting the resurrection of the elect. Apocalyptic developments tended to flourish beyond the influence of the priesthood, at least of the Jerusalem priests; apocalyptic, after all, did have a prominent place among the Essene priests at Qumran, who hated and rebelled against the temple priests and their influence. As apocalyptic developed, the symbolism became more fantastic and exuberant.

The *Book of the Apocalypse* is redolent of the apocalyptic style *par excellence*. Its message is a prophesy of what is to take place in the very near future. The revelation is mysterious and is conveyed to John[4] through angelic intermediaries in the form of visions. The symbolism conveys the ineffable and transcendent quality of the truths revealed to John. He presents himself as one persecuted for the faith — undoubtedly reflecting the oppositional and persecutory stance of the johannine community in the face of post-destruction Judaic Pharisaism. His mission is to explain the meaning of their trials and tribulations and reveal the glorious significance of their suffering. Elevated to the cosmic level, the struggle is not with the Jews or the Romans, but between the forces of God and the forces of Satan. The final victory is beyond doubt — Christ will conquer Satan — and then establish the New Jerusalem, the new world of divine promises that all the faithful are to enjoy.

Apocalyptic, then, was a development in exilic and post-exilic times of the prophetic style "in which heavenly secrets about a cosmic struggle and eschatological victory are revealed in symbolic form and explained by angels to a seer who writes down his message under the pseudonym of some ancient personage" (Stuhlmueller 1968, p. 343). The apocalyptic urge found expression in the nascent Christian church of the first century AD. The apocalyptic vision reached crisis and climactic proportions in the first Jewish revolt of AD 60-66, and again in the second revolt of AD 132-135. These dreadful defeats, especially the final defeat of Bar Kochba, left despair and hopelessness in their wake. The consequences were immense. Judaism abandoned its hope for the imminent intervention of Yahweh to save His chosen people and turned instead to the minute observance of the Law as the path to salvation. The consequences were equally as dynamic for the struggling Christian movement. The failure of Yahweh's intervention

---

4. Authorship of the Apocalypse is disputed. The disparity of style and content have persuaded some scholars that the gospel and the Apocalypse came from different hands. The traditional view holds to the identity of the author of the fourth gospel and the Apocalypse. The matter remains unresolved, but if the apostle John was not directly the author of the Apocalypse, it may reflect his influence and may well represent the work of disciples familiar with John's thinking. See the discussion in D'Aragon (1968).

brought home the realization that the parousia was not imminent; the Christian inspiration took the form of transposing the eschatological triumph into present terms — the church represented the eschatological triumph of God, expressed through the mission of Christ, transforming the world into the promised kingdom of the Spirit. The Book of the Apocalypse, the New Testament book of prophecy, ends with the words: "The one who guarantees these revelations repeats his promise: I shall indeed be with you soon. Amen; come, Lord Jesus" (Apoc 22: 20).

In the gospels, Jesus' preaching is not portrayed as apocalyptic, nor was his teaching esoteric. The only clearly apocalyptic material in the synoptics is found in Mk 13 and its parallels in Mt 24 and 25: 31-46 and Lk 21: 5-36. They speak of cosmic events and the coming of the Son of Man on the clouds of heaven — much in the Old Testament style. Probably the earliest apocalyptic texts in the New Testament, however, are found in Paul's letters to the Thessalonians, especially 1 Thess 4: 16-18 and 2 Thess 2: 1-12. The features are similar to Jewish apocalyptic, but they proclaim the second coming of Jesus, the parousia and the rapture of the saints. 2 Thess shares with the Apocalypse "the expectation of apostasy, the appearance of an impious character who parodies God Himself, the idea of the restraint of the evil one (cf. the chaining of Satan, Rev 20: 1-3), the slaughter of the impious one with the breath from the mouth of the Messiah, the activity of Satan, and the mimicking of signs and wonders together with deception" (Ford 1975, pp. 4-5).

These eschatological dreams and apocalyptic visions provide the historical, conceptual, and inspirational matrix for the development of religious beliefs and convictions that span the broad canvas of occidental religious thinking. The belief systems that owe their origin and sustaining vitality to these dreams and visions are legion — we shall trace a selection of them in the following pages — and they constitute a recurrent set of motifs and themes that resonate through the annals of religious history. If the original themes are sounded in the ancient religious views of Israelite prophets, the echoes continue to be heard through the centuries, even to our own time. While the themes are essentially religious, they at times spill over into the political realm and play out their destiny in those contexts of displacement. The dominant expressions of these themes that we will follow have to do with the coming of an expected and hoped-for messiah — whether in the end-time or beyond — and in the promise and vision of the thousand-year reign of the triumphant Christ in this world.

Section II

Jewish Messianism

CHAPTER 2

Ancient Messianic Themes

The messianic theme is nearly coextensive with the history of the Judaic and Christian religious traditions. The origins of the messianic ideal are undoubtedly ancient. Breasted (1933) noted that certain Egyptian sages, following destruction of the old order after the Pyramid Age, adhered to a vision of social justice and idealism that looked forward to a righteous ruler who would usher in an age of justice for all men (e.g., the so-called "Admonitions of Ipuwer"). This brand of messianism anticipates Hebrew messianism by a millennium and a half. Aspects of Hebrew messianism bear striking resemblance to these earlier Egyptian prototypes.

The word *mashiah* (messiah) in Hebrew originally meant "anointed with oil," but the term has limited currency in the Hebrew Bible.[1] The history of Israel is dotted with messianic (i.e., salvific) figures who emerge on the stage of history at times of Yahweh's definitive intervention in human history on behalf of His chosen people. The tradition began with Moses himself, who led the people of Israel to the Promised Land. Subsequent eras have looked for the coming of another prophet like Moses, who would fulfill the hopes and destiny of

---

1. The term appears 38 times in the Hebrew Old Testament, 29 of which refer to the Israelite king — primarily Saul, and secondarily David or one of the Davidic kings. Most of the Dead Sea Scrolls and pseudepigrapha and the whole of the apocrypha contain no references to "the messiah" (Charlesworth 1987; Green 1987).

Israel. The recurrent appeal to archetypal figures — the Suffering Servant, the Son of Man, the Anointed One, and others — sounds a symphony of eschatological themes that permeate the thinking and the pages of the Old Testament. If there are numerous messianic prototypes, there is nonetheless only one true messiah, specifically the anointed king of the Davidic lineage who would come in some future time to establish once and for all the reign of Yahweh.

The idea of the reign or the kingdom of Yahweh sums up the multiple components of the idea of salvation. The idea has its place in the Old Testament, but came to play a greater role in Jewish literature and later became a dominant theme in the New Testament writings. It became the designation for the hoped-for salvation that was to come through the universal acceptance of God's will. The universal knowledge of Yahweh and His commandments, communicated to men through His revelation of Himself to Israel, would lead to a dramatic revolution in mankind — a revolution that would include not only the interior man but the entire material world as well.

David and the Two Kingdoms

From the earliest days of the Davidic monarchy, the king, who was anointed (messiah), was regarded as a divinely appointed savior sent by God to guide His people. This early expression of the messianic idea corresponded to the emergence of the monarchy. Saul may at first have been seen as simply another, if more powerful, judge. The idea of royalty and kingship may have developed only gradually. His decisive victories over the Ammonites, Philistines and Amalekites consolidated his power. His jealous and tyrannical rule led to a break with Samuel and the famous quarrel with his son-in-law David, a hero in his own right.

Saul's death in the battle of Gilboa opened the way for David to ascend the throne (1000 BC). David's charismatic personality and personal gifts won him favor on all sides. He consolidated his power and successfully challenged the Philistines in war. He established his capital at Jerusalem, located outside the the Israelite tribal system and on the border between the northern and southern kingdoms. He was able to unite the two kingdoms under a single rule, and set the plans in motion for construction of the Great Temple in Jerusalem. His conquest of neighboring nations extended the boundaries of Israel to include most of the Middle East and resulted in handsome booty and tribute that filled the royal coffers.

David's success laid the foundation for the long reign of his son Solomon (961-922 BC), who presided over a powerful and wealthy kingdom. Solomon's royal construction projects were grand, if not grandiose. The Temple and the Royal Palace were completed — largely through the slave labor provided by conquered peoples. Politically he continued David's policies of centralizing and consolidating royal power, dissolving tribal ties and autonomy, and attaching the Temple priesthood to himself. His was the golden age of the Davidic monarchy!

The earliest kings of Israel, beginning with Saul and David, were anointed in assuming the kingly office. David's reign was the high-point of Israel's power and prestige, so that after the ruin of Israel and the first destruction of the temple later generations would look to the ideal of the Davidic reign as a golden age to which they would yearn to return in the face of their oppression and persecution. The death of Solomon was followed by centuries of dynastic struggles between the two kingdoms — Israel in the north and Judah in the south.

The Prophetic Vision

By the time of the 8th century BC, the luster of many of the visions of the glory of the Davidic line and the hope that each succeeding king would become the savior of his people had been dimmed by the rule of wicked and inept kings, like Ahaz. The prophets looked, therefore, more to the restoration of the glorious kingdom of the house of David. Isaiah gives that often frustrated hope a new twist — that the power of Yahweh would intervene to restore the dynasty to its former brilliance and insure its survival. He would raise up another David who would be a worthy successor to the first David and would restore the monarchy. The prophet grows rhapsodic in his praise of this expected heir to the throne (Is 7: 14-17; 9: 1ff). Isaiah might have thought optimistically that his hopes were fulfilled in the person of Hezekiah, who succeeded Ahaz; but the oracles proclaim a restoration ideal rather than any reality. Later generations were not slow to apply them to the continuing desires for the revival of the Davidic monarchy. Even Isaiah 11, which may come from a later date, seems to envision this coming in a more remote future. The longed-for leader was to possess charismatic power since the Spirit will rest on him and bestow the qualities of an ideal king. He will bring to pass the wonders of the lost paradise and establish a reign of universal peace. His reign will be based on the "knowledge of Yahweh" that Yahweh himself reveals to his chosen one. The notions of the return of the Davidic monarchy and universal salvation make their appearance here for the first time in the Old Testament (McKenzie 1968).

In Amos, the messianic promises are largely political, envisioning an ingathering of the exiles and the rule of the house of David over all of Israel. It was a vision of strong political power and wealth with the subjugation of other nations and peoples to the hegemony of Israel. There was no notion of an individual messiah, but rather a collective messiah embodied in the house of David. In contrast, Isaiah's messiah is a personal messiah, who embodies the highest ideals of the Davidic kingship (Goldstein 1987). His charismatic gifts are seen as the basis for a rule of idyllic peace, justice, and the supremacy of the law of Yahweh (Isaiah 11).

Oracles of similar messianic hope are attributed to the prophet Micah, Isaiah's contemporary, writing in the early 8th century BC (Micah 4-5). These passages may be postexilic, or if originating with Micah himself, may have undergone later revision and supplementation. The prophecy looks forward to a glorious reign of Yahweh, of universal peace. Zion would become the religious center of the world toward which converts from the whole world would turn, seeking instruction and salvation. Yahweh would become the sole ruler over a theocracy in which peace, calm, and security would reign supreme, and the instruments of war would no longer be needed. Yahweh becomes the good shepherd, who gathers his flock, carrying, seeking out the lost sheep and caring for them (Coppens 1968).

There is another theme which enters the messianic tradition at this point. Besides the vision of peace and tranquillity, Micah also speaks of the vengeance of the Lord which will fall upon those nations who had formerly persecuted Israel and refused to listen to the message of divine peace. It is a wish for vengeance of a people who had been beaten down and oppressed by the powerful nations surrounding them. But history trampled these hopes in the dust of Assyrian conquest.

Zephaniah prophesied in the 7th century, during the period of Assyrian domination. The theme of messianic universalism plays a major role in his prophecies, and once again it is Yahweh himself who is both king and redeemer. It is likely that the reigning kings of Judah of the time did not offer much of a basis for formulating messianic hopes in terms of a human king-messiah.

Jeremiah wrote in a turbulent period toward the beginning of the 6th century BC, when the decline of Assyrian influence was overtaken by the Babylonian conquest. Jeremiah prophesies a messianic age in which repentance would be followed by an ingathering of the exiles into Zion. The notion of the messiah is here collective, that is, represented by a series of kings, all of whom will be worthy servants of the Lord. The covenant with Yahweh involves the promise of material prosperity and an expansion of the reign of Yahweh to all the nations of the world. The "shoot" or "branch" (Jer 23: 5) is the savior-king who will affirm the salvific righteousness of Yahweh. This vision of political union embraced the union of the kingdoms of Judah and Israel. The redemption to come is described in terms analogous to the deliverance from Egypt, but this last redemption would far outstrip the earlier one in that it would bring with it a new spiritual life, a revolution in the spiritual life of Israel and in the hearts of true believers:

> Behold, the days come, sayeth the Lord, that I will make a new covenant with the house of Israel, and with the house of Judah; not according to the covenant that I made with their fathers in the day that I took them by the hand to bring them out of the land of Egypt; . . . . but this is the covenant that I will make with the house of Israel after those days, sayeth the Lord: I will put my law in their inward parts, and in their heart I will write it; and I will be their God, and they shall be my people. (Jer 31: 31-34)

The messianic ideal here involves more than political liberation and redemption, but embraces also a spiritual renewal of the heart.

Post-exilic Messianism

Any ambitions for a reunited monarchy died with Josiah. The emergence of the Chaldeans led to surrender to Nebuchadnezzar (598 BC). Jeremiah inveighed against paganism and the deterioration of morals. Wickedness and departure from the path of Yahweh had brought about political disaster, and avoidance of total catastrophe could be purchased only by submission to God's will and punishment as embodied in the Chaldeans. No flaming patriot he! But his prophetic message stirred opposition in royal circles — the Lachish Letters tell the story of efforts by royal officials to denounce Jeremiah to the king and to have him put to death. Jehoiachin was taken into exile, along with many of the leading men of Judah. Jeremiah had little good to say about his successor, Zedekiah (597-587 BC). They played their hand badly by conspiring with the Egyptians. Chaldean patience finally wore thin; Jerusalem was stormed in 587 BC, and most of the citizens and craftsmen led into the Babylonian captivity. Jeremiah's warnings had come to fruition.

Jeremiah's younger contemporary, Ezekiel, declaimed scathingly against the perversity of the men of Judah. Judah itself was devastated and its territory divided among the Chaldean tributaries. As long as Jehoiachin lived, even in captivity, hopes for the restoration of the monarchy lived on. After his death, they remained buried until the fall of the Chaldean empire to the onslaught of Cyrus and the Persians in 539 BC. Hopes for restoration surged along with a spirit of Jewish nationalism eloquently described in Deutero-Isaiah, who combined it with a theme of religious universalism. The Edict of Cyrus (538 BC), restoring the Jews of the exile to their homeland, was not met with universal enthusiasm. Many had become well-ensconced in their exilic homes and had established new lives. The return to Jerusalem would entail many hardships and deprivations, a long and dangerous journey, and at the end of the trip lay an uncertain future.

Exilic Prophesy

The first of the great exilic prophets, Ezekiel, was a witness to the failures of King Zedekiah and the inevitability of the destruction. His messianic vision was cast in terms of the period after the exile, of a return to Zion rather than the "end of days." A period of total devastation, national ruin and exile was to precede the period of messianic revival. His messianic hope took the form of a return of the exiled nation to its former political power, even becoming greater than before, recapturing and exceeding the glory of the Davidic kingdom. Yahweh will plant the dynasty like a cedar (Ez 17: 22), and David will once again reign as king (Ez 34: 23; 37: 24).

The second great prophet of the exile was Deutero-Isaiah, whose prophecies are directed to the exiles in Babylon. Jerusalem has been destroyed, and Israel can only now wait for a new and glorious future. Since there was no king and no kingdom, there is no place in Deutero-Isaiah for an individual political messiah. The exalted ethical and spiritual virtues of the messiah are transformed into a collective ideal. The songs portray the ideal servant of the Lord, whose consecration to Yahweh's will, even in the midst of suffering, brings redemption to many. But this "suffering servant" is the whole people of Israel, who become the messiah of the world and the redeemer of all mankind. The suffering and punishment of this messiah must precede the redemption. Thus, Israel's suffering will bring redemption to the world, so that it becomes "a light to the Gentiles."

Many did return, however, under the leadership of Zerubbabel of the Davidic line and the high priest, Joshua (ca. 538 BC). Under the urging of the prophets Haggai and Zechariah, the reconstruction of the Temple was undertaken. Zechariah takes up the messianic themes now in the context of the postexilic reconstruction of Jerusalem. Yahweh is eager to fulfill the messianic promises through glorification of the great temple of Jerusalem. He promises to make his dwelling among his people and to fulfill frustrated messianic hopes with their expectations of universal peace, prosperity and power. Haggai declaimed the downfall of Persia and declared that Zerubbabel was the Lord's anointed. Haggai and Zerubbabel were followed by Ezra and Nehemiah in the 5th century BC. Ezra brought about a cultic reform and probably was responsible for establishing the canonical Torah as normative for Israel's faith.

The following century becomes even more obscure in the historical record — we know little of the fate of Judaism until the Alexandrian conquest. Throughout this period the longing for the restoration of Israel took the form of a messianic hope, namely, that Yahweh would send his anointed one, his messiah, presumably a descendant of the line of David, who would redeem Israel, relieve her from her oppression and bring her enemies to their knees. This fervent hope has persisted through the centuries and has been transformed, even in modern times, for example, into the Christian belief that Christ is the promised messiah, and within Judaism itself into the Zionist movement.

The second part of Zechariah, known as Deutero-Zechariah (9-14), may have been compiled at a later date (somewhere between 300 and 180 BC). The messianic vision conveyed in these chapters may have been the result of the disintegration of the Persian empire before the onslaught of Alexander. The prophet believed that the day of the Lord was near, and perhaps even that Alexander himself may have been a divine instrument for establishing the messianic kingdom. The vision is predominantly one of great material prosperity and political power, the reestablishment of the Davidic kingdom of old, headed by a meek and humble king who would abolish war and establish peace among nations. God's people will overcome all opposition, bringing about the final struggle between the forces of Yahweh and his demonic enemies. Victory and salvation are brought about by the power of God's presence. The final titanic battle for Jerusalem describes the mortal agony that must take place before the day of the Lord. Jerusalem must suffer the worst agonies and thereby be purified in order to enter into its final glory. .

Ancient Judaism

The elements of messianic expectation have continually evolved under the influence of historic events and circumstances. Any effort to focus a messianic belief as a focal category in ancient Judaic religion immediately runs afoul of the multiplicity of meanings and its scanty and inconsistent usage in Jewish texts (Green 1987). As Charlesworth (1987) comments: "We must not treat the extant early Jewish texts as if they are," using Neusner's [1985] words, 'testimonies to a single system and structure, that is, to Judaism.' Since we are dealing not with one normative structure, but with many structures and substructures, each conceived as normative in its own way and to its own religious group, we must resist the old methodological approach that assumed a coherent messianology in Early Judaism." (p. 227)

In periods of political independence, ethical ideals were emphasized, while during periods of oppression and exile the longing for political freedom became predominant. By the same token, when some degree of political freedom was available, the universalistic aspect of the messianic design came to predominate over more nationalistic ambitions, which flourished in times of political oppression. The influence of Judaic ideas on the nascent Christian movement[2] led early Christians to believe that Christ, the promised messiah, would return in the longed-for *parousia* with its promised joys and graces. While the Christian view of the messiah tended to remain predominantly ethical and spiritual, the Jewish belief always envisioned the messianic kingdom as a kingdom of this world. If that messianic vision became in part ethical, idealized and even spiritually exalted, it remained a terrestrial kingdom. The tension remained a constant part of Jewish messianic beliefs, embracing a dualism of a messiah who was not only spiritual but at the same time political (Klausner 1955; Scholem 1971).[3] Neusner (1984) puts the difficulty in graphic terms: "Does Judaism present a messianism, and may we therefore speak of the messianic idea or doctrine of Judaism? The answer . . . is a qualified negative, yielding a flat no. Judaism as we know it contains numerous allusions to a Messiah and references to what he will do. But so far as we examine the original canon of the ancient rabbis, framed over the sec-

---

2. See chapters 5 and 6.
3. As Mack (1987) notes, the work of Neusner (1984) and others has made it impossible to speak of a Jewish "messiah"; we must speak of "messiahs" instead. The more definitive Christian formulation of the messianic idea has historically become a lens through which Jewish traditions have been interpreted. The picture looks different without that lens.

ond through seventh centuries, we find these inherited facts either reformed and reshaped for use in an essentially non-messianic and ahistorical system, or left like rubble after a building has been completed: stones that might have been used, but were not. So Judaism as we know it presents no well-crafted doctrine of the Messiah, and thus its eschatology is framed within the methods of an essentially ahistorical teleology." (p. ix)

The messianic ideal has been a source of powerful religious motivation and stimulation for centuries. It is a powerful and enduring belief system that has touched the lives of millions profoundly, and from a psychological perspective finds its conviction and enduring power by reason of its capacity to mobilize the deepest and most telling psychological motivations in countless believers. While the messianic belief represents a traditional and ancient belief system, its multiple aspects have received varying degrees of differential emphasis, depending on the psychological needs generated in given historical contexts.

Messianic Belief

It is within the context of these divergent trends that the cultic phenomenon and its related cultic process can be identified. The messianic belief in Jewish history persisted under conditions in which the exile was the primary reality of Jewish experience. Scholem (1971) describes the interplay of three forces influencing the shape of messianic expectations: conservative, restorative, and utopian. The conservative forces sought to preserve the law and religious traditions during the period of the exile. The restorative forces aimed at return to the idealized conditions of the ancestral past. The utopian forces press forward toward a vision of the future, the object of hope and utopian wishes.

Conservative tendencies played a major role in the preservation of the Jewish religious community, but a lesser role in the genesis of messianism. There the forces of restoration and utopian desire mingled in complex patterns of mutual interaction to determine the historical course of the messianic idea. The proportion between them fluctuated wildly, but never one to the exclusion of the other. They operated on the common ground of messianic hope. The utopian vision of the future is the realization of an idealized past. As Scholem (1971) observes: "The completely new order has elements of the completely old, but even this old order does not consist of the actual past; rather, it is a past transformed and transfigured in a dream brightened by the rays of utopianism." (p. 4)

In addition, the messianic belief provides a significant example of the manner in which belief systems are formed and continue to function with profound psychological effect. In this respect as well, the cultic process comes into play as an expression of underlying psychological dynamics. My contention here is that these dynamics can be expressed in terms of the paranoid process (Meissner 1978b, 1984a), and that the messianic belief system functions as a form of paranoid construction, based on and incorporating powerful psychological motivations. With these purposes in mind, then, I will examine the origins and development of the messianic ideal in both Jewish and Christian sources, and then trace some of its doctrinal developments into medieval Judaic thought, particularly in the development and evolution of sabbatianism in which the dimensions of the cultic process come dramatically into focus.

Although the notion of the messiah has an ancient history, the term is not found as a designation for the expected redeemer either in the Old Testament or in the Apocrypha; its first use in this precise sense is found in the book of Enoch (161-164 BC) (Klausner 1955). But elements of the messianic belief can be traced to early strata of the Hebrew traditions. Coppens (1968) observes that even in the books of the Pentateuch, premessianic elements can be identified in the form of hopes for the possession of the Promised Land, promises of the growth and prosperity of the nation, foretellings of the supremacy of the tribe of Judah and of a brilliant monarchy later identified with the reign of David.

In the early days of the Davidic monarchy, every anointed king was regarded as a savior sent by God. The promises of victory and dominion reflected the covenant between Yahweh and David and his successors, together with the assurance that the Davidic line was the chosen human agency through which Yahweh was to bring about salvation in human history. The same motifs are echoed in the royal psalms with reference to any Davidic monarch, not necessarily to David himself. The king was held to be Yahweh's representative, and his priesthood (according to the order of Melchizedek, Ps 110: 4) probably reflected a hereditary title given to the Canaanite kings of Jerusalem, for example, the priest-king Melchizedek (Gen 14). References to divine origin (Ps 110: 3) or divine sonship (Ps 2: 7) seem to derive from the symbolic court language used to describe Yahweh's representative. Ideas of the eternal and universal reign of the king expressed a wishful fantasy of his long life and victories, as well as the sense of enduring greatness of the Davidic monarchy.

Perhaps the clearest expression of the notion of the king as savior of his people may be found in Psalm 72 (Coppens 1968). As McKenzie (1968) comments: "The king governs with the justice that becomes a ruler; he is the savior of the poor and the needy. He is victorious over his enemies, who are also the enemies of his people; he is the savior of his people from external danger. During his reign the blessing of Yahweh brings fertility to the land. Nowhere in the Psalms is the king presented as a future eschatological deliverer. He is the reigning successor of David and the heir of the covenantal promises made to David." (p. 763)

CHAPTER 3

Apocalyptic Messianism

The rise of the power of Macedonia under Philip II in the 4rth century set the stage for the next significant development. Philip's son, Alexander, was born in 356 BC and succeeded to his father's throne in 336. When Alexander assumed control, some of the Greek city-states revolted. The young king lost no time in crushing the rebellion, destroying Thebes and enslaving its inhabitants. In short order he crossed the Hellespont and confronted the Persian armies. At the battle of Issus in 333 BC, he roundly defeated Darius III and swept all opposition before him. Palestine was in Greek hands as of 332 BC. Alexander drove his army eastward as far as the banks of the Indus, leaping like an insatiable fire that consumed everything in its path. Alexander, the Great as he is known, died in Babylon on June 13, 323 BC.

The outcome of the Alexandrian conquest for Judaism was both benign and filled with dire consequence. As long as Alexander was preoccupied with his campaigns, the Jews were left more or less to themselves. Alexander's policy of fusing Greek and Asian peoples and cultures brought with the horses and chariots and glistening arms an infusion of Greek culture and ideas that was to play a dominating role in the subsequent centuries of Palestinian history and was to have far-reaching and powerful effects on the course of ensuing religious history.

In the wake of the Alexandrian conquest (332 BC) and the death of the conqueror (323 BC), Palestine fell under the control of the

Egyptian Ptolemies. The Ptolemies wisely interfered little with Palestinian life beyond the payment of taxes; the internal government remained largely in the hands of the high priest and his council. But with the subsequent Seleucid conquest came a gradual process of hellenization, which introduced important social changes into the fabric of Palestinian life. The Ptolemies and later the Seleucids had set up an efficient imperial bureaucracy for collecting the hated taxes. Judea's importance was more strategic than economic, but these dynasties had to maintain a military presence in order to preserve their position. The Seleucids only gradually imposed hellenizing measures as the need for funds increased and their position became more tenuous. Taxes were collected through the Judean high priesthood, which established itself as a virtual dynasty.

Messianic Vision

The last sampling from the prophetic literature is the book of Daniel, probably composed somewhere in the 2nd century BC during the decline of Seleucid power in Palestine. It probably arose—along with the apocryphal Book of Enoch—among the *hassidim*, the "pious ones" who were devoted to the purity and respect for the law and had early on joined forces with the Maccabees against the hellenizing influence of the Seleucids (Eliade 1982). It prophesies the overthrow of the Greek empire and the domination of Israel over all other nations. The messianic vision is apocalyptic, rather than prophetic. The prophet's words are cast in the context of the encroaching hellenization and its associated paganism, along with the vicious persecution under Antiochus IV Epiphanes, who tried to force the Jews to abandon the law of Moses and accept pagan worship. The portrayal of the Seleucids in the book of Daniel is graphic enough: the fourth beast, representing the hellenistic empire, was "terrible and dreadful and exceedingly strong, and it had great iron teeth; it devoured and broke in pieces, and stamped the residue with its feet" (Dan 7: 7).

But Yahweh will rescue his people from their persecutors. The hope for political power is predominant, but not necessarily material prosperity. Yahweh will extend his political and religious authority over all the Gentiles. The hopes for an individual messiah and the restoration of the Davidic kingdom were dimmed at this time, so that the messianic vision was applied to the people of Israel as a collective entity. The need for a reward for those who had suffered martyrdom in the establishment of the kingdom led to a belief in the resurrection of the dead, mentioned here for the first time in the Bible. The book of Daniel thus serves as an introduction to the apocrypha and the pseudepigrapha, announcing a world to come in which the dead rise and the righteous are enthroned in glory. The connection between the messianic idea and the realization of eschatology is a theme that was further developed, not only in the pseudepigrapha but in the Talmud and subsequent Midrash.

The messianic teaching of the prophets mirrors rather consistently their attitudes toward the monarchy. In general, the royal messianism of the pre-exilic prophets gives way in the later classical prophets to a process of spiritualization, which no longer emphasizes the role of the king as the anointed and chosen one of Yahweh, but stresses the king as the bearer of Yahweh's election and power. Where glorious expectations are attached to the messianic ruler, the emphasis falls almost exclusively on the power of Yahweh acting through him. There is little emphasis on royal messianism in the exilic prophecies; in Deutero-Isaiah, the messiah is no Davidic king at all, but rather Cyrus, the king of the Persians. The redeemer is no king, but Yahweh himself. Davidic messianism, however, enjoyed some revival in the post-exilic period (Klausner 1955; Coppens 1968).

The prophetic messianic vision has been summarized by Klausner (1955) in the following points:

1) Sin begets punishment, and without sin there would be no place for the idea of redemption. The punishment takes place in the day of the Lord or the day of judgment, which falls either on Israel alone or on the pagans or in other accounts on both. The day of judgment involves frightful wars, destruction, exile, humiliation and oppression, even the elimination of the Torah ("the birthpangs of the messiah").

2) The day of judgment brings about repentance, the result of Yahweh's mercy, which prepares and purifies his people for the redemption to follow.

3) The redemption was thought to be heralded by a messenger of the good news, who later was identified with Elijah. This redemption may be accompanied by a victory over the Gentiles, but the later prophets (from Zephaniah on) also hoped that Israel would triumph without resorting to war through the power of Yahweh.

4) At the time of the redemption, only the "remnant of Israel" will remain, namely, a small group of the righteous, blameless

and humble among the sons of Israel. The remnant will be drawn from the sons of Judah and the sons of Ephron, a union which will be joined by an ingathering of the exiles into Zion.

5) The political power of Israel in messianic times is portrayed by all the prophets, but with varying emphasis: some seeing it in terms of the superior power of Israel over the rest of mankind, others as a condition of peace and prosperity in which Israel would be neither subservient to any other nation nor fearful of any foreign power.

6) Material prosperity holds a prominent place in most of the prophetic accounts, but in those prophets in whom the spiritual messianic expectations play a greater role, the element of material prosperity holds a lesser position. Material prosperity includes peace among nations, the abolition of wars, the elimination of conflict in nature, extraordinary fertility of the soil, an increase in the number of human beings, the resettlement of ruined cities, the healing of the sick and handicapped, the prolongation of human life, and finally the extension of the borders of Judah, including Jerusalem.

7) Redemption is accompanied by spiritual welfare, which includes (a) a knowledge of God, not only among the Jews but among all peoples, (b) the predominance of good deeds and righteousness and a love of justice and mercy, (c) a new heart and spiritual renewal in terms of a new covenant, and (d) the perpetuity of the Jewish nation and the Torah.

8) The war against Gog, King of Magog, ("the war of Gog and Magog" in later writings) would take place after the redemption. Yahweh would go to war for his people and win a great victory.

9) In many of the prophet accounts, there is no mention of a human messiah at all; the Lord himself is the redeemer and savior. In other accounts, the messiah is not individual but collective, namely, the kingdom of the house of David. Zechariah probably had in mind an actual person, Zerubbabel, of the Davidic line, but in the rest of the prophetic accounts there is a description of an idealized human messiah, complete with the highest spiritual and ethical characteristics. While he himself may not be a redeemer, this king-messiah is the head of the redeemed people, its political and spiritual

king. A significant shift took place in the teaching of Deutero-Isaiah and Daniel, who spoke not of one man from the
house of David as the messiah, but rather the whole people of
Israel. The people become a spiritual and suffering messiah,
portrayed in Daniel as the "son of man" coming with the
clouds of heaven — the people of Israel at the highpoint of
their eschatological triumph.[1]

The Maccabean Revolt and the Hasmonean Dynasty

The repressive hellenizing measures of the Seleucids were building pressures toward a revolution. When he returned from a campaign
in Egypt (169 BC), Antiochus profaned and plundered the temple. A
year later, when the Romans forced him out of Egypt, Antiochus began
an official persecution in which traditional Jewish practices, for example, temple sacrifice and circumcision, were prohibited under the penalty of death. The ultimate ignominy, the erection of an altar to the
Olympian Zeus, the "abomination of desolation," was the final straw.
The revolt was spurred by the Maccabees and their Hasidean and other
traditional followers.

The revolt, directed against the Seleucids and the apostate
priestly aristocracy, went from initial successes to increasing strength.
In 164 BC, Judas moved boldly to remove the "abomination of desolation" from the temple and thus to wipe out three years of ignominious
blasphemy. The fires of revolution and the spirit of independence
burned brightly. The Maccabees were succeeded by the Hasmonean
Dynasty (134-63 BC), formed by John Hyrcanus I (134-104 BC) and
his successors. The years 63-37 BC witnessed the establishment of Roman power in Palestine and the end of the Hasmonean dynasty. The
Hasmoneans were gradually replaced through a complex process of deception and intrigue by the Herodians.

---

1. According to Eliade (1982), the Son of Man theme is connected to the Anthropos or
Primordial Man of hellenistic mythology. The origins of the myth are buried in Indo-Iranian
sources, mediated through Irano-"Chaldean" religious syncretism. He points out that "The
Idea of the First Man invested with an eschatological mission is not biblical. It is only in late
Judaism that the notion appears of an Adam who existed before the Creation." (p. 268)

The Apocrypha and Pseudepigrapha

The apocryphal literature arose during the period of the Second Temple and was written, for the most part, during the period of the Hasmonean dynasty. The apocryphal works contained little of the apocalyptic (e.g., revelations, prophetic visions) and eschatological elements (e.g., descriptions of life after death, the world to come, the resurrection of the dead, etc.) that would play such a prominent part in the subsequent pseudepigraphal literature. Even the idea of the messianic realm plays no great role in the apocrypha. It was only after the splitting off of the major sects in Israel, the Pharisees, the Sadducees and the Essenes, from the Hasidim and the Hellenists, and especially after the opposition of the Pharisees to John Hyrcanus and the subsequent struggle between the Pharisees and Alexander Janneus, that the religious imagination of the Pharisees and, particularly, the Essenes began to weave visions of messianic grandeur and to further elaborate the messianic message of the prophets. The apocryphal books preceding the reign of John Hyrcanus are filled with historical accounts, legends and ethical precepts, but have little to say about the "days of the messiah," and add nothing to the messianic vision of the canonical scriptures (Klausner 1955).

In contrast, the pseudepigrapha form a kind of transition to the Talmudich *Haggadah* and even to the early Jewish forms of Christianity. Prophetic visions and revelations abound, along with elaborate descriptions of the days of the messiah, including a developed eschatology. When the messianic idea takes on a living force, it is usually in close connection with apocalypticism — "Apocalypticism appears as the form necessarily created by acute Messianism" (Scholem 1971, p. 4). The new eschatology moves beyond the ancient prophets. The prophetic vision was national, this-worldly, envisioning the return of the kingdom of David in renewed glory and a universal reign of religious peace under the suzerainty of the one true God of Israel. The apocalyptic vision contained two antithetical worlds — this world and the world to come, the reign of darkness versus the reign of light. The drama is cast against a cosmic background, the stage on which the final struggle between Israel and the heathen world will be fought out in the end of days (Scholem 1971).

Undoubtedly, the persecution in the time of Antiochus Epiphanes intensified messianic reflections about the day of judgment and the messianic birthpangs. The persecution and afflictions imposed on the nation required a vindication of divine justice along with a deepening desire for vengeance. The seeds of apocalypticism were being sown (Segal 1990). The success of the Maccabees and the subsequent Hasmoneans stirred visions of the realization of the power of the Lord and the destruction he would bring upon the enemies of Israel in the days of the messiah. Early Hasmonean writers saw a vision of ancient glories reviving along with the hope of a personal messiah to rule the new age. The present age was seen as the beginning of the hoped-for messianic era. The apocalyptic literature of the period (the Book of Jubilees, the Testaments of the Twelve Patriarchs, and the Vision of the Weeks of Henoch) emphasized the role of the Hasmonean priest-kings, the sons of Levi, from whom the messiah will come, rather than from the tribe of Judah.

Questions remain, however, as to the extent to which this shift reflects the influence of later Christian interpolations. The ideal figures in the Testaments include the figure of the "savior-priest" of the Testament of Levi (18: 2-14) who ". . . must be ranged among the great messianic figures propagated by the Judaism of the late Second Temple period: the royal messiah in the Psalms of Solomon 17, the figure of Melchizedek in 11Q Melch and the Son of Man figure in the similitudes of Enoch" (Hultgard 1980, p. 105). Yet question remains as to the criteria for judging such messianic status, whether they are or can be dissociated from the Christianizing lens (Mack 1987).

Elements of the traditional view that the messiah would come from the tribe of Judah, as in the Testaments of Judah and Joseph, were cast in doubt. The failure of the Hasmonean dynasty and the rift between the Hasmoneans and the Pharisees with the withdrawal of the more radical Essenes into the desert not only brought the realization that a different conception of the messianic promises was called for, but set the stage for a mighty upsurge of messianic ambitions and dreams.

The failure of the Maccabean revolt had revealed the desperation of mere human efforts at liberation. The writer or writers of Maccabees 1 and 2 nowhere mentions David or the Davidic line. The omission suggests this sect no longer even considered the possibility of a Davidic revival, unlike the seer of 1 Enoch. The Hasmonean propagandist seems to have abandoned the promises of the prophets that centered on the restoration of Davidic rule as part of the messianic kingdom (Goldstein 1987). The traditions of Davidic messianism had faded into the background, and the presence or absence of any messianic residues was largely a matter of the political circumstances of different groups. The Maccabees, focused on their own political fortunes, were little interested in messianic concerns. Apocalyptic groups turned to a concept of a transcendent savior to complement the earthly messianism. But it was not until the rise of the Qumran Essenes and the 1st-century BC Psalms of Solomon that there was a resurgence of messianic interest (Collins 1987).

The defeat of the Maccabees dashed hopes for such a nondavidic restoration so that Israel's only hope was to await the manifestation of divine power that would inaugurate the messianic kingdom. The tribulations of the Hasmonean period were followed by even greater anguish under the harsh rule of the Herodeans in league with the power of Rome. The harsh and uncompromising rule of the Roman procurators brought about the revolt of the Zealots and the catastrophe of the destruction of the Second Temple. Messianic expectations and descriptions of life after death held a predominant place in the later pseudepigrapha. The *Assumption of Moses* comes from the time of the Herodean dynasty, and the *Syriac Apocalypse of Baruch* and the *Book of IV Ezra* from the years immediately following the destruction of the temple.[2]

In the Enoch corpus, for example, two dominant myths share the stage, both set in primordial times. The first tells the story of Enoch's excursion through the cosmos, where he learned the secrets of heaven and earth that he recorded for posterity. The second recounts the fall of the heavenly watchers and the consequences in the deluge. The watchers, their offspring the giants, and the deluge itself will be reflected in the evils of the end-time. The evils that afflict Israel in present times are not the result of the evil deeds of men, but are the result of a more radical evil born of an act of rebellion in another realm beyond human knowing. The real forces of evil are the principalities and powers: the warrior kings are one form of the personification of these evil forces; magicians and soothsayers possess forbidden knowledge and act as the agents of the malevolent forces. And mankind

---

2. Klausner (1955) divides the pseudepigraphal books into the Palestinian and the Hellenistic. The Palestinian were written in Jerusalem and in the Hebrew language. Important messianic expectations are found in the *Book of Enoch*, the *Book of Jubilees*, the *Psalms of Solomon*, the *Assumption of Moses*, the *Syriac Book of Baruch*, and *IV Ezra*. The Hellenistic books were composed for the most part in Alexandria in Greek. The most important messianic expectations are found in the Sibylline books. In some of the later pseudepigrapha, especially in some *Sibylline Oracles*, *IV Ezra*, the *Martyrdom and Ascension of Isaiah*, the *Testaments of the Twelve Patriarchs*, *2 Enoch*, the *Apocalypse of Abraham*, and the *Testament of Adam*, there is evidence that Christian corruptions have crept into the texts in the second and third centuries and even later (Charlesworth 1987).

itself is no more than their helpless victim. Such supernatural evil can only be overcome by divine intervention acting through angelic agents of judgment and salvation. As Nickelsburg (1987) summarizes: ". . . a myth set in primordial times explains the demonic origins of evil in the present time and promises its extermination. The agents of that judgment and the salvation that will follow are transcendent figures from the heavenly realm, who are commissioned with functions that parallel those of human agents: prophet, healer, warrior, high priest. Each of these roles reflects a particular model of salvation, which is here construed in eschatological dimensions." (p. 52)

A New Messianic Vision

Such pseudepigraphal elaborations of the messianic ideas were basically extensions of the messianic vision of the prophets. The "birthpangs of the messiah" were based on ideas of the day of the Lord, as were visions of material prosperity and spiritual enlightenment — all previously expounded in the canonical scriptures. The imaginative elaboration of these ideas gave rise to a new messianic vision. As Klausner (1955) describes it, "And thus was forged that complete messianic chain whose separate links are: the signs of the Messiah, the birthpangs of Messiah, the coming of Elijah, the trumpet of Messiah, the ingathering of the exiles, the reception of proselytes, the war with Gog and Magog, the Days of the Messiah, the renovation of the world, the Day of Judgment, the resurrection of the dead, the World to Come." (pp. 384-385)

The new eschatology moved beyond the limited perspectives of the prophetic vision of the restoration of the House of David with the resulting universal peace under the God of Israel. The apocalyptic vision was cast in terms of two aeons that stood in contradiction — the present world vs. the world to come, the rule of the messiah belonging to this world and the new aeon beginning with the Last Judgment, the reign of darkness vs. the reign of light. The national eschatology is projected to a cosmic stage on which the struggle between the sons of light and the sons of darkness takes place. The utterances of the prophets are recast in the mysterious terms of apocalyptic allegory; the framework of biblical prophecy gives way to more esoteric forms of apocalyptic gnosis. As Scholem (1971) observes:

> It cannot be coincidental that for nearly a millennium this character of apocalyptic knowing has also been preserved by the heirs of the ancient apocalyptists within rabbinic Judaism. . . . The

stronger the loss of historical reality in Judaism during the turmoil surrounding the destruction of the Second Temple and of the ancient world, the more intensive became consciousness of the cryptic character and mystery of the Messianic message, which indeed always referred precisely to the reestablishment of that lost reality, although it also went beyond it. (p. 7)

These ideals and visions undoubtedly played a profound role in the life of the Jewish nation, providing consolation and hope in the turmoil of political oppression and religious persecution. The messianic ambitions may also have fanned the flames of rebellion and served as an intensely cathected ideology that led to the revolt against the power of Rome and ultimately the second destruction of the temple (Meissner 1988). Klausner (1955) has noted that many of the apocrypha and pseudepigrapha are products of the spirit of the Zealots and the Sicarii, whose revolutionary zeal and rebellious attitudes led to the Roman-Judaic war and the destruction of Jerusalem. As Scholem (1971) notes:

> These two aspects [of the messianic idea], which in fact are based on the words of the prophets themselves and are more or less visible there, concern the catastrophic and destructive nature of the redemption on the one hand and the utopianism of the content of realized Messianism on the other. Jewish Messianism is in its origins and by its nature — this cannot be sufficiently emphasized — a theory of catastrophe. This theory stresses the revolutionary, cataclysmic element in the transition from every historical present to the Messianic future. (p. 7)

CHAPTER 4

Qumran
and the Later Tradition

Qumran Messianism

The discovery of the Dead Sea Scrolls at Khirbet Qumran has added a new and important dimension to the understanding of messianic and eschatological ideals in the period immediately preceding the second destruction of the temple. The origins of the Essene community have been described elsewhere (Meissner 1988, in process) as a radical wing of the Pharisaic movement that split off in the face of the politicization of the Maccabean-Hasmonean movement. Linked to this eschatological context, the messianism of the Qumran community took a particular form. The scrolls manifest a credal form of messianism that was not only divergent from but rebelling against proto-pharisaic Judaism.

The life of the later Qumran community was lived largely within an eschatological context. They looked forward to the new covenant that would be realized in the day of judgment, but the rewards of this messianic era were reserved to those who remained pure in the observance of the laws and firm in their belief and commitment to the Righteous Teacher. As Talmon (1987) notes,

> Viewed from the angle of typology, they represent the most decidedly millenarian or chiliastic movement in Second Temple Judaism and possibly in antiquity altogether, Christianity included. . . .

However, they did not live to see their hopes materialize, and thus were suspended in limbo between the real and the visionary stage of history. They present to us a prime example of stunted millenarianism. (p. 115)

The Teacher of Righteousness was not in any sense a messiah, nor did he claim any messianic title, but proposed his teaching as leading Israel to salvation (Coppens 1968). As long as the Teacher of Righteousness was active and functioning, the Qumran writings of the period are caught up in enthusiasm over his teachings and pay little attention to the future promise of a messianic era. But with his death (circa 120-110 BC), the stage was set for a rebirth of messianic expectations. The realization that deliverance had not come in the Teacher's lifetime and the conviction that they were living in a period before the final cataclysm led to the persuasion that God would raise up his anointed messiahs to accomplish the ultimate victory of the forces of light over the forces of darkness. The early writings, presumably composed in the early years of enthusiasm about the teachings of the Righteous Teacher, say little or nothing about the coming of the messiah. Rather than a future community of eschatological expectation based on the teaching of a future prophet, the Qumran community saw itself as the fulfillment of traditional prophecies concerning the new covenant under the guidance of the new Moses, the Teacher of Righteousness.

The renewed interest in messianism at this time may have been fostered by the addition of new members who found themselves dissatisfied with the pharisaic movement. The community looked for the coming of a messiah who would arise from Aaron or from Israel. The life of the later Qumran community was lived largely within an eschatological context. The original expectations were for a relatively short period of time between the death of the Righteous Teacher and the coming of the messiah — 40 years in the *Damascus Covenant*. But this optimistic estimate was rapidly revised, so that by the time of the appearance of the Roman legions in AD 83, the notion of God's indefinitely prolonging the period of waiting had been accepted. The parallels to later Christian expectations and rationalizations regarding the *parousia* are clear.

The Qumran documents speak of the expectation of "the coming of a prophet and the messiahs of Aaron and Israel." The expectation of a prophet follows traditional motifs, namely, the expectation of a prophet like Moses or Elijah announcing the dawn of the messianic era. The messiahs of Aaron and Israel reflect the expectation of two individuals to carry out the messianic mission. The messiah of Aaron would be the anointed high priest, and the messiah of Israel the anointed Davidic king. This form of messianic expectation may have arisen in post-exilic Judaism. Zechariah (Zech 4: 14) imagines two figures anointed by the Lord, namely, Zerubbabel of the Davidic line and Joshua, the priest. It is reasonable to assume that in a community so devoted to the priestly life as the Qumran community, the hope for a priestly messiah to stand alongside the more traditional Davidic messiah is to be expected. In the messianic banquet, the two presiding figures are the priest and the messiah of Israel. In the later works of the community, an even greater role was assigned to the eschatological high priest than to the Davidic messiah. As Charlesworth (1987) observes:

> What is novel and important in Qumran messianism is not the denial of a kingly Messiah, but the addition of a priestly Messiah who shall not only accompany the messianic king but also dominate him. The tendency to elevate the priesthood and place all others, especially the ruling king, in subordination to it is to be expected among priests in exile and in tension with the ruling body; this tendency has now been clarified impressively in the Temple Scroll. (p. 230)

Thus, the Qumran elaboration of the messianic motifs has entered Jewish history and thought as a separate line of development and influence. This notion of a dual messiahship assumes a more dominant position in the Qumran literature than in any apocryphal work. The pattern evolved from a biblical pattern that emerged in the post-exilic period, and was not the exclusive legacy of the Qumran Covenanters. Talmon (1987) summarizes the millennarian-messianic ideology of the Qumran community:

> The expected *New Aeon* will unfold at an age in which terrestrial-historical experience coalesces with celestial-spiritual utopia. Salvation is viewed as transcendent and imminent at the same time. The New Order to be established by the Anointed is not otherworldly but rather the realization of a divine plan on earth, the consummation of history in history. Qumran Messianism reflects the political ideas of the post-exilic returnees' community. It is the *politeia* of the New Commonwealth of Israel and the New Universe. (p. 131)

All of this must be taken with the usual grain of salt. The life of the Qumran community extended over three centuries and involved different groups with different and evolving beliefs. Rather than a monolithic belief system, it is difficult to discern any consistent content or development in Qumran messianology. The scrolls do not present a unified picture, certainly not one that would easily lend itself to translation into a Christian christology (Charlesworth 1987).

The messianic expectations at Qumran were current in Palestine even a century later, and were applied in the New Testament to the figure of Christ. There is not total agreement about the meaning of Qumran messianism. The priestly traditions extant at Qumran could well have stirred hopes for a priestly messiah to accompany the more general wish for a Davidic messiah. In the account of the messianic banquet in the appendix to the Rule of the Congregation (1QSa), the two presiding figures are the priest and the messiah of Israel. And in later works, for example, *The War of the Sons of Light Against the Sons of Darkness*, the role of the eschatological high priest seems to be raised above that of the Davidic messiah, but the documents themselves are incomplete. The theory of the two messiahs seems to have found its way into the apocryphal Testaments of the Twelve Patriarchs, possibly reflecting the influence of Qumran thought. While the New Testament clearly pictures Christ as the expected Davidic messiah, there are also grounds for a theology of Christ as the anointed eschatological high priest (Hebrews 4: 14).

The Herodian Dynasty and the Judean Revolts

The period of Herodian rule in Palestine had important implications for the understanding of the incidence of messianic ideas of the time. The historical impact was felt more decisively in the development of Christian views of the messiah than in contemporary Judaism. Herod had suppressed rebellion by tight control, but the populace was seething with revolutionary ferment. After his death, acts of defiance and popular revolts broke out everywhere in his domain. Popular messianic movements sprang up in every district and spawned peasant revolts.

In the wake of the Herodian misrule, the Romans took over governance of Palestine and ran it with an iron hand. The burdens imposed on the populace were more burdensome than ever. Revolutionary messianic movements sprang up everywhere. Presumably the accusations brought against Jesus that led to his crucifixion were cast in terms of such a messianic revolt. In any case, the deep resentment and desperation of the Jewish people, crushed under the Roman heel, festered during the early part of the first century and finally reached the flash point in the revolt of AD 66.

The destruction of Jerusalem and the Temple had symbolic significance far beyond the actual demolition. It brought to an end a tradition of centuries in which sacrifice could be offered to Yahweh only in the Jerusalem temple. In these terms, the Temple had been the center of the Jewish world, but now it was no more. The fall of Jerusalem and the destruction of the Temple created a decisive and irrevocable break with the past, such that Judaism was forced to turn in new directions and, in some sense, to seek a new destiny.

The destruction had its effect on the Christian community as well. For the Romans, the Christians were for all practical purposes indistinguishable from the Jews and were lumped with them as subject peoples. But to the Jews they were traitors, because they had failed to support the Jewish cause and had turned their back on Jewish religious traditions. In large measure, many of the Jewish Christians became refugees from Palestine and carried with them into the Gentile world the kerygma of the gospel in the primitive church.

After the destruction of Jerusalem, Palestine remained under Roman military control, but the yearning for the restoration of Israel remained alive, nourished by the recollection of the events following the destruction of Jerusalem in 586 BC. Revolts among the Jews continued to erupt, usually stemming partly from Roman oppression, but also stirred by messianic expectations. In Palestine, a constant level of unrest continued to smolder beneath the surface. These unsettled conditions in Judea finally came to a climax in the so-called Second Revolt (AD 132-135) under Simon bar Kochba. Sextus Julius Severus had to be recalled from his command in Britain to put down the revolt, but only after a long, tedious process of starving out the Jews who had taken refuge in desert strongholds and caves. Jerusalem was once again taken, razed, and on its ruins Hadrian built his Aelia Capitolina.

With the defeat of Simon bar Kochba, Jewish hopes for the restoration of Israel and for the reconstruction of the temple were dashed irrevocably. After the destruction of AD 70, hope had lingered on, and messianic expectations had risen to a new crescendo, centered on the figure of bar Kochba. But he proved to be the last major Palestinian political leader of the Jews until modern times. The frustrated hope and longing for a return to Jerusalem and for the restoration of the temple has been part of Jewish life and culture for the ensuing 1800 years.

The Period of the Tannaim

The period of the Maccabean revolt and the gradual hellenization of Palestine saw the emergence of various sects in Judaism, particularly the alignment of the Pharisees in opposition to the Sadducees. The Pharisees espoused a tradition of oral law based on the opinions of the great teachers, a development that was rejected by the more conservative Sadducees, who insisted on the observance of the written law exclusively. In the time of the emergence of Christianity, two divergent schools of jurisprudence had developed: the stricter approach followed the teachings of Shammai, and the more lenient group the teachings of Hillel.

The period of the Tannaim extended from the teachings of the last of the great teachers until the formation of the Mishnah in AD 200. There was need for these oral teachings to be collected and preserved. Primitive collections may have existed, even in Hillel's time, but the destruction of the Temple and the subsequent failure of the second Jewish revolt (AD 135) served as further stimuli toward the definitive collection of these oral teachings. The failure of the Second Revolt had placed the very survival of Judaism in jeopardy. The Jabneh Sanhedrin was abolished, study of the Torah was banned under penalty of death, and the religious leaders were persecuted — Aqiba died from torture.

There was thus desperate need for compilation of the oral traditions, a goal that became possible after restoration of the Sanhedrin by Antoninus Pius (Eliade 1985). The predominant influence in this codification was the great Rabbi Aqiba, whose collection was subsequently expanded by his disciple, Rabbi Meir. By the end of the century, the final official codification of the previous centuries of oral law was accomplished in the Mishnah.

During the period of the great teachers, prior to the first Jewish revolt and the destruction of the temple, the messianic idea was preserved, but more in the popular mind than in official circles. As long as Judea maintained some degree of political autonomy, and the Temple in all its glory was still standing, the Pharisees must have had little reason for further elaboration of the messianic ideas. The Scribes, the precursors of the Tannaim, were immersed in the study and exposition of the law and its adaptation to practical everyday affairs. There was little need and little room for messianic speculation or apocalyptic elaboration, as had been characteristic of pseudepigraphal works (e.g., 2 Baruch and 4 Esdras).

The Torah became the center of Jewish life and thought, so that the messianic age could not be imagined without reference to it. The influence of pharisaism had become firmly established in the first century. The impact of historical selection is significant here, since what we are left with is the remnants not just of pharisaism, as one among the wide variations of Jewish beliefs, but one brand of pharisaism derived from the work of Johanan ben Zakkai. For this group, loyalty to the Torah became the binding force in Judaism after the destruction of the Temple. The regulation of all aspects of Jewish life by reference to the Torah ultimately led to the need for codification in the Mishnah. The place of the Torah in the messianic vision became a matter of debate. A dominant view was that the Torah was immutable: it had been given to Moses by Yahweh and was therefore perfect and unchangeable. No prophet would ever appear to change it and no new Moses would ever provide a different law to replace it. This belief was common not only in Palestine but in hellenistic Judaic circles as well, as for example in the writings of Philo (Davies 1966).

Certainly obedience to the Torah would be a prominent aspect of the messianic age. The Torah would persist into the messianic age, but room was left for a new and deeper understanding of it so that the many obscurities would be made clear. Even the Gentiles in this view would come to accept the Torah and obey it. There is some doubt whether the opposing notion of a new Torah as part of the messianic dispensation was a late Christian accretion or not. Even without this influence, however, there were elements in the messianic attitudes of some groups that would accept the idea of a new Torah, but how this new rendition would relate to the old was left obscure at best.

But the messianic expectations lived on. Both in Palestine and the diaspora, there was a yearning for the restoration of Israel. Pain and oppression gave new vitality to the messianic hopes, despite the painful disillusionment of the failure of the second revolt. The political aspect of the messianic ambitions had suffered a severe blow in the tragedy of bar Kochba, so that subsequent elaborations of the messianic ideal tended to emphasize the spiritual side more strongly. The birth of new hope from the ruins of despair produced the idea of the occultation of the messiah — the messiah is present but hidden, waiting for the moment of redemption — a leading idea of the Messianic Haggadah (Scholem 1971, p. 11). The failure of bar Kochba brought a new sense and a new concreteness to the notion of the "birthpangs of messiah." The notion of suffering preceding the messiah's advent had been a traditional concept, but the imagery had remained somewhat nonspecific and general. The idea now received a concrete form of a messiah who must die. The figure of the messiah ben Joseph emerged with greater clarity as one who was fated to die in the war with Gog and Magog, just as bar Kochba had fallen in the war with the Romans.

The Period of the Amoraim

The period of the Amoraim, the Talmudic masters (AD 200-500), spans the period from the formation of the Mishnah to the completion of the Talmud. This period also saw a gradual shift of the center of Jewish intellectual activity from Palestine to Babylonia. The Palestinian schools continued their activities, while the Babylonian centers gradually became more active and influential. By the early 3rd century, the Mishnah was brought to Babylon and served as the focus of scholarly study and comment. Two independent traditions grew up of commentary on the Mishnah and ultimately produced the great Talmuds, the Palestinian Talmud and somewhat later the Babylonian Talmud.

Along with the shift in leadership from Palestine to Babylonia, there was an important shift in the messianic idea. The Babylonian Talmud pointed the way for Jews to achieve greater adaptation to the diverse environment of the diaspora. Babylon became the center of diaspora Judaism, and the Babylonian Talmud became the universally accepted authoritative teaching of rabbinism. The cult of the synagogue came to replace the worship and sacrifice of the temple. This authority remained unchallenged until the 9th century, when a dissident movement arose led by Anan ben David, called the Karaites. They rejected the oral traditions and recognized only the authority of scripture; they also called for a return to Palestine in order to hasten the coming of the messiah (Eliade 1985).

As time passed, the Jews became more and more removed from the source of their political life and hopes in Palestine, so that the desires for political redemption were replaced by more mystical and religious fantasies. The emphasis in the messianic ideas also seemed to shift. In literature of the Tannaitic period, there is no trace to be found of references to the "suffering messiah." These belong entirely to the post-Tannaitic period, when influences from Christian sources may have played a role. In addition, the personality of the messiah takes on an increasingly important function. In the biblical development of the messianic idea, emphasis is laid on the redemption of Israel, while the person of the messiah seems to play a relatively minor part. In the post-biblical literature, the messiah seems to step into the foreground. It is through him that the days of the messiah and the messianic era are realized.

This emphasis is evident in the Tannaitic period, but in the later post-Tannaitic period the characterization of the messiah to come becomes highly elaborated and detailed. Part of this evolving picture was an increased appreciation of the role of suffering in relation to messianic hopes. The sufferings of the Jewish nation were seen as punishments for its sins, but redemption from such suffering implied the redemption from sin. Such redemption required sincere repentance and observance of the law as essential changes required before the dawn of the messianic era. Thus, the birthpangs which were to precede the coming of the messiah were an essential aspect of the notion of redemption. The messianic idea itself was closely connected with the history of affliction and oppression, which was Israel's lot from the beginning. Basic elements in the "messianic travail" were the forgetting of the law and the loss of disciples. Persecutions directed against the law in the schools did not come until the time of Hadrian, so that it was only in this period of persecution that the distinctive aspects of the messianic travail took their final form.

The glorification of the personality of the messiah is a characteristic of the later Amoraim period. In contrast, the Tannaim remained true to the prophetic tradition and emphasized the messianic age rather than the messiah himself. The messiah in the Tannaitic literature is only an instrument of Yahweh, and only Yahweh himself can bring redemption. Similarly, in no authentic Tannaitic source is there any description of the messiah that indicates anything beyond human capabilities. While the portrait is idealized as a mighty ruler of exalted moral perfection, he remains a human being, and his kingdom is a kingdom of this world. Suggestions as to the possibility of the divine nature of the messiah may be found in later Midrashim. But these post-Tannaitic divine attributions probably reflect the indirect and unconscious influence of the teachings of Christianity.

The later tradition developed the idea of two messiahs, rather than one, as in the Essene version of messianism. However, Klausner (1955) suggests that this idea arose out of the twofold character attributed to the essentially single messiah of the earlier tradition. The traditional idea of the messiah contained both a spiritual and a temporal dimension, and in the earlier literature the messiah was thought of as a king and a warrior. The messiah had to be, in some sense, a military hero, and this imagery was perfectly consistent with the role of the kings who not only ruled, but took the position of leadership in battle. However, the vision of a spiritual and ethical messiah found in Isaiah and in Zechariah, for example, was increasingly difficult to reconcile with the notion of the warrior messiah. As long as political hopes could be maintained, the political aspect of the messiah could be consistently maintained. But after Aqiba committed himself to the notion of a purely political messiah, without any spiritual qualities whatsoever, and after the bitter failure of the bar Kochba rebellion, political hopes and ambitions were destroyed, and only then could the contradiction in the notion of the messiah be felt with its full impact. The spiritual and religious aspect of the messianic faith gained the upper hand and could not coexist with the destructive and warlike qualities of the warrior messiah who would reek vengeance and destruction on the enemies of the nation.

The tension was resolved by assigning the warrior functions to one messianic figure, leaving the other messianic figure as the bearer of more authentically spiritual and religious values. The Messiah ben Joseph flourishes during the messianic catastrophe — he fights the good fight but loses. With his defeat and death, the period of history ends. The utopian desires are focused on the Messiah ben David, who arose from the ashes of defeat to bring about the final victory and establish the messianic era (Scholem 1971). Thus, the spiritual messiah was the messiah ben David from the tribe of Judah, and his opposite number was the messiah ben Joseph, representing the tribe of Ephraim. This messiah, it was also thought, would have to be slain in his struggle with the enemies of Israel, probably after the model of bar Kochba. After the wars of the messianic age have been fought and victory has been achieved, the messiah ben David will come to claim his throne.

The Messianic Belief System

The tradition of messianic beliefs provides a rich tapestry of psychological motifs and thematic symbols. The overriding theme expresses the hope for redemption and restoration. These expectations arise first in the face of the demise of the glories of the Davidic monarchy and continue to evolve through the subsequent centuries of defeat and oppression. The belief system thus carries with it a restitutive connotation in the face of profound and continuing loss. As such it provides a remarkable example, painted in gigantic form over the huge tapestry of human history, of the dynamics of loss and restitution, of the restorative capacity of human psychic potential in the wake of powerful and destructive loss (Rochlin 1965). This dynamic configuration is well expressed by Mack (1987) in a summary statement:

> [There is] a kind of intellectual effort even in the most fantastic constructions that diverse groups placed upon their ideals. Some of this fantasy would border on madness, were we not able to see its cogency. But a certain toughness of the intellect marks the limits to which the flights were allowed to go. A realism about the way things were going in actual social history was never denied. It was in fact that acknowledgment which placed the questions and generated the energies that produced these marvelous visions. If we see them constrained both by a painful analysis of social events — the careful sifting of the epic traditions and ideals — and studied reflection on the options available for remedial or alternative social formations, this imaginative labor had not lost touch with reality. It was marked, in fact, by a stubborn capacity not to give up the archaic ideals even in the face of events and circumstances that could only be seen to reflect them in the furthest stretches of the imagination. (p. 47)

The redemption is not without destruction and ruin, but its utopian impulse incorporates all restorative hopes for return of the Davidic monarchy, but in a form more perfect, more pure, complete, immeasurably richer than any beginning — something entirely new and more glorious. This utopian vision became the basis for mystical beliefs. As Scholem (1971) notes:

> The world of *tikkun*, the reestablishment of the harmonious condition of the world, which in the Lurianic Kabbalah is the Messianic world, still contains a strictly utopian impulse. That harmony which it reconstitutes does not at all correspond to any condition of things that has ever existed even in Paradise, but at most to a plan contained in the divine idea of Creation. (p. 13)

A second striking aspect is expressed in the constantly evolving variations on the theme in relation to the shifting kaleidoscope of historical actualities. The belief system shows remarkable adaptability to the political and historical contexts in which it lives. In the context of political defeat and oppression, the messianic hopes assume a highly political flavor, looking forward to the restoration of Israel, to the regaining of the glories of the Davidic kingdom, and, if not political hegemony, at least political invulnerability. In periods of relative political tranquillity and autonomy, the pressure of political needs recedes and gives way to a more specifically religious and spiritual vision of the messianic realization. When faith and confidence in the promise of the Davidic kingship weakens and falters, the messianic vision becomes collective and less personal; salvation is sought in the people of Israel rather than in any individual, or failing that, in Yahweh himself, who is able to realize the fruits of the messianic revival regardless of the failings of his merely human instruments. Within this welter of usages, the meaning of the messiah is a shifting, changing chameleon reflecting more of the coloration of its religious and political background than any of itself. Green (1987) cites a passage from Morton Smith (1959) that catches the flavor of this heterogeneity:

> Now all this variety in the matter of messianic expectations is merely one detail — though a particularly striking one — of the even greater variety of eschatological expectations current in the two centuries before and after the time of Jesus. To say nothing of mere differences in personnel and program, these expectations run the whole gamut of concepts, from ordinary kingdoms in this world, through forms of this world variously made over and improved, through worlds entirely new and different, to spiritual bliss without any world at all. But the point to be noted is that these contradictory theories evidently flourished side by side in the early rabbinic and Christian and Qumran communities which copied the texts and repeated the sayings. What is more, quite contradictory theories are often preserved side by side in the same document. (p. 3)

When persecution wanes and some degree of relative political freedom and material prosperity waxes, messianic speculation pales and fades, only to be revitalized and rejuvenated when oppression and persecution reassert their painful sting. And as hopes for any messianic realization in this world become remote and dim, they are replaced by apocalyptic visions and eschatological expectations. The squelching of hopes in the Teacher of Righteousness by his death lights the fires of messianic speculation among the Essenes. Roman repression stirs the Zealots to violence and rebellion in the service of a political vision of messianic triumph. This strain of political messianism finds its explosive fulfillment in the revolt under bar Kochba; the pain and disillusionment of his defeat and death turns the messianic hopes away from political dreams of conquest and glory to a more spiritual and mystical vision in which suffering and repentance for sin become the vehicles for redemption and salvation. The radical tension of conflicting ideological commitments even produces a doctrine of two messiahs, one who suffers and dies for the realization of the messianic kingdom, the other who brings it to fruition and rules it.

A third important component of the messianic belief system, in addition to its utopian idealism and hopes, are the themes of vengeance, revolutionary zeal and rebellion that seem to pervade its motivational structure. The messianic doctrine is a theory of catastrophe and destruction that stresses the element of cataclysmic revolution as the means of transition to a messianic future. This catastrophic doom is applied in the first instance to the destruction within which the messianic redemption arises ("the birth pangs of the messiah"), but in the second instance it focuses on the terrors of the last judgment that concludes the messianic period. This revolutionary strain of the messianic tradition came to its greatest fruition in the Zealot movement and later in the rebellion of bar Kochba that culminated in the second destruction of Jerusalem and the Temple. The revolutionary messiah is a warrior-king who will drive the enemies of Israel into the sea and who will establish the hegemony of the new messianic order over all the nations of the earth. The apocalyptic emphasis, however, tended to view this messianic utopia as twofold: the conquest and rule of the messiah still belong to this world, but the secondary period, inaugurated by the Last Judgment, is a totally new aeon of other-worldly fulfillment.

Aspects of the Cultic Process

Traditional messianism carries within it the characteristics of the cultic process.[1] The cultic elements come into play in varying degrees and in varying proportions in different contexts. The messianic hope was cast in opposition to the prevailing forces and institutions of the surrounding society. The messianic belief system was maintained in a state of high tension with the surrounding sociocultural environment. This was particularly the case under the conditions of political defeat, humiliation and subjugation that characterized Jewish life in the exilic and post-exilic periods. The straining against extant social forces, even though they were imposed from the outside, was relatively diffuse and anarchical, without an emphasis on social structure and organization other than commitment to an idealized messianic king. My argument here is based on the supposition that much of the dynamism that powered these beliefs came from underlying psychological needs and yearnings, so that the motivational drive came as much or more from internal psychic needs than from purely social imperatives. This is re-

---

1. The cultic elements are reviewed in chapter 15.

flected both in the yearning for mystical experience that expressed itself in eschatological and apocalyptic visions, and in the yearning for the idealized and charismatic messiah leader.

The typology of the messianic cult is mixed rather than pure. Conversionist elements do not play a very great role since the cult membership included the chosen people to the exclusion of others. Jewishness was the basis of belonging and membership was more or less taken for granted. Other nations might share in the benefits of the messianic renewal, but only as secondary participants and beneficiaries of the messianic reign. The adventist strains played a more prominent part, largely stimulated by political oppression. This aspect became most poignant in regard to the anticipation of a future order of peace and justice that would be achieved by the overthrow of the extant order and its replacement, even by violence and conquest, of a utopian messianic reign. Introversionist and gnostic elements also played a telling role insofar as the emphasis fell on the internal life of the Jewish community and its attainment of justice and peace. This enlightened expression was to be attained under the guidance of the spirit which would renew and create within the members a new life and spirit by which they would become an enlightened elect. Aspects of this belief were decidedly gnostic, emphasizing an esoteric body of wisdom, an elevation through the power of the spirit to new levels of mystical experience and divine communion (Meissner, in process).

The sectarian response can take the form of acceptance, aggression or avoidance. Certain segments of Jewish society were inclined toward acceptance; these were usually the established power groups who had something to gain from acceptance of prevailing social structures. The political involvement and collaboration of the Sadducees and temple priests with the Romans is a case in point. But by and large, the more common response was to seek aggressive opposition or to follow a more avoidant pattern of withdrawal into eschatological beliefs, apocalyptic expectations, and mystical contemplation. The more oppressed, humiliated, deprived and violated the believers felt, the greater tendency there was for messianic expectations to take an aggressive revolutionary turn. The more these forces came into play, the greater was the tendency to consolidate ideological convictions and to seek a more unified commitment and submission to a charismatic leader.

I would argue, therefore, that the Jewish messianic tradition carries within it the elements of the cultic process. These aspects of the messianic belief system derive from profound human needs and reflect the influence of powerful dynamic processes. Powerful narcissistic and

aggressive forces are called into play in response to oppressive subju-
gating influences which violated traditional political structures and undermined the structure of religious beliefs and practices. These constituted narcissistic traumata not only on the level of national and social
organization, but in the souls of individual Jews who were deprived of
their freedom, were violated physically and spiritually, and even threatened with banishment, torture, imprisonment, slavery, and death. Messianic beliefs became the channel for restitutive forces that provided a
compensation for narcissistic loss and mobilized aggressive capacities
in the service of that restitution. The same elements came into play in
the later evolution of messianic traditions, as we shall see in the following section.

Section III

Christian Messianism

CHAPTER 5

Messianism in the Gospels

From Judaic to Christian Messianism

Out of the welter of meanings attributable to Old Testament messianic ideas there evolved a more consistent and specific messianic vision that centered the messianic doctrine on the person of Jesus Christ. The expectation of the messiah can be found in post-exilic Judaism, although the word was not used as a title in any sense. From the evidence of the New Testament and Jewish postbiblical apocryphal writings, it seems that messianic expectations were common coin in late intertestamental Judaism, even to the point of becoming a national hope. But for many, discouragement was more the order of the day. In the 1st century AD, hopes of the return of the Davidic monarchy had begun to fade — they had endured for half a millennium. Eschatological visions had begun to be entertained without any reference to the messiah. As McKenzie (1968) has written:

> In particular, the Christian must be warned that while the late Jewish hope of the Messiah was highly idealized almost to the point of making the messiah a figure of superhuman abilities there was no expectation of a divine Messiah in the sense in which Jesus is professed as Son of God. Moreover, nationalistic coloring was never absent from any stage of the pre-Christian development of messianic thought, any more than the OT [Old Testament] concept of salvation itself was devoid of materialistic and nationalistic aspects. It is inaccurate and unjust to say that the Jews of Jesus' time had corrupted the idea of the Messiah as a spiritual

savior by making it secular and nationalistic and that Jesus restored the concept to its pristine meaning. The Christian understanding of a spiritual Messiah represented a change rather than a
restoration. . . . (p. 762)

The transition from Judaic to Christian usage may have seen a
syncretism of messianic images with pre-existing salvific figures — the
Suffering Servant, the Son of Man, etc. — resulting in a composite
conception (Stanley 1968b). This was clearly the case in the Christian
era, but uncertainly so in pre-Christian Judaism. No pre-Christian writings ever described a suffering messiah (de Jonge 1991) — an idea that
became central to Christian understanding. The transposition of the
messianic idea from Judaism to Christianity had to involve considerable modification.

Christian messianism derives from and builds upon the roots of
the traditions of the Jewish messianic belief system. As Green (1987)
notes:

> A broad academic and popular consensus holds that the messiah, a
> term conventionally taken to designate Israel's eschatological re-
> deemer, is a fundamental Judaic conception and that conflicting
> opinions about the messiah's appearance, identity, activity, and
> implications caused the historical and religious division between
> Judaism and Christianity. . . . That Jewish anticipation of the
> messiah's arrival was unusually keen in first century Palestine and
> constituted the *mise en scene* for the emergence of Christianity is
> a virtual axiom of western history. The study of the figure of the
> messiah thus is inextricable from the quest for "Christian origins"
> and persists as a major scholarly strategy for discerning early
> Christianity's filiation and divergence from the Jewish religion of
> its day. (p. 1)

The heterogeneity and multiplicity of messianic traditions and
their relation to the more unified Christian messianic vision is only part
of the problem. Other difficulties arise from the translation of relatively narrow Palestinian Jewish sectarian views to the broader proclamation of belief to the far-flung Greco-Roman empire. The transition
is already evident in the earliest Christian sources, as for example in
the hellenistic Jewish letters of the apostle Paul or the gentile Christian
writings of Luke. How does the notion of the messiah translate from
its essentially Jewish origins to the language and categories of hellenistic thought (MacRae 1987)?

The line of development in the messianic doctrine is parallel and
mutually influential in both the Jewish and Christian traditions. The

political and chiliastic messianism of religious movements within Christianity contains often hidden strains of Jewish messianic doctrine of one sort or another. The messianism of the Taborites, the Anabaptists, or the radical Puritans finds its inspiration more in the Old Testament than in Christian sources. The Christian conviction regarding the resurrection and its associated redemption lends special vehemence to these messianic illusions. Within Judaism, the messianic inspiration becomes ineffectual and powerless due to the radical difference between the reality of the unredeemed world and the vision of messianic redemption. Within Christianity, the dialectic of messianic interiorization and mysticism continues to run its historical course. As Scholem (1971) observes:

> Parallel to this line, along which Judaism has again and again furnished Christianity with political chiliastic Messianism, runs the other one, along which Christianity, for its part, has bequeathed to Judaism or aroused within it the tendency to discover a mystical aspect of the interiorization of the Messianic idea. To be sure, this aspect comes to the same degree from the inner movement and development of mysticism in Judaism itself, for which the Messianically promised reality must in addition appear as a symbol of an inner condition of the world and of man. (p. 16)

I will develop the argument in the present chapter that Christian messianism not only has preserved a historical and doctrinal continuity with the Jewish tradition, but that the same psychological forces and dynamics that were identifiable in the Jewish messianic tradition are at work in variant form in the Christian tradition as well. The messianic aspects of early Christian belief were an expression of the cultic aspects of the development of the early Church. As such they form a vehicle for the expression of the dynamics of the paranoid process.

Messianic Doctrine in the Gospels

The Jerusalem catastrophe left its mark on the Christian church as well as on Judaism — particularly in the resurgence of messianic expectations and apocalyptic enthusiasm, along with the longing for the return of Christ in the parousia. The gospel accounts represent two distinct movements, that of John the Baptist and that of Jesus, both qualifying as apocalyptic and millennarian cults (Segal 1990). The gospel accounts were written, after all, in the wake of the destruction of the Temple. It is no surprise, then, that the eschatological themes of early apostolic preaching find their echoes in the synoptic gospels;

there was as yet no clear expression of the realized eschatology that finds its way into John. In the synoptics, John the Baptist preaches an apocalyptic judgment in Old Testament terms: he proclaims an imminent judgment (Mt 3: 10) by one who is the mediator of divine wrath (Lk 3: 15-18). The judgment is meant to purify those who repent (Mt 3: 10, 12) and punish those who rebel against God (Mt 3: 12). Even the corrupt leaders of the people will not escape this universal judgment of God. John's preaching seemed to echo the spirit and themes of the messianic doctrine of Qumran (Stanley 1968a).

The picture of the Son of Man in the synoptics is twofold. On one hand he is humble and poor, the embodiment of the Suffering Servant. At the same time he is the glorified Son of Man who will serve as the judge of all men (Mk 8: 38; 13: 26; 14: 62; Mt 25: 31-46). If Jesus' suffering and the related persecution of his followers is patterned after the persecution of the prophets (Lk 6: 22-23; Mt 5: 11-12), it also provides the basis for joy since their reward will be great in heaven. The beatitudes promise that when the kingdom has arrived, hunger, poverty and sorrow will have their rewards. Mark (Mk 13: 9-13) predicts the struggles of those who remain faithful to the gospel, but in the end they will be saved. "For anyone who wants to save his life will lose it; but anyone who loses his life for my sake, and for the sake of the gospel, will save it" (Mk 8: 35). Thus, as de Jonge (1991) notes, "According to these words of Jesus found in Mark and Q, those who follow Jesus, bringing his message and serving his cause until the very end, will be vindicated. They may expect to suffer and must be ready to give their lives, but they may also expect to share in the blessings of God's Kingdom, due to be revealed in the near future." (p. 38)

While Luke tends to mute the eschatological and apocalyptic tones of Mark's gospel (Mk 13: 14 vs Lk 21: 20; Mk 14: 62 vs Lk 22: 67-69), Matthew moves in the opposite direction (Mk 8: 38 vs Mt 16: 27; Mk 13: 4 vs Mt 24: 3). Mark records the eschatological discourse (Mk 13: 1-37) with a degree of confusion, but Matthew (Mt 24: 1-44) applies it to the destruction of the Temple and Luke divides it into two discourses, one dealing with the second coming (Lk 17: 22-37) and the other with a prediction of the destruction of Jerusalem and the Temple (Lk 21: 6-36). Thus, in the synoptic gospels at least, the views of the messiah are cast in terms of the eschatological framework that pervaded their thinking.

Even though the primitive kerygma suggests that Jesus proclaimed himself as messiah and son of God, this view has been questioned, especially at the hands of liberal theological critics. For Karl

Barth (1972), any connection of the content of faith with historical data was suspect, since faith was meant to be a response to the gospel message rather than to any results of historical investigation. For Bultmann (1952), Jesus' announcement of the kingdom takes place in the context of Jewish eschatological expectations, but he emphasizes the immediate presence of the kingdom as an existential call to a radical commitment to God and a new life rather than an argument based on apocalyptic constructs (de Jonge 1991). If Jesus was aware of his messianic mission, he was not very forthright about it. The fact that the gospels reflect the influence of the post-resurrection faith of the Christian Church makes any assessment of Jesus' preaching difficult. Christian apologetics would argue that Jesus was unwilling to declare himself because he would risk being understood in terms of the prevailing views of the messiah (Léon-Dufour 1968).[1]

On the other hand, it should not be ignored "that the earliest Christians, Jews of Jerusalem, constituted an apocalyptic sect within Palestinian Judaism. They were in daily expectation of the Second Coming of Christ, the parousia; it was the *end of history* that preoccupied them, not the historiography of the eschatological expectation. In addition, as was to be expected, around the figure of the resurrected Master there had early crystallized a whole mythology reminiscent of that of the savior gods and the divinely inspired man (*theios anthropos*)" (Eliade 1982, pp. 337-338).

Each of the gospel accounts, the three synoptics and John, has a specific origin, historical context and theological message to convey. Before the writing of the gospel accounts, in Paul's letters or in Q,[2] the doctrine of the messiah does not occupy a central position. In Q, Jesus is never referred to as the messiah (MacRae 1987). MacRae (1987) has suggested six theses that summarize the emergence of messianic ideas in the gospels:

> 1. The earliest recoverable strata of the Christian proclamation of the gospel are aware of the claim that Jesus was (is, or will be; see below) the Messiah of Israel; this claim is not the primary focus of their message.

---

1. Critical opinion regarding early Christian views of the mission of Jesus are discussed in de Jonge (1991).

2. The earlier source of sayings about Jesus that served as one of the important sources of the gospels of Matthew and Luke.

2. The earliest Palestinian Jewish preaching of the gospel probably emphasized the messianic idea, but there is no adequate evidence to support this probability.

3. The further one gets away in time from the earliest preaching, whether Palestinian or Hellenistic, the more the issue of Jesus as Messiah gains in prominence.

4. This development takes roughly two forms:

   a. a movement away from traditional Jewish understandings of the Messiah and his role, evidenced in the Gospels of Mark and John, and

   b. a movement toward some aspects of the traditional Christian understandings, with an emphasis on the continuity of promise or prophecy and fulfillment, evidenced in the Gospels of Matthew and Luke.

5. These trends are not to be explained simply as diverging views of gentile as opposed to Jewish Christians, for the Gospels of Mark and Luke represent mainly gentile concerns, while those of Matthew and John arise out of originally Jewish Christian churches.

6. The Gospels of Mark and John, and to a certain degree those of Matthew and Luke, illustrate the fact that to the extent that the title *Christos* became progressively more central to early Christian proclamation, to that same extent it departed further from the Jewish understanding of the Messiah. (p. 174)

Mark's gospel is the oldest of the four, and he portrays the history of Jesus as a cosmic eschatological struggle with the forces of evil. The Baptist heralds Jesus as the powerful figure who has come to do battle with the common adversary, Satan. The first skirmish takes place in the temptations in the desert (Mk 1: 12-13), but the battle is really joined in the various exorcisms in which Christ displays his power over Satan (Mk 1: 21-27; 3: 11-12; 5: 1-17; 7: 24-30; 9: 14-29). The miracle stories are cast as part of the fight against evil (Mk 1: 40-45; 4: 35-41; 7: 24). The opposition is also found in the debates with the religious leaders of Israel (Mk 2: 1-3: 6), as well as in his struggles with the ignorance and timidity of his own disciples (Mk 8: 34-37; 10: 38-45).

Although Jesus is recognized as messiah, the designation has problems. As Kee (1987) points out, the assumptions that Jesus used extant messianic titles from pre-70 AD Judaism to articulate his mission, that there was an established messianic understanding that was concealed in the messianic secret[3] in Mark, that messianic titles and ideas were consensually accepted in Judaism of the Second Temple, and that the argument between Jesus and the Jewish leaders was over his claim to fulfill a commonly accepted messianic perception, are all open to serious question.[4] Mark was the disciple of Peter and his gospel reflects the influence of the Jerusalem community, probably for the benefit of non-Palestinian Christians of pagan origin. Mark's gospel is a proclamation of Christ's messiahship, emphasizing the mystery of Jesus' true identity, its misunderstanding and the "messianic secret," as well as the mystery of his role as Son of Man (Kee 1987). Mark clearly proclaims Jesus as the messiah, but the proclamation is not put in the mouth of Jesus (Borg 1987). The scholarly consensus is that Jesus did not make any claim to be the messiah and did not accept the efforts of his followers to designate him as such. The matter of his identity as messiah was a matter of doubt and debate. The disciples in Mark were more confused about who Jesus was or what his program was about (Charlesworth 1987; de Jonge 1991).

For Matthew, Jesus is the new Moses who brings with him a new revelation and the promise of a new Israel. Matthew preserves the semitic tone of Jesus' sayings, along with the imagery and futurist eschatology characteristic of apocalyptic language. This is especially noteworthy in the eschatological sayings which are found nowhere else in the gospels (Mt 10: 21-23; 13: 24-30, 37-40; 25: 1-13). But there is also movement toward a realized eschatology in which Christ's words and actions point toward the realization of the kingdom of heaven in this world, specifically in the form of the Church. Matthew's view of salvation has an eschatological cast: Jesus' death and resurrection are the realization of eschatological hopes and expectations. He uses the language of apocalyptic to proclaim that with the death and resurrection of Jesus the general resurrection of the just has already begun (Mt 27: 51-53).

The Hebrew scriptures become the tapestry against which the drama of Christ's life, career and death are played out. The motif of promise and fulfillment is a major contribution of New Testament apologetics (Green 1987). Matthew's work is a Jewish Christian gospel that identifies Christ[5] as the messiah, not the messiah of Jewish

---

3. This refers to Christ's supposed concealment of his messianic status and mission from his disciples, a realization that was achieved only in the light of post-resurrection faith.

4. See also Charlesworth (1987).

5. Although the Greek word *christos* originally translated the Hebrew *mashiah*, it was probably regarded early on as a proper name. In most instances in the New Testament, there

tradition and expectation, but a suffering messiah who died on the cross and whose kingdom is not of this world. From the beginning he is acknowledged as the son of David, the messianic king, the agent of the messianic age (Davies 1966; Brown 1977). He is presented as the savior of Israel — his very name means "Yahweh saves" (Stanley 1968b). Fulfillment formulas abound and ancient prophesies are put to use predicting Christ's birth and death. Since so many of these utterances are not prophecies at all, but statements about past or present events, their application in the gospel takes the form of strategic adaptation in the service of the Christian ideology. This promise-fulfillment strategy and the infancy narratives, both in Matthew and Luke, forge a link of continuity between the early Christians and Israel (Lyonnet 1968b).

Matthew's gospel was probably written for an audience predominantly, but not exclusively, composed of Jewish Christians, about a decade and a half after the destruction of Jerusalem and the temple (about AD 80-90) (Viviano 1990). His community was in all likelihood situated in Palestine or Syria, where post-destruction developments in Judaism, most notably the emergence of Jamnia Pharisaism,[6] colored the religious landscape. The membership was largely converted from Judaism, and would have held on to their hopes for the promised and longed-for messiah, the son of David.

Luke, writing as the disciple of Paul about the same time (the mid-80s of the 1st century, circa AD 80-85) (Karris 1990), and addressing a Gentile community centered in Antioch, from the perspective of the church in Rome, has a message more universal in scope. Rather than the crisis of identity created by the Jamnian reforms that Matthew confronted, Luke is dealing with the growing distance between the Gentile churches and the Jewish origins of the faith and the growing need to find a place in the Greco-Roman world of the Mediterranean basin. His message concerns the coming of the kingdom in the establishing of the church, the fulfillment of Jesus' prophetic ministry in the guise of the Son of Man. The church is the fulfillment of messianic promises under guidance of the Holy Spirit.

The eschatological themes do not have the same semitic coloration as in Matthew, but they are there nonetheless. Luke stresses the theme of salvation (Lk 1: 69, 71-77; 2: 30; 3: 6; 19: 9) and Christ as

---

is little agreement on its interpretation, i.e., as title or name (MacRae 1987).

6. See chapter 6.

savior (Lk 1: 47; 2: 11). Jesus' death and resurrection carry eschatological overtones — cast in the imagery of the exodus as God's definitive act of deliverance (Lk 9: 31) and the apocalyptic account of Elijah's assumption (Lk 9: 51).

John's gospel comes from the end of the 1st century, probably written by the beloved disciple, and reflects a more advanced stage of reflection on the mystery of Christ's mission (Perkins 1990). Emphasis falls on Jesus' divine origin and on the spiritual nature of his mission and preaching. The messianic mission is cast in more specifically spiritual and eschatological terms. Christ as the light of the world is the primary eschatological reality for John. Christ's miracles have eschatological import since they manifest the glory of the Lord (Jn 2: 11; 12: 37ff). The Johannine christology hails Jesus as the "Son of God" (Jn 20: 31) and faith in him as the source of salvation.

Collection of messianic titles from early traditions in the Christian churches (Jn 1: 19-50) — messiah, Elijah, prophet, lamb of God, Son of God, king of Israel — culminate in a messianic vision of the Son of Man with the angels of God ascending and descending on him (Jn 1: 51). The apocalyptic vision of Daniel and Jacob's vision at Bethel are united into a messianic expression in which Jesus fulfills and transcends any messianic hopes that may have been incorporated in them. As Perkins (1990) concludes,

> Johannine Christology seems to be more than a simple expansion of possibilities already in Jewish or earlier Christian sources. One cannot escape the novelty of the evangelist's use of categories previously felt appropriate only to the transcendent reality of God in conjunction with a narrative which describes the earthly career of a human being. Johannine christology poses the problem of redefining monotheism. (p. 948)

Messianic allusions abound in the gospels. The genealogies in Matthew and Luke are cast in messianic terms. The name "Christ" in Mt (1: 1-17) is not used as a proper name as in the later tradition, but as the Greek equivalent for the Aramaic term for messiah. The aim is to place Jesus in the line of Davidic succession (Brown 1977). Brown (1977) comments, "The name 'Jesus Christ' binds the title 'Messiah' indivisibly to Jesus and serves as a good preparation for a genealogy and a narrative both of which will stress that Jesus is the fulfillment of Jewish messianic hopes." (p. 67) Even the 'virginal' conception (Mt 1: 18-25; Lk 1: 34-8)) connects the birth of Jesus with the prophecy of Isaiah (Is 7: 14). The name Jesus itself means "Yahweh is salvation" and Emmanuel of the prophecy means "God is with us." In Lk 3:

23-38, Christ's origins are traced not merely to Abraham, but to Adam as befits a universal savior.

But even here, at the very beginning of the story, traditional Jewish notions of the messiah are challenged. The Christ comes from the Galileans, the country bumpkins held in contempt by the Judean rabbis, and from an obscure town never mentioned in the Old Testament. Zechariah addresses the baby John as the "prophet of the Most High," the Elijah who would proclaim the coming of the messiah and salvation. Even if the savior comes from the line of David (Lk 1: 26-38), the salvation promised is no longer earthly and national but spiritual, and the messianic kingdom is not of this world but of the world of the spirit (Coppens 1968).[7]

The baptismal narratives declare that the Old Testament promises about a Davidic messiah, the Lord's anointed who is savior and Lord, have been fulfilled in Jesus (Lk 2: 1-20) (Stanley 1968b). The allusions are reminiscent of the Psalms of Solomon, whose messianic aspirations echo through Luke's narrative (Bruce 1969; Brown 1977). When his parents bring the child for presentation at the Temple, Simeon declares him to be the promised messiah and prophecies a mission of universal salvation accomplished through sorrow and tragedy (Lk 2: 25-35), echoing the message of the Servant Songs of Isaiah. Brown (1977) adds a further note on the accounts of the annunciation: "Since it is almost unanimously agreed by scholars that the Matthean and Lucan infancy narratives are independent of each other, and since so many similarities can scarcely have arisen by accident, we are led to the probability of a basic pre-Gospel annunciation tradition that each evangelist used in his own way. And since both annunciation messages mention David (Mt 1: 20; Lk 1: 32), this pre-Gospel tradition presumably concerned the birth of Jesus as the Davidic Messiah." (p. 159) That such an idea of the announcement of the birth of a Davidic messiah may have existed in pre-Christian Judaism is supported by a Qumran *pesher*[8] harkening back to 2 Sam in which the salvation of Israel is to come from the lineage of David (Brown 1977).

The preaching of John the Baptist is presented as preparing the way for the coming of the messiah (Mk 1: 1-8; Mt 3: 1-12; Lk 3: 1-20; Jn 1: 19-34). John is the herald, in the image of Elijah (Mt 11: 2-15;

---

7. See also the discussion of the Davidic descent in Brown (1977), especially appendix II.
8. In 4QFlorilegium.

Jn 1: 21), who proclaims the coming of the messiah — a voice crying in the wilderness, "Prepare a way for the Lord" (Is 40: 3-5).

When John baptizes Jesus, the messianic references are unmistakable, a public manifestation of Jesus' messianic claim (Mk 1: 9-11). The anointing takes place through the descent of the Spirit (Lk 3: 21-22). He is the anointed one, beloved of the Lord (Mt 3: 13-17; Lk 3: 21-22; Jn 1: 31-34) (de la Potterie 1968). Particularly in the gospel of John the messianic titles are given a prominence that can be found nowhere else in the New Testament — the Chosen One of God (Jn 1: 34), Christ [messiah](Jn 1: 41), king of Israel (Jn 1: 49), son of God (Jn 1: 49), son of Man (Jn 1: 51) (Dodd 1968).

The temptations in the desert (Mk 1: 12-13; Mt 4: 1-11; Lk 4: 1-13) are invitations by the evil one for Christ to use his messianic powers, perhaps in a manner corresponding to current popular messianic expectations. To respond to these temptations would have cast Jesus' ministry in terms of temporal prosperity and power. The implications of political power in the last temptation would have suggested some reference to the fanatical Zealots who looked to the messiah to overthrow the power of Rome with a military victory.[9] Christ's resistance to these blandishments were meant to convey the message that his mission was not to meet the wishful fantasies of Jewish messianic hopes.

The miracle accounts are presented with overtones that call to mind the messianic promises. The feeding of the 5,000 is the only such account that is rendered by all the evangelists (Mk 6: 30-44; Mt 14: 13-21; Lk 9: 10-17; Jn 6: 1-13). In Mark, Jesus is cast as the eschatological shepherd (Mk 6: 34) who cares for the lost sheep and who was foretold in Ezekiel (Ez 34: 23). The feeding itself, besides the miraculous quality of the account, holds a promise of the messianic banquet. According to Matthew 8: 11-12, the messianic banquet will be open to not only the Jews, but to the Gentiles as well.

A high point in the profession of Christ's messianic role comes in the confession of Peter at Caesarea Philippi. In Mark 8: 27-33, this episode climaxes Jesus' self-revelation and marks a turning point for the disciples who, for the first time, recognize Jesus as the messiah. But if Peter's confession acknowledges Christ as the promised messiah, it is as a different kind of messiah than traditional Jewish beliefs had looked for. The same motifs are repeated in Matthew 16: 13-23, and

---

9. See chapter 9.

Luke 9: 18-27. Peter's acknowledgment recognizes at least dimly that the messiah he follows is not a triumphant conqueror, but one whose lot is suffering and death (Mk 8: 31-33; Mt 16: 21-23; Lk 9: 22) (Bruce 1969).

Jesus cautions them to keep the messianic secret (Mk 8: 30; Mt 16: 20; Lk 9: 21). The messianic secret of Mark is transformed in Luke into the mystery of a suffering messiah. But even here Peter's acceptance was limited, his vision myopic. He objects to this stunning reversal of messianic hopes, but for his trouble is sternly rebuked (Mt 16: 22-23). It was easier for Peter to accept that Jesus was the messiah than to come to terms with the idea that the messiah was to suffer and die.

This shattering revelation of Christ's suffering mission is followed in the synoptic accounts by the account of the transfiguration (Mk 9: 2-8; Mt 17: 1-8; Lk 9: 28-36). The transfiguration has no parallels in the synoptic gospels, except perhaps for the baptismal narratives in which a divine quality is attributed to Jesus and his mission. Some scholars have suggested that the account may represent a post-resurrection narrative transplanted to this position. Certainly the glory attributed to the risen Christ is foreshadowed in this account. There are echoes of the appearances of the Son of Man in the apocalyptic literature in the book of Daniel, Enoch and 2 Esdras. The heavenly voice resonates with the voice from heaven in the baptism account. The account is highly symbolic and, coming in the wake of Peter's confession and the predictions of the passion, serves to reaffirm Christ's messiahship and his messianic glory. There is more theological interpretation here than history. The tension is obvious, and the implication seems to be that the disciples, for all their good will, had not fully grasped the implications of these events.

The paradox of Christ's messianic mission is again reflected in the discourse about the relation between Christ and David (Mk 12: 35-37; Mt 22: 41-46; Lk 20: 41-44). Jesus poses the dilemma: how can the Christ be the son of David when David calls him Lord? The question is obviously concocted to discredit the scribes and Pharisees, who proclaim themselves the true expositors of the tradition. It challenges the currently accepted teaching among the teachers of Israel. The long-standing belief was that the anointed one was to be a descendant of David, a belief that was elaborated in the last two centuries BC into a full-blown messianic doctrine of an ideal Davidic king to come. The quotation put in Jesus' mouth comes from Ps 110, a hymn of royal messianism believed to have been authored by David. The passage,

which is essentially the same in all three synoptics, has been interpreted to mean (a) that Jesus was calling into question the Davidic
origins of the messiah, (b) that the origins of the messiah are more
exalted and transcendent than David's, or (c) that the reference is to the
Son of Man passage in Daniel 7: 13, asserting that the Christ is more
than a son of David — Son of Man in a unique sense (Léon-Dufour
1968). The second of these seems to carry the most weight — that the
messiah may come from the line of David, but that his messianic character transcended mere blood ties with David (Fitzmyer 1974). Matthew makes the debate with the Pharisees more explicit: the immediate
point of the story in this context is the implication that they cannot
resolve this simple exegetical problem so that they cannot be taken as
valid judges of the identity of the messiah.

The account of Jesus' meeting with the Samaritan woman is
found only in John (4: 1-42). The revelation of Christ's messianic
identity seems quite direct, but not only does it involve the confession
of his messianic mission, but the revelation to the Samaritans implies
that the salvation to come transcends national boundaries and extends
beyond the Jews to include all nations. The realization of messianic
hopes in the mission of Christ is to be found in universal salvation.
The parable of the wedding feast (Mt 22: 1-14; Lk 14: 16-24) seems to
strike an even further discordant note. Those who are invited to the
feast do not come; they offer frivolous excuses or abuse and even kill
the king's servants. The king retaliates by destroying them and invit-
ing other guests who would be willing to come to the feast.

In Jewish literature, the messianic era was compared to a feast (Is
25: 6) and the messiah himself to a bridegroom who would take Israel
to himself as his bride. The message is that not all will be included in
the messianic kingdom. To fill out the allegory, the king is God, his
son the messiah, and his servants the prophets. The religious leaders or
the chosen people may not be among those who sit at the banquet table
in the messianic kingdom. John's messianic doctrine shares with Matthew an uneasy designation of Christ as the messiah unless it is understood in specifically Christian terms.

The messianic doctrine of the synoptics is expressed in their
thinking about the parousia, the time of the coming of the predicted
messiah in his messianic splendor. Matthew 24: 4-8 lists the signs of
the parousia as part of the eschatological discourse. The account is
cast in similar terms in both Mark 13: 5-13 and Luke 21: 8-19. The
usual apocalyptic disasters are included: wars, earthquakes, famine.
But a warning is included against the false messiahs, those who lay

claim to the messianic title but are not the true messiah (Mt 24: 26-28; Mk 13: 21-23; Lk 17: 22-25). The coming of the Son of Man (Dn 7: 13-14) will be clear to all, like lightning flashing across the sky. The warning is set in a context of sudden, unexpected and total disaster. The account is linked with warnings about the destruction of Jerusalem and the temple. The references to the "abomination of desolation" echo the reference in Daniel to the statue of Zeus Olympios erected in the temple by Antiochus IV Epiphanes in 168 BC. The material in these citations is undoubtedly retrospectively based on the events of the Jewish War and the destruction of Jerusalem and the desecration and destruction of the temple by the Romans in AD 70. The expectations for the time of the parousia and the expected messianic renewal were that all these predictions would take place within the present generation — a belief that had to be revised as time went on. The vision of the coming of the messianic king to establish his messianic kingdom is set forth in Matthew as the last judgment (Mt 25: 31-46) — the messianic judgment and the kingdom he came to establish are far removed from contemporary expectations. This final judgment is not unlike the contemporary Jewish idea that a judgment would inaugurate the messianic era (the last "days of the messiah"), and would be followed by a final judgment introducing the eschatological era. Even this last judgment has a nationalistic flavor — God, the divine judge, would give the chosen people preferential treatment. In Matthew, the messiah himself judges, and his judgment is based on religious rather than nationalistic grounds.

All of the synoptics trumpet the triumphal coming of the Son of Man (Mk 13: 24-27; Mt 24: 29-31; Lk 21: 25-27). The allusion is to the apocalyptic vision of the Son of Man of Dn 7: 13-14, coming in his messianic glory at the end of the world to pass final judgment (Léon-Dufour 1968). The title "Son of Man" is of interest here. In Old Testament usage, the phrase seems to mean little more than "human being." Here it can be interpreted as referring to Christ as the representative head of redeemed humanity and in connection with the judgment to come. There is little to suggest that in pre-Christian Judaic usage it served as a messianic title; even the question of an individual reference in Daniel, as opposed to a more symbolic corporate reference, e.g., to the company of the elect, has not been settled. Dodd (1968) argues that even apparently messianic uses of the title in the apocalyptic literature have more symbolic than personal implication. Thus the "Son of Man" title is capable of both individual and corporate reference and may be used with both implications simultaneously in mind.

The messianic implications of Christ's mission reach a crescendo in the final journey to Jerusalem and in the events of the passion. The entry into Jerusalem (Mk 11: 1-11; Mt 21: 1-11; Lk 19: 28-38; Jn 12: 12-16) is an account of messianic display. Mt refers the scene of the triumphal entry to Zechariah 9: 9, omitting the phrase that alludes to the victory of the messianic king. The king here is among the lowly and lacks the trappings of a royal messianic figure. The procession becomes a messianic parade complete with crowds and cheers, and the messiah is saluted as the son of David. The procession is succeeded by the cleansing of the Temple, an act of direct aggression against the Temple priests and hierarchy. By implication, Jesus does not recognize the existing authorities and asserts his own higher messianic authority.

The narratives of the passion are also used to reinforce the messianic character of Christ's mission. In Mk (14: 53-65), the high priest puts the question to him directly: "Are you the Christ . . . the son of the Blessed One?" Christ replies in the affirmative and identifies himself with the Son of Man of Daniel 7: 13. In Matthew 26: 57-68, Jesus' answer appeals not only to Daniel but to Ps 110, thus declaring himself to be not only the royal messiah but Son of Man as well. The implication, however, reaches beyond a mere claim to be the messiah; it is equivalently a claim to be the Son of God (Bruce 1969). The high priest tears his robes and declares the reply a blasphemy worthy of death. Luke's account (Lk 22: 66 - 23: 1) seems to connect the titles given to Jesus — messiah, Son of Man, Son of God — to imply the supereminence of the last title. The words to the Sanhedrin are probably meant to convey no more than the connotation of the title in the Old Testament — the anointed, the chosen one, the Davidic king. For the post-resurrection Church, viewing these events from the perspective of the Easter faith, the implications were much greater.

When Jesus appears before Pilate, the charge is specifically his claim to be the messianic king (Mk 15: 2-5; Mt 27: 11-14; Lk 23: 2-7; Jn 18: 28-40). Undoubtedly for Pilate, Jesus was just another of many messianic claimants who were causing trouble. He was more interested in placating the Jewish authorities and avoiding a public disruption than he was in seeing to it that justice was done. Again Jesus makes his messianic claim in other terms — he is indeed a king, but his kingdom is not of this world. The ancient themes of classical messianic royalism are transposed to a superior spiritual level, especially in John where his kingdom is cast in purely spiritual terms (Coppens 1968).

In John, as in the synoptics, messiah is a royal title — Jesus is king of Israel (Jn 1: 49). The discussion of Jesus' messiahship in chapter 7 focuses on three criteria: (1) his hidden origin, (2) the performance of signs, and (3) Davidic lineage. The argument is left without closure, as if to say that John is less interested in defending Jesus' claim to fulfill Jewish messianic expectations than to assert his claim to a more spiritual messiahship in the new dispensation. Then, to Pilate's question, Jesus replies that if Pilate means a king in the Roman sense as a political leader of this world, the answer is No. If it was meant in the sense of the Jews, then Jesus was a king, but not of this world. His claim was not to political power, but to spiritual authority — a meaning that was ultimately alien to the Jewish mind (Dodd 1968). Dodd concludes:

> The conclusion we draw is that the Fourth Evangelist, even more definitely than the Synoptics, is developing his doctrine of the person and work of Jesus with conscious reference to Jewish messianic belief. The Messiah of the Jews is to be a descendant of David, He is to appear no one knows whence, He is to work signs and to reign as king, and He is to abide forever. Of Jesus the evangelist will not affirm that He is the Son of David; if He is a king, His kingship is of an entirely different order; His origin is mysterious indeed, since He comes from another world; He works signs, in a more profound sense than the Jews imagined; and the death which appears to be the end of Him is in fact the climax and seal of His manifestation as the eternal Savior of the world. Thus while formally the evangelist claims for Jesus the Jewish title *Messias*, in fact the Jewish conception of Messiahship is set aside, and his doctrine of the Person of Christ is mainly worked out under other categories, which are not those of Rabbinic Judaism. (p. 92)

CHAPTER 6

Messianism in the New Testament

Acts of the Apostles

The narrative of Acts takes place in the context of a post-crucifixion, post-resurrection faith. The disciples at the beginning have no more than a dawning awareness of a doctrine of divine sonship. The primitive kerygma proclaims that Jesus is both Lord and messiah. His messiahship is demonstrated by prophecy, miracles, and especially by the resurrection. He is the Lord, the Son of God, the Suffering Servant. Salvation is gained through no other name, and the work of salvation is wrought by the Spirit of Jesus who is sent by the resurrected Christ to dwell in the hearts of true believers.

The handicaps to this mission were considerable. The disciples set out to proclaim as messiah one who had been crucified by the Romans on a charge of sedition. A crucified messiah was a contradiction in terms. How could the crucified be the anointed one, the chosen one of Yahweh, on whom all Yahweh's favor was to rest? One who was hanged on a cross was accursed by God (Bruce 1969).

Peter's speech at Pentecost (Acts 2: 14-36) bases this messianic claim on the resurrection. The wonders of Pentecost itself manifest the outpouring of the spirit that was to herald the establishment of the messianic kingdom. Then Peter's temple discourse (Acts 3: 12-26) proclaims the Isaian theme of the suffering messiah and identifies Christ as the Holy One, the Just One, announced by the prophets.

It is in Acts 11: 26 that Christ's followers are first designated as Christians — the servants and followers of the *Christos, Christianoi.* The designation could not have arisen in a Jewish setting; the designation would have implied to Jewish ears an admission of the disciples' claim that Christ was the messiah. To Gentile ears, however, the name *Christos* held less of a religious connotation and sounded more like a personal designation (Bruce 1969). The designation *Christianoi* arose in the hellenistic center Antioch.

The messianic theme emerges again in the account of the Ethiopian eunuch (Acts 8: 26-40). Philip meets the eunuch on the road to Gaza and explains the Isaian text as applied to the suffering messiah. The eunuch is converted and baptized. The part of the Servant of Yahweh song cited refers to the death and suffering of the Righteous One (Is 53: 7-8). The same motifs echo throughout the speeches of Paul in Acts. In his speech in the synagogue at Antioch (Acts 13: 16-41), Paul preaches the suffering, dying and resurrected Christ. Christ was raised by the power of God from the dead and was not allowed to experience corruption — one of the promises made to David (Ps 16: 9).

When Paul preaches in Thessalonika (Acts 17: 1-9), his message is again that Jesus is the messiah who was destined by God to suffer and die and to rise again from the dead. This message no doubt contributed to the violent reaction of the Jewish contingent, who dragged Jason and some of the brothers before the city council with the charge of setting up another emperor to rival the emperor of Rome. Even though Paul and the disciples were careful to avoid any use of imperial titles, preaching only that Jesus was the messiah and Lord, the Jewish reaction instinctively translated these terms into royal and imperial connotations consistent with the established expectations of the davidic messiah. Later, when Paul is imprisoned and brought before the Sanhedrin, he tries to engage Jewish sensibilities by appealing to the Pharisaic belief in the resurrection of the dead. The Pharisee and the son of Pharisees argues that the messianic hope, cherished by the Pharisees, for the resurrection of the dead was the basis of his belief in Christ and the reason for his being on trial. A violent argument broke out between the Pharisees and the Sadducees, who did not believe in life after death or the resurrection of the dead (Acts 22: 30 - 23: 11).

Further on, Paul is dragged before King Agrippa, Herod Agrippa II, to plead his case. Once again, it is the suffering and risen Christ he proclaims (Acts 26: 1-23). The conflation of the messiah with the Suffering Servant of Isaiah is a characteristic Lucan theme which occurs in Luke's gospel and again here; the authorship of Acts is traditionally ascribed to Luke, the companion of Paul and evangelist. Certainly both Luke and Acts seem to constitute a continuous account from the same source (Dillon and Fitzmyer 1968). The connection of these themes is not explicit in the Old Testament but seems to have been a constant and powerful motif in the early Christian kerygma. Paul does not hesitate to present his case to Agrippa, basing it once again on the messianic hope for the resurrection and appealing to Christ's death and resurrection as proof of his messiahship. As Segal (1990) notes, "To read Paul properly . . . one must recognize that Paul was a Pharisaic Jew who converted to a new apocalyptic, Jewish sect and then lived in a Hellenistic, gentile Christian community as a Jew among gentiles." (pp. 6-7)

A definitive event in shaping the messianic vision was the ascension of the Lord. As presented in Acts, the account suggests that the full significance of Christ's messianic role and the nature of his kingdom had not yet dawned on the disciples. Their vision was of an earthly theocracy, the restoration of Israel (Acts 1: 6). Jesus' ascension would have dashed any hopes for a terrestrial kingdom, even as his death had shattered any thoughts of a glorious earthly messiah. Only the announcement of his second coming preserved any glimmer of hope, but with it the radical revision of their theology of history. The messiah would have to come a second time, not just once; and the day of judgment would have to be postponed until that unknown day of the glorious parousia (Stanley 1968b). Moreover, the ascension comes to represent the final messianic anointing declaring his enthronement at the right hand of the Father as the messiah, the son of God. As de la Potterie (1968), commenting on the references to anointing in Heb 1 with their allusions to the royal psalms, wrote: "This anointing should therefore not be understood as the Messianic investiture at the moment of the incarnation, much less that which Christ received at baptism. The subject here can only be the moment when Christ by his ascension takes his place at the right hand of the Father. By this very fact, the character of this anointing is clearly indicated — it is a *royal* anointing. It symbolizes the heavenly royalty of Christ, his universal supremacy." (p. 181)

Pauline Messianism

In Paul's theology, Jesus is the new Moses who came to replace the old Mosaic law with a new law, the law of the new dispensation. Sin entered the world through Adam, and the reign of sin lasted through the period of the mosaic law, to be finally dissolved after the coming of the Christ messiah (Rom 5: 12-14). In the rabbinic tradition there were three eras: from Adam to Moses, 2,000 years of chaos; from Moses to the messiah, 2,000 years of the law; after the messiah, 2,000 years of bliss. In this last period the messiah would bring the new law that would govern the messianic era.

The problem Paul faced was the failure of the revelation of Christ to convince the Jews. How can the Christian gospel be the true fulfillment of the messianic promises when the messiah himself has been rejected by Israel? The issue of the separation of the nascent church from Israel can be viewed in the context of Paul's mission to the gentiles and the division of orientation and purpose in the ranks of the early Jerusalem church.[1] Behind the tension in Paul's thought lies the tension between the Jerusalem church of James and his group, who wanted to maintain their identity and attachment to the Jewish origins of Christianity and who insisted on continuing the Jewish practices of fasting, circumcision and so on, and the emerging churches of Rome and Antioch that were more decidedly gentile in orientation, hellenistic in background, and even sociologically different from the more pastoral focus of the Jerusalem church. The church of James was essentially rural and agricultural in its roots; the church of Paul was urban, middle class, and upwardly mobile. It is not unlikely that these more hellenized Christians were anxious to dissociate themselves from the Jewish origins of their faith, if only to distance themselves from the connotations of the Jewish revolt and the fact that their messiah had been crucified by the Roman authorities. Paul's apologetic in Romans 9-11 is the first effort of the new theology to confront the traditional theology of the synagogue.

In 1 Corinthians, Paul takes up the theme of the suffering messiah. The Jews demand miracles and the Greeks look for wisdom, but Paul preaches Christ crucified. For the Jews the messiah was a figure of power and might, an emperor greater than the emperor of Rome. The suffering messiah was far from that image; for them a suffering

---

1. See Meissner (in process) for a detailed explanation of these issues in the early development of Christianity.

messiah was a stumbling block. The Greeks sought knowledge and understanding, not mystery. They could not accept anything on another's authority. To prefer suffering and mystery to wisdom was merely foolishness for them (1 Cor 1: 22-25). But this suffering messiah is the messianic king, the royal descendant of David, who offered his death for the salvation of many (2 Tim 2: 8-10). This suffering looks forward to the day of eschatological redemption in the parousia when Christ's suffering will be crowned in glory. The work of redemption that was begun on Calvary will be completed in the parousia — as Lyonnet (1968a) comments, ". . . according to the usual twofold meaning of Messianic notions which theoretically can be applied, and practically almost always are, indifferently to the first or to the second coming of Christ, as is clear with the notions of salvation and kingdom of God, even adoptive filiation, perhaps even justification." (p. 208)

The Epistle to the Hebrews is probably not from the hand of Paul, despite its early ascription to him in the church of Alexandria. The style and vocabulary are not Paul's, the manner of citation of the Old Testament is different, and the theological emphases strike another chord. The overall tone, however, is quite Pauline. The consensus view is that the author was probably a Jewish Christian of hellenistic background, especially insofar as many influences of Plato and Philo of Alexandria can be detected. Hebrews treats the role of Christ in terms of the themes of royal and priestly messianism. The theme of royal messianism is cast in terms of the messianic enthronement (Heb 1: 5-14). The relationship between God and the messiah is that of father to son. The reference is to Ps 2: 7, one of the royal psalms probably celebrating the enthronement of one of the kings of Judah. The day of the king's accession to power was the day on which he was "begotten" as the son of God. Christ was the son of God, the Davidic king who embodies the promises and fulfillments of the tradition of royal messianism. Appeal is also made to the royal nuptial psalm (Ps 44); the royal prince is another prototype of the messiah.

Hebrews also emphasizes the priestly character of the messiah. Jesus is a priest according to the order of Melchizedek and the Levitical priesthood (Heb 7: 1-28). The author ignores the fact that the lines of priestly and royal descent were joined in Melchizedek. He is apparently not interested in the royal aspect, but in the priestly function. The roles were separated in the later tradition, but in the royal Ps 110, so frequently cited in Hebrews, the union of these functions is regarded as the normal state of affairs. The emphasis there is not on the fact that Melchizedek was priest-king, but that he was priest-king of Jerusalem. Hebrews emphasizes not only the continuity of the messianic line, but the eternal priesthood of Melchizedek which makes him both a prototype of Christ and superior to the Levitical priesthood. The account of Hebrews represents an attempt to spiritualize and sanctify the messianic tradition. The establishment of the kingdom is the victory of the messiah over the devil and the forces of evil. Christ is not only the preserver of the messianic kingship, but the high priest of the new dispensation (Coppens 1968). The coming of the messiah is the occasion for spiritual renewal and moral perfection (Heb 5: 11-6: 20).

For all this, it is surprising that in Paul's writings the messiah is not an issue. This is surprising in view of Paul's strong Jewish background, but of course the letters are addressed primarily to gentile churches for whom the issue of Jesus' messiahship was not as pressing. But, on the other hand, Luke who also wrote for a gentile audience is hardly bashful about asserting Jesus' messiahship, and in other ways Paul is not reluctant to assume the interest of his gentile converts in Israelite traditions. Even so, no New Testament author uses *christos* more frequently than does the Apostle to the Gentiles, but usually as a proper name and virtually never as a messianic title. Despite this linguistic usage, there is no doubt that in Paul's thought Christ fulfills the functions of the messiah — he is the agent of eschatological salvation through liberation from the law — clearly a messianic function but not necessarily in the terms of the messianic tradition, but as an interpretation of the messianic function in transcendent terms (MacRae 1987).

The Apocalypse

The Apocalypse was written, possibly by the apostle John or a school of his disciples, toward the end of the 1st century, possibly during the persecution that raged toward the end of the reign of Diocletian (AD 81-96)(D'Aragon 1968; Collins 1990). Its title connects it with the post-exilic apocalyptic tradition: its visionary revelations have to do with the times to come, particularly with the realization of the messianic promises in the eschatological period. The symbolic language borrows from the prophetic tradition as distilled through the apocalyptic filter. Woman comes to represent a people or city, horns refer to power, and the word of God is a sharp sword. The vision of the dragon and the lamb (Apoc 12: 1-14: 20), for example, pictures the struggle between the power of evil represented by the monster and the messiah and his people, between the devil and Christ and his church. The power of evil tries to destroy the woman and her son, a recapitulation of current Eastern myths. The woman with child is pursued by a horrible monster, but she is miraculously preserved to give birth, and her child in turn slays the evil monster. The Christian myth deviates from its pagan counterparts insofar as the child does not immediately destroy the monster; rather, he is taken up to heaven where he reigns with God, while the woman remains in peril of the dragon's hatred. The story is at once an allegory for the suffering and persecuted church (the woman is the people of God, the true Israel of both Old and New Testament) (D'Aragon 1968; Collins 1990) and for Mary, the woman of Israel who brought the messiah into the world. The pangs of birth become the prototype of the birthpangs of the messiah that introduce the eschatological era.

The messiah was to destroy the power of the dragon over the world. The beast (Apoc 13: 1-10) is the representative of the dragon on earth and is invested with his power. The reference harkens back to Dn 7 in which the 10-horned beast represents Antiochus IV Epiphanes, the archpersecutor of Israel, but is then transferred to the Roman Empire which epitomizes all those secular powers that persecute the Church. The second beast or "false prophet" probably refers to Nero, the first emperor to persecute the Christians. It is the risen and glorified Christ who leads the hosts of heaven in the final triumphant battle against God's enemies and thus establishes God's eschatological kingdom. It is the Christ of the parousia who emerges in all his power and glory to smite the enemy and declare the messianic era. The vision is graphic:

> And now I saw heaven open, and a white horse appear; its rider was called Faithful and True; he is *a judge with integrity*, a warrior for justice. His eyes were flames of fire, and his head was crowned with many coronets; the name written on him was known only to himself, *his cloak was soaked in blood*. He is known by the name, The Word of God. Behind him, dressed in linen of dazzling white, rode the armies of heaven on white horses. From his mouth came a sharp sword to strike the pagans with; he is the one *who will rule them with an iron scepter*, and tread out the wine of Almighty God's fierce anger. On his cloak and on his thigh there was a name written: *The King of kings and the Lord of lords*. (Apoc 19: 11-16)

This "battle of the messiah" is a grandiose portrayal of Christ in his full messianic majesty and power, but precisely as the "anointed one" who is the instrument of divine purposes acting as God's special agent.

In this ultimate battle with the beast and the false prophet Christ will emerge triumphant (Apoc 19: 11-21). The apocalyptic tradition taught that the establishment of the messianic kingdom would follow a violent battle in which the messiah would triumph over the powers of evil. The messianic victory will inaugurate a thousand-year reign of peace and justice (Apoc 20: 1-6). This belief has become the basis for a series of millennial cults that look forward to the thousand-year reign of Christ on earth, e.g., Joachim di Fiore and the Fraticelli, and later Protestant sects like the Anabaptists, Adventists, and Jehovah's Witnesses (Bettencourt 1969).[2]

Messianic Doctrine in the New Testament

The messianic transformation from the Old Testament to the New involves movement from a view of the messianic promises in material, temporal and nationalistic terms to an understanding that was spiritual, eternal and universal. The "days of the messiah" of the contemporary Jewish view looked forward to the national restoration of the Jewish nation. Salvation would be the work of divine intervention, rather than simply from the messiah himself. The coming of the messiah was to be heralded by the messianic tribulations, a series of temporal and spiritual calamities; it would mark the end of the world and the beginning of the eschatological era. The messianic kingdom was to last for a thousand years.

The conceptions of the messianic kingdom came in several varieties. One view divided the messianic era into two periods: one terrestrial in which the kingdom of Israel would be restored, the other superterrestrial. The transcendental view held that there was to be no messianic kingdom in this world but only in the next — salvation was to be found in heaven or paradise. In the eschatological view, the resurrection and judgment would take place in this world in the "days of the messiah," but would be transformed into a transcendental form still in this world. This was probably the dominant view in the New Testament context of early Christian preaching. The primary beneficiaries of the messianic blessings were the chosen people, the fate of the heathen nations remaining uncertain. In some accounts they are destroyed by the triumphant return of the messiah, in others they continue to wage war against the messiah and his kingdom on this earth, finally to

---

2. See chapter 14 below.

be judged and destroyed in the catastrophe at the "end of days." The center of the messianic kingdom, nonetheless, was Jerusalem, transformed in suitably messianic style.

The contemporary view of the messiah himself was cast in terms of the kingly and priestly offices. In Esdras and Enoch, the messiah is preexistent and somehow suprahuman. He occupies a position between God and man, possessing transcendent characteristics but not identified with God. He is the warrior-king who establishes the messianic kingdom on earth. There is little room here for a view of a suffering messiah. The only allusions come from Is 53, but these hints are irreconcilable with the view of a triumphant and conquering messiah. Thus arose the idea of a second messiah, the Messiah ben Joseph. Contemporary Jewish views of the messiah were, therefore, somewhat vague and even at times contradictory.[3]

There is little hesitation among New Testament authors to apply messianic titles to Jesus. He is referred to as "the son of David," a title that asserts his claim to royal messianic lineage. The most frequent usage is "the son of Man," a title that does not lend luminous clarity to the messianic claims. While it asserts an anthropomorphic connotation, it also seems to advance more exalted claims — we are puzzled to see the high priest rending his garments and screaming "blasphemy" at a mere anthropomorphism. While there are significant doubts regarding the messianic status of the title in Old Testament usage, there seems little doubt that in the hands of the New Testament writers the title is meant to be messianic. The obvious reference point is Dn 7, but the additional association placed in Jesus' mouth is the suffering servant of Isaiah (e.g., after the confession of Peter, Mk 8: 31ff; Mt 16: 21ff; Lk 9: 22ff). Clearly this title in the New Testament implies more than is involved in its Old Testament connotations. Jesus is called "Lord," a title of royal address, reflecting the court language of Syro-Greek royalty and emphasizing the royal messianic claim.

More difficult is the title "son of God." Nowhere in the Old Testament or later Jewish literature does this title appear to have messianic overtones. When Peter says, "You are the Christ, the son of the Living God" (Mt 16: 16), the Christian tradition has interpreted this in a theological sense, in conjunction with the theophanies of the baptismal accounts, to imply that Christ is more than human, that he is actually divine. He is more than a human messiah, he is God's son and shares

---

3. See section II above.

in God's nature and power. He is the son of God as sharing in God's nature, not merely son of God as was every good Jew. Repeatedly, especially in John's gospel, the relation of the Son to the Father is stressed, and the links to the power and glory of Yahweh implied. These elements have been elaborated theologically into the doctrine of Jesus' divine sonship, so that the messianic claims at this point in the Christian kerygma reach far beyond anything conceivable in the pre-Christian dispensation to assert the divine nature and origin of the messiah.

To the eyes of Christian faith, then, Jesus gathered in his own person the heterogeneous and variegated messianic allusions of the tradition and amalgamated them into a new synthesis. He was the embodiment of all the hoped-for fulfillments of the end days; he was the prophet, the servant of Isaiah, the priest-mediator in the line of Melchizedek, the Savior, the royal king-messiah of the line of David, the Son of Man, the Son of God, and even, for John, the Word of God (Coppens 1968). He was all these and more. He was the divinely given answer to the messianic dreams of the past. He was "anointed by the Holy Spirit and power" (Acts 10: 38). While all of this was subjected to the workings of the post-resurrection faith, the presentation of Jesus himself is more muted and qualified. The picture presented in the gospels is that he more or less avoided publicizing his messianic role during the public ministry. He rejected the popular imagery of the triumphant and glorious messiah, and to his disciples stressed the image of the humble king in Zechariah 9: 9 (Mt 21: 4-5) and the role of the suffering messiah. This may explain the preference for the title "son of Man." The more jubilant and triumphant procession into Jerusalem stands out as an exception where acknowledgement of his messianic status breaks out in a public way. He was crucified as a messiah-king, and inevitably the disciples took the events surrounding the resurrection as proof of his messianic role and ultimately divine origin.

The events of Christ's life left little room for proclaiming him as the messiah of Jewish expectations. There had been nothing regal or royal about it: there were no victories, no kingdom, no defeat of the hated Romans, no deliverance of Israel, no miraculous transformation of the world as the extant messianic expectations dictated. The resolution of these difficulties was twofold: Christ's messianic mission was elevated to the level of the spiritual and the divine, and the fulfillment of messianic expectations was postponed to the second coming in the parousia. This made it possible to maintain the traditional expectations intact, and to allow the messiah to remain glorified and triumphant, now as the ascended and glorified Christ who reigns in heaven rather than on earth. In any case, it is clear that messiah was his predominant title, such that it became in its Greek form his proper name and title — the Christ.

Christian Messianism and the Cultic Process

The burden of the above review seems clear enough, namely that the motifs of the messianic vision in the Christian redaction derive from and in large measure echo those of the Jewish milieu within which they arose. The earliest strata of the Christian church were decidedly Palestinian in origin and are probably best exemplified in the early Jerusalem church as embodied in the figures of Peter and James and their disciples. Only subsequently did the broader hellenistically influenced vision of Pauline Christianity come into being (Meissner, in process). Christian messianism, therefore, replays the themes of its predecessor, Jewish messianism, but not completely. The messianic vision undergoes a change that translates and transforms the accents of the earlier Jewish hopes into a Christian form that adapts it to the mission and reality of the ministry and life of Jesus. Thus, while the parallels between Jewish and Christian messianism are striking, the transposition to a new key brings with it entirely new and distinguishing elements that do not exist at all in the older versions.

It would seem logical to conclude, then, that the same psychological processes and mechanisms that we have identified in the older Jewish tradition are also at work in the New Testament tradition. My effort here will aim at delineating the aspects of the cultic process as they are embodied in the phenomenon of New Testament messianism and then to make explicit the elements of the paranoid process that find expression in it.

One of the characteristics of a sect or cult is the degree of tension that obtains between the religious group and the surrounding social milieu. The cult typically stands in opposition to or is distanced from the prevailing social environment, distinguishing itself thereby from more established religious structures that tend to be more congruent with and to reinforce existing social structures. The Christian movement, as the story emerges on the pages of the New Testament, was more or less a deviant movement in social terms. The ministry of Jesus was cast in terms of his progressively deepening opposition to the established religious groups, especially the Pharisees and Sadducees. The connec-

tions between the emerging Christian movement and other extant religious groups, like the Essenes or the Zealots, remains somewhat obscure
and conjectural, but the essential differences shine through the mists of
obscurity anyway. In essence, the movement that came to life under
the leadership of Jesus was independent of and separate from the company of religious structures that already existed in Palestine. The tension between Jesus and the Sanhedrin and the Roman authorities came
to a head in the trial and crucifixion. Those circumstances of the
rebellious and deviant origins of the Christian inspiration remained a
significant embarrassment as the disciples spread throughout the Mediterranean world of the Roman empire to begin the work of conversion.

While established religious institutions are inclined to adapt to
the existing social order, the cultic impulse is toward change — either
advancing or preventing modifications in the existing system of beliefs,
values, symbols and religious practices. Christianity came on the Palestinian scene as a movement of conversion, pronouncing the "good
news" of the Christian gospel and striving to convert first the Jews and
later the pagan gentiles to the way of salvation through faith in Jesus
Christ. It was this basic alloplastic drive to transform the world of the
old dispensation and pagan belief that brought the nascent church into
such dire conflict with the Jewish and Roman authorities. The inevitable conflict of value and belief systems lies at the root of the persecutions that accompanied the origins of Christianity and dogged its early
steps until the time of Constantine. Part of the need to transform the
world of Jewish belief from which Christianity derived was to modify
the core of belief that surrounded the messianic convictions.

Descriptions of the cult phenomenon have emphasized that cultic
movements tend to be more responsive to individual human needs
which often have been ignored or obscured in the existing order of
things. This aspect of the cultic process in early Christianity does not
emerge with stunning clarity, but there is detectable a certain differential emphasis. The Christian kerygma seems to have a certain individual appeal that may mark it off from the emphasis to conformity to the
law and the legalized forms of religious expression that characterized
contemporary Jewish religious life. The gospel accounts in which
Christ challenges existing beliefs regarding observance of the sabbath
or fasting are a case in point; the Pauline tension between the freedom
of the followers of Christ and the observance of the law seem to underline this aspect as well. Even the messianic emphases carry a more
individual connotation in the Christian translation than the Jewish emphasis on the nationalistic overtones of the messianic salvation of the

chosen people. The differences are more a matter of accent and emphasis than radical contrast. By implication the internal drive toward division, or as Yinger (1957) puts it, "anarchy," was tempered by the cohesive forces of organizing structure that obtained among the disciples from the first. The Twelve were tightly knit around the figure of Jesus to begin with, and the mantle of succession and authority was firmly placed on the shoulders of Peter, who proved to be a powerful unifying figure in resolving the early tensions and splits, most notably between the Jewish Christians of the Jerusalem church and the hellenizing faction under the leadership of Paul. While divisive forces were not absent from the early church development, the major focus of opposition and conflict remained between the church and the outside world.

As a religious movement, the early Christian church manifested aspects of all the major forms of cult expression. It was conversionist in that it sought to bring about change in the minds and hearts of men by converting them to the message of the Christian gospel, and the approach was evangelistic and devoted to the theme of salvation through faith in Jesus Christ. It was introversionist insofar as it rejected the values of the pagan world and sought to replace them with a higher form of Christian ethic. It was adventist by reason of its insistence on the end of this world and the renewal of all things in the world to come. The messianic themes were well adapted to this aspect of Christian thought, the difference lying in the gradual displacement of the messianic expectations not only to the end of time but even beyond into a realm of eternal bliss. There was a revolutionary accent in this dimension of the Christian outlook, seeking to overthrow the order of things in the present world and replacing it with a new, sanctified and salvific Christian dispensation. And finally, it was in some degree gnostic in that the central tenets of Christian belief were shrouded in mystery that was open to the deeper understanding only of an elite. It can safely be said that the original cult, that took form within the small and devoted band of followers who gathered around the charismatic figure of Jesus, gradually was transformed into a sect after the traumatic events of the passion, death and resurrection. According to Yinger's (1957) classification, the cult, which is small and focused around the teaching and influence of the charismatic leader, can evolve into a sect which is to a greater degree socially oriented, responsive to unsatisfied needs in the social milieu, and may take up a position of aggressive opposition or avoidance in relation to the social order. While the charismatic influence of Christ was extended in the subsequent evolution of the church, there were also gradually emerging elements of structure and redistribution of the charismatic influences. After Pentecost, the apostles increasingly assumed the mantle of authority and religious inspiration.

The upshot of this development was an increasing emphasis on the divinity of Jesus and a displacement of the messianic expectation to an eschatological future and an increasing emphasis on realized eschatology. This process involved a distancing from the messianic emphases of the traditional doctrine of the messiah. Rather than a king after the model of David and a kingdom envisioned as a restitution of an idealized kingdom of this world, the messianic kingdom became spiritualized and the messianic king became the Son of God. These transformed messianic beliefs became the centerpiece of the Christian belief system as it emerged from its Palestinian origins and engaged with the pagan and hellenistic world of the time.

Thus the sectarian aspect of the religious community founded by Jesus seems clear enough. It was born in oppression and protest, it rejected the legitimacy and authoritative claims of the existing religious establishment, it established an egalitarian communal life, it was a form of voluntary association demanding total commitment from its members and proposing an apocalyptic or adventist prospect (Scroggs 1975). Even the Pauline churches were marked by a fundamental ambiguity of their social character. On one hand they were eschatological communities endowed with a strong sense of group boundaries, while at the same time they were open to prospective new members, hoping to draw them to conversion and acceptance of the gospel message and membership in the fellowship of Christ (Meeks 1979). If the mix was unstable, it was also creative. As Harrington (1982) comments: "The boundaries between the Pauline churches and the society around them were defined by special language emphasizing separation (the chosen, brothers and sisters, the saints, etc.), rules, the penalty of exclusion from common meals, the creation of autonomous institutions to serve the members, and sanctioned interactions with the society at large" (p. 158). A particularly noteworthy example of this sort of social interaction, segregation, exclusiveness and internal division can be found in Paul's relationship with the community of Corinth (Theissen 1982; Schreiber 1977).

Evolution of the Messianic Ideal

The messianic vision has undergone profound transformations in the course of its history. If we start with the yearning for the restoration of the Davidic monarchy, the original impulse took the form of a profound desire for the return of a time of political independence and relative security from the predatory incursions of hostile nations. The vision was one of material prosperity and power, instituted in this world at the good pleasure of Yahweh. In the cultural matrix of the world of the time, Israel could look for little else. But the continued frustration of this desire and the mounting pressures of defeat, captivity, exile, suffering and oppression, dimmed the hopes for a political restoration. But hopes, particularly messianic hopes, are difficult to kill — they may fade for a time, seemingly buried in the wreckage of historical catastrophe, only to rise again like the mythical phoenix to shine brightly and stir the hearts of men.

Israel's Davidic destiny faded before the onslaughts of history, but the messianic dream — like Freud's repressed — found a displaced pathway to revivification. The vision evolved into a modification of the messianic ideal that took several forms. The character of the messiah changed — he was no longer a mere human king, but now took on a collective identity with the people of Israel themselves, or, even better, became identified with Yahweh himself. Another theme which entered the picture was the idea of a suffering messiah — so poignantly expressed in the Isaian Servant Songs. Thus in the Israelite framework, the messiah theme became diversified and complexified. As Neusner (1984b) has pointed out, if we ask what the meaning of the messiah was in Israel, we would have to provide many answers with quite divergent meanings and implications.

With the entrance of Jesus Christ on the stage of history, the messianic theme entered another phase of its evolution. The extent to which Jesus himself took on the role of messiah and proclaimed himself as such is disputed. If he did at all, it was in obscure, muted, and unfamiliar terms — certainly unfamiliar to his Jewish disciples and listeners who would have had a very different concept and expectation for their messiah. From the perspective of history, we are trapped in the uncertain web of not knowing how much of what we read in the gospels is authentic history and how much falls under the rubric of retrospective distortion or interpretation deriving from later Christian belief and understanding of the role of the Christ-Messiah. Certainly after Christ's death and resurrection, the direction of Christian thinking about the messiah shifted. In the light of post-resurrection faith, Jesus was declared to be messiah and Lord. As Schnackenburg (1963) notes: "But even the eschatological and final gospel of Jesus enters yet another stage of its preaching after Easter. In the early Church Jesus was regarded as raised to the right hand of God and established as the "Lord" who, in a special manner, exercises God's royal power until his Parousia inaugurates God's perfect kingdom." (p. 9) He was not messiah in any sense to be identified with Judaic prototypes, but he was a spiritualized messiah, part of whose messianic mission was to suffer and die on the cross and to be raised again to glory by his heavenly Father. "But the messianic titles, in which this identity of Jesus in cross and resurrection is claimed and described, all anticipate at the same time the not-yet apparent future of the risen Lord. This means that the Easter appearances and revelations of the risen Lord are manifestly understood as foretaste and promise of his still future glory and lordship" (Moltmann 1967, p. 85). The process of spiritualization that was the product of the higher christology that evolved in the Johannine community particularly (Meissner, in process) led to the ultimate of spiritualization in the doctrine of Jesus as Lord and the Son of God, equal to the Father in power and divinity.

As the pages of history continued to turn, the eschatological dream developed and diversified as well. The eschatological future and the hopes for the fulfillment of divine promises and the longed-for parousia faded, the impact of the events of the final time were diluted and diminished. As Moltmann (1967) comments:

> The more Christianity became an organization for discipleship under the auspices of the Roman state religion and persistently upheld the claims of that religion, the more eschatology and its mobilizing, revolutionizing, and critical effects upon history as it has now to be lived were left to fanatical sects and revolutionary groups. Owing to the fact that Christian faith banished from its life the future hope by which it is upheld, and relegated the future to a beyond, or to eternity, whereas the biblical testimonies which it handed on are yet full to the brim with future hope of a messianic kind for the world, — owing to this, hope emigrated as it were from the Church and turned in one distorted form or another against the Church. (pp. 15-16)

This evolutionary pattern came to realization in the messianic and millennarian sects that arose in the medieval context, and found renewed vitality in the Protestant reformation that tore the fabric of Christendom to pieces.

While the theological ramifications of this doctrinal evolution are immense and articulate very different religious orientations and traditions, I would argue that from a psychoanalytic perspective they form a common thread that builds upon and articulates common underlying psychic needs and mechanisms. The needs in the perspective I have been developing here are concerned with basic narcissistic dynamics and the formation and sustaining of identity. They involve not only basic narcissistic investments and defenses, but also have a direct impact on the sense of communal belonging, participation, identification, and the purposefulness of existence that reflect the deeper levels of implication in the sharing of values and meanings that unite the individual with his fellow believers. To the extent that they share a common faith, a mutual system of beliefs, a common goal, and a mutually reinforced system of values and hopes, they find the resources for developing and sustaining a sense of personal identity and destiny. The messianic vision, in whatever form it has manifested itself in the course of history, serves these basic functions.

Section IV

Medieval Messianism
and Mysticism

CHAPTER   7

Medieval Messianism

Background

The second destruction of the Temple and the bitter disappointment of the messianic claims of Simon bar Kochba set the stage for the ensuing diaspora and the subsequent evolution of messianic ideas. With or without the contamination from Christian messianic views, the notion of the messiah who was to bring about the restitution of Israel and restore the glories of the Davidic monarchy in eschatological times became increasingly individual and personal. As the centuries passed, the yearning for this anticipated messiah grew more intense and more desperate. As Scholem (1971) notes: "When the Messianic idea appears as a living force in the world of Judaism — especially in that of medieval Judaism, which seems so totally interwoven with the realm of the *Halakhah* — it always occurs in the closest connection with apocalypticism. In these instances the Messianic idea constitutes both a content of religious faith as such and also a living, acute anticipation. Apocalypticism appears as the form necessarily created by acute Messianism." (p. 4) It became the breeding ground for the origin of many claimants to the messianic title, who laid their spurious claims to be the anointed of the Lord before the eager expectations of the faithful and were in some degree accepted as the true messiah by their followers. I will focus here on the intersection of the frustrated faith of the believers with the psychopathology of the religious cult leader. The story I will focus on is that of the rise of sabbatianism (Scholem 1973).

97

As Jewish life of the diaspora passed into the second millennium, the Babylonian schools continued to hold a dominant position. But with the rise of Islam, cultural changes began to make their inroads. The language of discourse became Arabic, and with it the increasing influence of Greek philosophy. About the middle of the 8th century, following the lead of Anan ben David, the karaite schism arose, calling for a return to the scriptural tradition and a rejection of the rabbinic oral law. Increasingly, under the influence of Islamic transmissions, from the 10th century on, of ancient Greek thought, hellenistic rationalism became a challenge to traditional religious views. Neoplatonic influences, along with the ascetical and mystical influence of the East, came into play and interacted with traditional Jewish views.

The earlier influence of platonism on the philosophy of Philo of Alexandria and on Palestinian rabbis contributed to the foundations of Jewish mysticism, and may have its reverberations in the emergence of the *kabbalah*.[1] The decline of Babylonian influence was followed by the increasing influence of Spanish Jewry. Judaism had to protect its unique religious orientation against the forces of Islam on one side and those of Christianity on the other. Philosophical rationalism remained a challenge, but also provided an opportunity for being incorporated with traditional views in the service of strengthening the true faith. In the golden age of Spanish Jewry, the great poet-philosophers wove brilliant tapestries of philosophical reason and poetic vision.

The greatest rabbinic scholar and Jewish philosopher of the early centuries of the second millennium was Moses Maimonides (AD 1135-1204). His effort to reconcile Jewish religious teaching with Aristotelian philosophy demonstrated that faith and reason are not opposed, and that the teachings of Judaism can be presented in a reasonable and rational manner. He tried to steer a course among the rocky shoals of apocalypticism, the fantastic visions of the haggadists, and away from the popular midrashim of the end times and the final catastrophe. If the messianic age brings freedom in the form of the release of Israel from slavery, it does not abrogate the law. The messiah must prove his case not by cosmic signs and miracles, but by real success — only in such success can the identity of the messiah and the authenticity of his mission be established. In the mind of Maimonides the accent fell on

---

1. Idel (1988) seems to urge this view as an alternative understanding of the development of Jewish mysticism progressing more or less organically from ancient to medieval times. This is part of the argument with Scholem over the origins of Jewish mystical and particularly kabbalistic traditions.

the restorative element, with little play given to utopian visions. The messianic age must be a public event culminating in the restoration of the community. Only study of the Torah and the knowledge of God carried on in a world governed by natural causes is utopian (Scholem 1971).

Under the influence of philosophical trends and the surrounding culture, various traditions grew up among the Jews of the diaspora. Sephardic or Spanish Jewry came under the influence of Islamic culture. In Germany and Central Europe, a quite different cultural and national set of traditions influenced the emergence of Ashkenazic or German Jewry. The Sephardic Scholars wrote in Arabic and were largely systematizers; the Ashkenazim wrote in Hebrew and saw themselves more as commentators on the Torah.

The thread of mysticism which ran as a continuous, if often subtle, strain in all of Jewish thinking also differed. The mysticism of the Ashkenazim tended to be individualistic, emphasizing the role of personal ethics. Sephardic mysticism, however, developed the great speculative and practical systems of the *kabbalah*. The *kabbalah* was not born as a reaction to philosophizing trends, but once on stage it came to fulfill that role. The debate between the philosophers and the mystics continued unabated. God was regarded as the *En-Sof*, infinitely distant, the *deus absconditus* of the philosophers. The classic formulation of kabbalistic mysticism, the *Zohar*, was given its final form in the 13th century by Moses de Leon. The origins of the *Zohar* lay in a group of Spanish writers who reflected the gnostic strains in Spanish Kabbalism. This early expression of the *kabbalah* may have derived from the union of an earlier gnostic tradition and the more contemporary elements of Jewish neoplatonism (Eliade 1985).

The *Zohar* advanced another view of God as less transcendent and more imminent. For the Ashkenazic Hasidim, their pietistic vision saw the smallest actions and events of daily life as infused with the mystical glow. The *kabbalah* flourished in an atmosphere of allegory and symbolism. The symbol uncovers fresh meaning and makes the inexpressible transparent; through it the life of the Creator and the created become unified. As Scholem (1941) commented:

> Of such symbols the world of *kabbalah* is full, nay the whole world is to the Kabbalist such a *corpus symbolicum*. Out of the reality of creation, without the latter's existence being denied or annihilated, the inexpressible mystery of the Godhead becomes visible. In particular the religious acts commanded by the Torah, the *mitzvoth*, are to the Kabbalist symbols in which a deeper and

hidden sphere of reality becomes transparent. The infinite shines through the finite and makes it more and not less real. This brief summary gives us some idea of the profound difference between the philosophers' allegorical interpretation of religion and its symbolical understanding by the mystics. (pp. 27-28)

The mystical vision of the sephardic *kabbalah* embraced two major trends: the theosophical-theurgical and the unitive-ecstatic. The former espouses a highly theocentric theory of the structure of the divine world and its relations with the material world of man's experience, and the latter provided a highly anthropocentric doctrine of mystical and ecstatic experience as the greatest human good, regardless of its impact on the inner divine harmony (Idel 1988). The vision of both carried the potential for the redemption of the world.

The differences in emphasis were reflected in the attitudes toward symbolism. The mysticism of ecstatic *kabbalah* made more of the separation and division between spirit and matter, emphasizing the goal of liberation of the soul from the prison of the body. Ecstatic *kabbalah* sought to sever the connections between body and soul — the body played a minimal role as a point of departure for meditation. For theosophical *kabbalah*, on the other hand, the body was a powerful symbol of the realm of the *sefiroth*, so that contemplation of the body was a vehicle for discerning the dimensions of the deity — the body was the mystical stepping stone to the ascent beyond the material world (Idel 1988).

The world of the diaspora was not an easy or a kind world. The crusades led to repeated pogroms; bizarre and diabolical libels against the Jews abounded. In Europe, Ashkenazic Jewry was decimated. Some relief came in Poland during the reign of Casimir III (AD 1333-1370). But the sephardic community also suffered persecution and retrenchment. The persecution of the Jews in Spain finally led to their expulsion in 1492. Jewish communities became isolated and sought relief from their continuing trials and tribulations in mystical visions, in ritual and a kind of cultural involution. It was on the basis of this bedrock of frustration and despair that the false hopes stirred by messianic figures found their natural soil. Perhaps the most noteworthy of these false messiahs, as we shall see, was Sabbatai Sevi.

The Messianic Vision

Existing in this context of intellectual and cultural conflict, and in the conditions of torment and oppression of the exile, the messianic idea of medieval Jewry followed both popular-mythological and philo-sophical-rationalist traditions, which existed more or less side by side. Popular messianism was influenced not only by biblical traditions but by the popular and familiar legends and apocalyptic midrashim that sprang up during centuries of exile and oppression. Popular messianic views found room for both catastrophe and utopianism, both of which played an important role in the shaping of the messianic faith. Both had their roots in scripture, the catastrophic view in the vision of the end of days (Isaiah), and the utopian ideals in the "day of the Lord" (Amos). Unlike the apocalyptic scenario of Christian belief, Jewish messianism had no foundational text, no consensual scenario, no con-sistent or authoritative set of beliefs that might embrace the messianic expectations. The various messiahs that emerged during the course of Jewish history drew from various aspects of these competing views and emphases to substantiate their claims.

In general terms, the catastrophic aspects of the messianic vision created its own mythology of violent upheaval, wars, plagues, famines, an abandonment of Yahweh and the Torah, and unrestrained heresy and license. It was only on the ruins of history, through the "birthpangs of the messianic age" that redemption could be achieved. The centuries of alien rule, oppression and persecution fed into the violent and des-perate imagery of this eschatology, which can readily be traced back to the apocalyptic literature of the period of the Second Temple. In the final cataclysm, the persecuted and downtrodden people of Israel would turn on and realize vengeance against its torturers and persecutors, but not without suffering its own tribulation and burden of suffering in the process. In some versions, the Messiah ben Joseph was to fall in battle at the gates of Jerusalem and was to be the messiah of the catastrophe and not that of the utopia (Scholem 1973).

In contrast, the utopian elements were cast in terms of all the exaggerated qualities of a golden age, which implied not only miracu-lous and wondrous manifestations but a radical transformation of all of nature. These often idyllic and perfectionistic descriptions also con-tained within them explosive elements. The overriding intention of such ideals was to seek and realize the perfection and fulfillment of traditional religious law, but the latent forces they contained held the potential of undermining these very intentions. The messianic utopias offered the promise of something radically and miraculously different, and tended to open themselves to antinomian influences which were not at all foreign to many medieval messianic movements. The transla-tion of messianic hopes from the ideal into the real often found itself in tension with traditional rabbinic teaching. Thus, messianic movements produced leaders whose charismatic authority tended to challenge the established authority of the rabbis, even as the messianic claim presented a challenge to the claims for religious orthodoxy of the rabbinical establishment.

These apocryphal legends not only had a profound influence among the masses for whom they satisfied profound needs and longings by their descriptions of messianic catastrophe and utopia, but they often found their way into the writing of rabbinical authorities as well. Other scholars viewed this proliferation of apocalyptic imaginative visions with considerable skepticism and even hostility. Such utopianism not only arouses hopes and expectations, but it also threatens existing and traditional patterns. As Scholem (1973) comments, "Every utopia that is more than an abstract formula has a revolutionary sting." (p. 12)

It was against this revolutionary strain that Maimonides exercised his considerable dialectical skill. He emphasized the conservative function of the messiah and his role in safeguarding the Torah and traditional law. He was well aware of the disruptive and antinomian elements in prior messianic movements, and harbored no illusions about the dangers of such movements for traditional religion. His own utopian ideal, opposing the "beliefs of the rabble," took a more aristocratic form and seemed to aim at the abolition of messianism as a moving force in human life. Yet, even the authority of Maimonides could not match the power of the profound needs that lie behind the more popular apocalyptic views. His onslaught ran into powerful opposition of vested interests in the Jewish community and of deeply entrenched traditional mystical views.[2] The early kabbalists possessed great religious authority that tended to silence any opposition. Idel (1988) even links the rise of *kabbalah* with these rationalistic attacks; he argues

> that *kabbalah* emerged in the late twelfth and early thirteenth centuries as a sort of reaction to the dismissal of earlier mystical traditions by Maimonides' audacious reinterpretation of Jewish esotericism and his attempt to replace the mystical traditions with

---

2. Scholem (1971) describes the divergent trends of rationalist and apocalyptic messianism. The apocalyptists search the scriptures for anything that they can connect with the Last Days; every word can be connected in some sense to the messianic promises and events. The rationalists follow a diametrically opposed path: nothing is related to the messiah if it can be connected to something else. Prophetic predictions have already been fulfilled, and messianic utterances are meant to refer to the people of Israel (e.g., the suffering servant in Is 53). Part of this tendency was due to the ongoing polemic with Christianity, resisting the messianic claims of Christ.

a philosophical understanding. *kabbalah* can be viewed as part of a restructuring of those aspects of rabbinic thought that were denied authenticity by Maimonides' system. Far from being a total innovation, historical *kabbalah* represented an ongoing effort to systematize existing elements of Jewish theurgy, myth, and mysticism into a full-fledged response to the rationalistic challenge. (p. 253)

Other apocalyptic and eschatological writings found it necessary to readmit the elements of popular mythology, which had their profound influence on subsequent generations, even on the adherents of the Sabbatian movement (Scholem 1973).

Kabbalistic Theology

The expulsion from Spain brought in its wake a religious revival in which the influence of the *kabbalah* in Sephardic Jewry became increasingly prominent, particularly with its unique attitudes toward the messianic tradition. The earliest traces of *kabbalah* are found in the *Bahir*, an obscure and fragmentary text from the 12th century that echoes many of the familiar gnostic themes, along with Neoplatonic influences (Eliade 1985). Early kabbalism had had little to say about messianism, since it was preoccupied with the contemplative, mystical approach to God, including gnostic traditions and philosophical ideas. It was this mix of ideas that found its way to Spain and influenced the Spanish *kabbalah*.

An interesting question that seems to throw some light on these considerations has to do with the relationships, if any, between gnosticism and Jewish *kabbalah*. The accepted view had been that kabbalism had been a later development in Jewish mystical teaching that absorbed a certain portion of gnostic teaching in its course. But the question of priority between gnostic and kabbalistic influences is controversial. Scholem (1941, 1971, 1973, 1974) argues that the early kabbalistic movement incorporated gnostic influences that were flourishing in the hellenistic world in the period of the Second Temple. More current scholarship has come to appreciate the significance of ancient Jewish mysticism in the emergence of gnostic thought. It seems that gnosticism borrowed a good deal from more ancient traditions that were absorbed into the *Zohar*, the 13th-century classic of Jewish mysticism. The parallels between aspects of the kabbalistic doctrine and gnostic systems, especially those of Basilides and Valentinus, is striking — the gnostic view of the intermediary powers and the kabbalistic doctrine of the *sefiroth* especially so.

Scholem had taken the *kabbalah* to represent the merger of older gnostic motifs with neoplatonic philosophy. The gnostic elements in kabbalistic mysticism were explained as elements that had infiltrated Jewish beliefs and were carried along in esoteric heterodox circles, finally to surface again in the 12th century. Idel (1988) challenges this view, arguing that Scholem's perspective was influenced by the work of Hans Jonas (1963) that led to an understanding of *kabbalah* as a form of Jewish gnosticism and of the Heikhalot literature as gnostic.

More contemporary studies would reverse the sequence, seeing early *kabbalah* as infiltrating and influencing gnostic ideas — rather than seeing *kabbalah* as an outgrowth of gnosticism, it has been more impressed with the influence of Jewish thought on the emerging gnostic literature. The two traditions enjoy numerous parallels and utilize similar theosophic schemes. Thus many of the affinities between gnostic and kabbalist texts may have been originally Jewish views that had infiltrated gnostic circles and were also passed along in Jewish circles to finally come to light in the *kabbalah*. An example might be the myth of creation through the intermediary of a primal anthropos conceived as both monad and decad. Idel (1988) explains the evolution of this teaching as follows:

> . . . a hypothetical Jewish account of Creation consisted of a description of the first creature as man, who at one and the same time includes the ten things, or *logoi,* and is at the same time the monad. This creature is intermediary in the Creation of the world, which is sometimes envisaged as existing within him. This pre-Christian, pre-Gnostic view presumably underwent several metamorphoses in the various types of literature in which it was absorbed: (1) the Christian texts, such as Paul's epistle, identified it with Christ, thereby eliminating the motif of the decad; (2) Gnostic texts, which also showed their authors' awareness of the Christian versions of the Jewish idea, sometimes identified the man as the son of man, but *mutatis mutandis* reflected the original view; (3) rabbinic sources obliterated the anthropomorphic nature of the creating anthropos but preserved the innocuous term *logoi* as the principle means of creation; and (4) medieval *kabbalah,* inheriting these presumably ancient Jewish traditions, developed them in an elaborate form that is closest to the Gnostic accounts, albeit using rabbinic terminology: *ma'amarot,* or such terms as *Sefiroth.* (p. 122)

One can also note that many passages dealing with the Shekhinah as the divine consort and the concept of the exile of the Shekhinah in this world resonate with gnostic versions of the Sophia myth. But the religious contexts differ: for gnosticism, knowledge of the cosmogonic scheme was part of a salvific gnosis; for theurgical kabbalism, the theosophical scheme served more as a blueprint for life and behavior.

The kabbalistic view of the world was largely mystical and symbolic, seeking to find its way toward God by way of the ladder of spiritual ascent through which the mysteries of both God himself and of the Torah could be grasped. Their outlook was basically conservative and they shared the hopes of traditional religion, but the spiritual impulse carried with it no specifically messianic vision. The ecstatic ideal of contemplative communion with God did not require a messianic worldview. Rather than a collective phenomenon, redemption was individual, the redemption of the personal soul that was independent of the kind of national redemptive vision of traditional messianism.

Kabbalistic theology held a view of the hidden God (*En-Sof*), who was unrevealed and unknown in himself; but this God was revealed through his emanations, the ten *sefiroth*. The understanding of the *sefiroth* varied among writers of different theosophical traditions, variously influenced by neoplatonic philosophy, and in various scholarly conceptions. Idel (1988) describes three major views of the ultimate essence of the *sefiroth* dating from the 13th century: (1) the *sefiroth* are reflections of the divine nature and participate in the divine essence; these essentialist views tended to be more dynamic than static, but some more static essentialist views did arise, such as those identifying the *sefiroth* with the platonic ideas in the divine mind; (2) the *sefiroth* are not divine in essence, but are closely related to the divine as creative instruments or as vessels for the transmitting of the divine influx to the lower worlds; these more philosophical distinctions elaborated on previous kabbalistic distinctions between essential and instrumental functions of the *sefiroth*, a development that facilitated acceptance of *kabbalah* among Jewish and Christian intellectuals; and (3) the *sefiroth* are divine emanations within the created world, constituting the divine immanence; the identification of the emanations with their source lent itself to a pantheistic interpretation.

These conceptions were crystallized as separate views in the 15th and 16th centuries, but were more or less unified in the theosophy of Cordovero, so that the coexistence of the *sefiroth* as divine essences and instruments became a dominant theme in later kabbalist theosophy. Theosophical *kabbalah* rarely followed the immanence view, while pantheistic emphases were not hard to find (Scholem 1941). But even these writers held to a transcendent view of God: the transcendent layer of the divinity was more central to the divine essence, while pantheistic ideas occupied a more peripheral position as consequences of emanationist systems. Idel (1988) summarizes the view of theosophical *kabbalah* as *visio omnium in Deo*, while for ecstatic *kabbalah* it was *visio Dei in omnibus*.

Idel (1988) adds a fourth perspective on the *sefiroth* that viewed them as corresponding to aspects of human psychology. This latter view had more explicit appeal to ecstatic *kabbalah* and later hasidism. The mystical system emphasized inner experience rather than theurgical activity, so that "the entities to be activated are no longer the objectively existing divine Sefirot but rather the human spiritual Sefirot" (Idel 1988, p. 146). The shift from theosophical to human experience had its implications for the later development of Jewish mysticism, particularly that the *sefiroth* were less divine attributes than processes taking place within the human psyche. Idel (1988) concludes that Ba'al Shem Tov, the founder of Hasidism, "interpreted the entire sefirotic scheme as referring to mystical states on the human level." (p. 150)

In the more essentialist views of the *Zohar* and Moses de Leon, these *sefiroth* constitute the inner life of the Godhead and can be known from their reflections in the created order of beings. The *sefiroth* are emanations by which God reveals his various attributes; they contain the archetypes of all existence. The divine emanation, at least in one version, becomes increasingly less spiritual and more material, so that the sensible material world is the last and most peripheral realm of this "garment of the deity." Other versions saw the existence of matter and the world in more negative terms as reflecting the fallen and alien quality of worldly existence. This theory of emanation became more complex for the kabbalists of Safed. At every stage there was not only the direct light of divine emanation, but also a reverse "reflected" light which sought return to its source. The entire cosmos of divine emanation is structured by the dialectical interaction of the downward-directed direct light and the upward-directed reflected light.

True to its gnostic instincts, the 10 "holy" *sefiroth* are matched by a corresponding set of "unholy" or "impure" *sefiroth* that constitute the realm of Satan, a hierarchy of evil potentialities. Each of these was given a personal character and a name — in distinction to the divine *sefiroth* that represent abstract qualities (Scholem 1941).

Mysticism and Messianism

Thus, mystical contemplation reveals the symbolic character of the universe, and the inner meaning of creation; the law and the commandments are revealed through meditation on the mysteries of such mystical symbolism. By contemplative prayer, the human will attaches itself to the divine will and the sphere of the *sefiroth*. The mystic who achieves this communion with the source of all being through his contemplative ascent, or in some views through nonecstatic theological speculation (Idel 1988), achieves the endpoint of his individual redemption. Thus, for the kabbalist, contemplation was a form of participation in eschatological messianism. Thus, a new meaning was given to the concept of the "exile of the *Shekhinah*," the glory of God envisioned as his female consort. This disjunction in the Godhead parallels the exile of Israel, and only with the coming of the messianic redemption will the perfect unity of the divine *sefiroth* be reestablished.

In this vein, the eschatological teaching of the *Zohar* continued the apocalyptic and utopian elements against which Maimonides contended. The messianic events were essentially supernatural and implied a close link between redemption and a deepening knowledge of the kabbalistic mysteries. In the days of exile, the minds of men were beclouded, but in the end of time the mysteries of the *kabbalah* would be revealed. In this sense, the interests of apocalyptic messianism and *kabbalah* remained distinct and independent. Traditional messianism had its grim side since the coming of the messianic age was to follow the universal destruction of history. Over time this catastrophic view grew dimmer, and the messianic vision looked increasingly toward an ideal of man's infinite progress and perfectibility (Scholem 1971).

The failure of messianic prophecies, for example that in 1530, accompanied by intense propaganda by the kabbalists of Jerusalem, did not seem to diminish messianic fervor or belief. Creation of a new spiritual center of Jewry in Safed after the Spanish expulsion created a movement of spiritual and moral reform that had widespread influence. Apocalyptic expectations seemed to fade into the background and were replaced by doctrines of ascetic piety. The asceticism of the new kabbalism had far-reaching effects in stimulating enthusiasm for mystical salvation and a yearning for the time of redemption.

In Safed itself, kabbalism became a powerful force on Jewish spiritual life. In Scholem's reconstruction, while the teaching of the *kabbalah* was essentially esoteric, appealing to an intellectual and spiritual elite, it nonetheless had a powerful popular appeal. Its influence on the religious consciousness of the Jewish people in the 16th century was quite remarkable. The rise of kabbalism in such striking fashion can be explained by an appeal to the effects of persecution and suffering as preparing the way for mystical illusions. But Scholem (1973) rejects this view. He comments: "Kabbalism triumphed because it provided a valid answer to the great problems of the time. To a generation for which the facts of exile and the precariousness of existence in it had become a most pressing and cruel problem, kabbalism could give an answer unparalleled in breadth and in depth of vision. The kabbalistic answer illuminated the significance of exile and redemption and accounted for the unique historical situation of Israel within the wider, in fact cosmic, context of creation itself." (p. 20) Further, the theurgical dimension of kabbalism tended to narrow the gap between ordinary everyday prayer and the deeper spiritual needs with which the *kabbalah* resonated. One did not need to reach the levels of mystical or ecstatic experience in order to participate in the *kabbalah*.

The kabbalist view was that, had Adam not sinned, the divine emanations would have flowed down through all levels of creation, illuminating them so that the separation between the creator and his creation would have been obliterated. The cosmic exile would have been terminated and Adam would have functioned as the redeemer, whose mission was to restore the world to its unity. But with Adam's sin, the separation was prolonged and intensified. Thus, Adam was isolated from communication with God and became attached to the lower world and to the evil forces, which belonged to the "other side." The world sank into the realm of the *qelippah*, in which good and evil were mixed and compounded. In consequence, all natural beings, including man, were clothed in gross matter and physical bodies derived from the *qelippah*, instead of the spiritual bodies possessed before the fall. For this theological vision, *qelippah*, or "the shell," or "the other side" was a powerful reality, certainly in psychological terms.

Ultimately, evil in this view was derived from the deity and had its source deep in the divine essence. Thus, in the kabbalistic view, the messianic world retains its utopian traits, but such a world could not come into being until man had accomplished his *tiqqun* or redemption. The purification of souls was thus an ongoing process, extended in time through history rather than an event of the last stages of history immediately preceding the final redemption. For Lurianic *kabbalah*, the coming of the messiah could not be even considered until all of the purifications and the return of the divine light to its pristine state had been accomplished. The coming of the messiah would thus be a sign that Israel had completed its mission in the world.

Lurianic Kabbalism

Efforts of the Safed kabbalists to codify their teachings reflected the influence of older traditions of Spanish kabbalism, along with more current speculative and mystical contributions. The older generation tended more to speculation and commentary on the classic texts, for example, Moses Cordovero (1522-1570); the younger generation turned more toward symbolism and mythology, a path which found greater appeal for the untutored masses. Thus, Scholem (1973, 1974) argues, kabbalism came to provide the ideology for popular religious sentiments. A major contributor to this development was Isaac Luria Ashkenazi (1534-72), the "Lion" of Safed, whose teachings dominated kabbalistic theology for the next half-century.

The gnostic accents are not difficult to detect. As Scholem (1941) commented:

> To the student of religious history, the close affinity of these thoughts to the religious ideas of the Manichaeans must be obvious at once. We have here certain Gnostic elements — especially the theory of the scattered sparks or particles of light — which were either absent from or played no particular part in early Kabbalistic thought. At the same time there can be no doubt that this fact is due not to historical connections between the Manichaeans and the new *Kabbalah* of Safed, but to a profound similarity in outlook and disposition which in its development produced similar results. In spite of this fact, or perhaps rather because of it, students of Gnosticism may have something to learn from the Lurianic system which, in my opinion, is a perfect example of Gnostical thought, both in principle and in detail. (p. 280)

The notion of the ascent of the soul passing through spheres of hostile archons and rulers of the cosmos in order to achieve its heavenly abode and salvation is a central gnostic idea. The *sefiroth* are little different than the gnostic archons, namely hypostasized attributes of the divine. As Scholem (1941) comments:

> ... mysticism represents, to a certain extent, a revival of mythical lore. . . . The Jewish mystic lives and acts in perpetual rebellion against a world with which he strives with all his zeal to be at peace. Conversely, this fact is responsible for the profound ambiguity of his outlook, and it also explains the apparent self-contradiction inherent in a great many Kabbalist symbols and images.

The great symbols of the *Kabbalah* certainly spring from the depths of a creative and genuinely Jewish religious feeling, but at the same time they are invariably tinged by the world of mythology. . . . Failing this mythical element, the ancient Jewish mystics would have been unable to compress into language the substance of their inner experience. It was Gnosticism, one of the last great manifestations of mythology in religious thought, and definitely conceived in the struggle against Judaism as the conqueror of mythology, which lent figures of speech to the Jewish mystic. (pp. 34-35)

The new piety of Lurianic kabbalism created a mounting enthusiasm for ascetic devotions and intense piety. The Lurianic system brought with it an effulgence of exegetical literature in which the ritual and the significance of the *mizvoth* was reinterpreted in terms of Lurianic theosophy. This was the last of the greatest kabbalistic expressions of these themes — sabbatianism had no interest in such directives and the concern with theurgy and theosophy dwindled among Hasidic mystics. The objective was to hasten the work of redemption by an intensification of piety and the purification of a whole generation. In this system, the faintness of the image of the messiah is striking, even surprising. Lurianic kabbalism emphasizes the idea of redemption. But the messiah's role in this redemption is relatively pale and insignificant. If the messiah is mentioned at all, it is in a somewhat pedestrian recounting of traditional texts. The transfer of the messianic characteristics to the historical nation, Israel, tended to mask his distinctive personal traits. But at the same time, the traditional view of the messianic misfortunes and subsequent redemption retained their force.

The old apocalyptic tradition seemed to exist alongside the new kabbalistic conception of *tiqqun*. Both of these elements contributed to the sabbatian movement: the masses clinging to the ancient apocalyptic visions and messianic propaganda, while the spiritual elite emphasized the doctrine of *tiqqun*, thus minimizing the popular elements in their eschatology. The appearance of the messiah is no more than the consummation of the redemptive *tiqqun*. The essence of redemption was therefore mystical, and the historical or national aspects only secondary and external expressions of its accomplishment (Scholem 1941).

A particular kabbalistic belief was that God sent a potential messiah-soul into the world once in every generation. Such a perfectly righteous soul, like a Moses in his time, can exercise the redemptive function of the messiah, depending on whether the men of his generation have been sufficiently purified to merit the work of redemption.

The righteous soul could only come into full possession of his messianic nature when the general *tiqqun* had been achieved. Scholem (1973) also notes that even as the *qelippah* ultimately takes its derivation from the divine essence, so the messiah himself necessarily has an evil side to him. The *qelippah* was mixed in with the essence of all created beings, so that even the messiah had something of the power of the *qelippah* in him, even in his work of messianic redemption.

The elements of mystical and apocalyptic messianism existed side by side during the 16th century. The Safed kabbalists emphasized the spiritual aspects of redemption more than an external realization of messianic utopian ideals. But these latter were interpreted as symbols of spiritual transformation rather than obliterated. In the theurgical vision, spiritual acts became the vehicle for the realization of hoped-for messianic expectations. While the kabbalists seemed unaware of the tension thus created between their own mystical symbolism and a realized eschatology, they had in fact established a fundamentally-new conception. To the extent that the messianic idea, therefore, could remain untested in the harsh realities of historical experience, these different conceptions could stand side by side and feed eschatological speculation. But when put to the test, the contradictions became manifest. As long as the paradox remained unacknowledged, the political messianism of the masses and the mystical messianism of the spiritual kabbalists seemed to form a seamless robe. It was not until the challenge of sabbatianism that the paradox became apparent. Even there, political messianism was to take the lead until historical failures and disappointments replaced it with a new version of mystical messianism (Scholem 1973).

Scholem (1973, 1974) regards Lurianic *kabbalah* as a widespread popular movement in the generation preceding the rise of sabbatianism, one that sowed the seeds of messianic enhancement that were reaped in sabbatian messianism. He (1941) summarizes this movement in the following terms:

> To sum up, the *kabbalah* of Isaac Luria may be described as a mystical interpretation of Exile and Redemption, or even as a great myth of Exile. Its substance reflects the deepest religious feelings of the Jews of that age. For them, Exile and Redemption were in the strictest sense great mystical symbols which point to something in the Divine Being. This new doctrine of God and the universe corresponds to the new moral idea of humanity which it propagates: the ideal of the ascetic whose aim is the Messianic reformation, the extinction of the world's blemish, the restitution

of all things in God — the man of spiritual action who through the *Tikkun* breaks the exile, the historical exile of the Community of Israel and that inner exile in which all creation groans. (p. 286)

Idel (1988) takes issue with this interpretation on the following grounds. Lurianic *kabbalah* remained an esoteric, highly complex and intellectual system that appealed to a small elite and was never propagated to a larger public. Even those who were sympathetic to it did not interpret it as a messianic ideology. In addition, the messianic message of Lurianic *kabbalah* was no greater than it had been in previous kabbalistic teachings. The messianic elements of the *kabbalah* of Abulafia and of the *Zohar* were given no greater weight or intensity by Luria. For Luria, as for the *Zohar*, the coming of the messiah would result from the theurgical activity of the collective, and the individual messiah would reflect the attainment of the messianic age rather than its initiation. For sabbatianism, on the other hand, the messiah was a specific person whose redemptive acts would effect the eschatological age. These messianic views were essentially opposed and not easily reconciled. Consequently, the relations between Lurianic messianism and sabbatianism are probably more complex than in Scholem's view. As Idel (1988) comments:

> Notwithstanding this, I want to stress that Sabbatianism indeed benefited from Lurianic *Kabbalah*, primarily through the adoption of its theosophy and mythology. Although Sevi himself was not particularly interested in this type of *Kabbalah*, his prophet, Nathan of Gaza, can be considered as a Lurianic Kabbalist who employed Lurianic terminology creatively, giving it a special twist that "illuminated" the personal myth of Sevi. Moreover, the theological language of Sevi's followers was predominantly Lurianic, although again it was used and understood only by the very few. A perusal of Sabbatian documents demonstrates that they were as obscure as the Lurianic texts, far beyond the reach of the understanding of the masses. (p. 259)

Idel's (1988) critique of Scholem's work — which I have followed in the main in this discussion — deserves a hearing, if only to put Scholem's impressive contribution in perspective. A particularly trenchant part of Idel's critique rests on methodological grounds. Scholem assumes that a given cultural or religious phenomenon reflects the influence of its immediate historical predecessors. The historical sequence is Zoharic *kabbalah*, followed by Lurianic *kabbalah*, then sabbatianism, and finally Hasidism. This also postulates the progression of mystical phenomena by way of reaction and controversy: Hasi-

dism is a reactionary response to sabbatianism and a profound restructuring of Lurianic kabbalism. To this Idel argues that the historical
approach alone often leads to incomplete or misleading conclusions.
Nathan of Gaza was a Lurianic kabbalist, but Sabbatai was closer to
the Zoharic and ecstatic traditions. Another path to understanding the
evolution of religious systems is phenomenology.

In Scholem's approach, the expulsion from Spain becomes a focal
event that served to structure the concern of Lurianic *kabbalah* in issues of exile, messianism and evil. Reliance on the assumption that
historical change is the dominant influence in conceptual innovations
of this mystical system takes precedence over internal developments.
This is accompanied by neglect of extant Lurianic texts that never mention the expulsion. Given this lack, the interconnection of these developments is only one hypothetical option that could be considered. Idel
(1988) summarizes:

> To recapitulate, the far-reaching impact of the Expulsion is a cor-
> nerstone of Scholem's historiosophy. It was supposed to have in-
> spired the messianic expectations that . . . were articulated by Lu-
> ria's *Kabbalah*. The latter then was considered to have paved the
> way for Sabbatianism, and this messianic movement, in turn, was
> the starting point for processes that generated not only Frankism
> but also, through the neutralization of the messianic core of Luri-
> anism, Hasidism and, in a dialectic way, the Jewish Enlighten-
> ment. The conviction that characterizes Scholem's statements,
> and the uncritical way in which they have been accepted by both
> the larger public and the scholars who deal with Jewish mysticism
> and history, have had little to do with the historical facts as I
> know them. No elaborate discussions based upon detailed analy-
> sis of all the pertinent material underpin these far-reaching histori-
> cal visions. (p. 266)

Messianism and the Paranoid Process

The history of messianic beliefs can be seen as reflecting aspects
of the paranoid process (Meissner 1978b). The conceptual task in establishing these connections is to find the basis for understanding the
relationship between historical and cultural patterns and individual psychological dynamics. The paranoid process is intended to provide that
foundation. The cultic process is itself an expression of the dynamics
of the paranoid process. So I would argue here that messianism not
only manifests aspects of the cultic process but that these processes

reveal the workings of the paranoid process on the level of individual psychological participation and realization.

The question concerns the psychological mechanisms by which such a persistent belief system comes to bear on and draws its strength from individual motivations. The messianic belief system provided a powerful response to forces of destruction and conquest that brought oppression and desolation to the Jewish community of believers. I would argue that the experiences of defeat, humiliation, exile and oppression were not merely historical or sociological events, but that they had a powerful impact on the souls and minds of individual Jews. The exilic events were not simply a crushing defeat and humiliation for the Jewish people, but were also a personal crisis for each individual Jew.

The crisis was a crisis of personal security and well-being brought about by the desperate conditions of exile and enslavement. The loss of one's home, separation from loved ones, the death and banishment of family and friends, impoverishment, and the harsh conditions of slavery and bondage took their inevitable toll. But in addition, the crisis was one of faith. Where was the powerful and protecting hand of Yahweh? He had guided them to the Promised Land and had sustained Moses, Joshua and the Judges against their enemies. Where were the promises of divine protection and assistance? Why had Yahweh turned his back and permitted the enemies of his chosen people to triumph? Why had he allowed such a cruel punishment and dissolution of his people? Not only were well-being and security placed in jeopardy, but the very fiber of faith and adherence to the God of their fathers was cast into doubt and uncertainty.

The Mystical Messiah

Introduction

The apocalyptic and eschatological aspects of the messianic vision provided fertile ground for false messianic hopes to flourish. Lurianic kabbalism issuing from the school at Safed in the 16th century, and subsequently becoming a dominant force in Jewish religiosity of the 17th century, was no exception. Within the religious context generated by Lurianic kabbalism,[1] there arose the most powerful, dramatic, influential and far-reaching of the false[2] messianic movements, certainly in the 17th century and quite possibly since the time of bar Kochba. It stands as "by far the most significant and extensive Messianic movement" in the history of post-Christian Judaism (Scholem 1971, p. 59). The story of the rise and fall of Sabbatai Sevi and the

---

1. Whether Lurianic *kabbalah* was effectively a breeding ground for sabbatianism, as Scholem (1973, 1974) would argue, or not, as others including Idel (1988) would contend, remains an open question as far as I can see. It seems safe to say that sabbatianism arose within the religious context partially shaped by *kabbalah;* the question of generative links remains undecided.

2. The falseness or truth of any messianic claim must be set in the context of the system of belief from which it is judged. To the devoted followers of Sabbatai, their belief was that he was the true and promised messiah. To the eyes of more traditional and skeptical rabbis, his claim to messianic status was false. Certainly, to the eyes of history a similar judgment can be made. In the view of Christians, Christ is the true messiah; in the view of believing Jews, he is not.

messianic movement connected with his name displays many of the aspects of the cultic process and its psychological underpinnings. As so often in matters human, pathological deviations provide a much more forceful and dramatic delineation of the psychological roots of complex phenomena than is available in the more common run of normal events.

I will recount here some of the highpoints of the life and mission of Sabbatai Sevi, the prophetic spread of the messianic movement, and finally its decline after Sabbatai's arrest and apostasy. The account here throughout will follow the thorough and detailed reconstruction of the sabbatian messianic movement provided by Scholem (1973).[3]

Life and Personality

Sabbatai was born in 1626. Accounts of his early life experience reflect a severe degree of emotional disturbance and sexual conflict. From his earliest years, he is said to have been tormented by nightmares expressing his severe sexual conflicts. Intense sexual temptations were described in the conventional kabbalistic imagery of demonic activity, particularly the demons arising from masturbation. An account of a dream in which a flame appears and burns his penis was displaced to the early age of six years, but probably reflect more adolescent temptations and tensions and undoubtedly allude to Sabbatai's later refusal to consummate any of his several marriages.

There seems little doubt that Sabbatai was severely disturbed. Contemporaries describe him as a madman or fool, and it seems, at least from the time of puberty on, his behavior largely warranted these descriptions. Scholem (1973) opts for a diagnosis of manic-depressive psychosis, marked by some paranoid traits.[4] Throughout the whole of his life, certainly beginning in his adolescent years, Sabbatai experi-

---

3. The emphasis throughout is on the pathological aspects of Sabbatai's role as cult leader and on the potentiality for messianic beliefs to be led down a pathological path. In the words of sociologist Daniel Bell (1979), Scholem's massive study of Sabbatai was hailed as "the most subtle and complex exploration I know of the character of messianic movements and messianic longings. . . ."

4. Falk (1982) accepts this diagnosis, but argues against Scholem's bias for a constitutional basis for the disease in favor of a more exclusively psychological explanation. The discussion between these viewpoints, organic vs. functional, continues in current psychiatry; my own view would take a more integrative tack, seeing manic-depressive disease as involving psychological, developmental and dynamic factors riding on a by now identifiable genetic and physiological basis.

enced the swings between periods of mental exaltation and illumination and other periods of dejection, passivity and depression.[5] This cyclical pattern began to emerge more clearly in his 20th year and became fully established by the time he was 22. In periods of manic exaltation, he would experience lofty and expansive emotions to the point of ecstasy, and even would imagine himself as floating in the air. When other observers failed to confirm the levitation, Sabbatai would argue that they were unworthy to witness this glorious revelation. Apparently, Sabbatai had experienced a number of such ecstatic states prior to his messianic self-revelation.

Nonetheless, the manic states were also states of contradiction. In the grip of his manic enthusiasm, young Sabbatai would be swept to the heights of euphoric exultation and the vision of himself as the promised messiah. But at the same time, this young rabbi who was so self-consciously devoted to mortification and the exercises of ascetical piety would begin to act in a strange manner that was at odds with his normal pattern of behavior and would involve bizarre forms of transgression of the law. These outbreaks of bizarre behavior were later called "strange acts" by his followers. The expression refers not only to actions which were bizarre and confounding, even absurd or foolish, but also refers to actual transgressions of Jewish religious law, some of them of a serious nature. These actions were a cause of consternation for those who would embrace his cause. But Sabbatai felt himself to be driven by a mysterious and supernatural impulse that compelled him to act in irrational ways, even if these behaviors meant breaking the law. Scholem (1973) comments that these behaviors undoubtedly revealed a hidden and unconscious opposition to the traditional law, expressing an underlying aggressive and rebellious attitude.

The alternating depressive periods presented a quite opposite picture. In these phases he suffered from a deep and paralyzing depression, from constant obsessions and doubts, and severe anxieties that prevented any form of useful or productive behavior, even making reading difficult. He would become despondent and dejected and incapable of carrying out even the simplest of everyday tasks. The cyclical

---

5. Falk (1982) links the emergence of Sabbatai's pathology to the death of his mother, a hypothesis that would put the origins of his pathology early in his childhood. At the root of it would be Sabbatai's early abandonment, depression and unresolved rage over this irreparable loss, and the frustrated yearning for symbiotic union with his lost and abandoning mother. His mother's death occurred sometime during his adolescence, and would have represented the rupture of the symbiotic bond.

pattern of shifting from illumination to depression and back again was a regular and recurring phenomenon. Days of anguish and depression would alternate with days of rejoicing and exultation, at times these phases being separated by periods of relatively normal behavior in which he returned to a pattern of quiet and pious religious devotion and ascetical practice.

The Messiah

In one of these states of manic illumination, he heard the voice of God telling him that he was the savior of Israel, the messiah, the son of David. From that time on he felt that the spirit of God was with him, particularly during his periods of illumination, and that the "strange actions" were part of the mystical *tiqqun* imposed on him by God. By the same token, the periods of anguish and despair were part of the temptations of the *qelippoth*. In the wake of these illuminations, he would return to a more normal state of mind and could no longer understand the meaning of his bizarre actions, which seemed so repugnant to reason. From the point of view of the pious ascetic, he could only regret these strange behaviors which were forced on him by the superior power which took possession of him (Falk 1982).

During periods of relative normalcy, in the interludes between his exaltations and depressions, Sabbatai seems to have possessed a considerable degree of personal charm. At such times he would impress others by his tact and kindliness and his capacity to gain the affection of his fellow men. His demeanor was noble, kindly and even dignified; at times he could even display considerable skill and tact in his dealings. Prior to his messianic revelation, he could even be thought of as a young rabbinical scholar, perhaps gifted, and certainly desirous of leading a holy life. But with the onset of his illness, his behavior becomes bizarre and alien. He is sunk in melancholy, hides from his family and friends in a dark little room, and behaves in foolish and irrational ways. He is persecuted and possessed by demons, and even his manic states seem like demonic possessions. Then the year 1648 arrived, the year that had been predicted in the *Zohar* as the year of resurrection and redemption. Instead of redemption, that year saw the horror of the Cossack insurrection in Poland and Russia that resulted in the Chmielnicki massacres.

It was in this context of the horrors of the bloody massacres and the shedding of Jewish blood, along with the intensification of messianic expectations, that Sabbatai received his revelation and proclaimed himself to be the promised messiah. But his announcement fell on deaf ears. There was no reaction to this first proclamation, and no one seemed to take him seriously. He was regarded as sick or as possessed by an evil spirit. In the vision, Abraham, Isaac and Jacob appeared to him and anointed him with oil, thus conferring on him the office of the messiah. This first revelation apparently created a sort of scandal, which ended in gossip and created opposition among the rabbis. The subsequent opposition and persecution of Sabbatai did not result in expulsion until three years later.

Sabbatai's provocative actions led to little public reaction. He was generally regarded as sick and his strange behavior of little consequence. For him the transgressions, such as uttering the ineffable name, were the result of commands and acts of *tiqqun*, performed under divine influence. This rationalization suggests the presence of latent antinomian tendencies, which were at this stage a matter of private paradox, but later would determine the pattern of the theology of his messianic movement. For Sabbatai the strange actions were merely mystical improvisations, whose mystery he could neither comprehend nor explain.

Whatever the character of his "strange actions," it seems to have been sufficient to cause the rabbis of Smyrna to lose their tolerance and to turn to outright persecution. It was finally decided to banish him from the city, probably in 1651. Sabbatai spent the next several years wandering from city to city. An incident at Salonika shed some light on the nature of his "strange actions." He invited a group of the most prominent rabbis to a banquet, and then carried out a ceremony in which he performed a marriage ceremony between himself and the Torah. The assembled rabbis were shocked and accused him of madness. Disturbed by his behavior and its possible consequences, they, too, forced him to leave the city. Scholem (1973) comments on Sabbatai's fondness for bizarre ceremonials and for the invention of rituals which carried a personal symbolic significance. Such actions were not, strictly speaking, transgressions of the law, but were disturbing because of their eccentric and somewhat provocative nature.

When he arrived in Constantinople, his periods of depression and illumination continued, and he gained some notoriety as a result of his "strange actions." But as his behavior became more extreme, the rabbis began to feel that a new sect was emerging that might prove to be a threat to traditional religious views. Rather than expelling him, they sent an officer of the rabbinic court to lash him with 40 stripes, and they forbade his company to all Jews on pain of excommunication.

Apparently, Sabbatai was no stranger to such floggings during the course of his wanderings.

In 1658 Sabbatai declared that the old law was abrogated, to be replaced by a new law and new commandments, and new rituals which would bring mystical perfection to the world. He declared himself to be beyond the authority of rabbinic Judaism and, in fact, subject only to the higher law of God. The latent antinomian character of his illuminations openly declared itself. The new law was distinctly messianic in flavor, a new law revealed through the messiah. In kabbalistic belief there was no room for a new law, but rather a new adherence to the mosaic law. Since it was only in Christianity that the messiah was to reveal new commandments, Sabbatai's utterances raised the question of possible Christian influences on him. Certainly, his own antinomianism and his revaluation of sin as holy were not Christian, but came from his own inner tormented conflicts. In his more normal periods, Sabbatai continued to observe traditional Jewish beliefs and practice. But when the spirit was upon him, he plunged into these forms of strange behavior and transgressions. Certainly, these "strange actions" were in no sense taken by the rabbis as signs of a messianic calling, since they deviated from the behavior expected of a messiah, whose mission would be to restore the full observance of the law and the commandments, rather than abolishing them.

Sabbatai's definitive revelation of himself as the messiah came in May, 1665. At the time, he had entered on a new phase of manic exaltation, seemingly more acute and frenzied than ever. Unlike the previous revelation, he was now surrounded by faithful followers who looked to him with the eyes of faith and credulity. He is described in terms of his awesome appearance, his nobility, his majesty, virtue and saintliness. Even so, it was not long before the usual "strange actions" made their appearance with even greater vehemence. He took to inventing mystical allusions by way of the numerological connections between his own name and the names of God, particularly the divine name, *Shaddai*. He sought to establish a connection between himself and the names of God that implied special union or intimacy, even identity.

But Sabbatai was not content with minor deviations, even though bizarre. As the fast of the seventeenth of Tammuz approached, Sabbatai took the unprecedented step of abolishing the fast on the basis of his messianic authority. His followers in Gaza obeyed his command, but the abolishment of such a hallowed and strictly observed religious custom sent shock waves through the neighboring Jewish communities.

It served notice to the rabbis of Jerusalem, who held themselves to be the preservers of Israel's religious traditions, that a crisis had arisen. The majority of the Palestinian Jews reacted to the new revelations from Gaza by casting their lot with the followers of Sabbatai.

But in Jerusalem opinions were divided. Sabbatai had his followers there, but the majority of rabbis closed ranks in opposition to the new faith and refused to accept Sabbatai as an authentic messiah. They knew Sabbatai and his "strange actions," and were not ready to accept his paradoxical mission, which found expression in the abolition of traditional laws and religious customs. Rather than being impressed by the rationalization for the new messiah's bizarre behavior, they were shocked and offended. Sabbatai's application of the names of God to himself was regarded as blasphemous.

When Sabbatai himself made his way to Jerusalem, his arrival was accompanied by the usual "strange actions." In Gaza, he appointed 12 rabbis to accompany him to the site of the temple, then occupied by the Mosque of Omar. His intent was undoubtedly to signal the beginning of the rebuilding of the temple, and the event was given a certain amount of publicity. Sabbatai's frequently noted fondness for making appointments and granting titles led him even to appoint a high priest who was to preside over the new temple. The threat of this event, however, threw the rabbis of Jerusalem into a panic, fearing the consequences for the Jewish community of such an invasion of a sacred Moslem place of worship. They managed to dissuade Sabbatai from this course, but not without desperation.

The obvious solution to these difficulties was to expel Sabbatai from Jerusalem, but the expulsion could not stem the rapid growth of the movement. The messianic message had an appeal and an explosive force that evoked a powerful emotional upheaval. It was as though the course of the movement had little to do with the personality or behavior of Sabbatai. Legends and miracle stories sprouted everywhere and became the vehicle of emotional conviction. In fact, the more the figure of the messiah himself seemed to recede into the background and become increasingly blurred, the better did the growth of the messianic legend flourish, substituting marvelous and religiously inspired accounts for Sabbatai's actual deeds. The messiah was more a symbolic image than a living reality.

By September 1665, Sabbatai was back in Smyrna, but was not heard of for the next few months, probably because he was in a depressive phase of his illness. But in the meanwhile, the progress of the movement was carried on by the feverish activity of his followers and supporters. In Smyrna, Sabbatai was received warmly by his family and friends, but nothing happened for the first few months. Nonetheless, the local rabbis who were aware of Sabbatai's excommunication by the Jerusalem rabbinate adopted a wait-and-see attitude. As long as he was depressed, there was little that would provoke opposition or unrest. Before long a delegation arrived from Aleppo, where the messianic fervor had been particularly strong, to honor the new messiah. Whether stimulated by this event or merely in conjunction with it, the onset of another manic phase led to an outburst of messianic fervor. For the first time, accusations were brought against Sabbatai and his followers of sinning publicly and encouraging others to sin by their mystico-kabbalistic rationalizations. The allegations of sexual libertinism were accompanied by testimony of the adulterous behavior of Sabbatai's wife, Sarah.[6]

Contemporary accounts portray the contrast between the new messiah's predilection for solemn rituals and pomp and his sudden emotional outbursts of sexual libertinism in which all restraints seemed to have been lost. He often appealed to the blasphemous benediction, "Blessed is he who hath permitted things forbidden," reflecting a license that was hardly satisfied by an occasional antinomian outburst, but sought to invent new cultic practices in which the sublime and the ridiculous came into curious conjunction. The "strange actions" seemed to follow each other in rapid succession, intensifying the mass hysteria, which in turn drove Sabbatai into even more frenzied ecstasy and bizarre behavior. The enthusiasm of the believers grew daily, unleashing a fountain of joy and elation.

Tensions mounted between the followers of Sabbatai and his opposition. The believers had a vision of a new messianic world, and whatever seemed strange or inexplicable was taken as a part of the mystery of the new revelation. The need to believe created new miracles to confirm the new-found faith. Tales of miraculous events and signs became unquestioned facts. Accounts of the appearance of a pillar of fire and even the appearance of Elijah in the synagogue at

---

6. Sarah's role in Sabbatai's messianic career is clouded by the obscurity of facts and the accretion of legend. She may have had a role in Sabbatai's decision to declare himself the messiah. Her own aberration seems to have included the delusion that she would marry the messianic king. Her reputation for licentiousness and prostitution was general. Sabbatai may have married her for this reason, fulfilling the words of Hosea: ". . . take unto thee a wife of whoredoms" (Hosea 1:2). Scholem (1973) recounts the details of her life and relationship to Sabbatai. She too was severely disturbed, probably psychotic.

Aleppo were circulated and accepted as factual. It was even said that Elijah walked the streets of Smyrna, and had been seen by dozens, even hundreds. Sabbatai continued his practice of conferring royal titles on his followers. In Smyrna, the titles were taken seriously and the dignitaries were addressed by their new names. One beggar who had been granted a kingdom refused to sell it, even when offered a large sum of money. It is not known whether Sabbatai left Smyrna of his own choice, or whether he was expelled by the Turkish authorities because of the civil disruption he was causing. In any case, at the end of December 1665, he departed from the city and made his way toward Constantinople.

The messianic awakening that he had triggered had begun to spread over the European continent, carried by letters and reports of the new messiah and the religious renewal that had arisen in Gaza and taken hold in Palestine. The penitential awakening in Europe was widespread. Repentance and the hope of redemption spread to all corners of the diaspora. Everywhere the faithful gave themselves over to fasts, meditations, elaborate confessions of sins, devotion to good works and penitential practices. Alms were given to an extent previously unknown, and the distinctions of rich and poor seemed to be erased. In consequence, business was neglected, shops were closed, and the artisans were busy doing penance instead of plying their trade. People everywhere put themselves in readiness for the moment when the messiah and the prophet Elijah would appear and announce the end of days. There were also violent conflicts between the believers and the unbelievers, with the upper hand resting with the majority of believers against an obstinate minority of unbelievers. Even Sasportas, the leading spokesman for the stubborn infidels, grudgingly admitted that the rabble had gained the upper hand, and that in every community the rabbis had had to keep quiet for fear of the rabble.

The Prophet

The widespread appeal and the profound impact of sabbatianism could hardly rest on the bizarre and even provocative antics of Sabbatai alone. In order for the sabbatian doctrine to gain a hearing in more sophisticated and scholarly circles, there was need for theological reflection and for casting the messianic message in a more formal and rational guise. If Sabbatai was the messiah-king, there had to be a prophet, and his name was Nathan. Nathan of Gaza, as he was known, must have first encountered Sabbatai in Jerusalem. He must have known about the strange behavior, the ascetic practices and the kabbalistic teachings of this persecuted rabbi, who led such a saintly life until the spirit of madness came upon him and forced him to do the bizarre and forbidden actions. Whatever the contact between the two men at that time, and Sabbatai was roughly twice Nathan's age, the self-declared messiah must have made a profound impression on the young rabbinic scholar. When Nathan moved from Jerusalem to Gaza, the smoldering flame burst forth in a brilliant light as he began to immerse himself in kabbalistic studies.

For many years Nathan had devoted himself to Talmudic studies and deepening his knowledge of rabbinical teachings. In time he began to have prophetic visions and immersed himself in Lurianic writings under the tutelage of divine inspiration without any human master. Whatever seeds had been smoldering in his unconscious mind now burst forth in a tremendous emotional upheaval, which took the form of a messianic prophecy. In this vision he beheld the image of Sabbatai, who was announced as the savior who was to come. This vision, which took place in the summer of 1665, was a watershed in the sense that for the first time someone else had acknowledged Sabbatai in an ecstatic vision as the messiah. That the eccentric and somewhat mad kabbalistic rabbi had been able to make an impression on someone of substance and intellect changed the course of the messianic movement.

Nathan was a gifted theologian, who had mastered the language and the literature of Judaic lore and who brought these powerful capacities of intelligence and untiring energy to the service of the newborn messiah. He became the predominant ideological and theological proponent of the sabbatian faith. He was both the John the Baptist and the Paul of the new messiah (Scholem, 1973). He became the first great theologian of sabbatian kabbalism. His remarkable gifts and capacities complemented the ecstatic inspiration of Sabbatai. Scholem (1973) comments:

> Sabbatai was a poor leader. Devoid of will-power and without a program of action, he was a victim of his illness and illusions. But his paradoxical personality inspired Nathan and provided him with the impetus for his actions and ideas. It is idle to speculate what might have become of the brilliant young scholar had he never met Sabbatai Sevi. It is certain that only the encounter of the two gave birth to the Sabbatian movement. The hidden, revolutionary tendencies of his generation crystallize in Nathan Ashkenazi. He functioned as a kind of "transformer" — concentrating in his person, articulating, and transmitting the historical forces at work. In the eyes of Nathan, the curious, ascetic sinner

and saint, who occasionally dreamed of a messianic calling but who lacked the strength to believe in himself consistently, assumed the quality of an ultimate symbol. By making himself the herald and standard-bearer of the messiah, Nathan gave the crucial impetus to the formation of the Sabbatian movement. (p. 208)

Moreover, Nathan's prophetic contributions gave new strength and illumination to the faltering Sabbatai. He was no longer an isolated and pitiful object of derision, but with the respected, even famed, man of God at his side, the messianic vision could assert itself with renewed strength. With Nathan's support and encouragement, in the flush of manic exultation, Sabbatai finally declared himself to be the "anointed of the God of Jacob," the long-awaited messiah.

Needless to say, Sabbatai presented Nathan with two crucial problems. The first was the question of the justification of the "strange actions"; Sabbatai could do no better than to appeal to a principle of special dispensation, granted to him by reason of his messianic mission. The second problem was that of the mystery of his special and intimate relationship with God, reflecting an element of self-deification and identification with the divine principle in Sabbatai's understanding of his messianic role. Nathan's solution to these problems came in the form of his discovery of a leaf from a supposedly ancient apocalypse, which declared and defined the messiahship of Sabbatai Sevi. Accounts of the origin of this *Vision* vary, but Nathan would later describe it as a prophetic revelation. Undoubtedly the Vision was a literary forgery or perhaps, more appropriately, a form of pseudepigrapha familiar to apocalyptic midrashim.

In the *Vision*, Nathan refashions the understanding of the messiah to fit a kabbalistic mold. The messiah is made to correspond less to the traditional expectations and legends, and more to the concrete personal experience of an individual messiah. Recurring to a Lurianic pattern, the messiah is portrayed as joined to the divine power so that he might restore the divinely inspired order to the world. In virtue of his clinging to the divine life, every behavior of the messiah is restorative and redemptive. As Idel (1988) notes, "Cleaving and adhering are strikingly presented as enabling the Messiah to play a restorative role on all levels of reality, the theurgical goal being achieved only after the accomplishment of the mystical experience." (p. 57)

The apocalypse seeks to explain the mystery and the strange personality of this concrete messiah. He will not come in power and majesty, or at the head of an army to wage the messianic battles, but rather he will appear without military strength, and the real war will be against the demonic powers of the *qelippah*. The messianic struggle was to take place in the depth of his soul, where he must subdue the powers of evil and, in so doing, even fall into the bottomless abyss. The ultimate messianic task was not merely the defeat and annihilation of the powers of evil, but raising them to the sphere of holiness through the exercise of *tiqqun*. The wondrous and awesome deeds of the messiah were the "strange actions" through which transgressions were sanctified, and the *qelippah* was transformed and sanctified at its very root. Thus, the messiah of the *Vision* is not at all the vague and somewhat generalized figure of the Lurianic *kabbalah*, but was a specific and personal figure.

Without doubt, Nathan's formulations about the nature of the messianic mission had a profound impact. His formulations undoubtedly impressed and profoundly influenced the rabbis in Jerusalem and tended to neutralize some of the disruption created by the messiah himself. Examination of the prophet and his teachings by the rabbinic scholars did not find him wanting. The evaluation of Sabbatai's messianic mission hinged on the degree of credibility granted to the prophet. If Nathan was indeed a true prophet, then his prophecy would verify Sabbatai's messianic mission, so that some plausible kabbalistic explanation had to be found for the "strange actions."

Sabbatai's opponents were powerful enough to issue a ban of excommunication, but their influence was countered by the prophetic mission of Nathan. It seems that Nathan's extraordinary capacities were equal to the challenge. His teaching had great spiritual power, appealing to the deep longings for redemption and calling for repentance and mortification. He also found a way of explaining the mystical significance and bizarreness of the messiah's personality. The result was a splitting of the kabbalist camp, some accepting Nathan's doctrine that the "strange actions" were essentially a *tiqqun* of profound mystical significance.

Nathan himself continued his theoretical speculative activity, creating a new messianic legend out of his visionary insight and kabbalistic theorizing. Part of Nathan's emphasis was on pure faith as a religious value, without the need for signs or miracles. Scholem (1973) speculates that this strikingly sacramental conception of faith may have reflected the influence of Christian doctrines on Nathan's theological thinking. Even without such influences, early sabbatianism and early Christianity seemed to have followed similar paths dictated by the same psychological laws. In any case, ". . . the fact remains that at the very beginning of the movement, pure faith, independent of the observance of the Law, was proclaimed as the supreme religious value which secured salvation and eternal life for the believers" (Scholem 1973, p. 283).

Nathan's major work was a tract called the *Treatise on the Dragons.* It represents a transition from Lurianic kabbalism to sabbatian kabbalism and is an important contribution to the understanding of the spiritual development of sabbatianism. Sabbatian kabbalism reinterprets traditional Lurianic doctrines, applying them to the new faith in Sabbatai's messianic calling. Nathan shows himself to be an expert in the schools of Lurianic *kabbalah*, and demonstrates his originality and depth of theological reflection. He describes Sabbatai's periods of illumination and spiritual joy, contrasting these to the persecution by the *qelippoth*, in which his soul was thrown into darkness and anguish. Even when he had extricated himself from the power of the *qelippoth*, his soul, even though the holiest of human souls, was still subject to them and persecuted by them. It was the messiah's lot to continue this struggle until the glorious manifestation of his kingdom.

Nathan skillfully weaves elements of kabbalistic and metaphysical doctrine with psychological and biographical elements into this formulation about the messiah's soul and character. Within this perspective, the "strange actions," far from contradicting his messianic role, actually are taken to confirm it. No ordinary human soul would dare seek expression in such behaviors. These were "hidden acts of *tiqqun*" by which the messiah carried on his warfare against the *qelippah*. Only the messiah, who had been able to free himself from the depths of the abyss, understood the paradoxical ways in which this realm of darkness could be subdued. This theme became a dominant motif in nearly all of Nathan's subsequent writings.

Sabbatianism

The Movement

The movement that had begun to gather around the figure of Sabbatai Sevi enjoyed widespread success. The messianic revival spread throughout the diaspora, generating a new spirit and expectations that were not constrained to the visions of political deliverance. Along with the persistent hopes for divine deliverance from bondage and exile, there was a belief stirring that a new era of history was being realized and that the believers were beginning to experience their longed-for redemption. The influence of "spiritualists" or "pneumatics" became a major force in the movement; they were regarded as the privileged, the elect, who had realized the divine light within themselves and were, in consequence, no longer subject to the laws of reality. They took on the form of a special group with a special sense of their own superiority — a sectarian trend that separated them from the unenlightened masses and stamped them as the vanguard of the new reality. As Scholem (1971) observes: "The Sabbatian movement soon developed all the psychological characteristics of a spiritualist sect, and before long many of its followers proceeded to organize themselves along such lines. The persecutions against them on the part of various rabbinical and congregational authorities, their own special feeling of apartness and of the need to preserve their secret, and the novel practices which their beliefs eventually compelled them to pursue, were all factors in bringing this about." (p. 92)

In Leghorn, Italy, an important commercial center where the Jewish population was largely well-to-do, the sabbatian doctrine was received with enthusiasm. A significant portion of the population were former *marranos* who may have, in part, been atoning for the hypocrisy of their Christian past in Spain and Portugal by embracing the devout messianic fervor.[1] Elsewhere in northern Italy, the messianic movement dominated the life of Jewish communities. In city after city, the gap widened between the adherents of the new messianism and the reactionary conservatives who clung to traditional religious views.

Occasionally, the antagonism flared into physical violence. Scholem (1973) cites a letter of Samuel Primo, who was Sabbatai's secretary in Gallipoli, which fanned the flames of revolutionary fervor. The promises coming from the messiah had a royal and imperious tone. There was an artful blurring of past and future, references to promised eschatological events, for example references to the resurrection as a future event, as if they were happening in present time, which effectively translated the messianic vision into a present psychological reality that blurred the fringes of reality and brought the messianic fulfillment into conjunction with intensified expectations of the believers. Moreover, the letter invited its readers to terrorism and violence, an inevitable consequence of the proximate realization of the utopian dream. This new revolutionary authority threatened traditional religion and replaced the authority of the law with the new revelation and the implied authority of the messiah. The use of force was necessary to reinforce this new authority.

Opponents were regarded as enemies and outlaws, while more passive unbelievers were terrorized into compliance with the new faith. On a number of occasions, opponents to the new faith were turned over to the Turkish authorities for judgment and imprisonment. As the movement grew, these attitudes became increasingly intransigent among the followers of Sabbatai, and the intensity of their belief in Sabbatai as the king of Israel and the Lord's anointed knew no bounds. But these revolutionary and reformational elements of the sabbatian

---

1. Scholem (1941) argues that the Sephardic influence was an important contributing influence on the wide acceptance of sabbatianism. The *marranos* had carried on a double religious existence for generations, driven into Christianity by persecution. This did not destroy their ties to Judaism. For them the idea of an apostate messiah legitimated what was most tormenting to their own consciences. The arguments that they put forth to justify their apostasy seemed to surface again in the ideology of sabbatianism.

movement became only gradually more apparent, masked largely by Nathan's penitential and ascetical teachings.

The new fervor also spread to the Jewish community in Amsterdam, where it found an enthusiastic reception. The sephardic community formed by *marranos* from Spain and Portugal were survivors of the Spanish Inquisition; the Ashkenazim had hardly forgotten the ravages of the Cossack massacres of 1648, many of the survivors of which had found safety in Amsterdam. The prestige of the wealthy sephardic community provided an important boost to the sabbatian movement. There were no indications of persecutory tactics or intimidations; rather, both here and in Salonika, where the Jewish community enjoyed greater freedom and prosperity, the new movement was embraced u-nanimously by believers and religious leaders. Similar reports of the ascendancy and success of the new religion came from Germany and Poland. Conditions for the seeding of the messianic vision were particularly ripe in Poland. Polish Jewry was living in the aftermath of the 1648 massacres, a year that had been predicted as the year of messianic fulfillment. The Jewish community was ruined and pauperized by the effects of the Chmielnicki uprising. The resulting oppressive conditions and the frustrated despair made the remnant of the Jewish community open to the influence of the *kabbalah*, so that the messianic tidings fell upon fertile soil (Scholem, 1973).

The Decline and Fall

We had left Sabbatai on his way to Constantinople, after his expulsion from Smyrna. His arrival in Constantinople was awaited with increasing tension. The controversial news from Smyrna had divided the community, and the prophecies of the new messiah's overthrow of Ottoman power stirred fears of reprisal in the Jewish community. Revolts were not uncommon, and they were usually dealt with by the Ottomans with ruthless cruelty. The Jewish authorities would have been held responsible for any uprising, so that their lives were on the line in any messianic revolution.

Sabbatai was arrested immediately on arrival and taken before the vizier. The boldness of the Jewish enthusiasm about the coming of the messianic kingdom and the overthrow of Turkish authority would have been sufficient grounds by themselves for Turkish anxieties. The accounts of this confrontation vary, but the bottom line seems to be that Sabbatai was given the choice of recanting his messianic mission and apostasizing to Islam or facing execution. He finally renounced his messianic pretensions and accepted conversion to Islamism. He remained in prison at Constantinople for more than two months, and then was removed by order of the vizier to the fortress of Gallipoli. It was not long before his followers, by means of appropriate bribes, were able to change Sabbatai's detention into an "honorable confinement," so that his prison became known as the "tower of strength."

The immediate results of Sabbatai's imprisonment were electric, but the long-term effects were profound. In Amsterdam, for example, the messianic fervor was not dampened by the news of his imprisonment, which even served as a stimulus for legendary tales of his resurrecting the dead and passing through locked and barred prison doors, which opened before him of their own volition. Moreover, the Turkish jailors were not slow to realize that Sabbatai's imprisonment could be a source of considerable profit. If paid an appropriate entrance fee, the jailors would allow the Jewish faithful to visit the imprisoned messiah, and they did so by the thousands. The numbers who flocked to Constantinople for this purpose even resulted in driving up food prices. Pilgrimages were organized, and the boats plied back and forth between the city and the Dardanelles day and night. Legendary tales and miracle stories proliferated wildly. Evidences that the jailors granted Sabbatai a certain measure of respect and freedom, and even the fact that he had not been immediately executed as a rebel, were taken as confirmations of his messianic status. Sabbatai responded with a burst of manic excitation, which even further fed the fantasies and expectations of his faithful visitors.

In Constantinople, the conflict between the believers and the unbelievers grew more intense. The tension between the renewed need for his followers to believe and the reports of his apostasy created an explosive situation. One would have expected the shock of the messiah's apostasy to have completely shattered the expectations and the faith of the believers in his movement. Other messianic movements had collapsed in failure with less provocation. But the sabbatian movement had swept through the whole of the diaspora and had struck deep roots in the masses of believers. Many had committed themselves too deeply, e.g., fathering children in group sexual orgies, preventing any return to the rabbinic fold, selling homes and businesses in the flood of messianic fervor, and so on. The psychological laws of cognitive dissonance (Festinger et al. 1956; Festinger 1957) would have ample room for realization under these circumstances. In addition, the personal peculiarities of the messiah remained relatively unknown in the broader frame of reference, so that the emphasis fell on penitential enthusiasm rather than a revolutionary messianic law. The expectation of a "trans-valuation of all values" as part of a realized messianic eschatology was not widespread. But the powerful messianic ferment soon acquired an autonomous life of its own. Many believers were committed to the enthusiastic view that the new age had already dawned.

But without doubt, the news of the apostasy dealt a critical blow. Critics of the movement trumpeted their "I told you so" claims, but the tragedy was real enough. For the first time since the destruction of the second temple, the entire Jewish people throughout the far-flung reaches of the diaspora had been roused to new hopes and expectations, all of which were dashed and crushed. Sabbatai himself was a pitiful leader, whose messianic enthusiasm spent itself in fits of illumination and on fantastic and highly idiosyncratic eccentricities. As Scholem (1973) comments:

> Even Nathan's testimony to the effect that Sabbatai considers his agonies as symbolic of the sufferings of Israel cannot alter the fact that his inner life was autistically centered upon himself, a paranoid streak in his psychosis. Sabbatai never freed himself from the narrow circle of his private world, even when he offered symbolic interpretations of his personal experiences. Also, in the extremes to which his mental illness led him, he remained essentially lonely. The messianic revival bearing his name became a mass movement, but the imprint of the founder's personality was barely noticeable. (p. 693)

For his devoted followers, Sabbatai's apostasy was a tragic moment in the history of Israel, but it was not long before rationalizing justifications came to the rescue of shattered illusions. The faith of many of the believers remained undaunted, and the apostasy was explained by claiming that Sabbatai's Islamism was a form of disguise that was necessary for greater achievement of his messianic aims, or that Sabbatai had not apostasized at all but rather had ascended into heaven, and only his shape or appearance was left behind in the guise of an apostate — a sort of docetic resolution. But believers everywhere had to face the proof that they had been caught in a web of error and delusion. Many thought that evil powers had gained hold over his soul or, as Nathan would propose, Sabbatai had willingly entered the realm of the *qelippoth* so that he could claim it for the messianic kingdom. This view of the role of the powers of the *qelippoth* was an application of more generally accepted Lurianic doctrines.[2]

The faltering and consternation among Sabbatai's adherents provided the opportunity for the Jewish authorities to institute stern measures. Any organized liturgical or other religious activity on the part of the believers or any public demonstration of their faith was no longer permitted. The movement was essentially driven underground, at least in Turkey. The sabbatians adopted an attitude of sectarian superiority, envisioning themselves as the bearers of the true spirit, in contrast to the rabbis who were filled with the wisdom of the world rather than the truth of the Lord.

The rabbis were predominantly concerned with restoration of the traditional law and ritual observance, so that proscriptions were directed against public demonstrations rather than matters of faith. But the fervor of the movement was not easily expunged. The believers were not impressed by the rabbinical anathemas, which seemed mainly aimed at appeasing the Turkish rulers. The infidels who issued such proclamations would be dealt due punishment after the coming of Nathan and the manifestation of the messiah. The rulers of the Jewish community were thus faced with continuing agitation, which endangered their political position and ran the danger of government reprisal. The ground was laid for an incipient heresy, even though Turkish rabbis had no thought of schism or the growth of a secret sect. Nonetheless, the believers began to meet in secret and to build up a clandestine network of communications. The rabbis paid little attention as long as there was no open rebellion against their authority.

The rabbis were also concerned about the potentiality for a mass apostasy to Islamism, following Sabbatai's lead. Some of the believers did apostasize, even though Sabbatai himself apparently had not generally urged such action. He contented himself with rationalizing his behavior without demanding that his followers do likewise; some reports, however, suggest that he may have ordered followers to apostasize in some of his manic fits. There is also evidence that at times he even preached conversion to Islam in the synagogues.

The beleagured followers turned to a desperate search of the scriptures and tradition for explanation of the unexpected turn of events. Not surprisingly, they found the Bible, the rabbinic Haggadah

---

2. A thoughtful reader called to mind the parallel in Catholic lore of Christ's supposed descent into hell (purgatory), during the three days in the tomb, to rescue the souls of the damned who were destined to join Him in heaven. Might there have been some influence from Christian sources on this sabbatian doctrine?

and the kabbalistic literature to be filled with allusions to Sabbatai and the mystery of his apostasy. Through the exercise of convoluted tropological and kabbalistic exegesis, they found the means for coming to terms with the contradictions in the mission of the disappointing redeemer. Paradoxical explanation of the fate of the messiah found a sympathetic vibration in deeply rooted religious needs and emotions of a believing public.

Particularly effective were the explanations advanced by Nathan, originally to account for Sabbatai's "strange actions," but now applied to the context of the apostasy. Nathan had taught that the messiah's soul had to be liberated from the prison of the *qelippoth*, where it was to be held in the period preceding the final *tiqqun*, which had to precede his ultimate self-revelation. He modified this teaching slightly, so that even after the self-revelation the messiah would have to suffer a period of captivity by demonic powers. Particularly useful was the motif of the suffering servant of Isaiah as a model for the submission of the messiah to the power of the *qelippah*.

The moderate sabbatians parted company with their more extreme brethren over the issue of whether the "strange actions" were meant to set an example for believers or not. The moderates insisted that the paradox of the new religion was limited to the person of the messiah; he alone must move beyond traditional values and endure the torments of the world of evil. Not only was he not to be imitated, but according to Nathan the "strange actions" provided proof of the authenticity of his messianic mission. They were acts of redemption whose value were to be measured by the degree of scandal they caused. But the radicals could not remain passively accepting of the paradox of the messiah's mission. For them the paradox was meant to be universal, so that the messiah was to be seen as setting an example that the true believer was bound in duty to follow. As Scholem (1941) puts it:

> The consequences which flowed from these religious ideas were purely nihilistic, above all the conception of a voluntary Marranism with the slogan: We must *all* descend into the realm of evil in order to vanquish it from within. In varying theoretical guises the apostles of nihilism preached the doctrine of the existence of spheres in which the process of *Tikkun* can no longer be advanced by pious acts; Evil must be fought with evil. (p. 315)

Thus sin and moral decadence were elevated to a glorified position. The religious nihilism and antinomianism of sabbatianism would lead to the gradual erosion of the moral substance of Judaism in the 18th century that came to fruition in the Frankist movement.[3]

Other theological elaborations developed the idea of the mystical union between the messiah and the *shekhinah*, the divine consort of the *En-Sof*.[4] This union would result after their release from the imprisonment by the *qelippah*, and the subsequent *apotheosis* of the messiah. These reflections seem to imply a deification of the messiah, an idea that was taking shape in Nathan's mind, but undoubtedly originated with the messiah himself.[5] His ascent to the sphere of the divine was anticipated in his present life rather than after death. His followers seemed slow to accept evidently blasphemous conclusions, but Sabbatai, in his fits of manic exaltation, was convinced. In time he was transformed into a mythological figure — any residues of his real person or personality faded into obscurity. Like the Christian beliefs in the divinity of Christ, some of Sabbatai's more radical followers came to believe that the messiah was not merely a superior human being, but an incarnated manifestation of God Himself in human form. This interpretation was cherished by the more radical groups, including the Frankists, and was regarded as one of the most profound mystical truths. The paradox of an apostate messiah may have found a solution similar to (if not modeled after) that of the even-more paradoxical and confounding phenomenon of a crucified messiah.

After the apostasy, Sabbatai's dealings became devious and deceptive, if not downright schizophrenic. With the Jews he maintained his messianic pretensions, yet with gentiles his denials were proportionally emphatic. True to his basically passive character, he waited for an illumination from heaven to vindicate his claims. There was logic and consistency in his denial, since if God had not yet revealed the kingdom of his anointed messiah, then obviously the time had not come for revealing the messianic secret to the gentiles. He had been charged with fomenting rebellion and civil commotion by his messianic pretensions. He chose conversion to Islam and thereby purchased his life at the price of apostasy.

His embracing the Islamic faith and his personal charm apparently won him friends and protectors at the court. But psychologically,

---

3. See chapter 10.

4. This would constitute a prime expression of Sabbatai's need to achieve symbiotic reunion with the abandoning mother (Falk 1982).

5. Another Christian accretion? It may have stemmed from the influence of *Marranos* and the Christian doctrine they had assimilated (Scholem 1971).

his condition deteriorated. He seemed utterly confused and lost, his depression was interrupted by occasional fits of exultation and an intensification of the periodicity of the manic-depressive cycles. His apostasy was gradually seen as the climax of his "strange actions," reflecting his captivity in the prison of the *qelippoth*. He kept in contact with his disciples, particularly Nathan and Primo. Many of his followers apostasized, following his example, some at his urging, others not. This group of early apostates often accompanied Sabbatai, causing consternation and anger among many traditional Jews. His Janus-like behavior was a cause of considerable confusion among his followers and others. At times he behaved like a Jew, at other times like a Moslem, giving rise to stories of him sitting with the Koran in one hand and the scroll of the law in the other.

His strange behavior often caused commotions and were regarded as blasphemous by both religious groups. He was arrested in September 1672 and again sent to Adrianople. He was accused of reviling Islam, an offense worthy of capital punishment. The vizier, who in 1666 had treated him with consideration and moderation, had apparently lost patience and was willing to cooperate with the Jewish leaders in ridding them of this apostate messiah. After some months, he was finally banished rather than executed. The leniency was probably a result of petitions by his more influential supporters in Turkish circles.

An unfortunate aspect of his post-apostasy career was the strains of sexual license and immorality that can be traced through various accounts. He was accused of having sexual relations with a number of his female followers, along with accusations of lewd behavior and debauchery. Evidence suggests that Sabbatai himself took pride in his capacity to have intercourse with virginal women without actually deflowering them. This strain of erotic perversity seems to fit well with other antinomian tendencies that gave scandal to faithful Jews. Sabbatai also divorced his wife, Sarah, shortly after she had born him a daughter. He announced his intention of marrying the daughter of a Jew, a marriage that was contracted in one of his manic illuminations.[6]

Sabbatai apparently regarded his sexual performances as acts of mystical *tiqqun*, and probably in 1673 performed such a mystical act with the betrothed of one of his followers. The young man protested that Sabbatai had made his bride with child, but without avail. The

---

6. It seems likely that the licentiousness, group sex, and other relaxations of traditional sexual taboos, may have been one of the attractive and appealing aspects of sabbatianism.

incident caused considerable scandal in Constantinople, and when it was apparent that the young woman was pregnant, the son that was born of this pregnancy was known as the son of Sabbatai. The faith of many believers was shattered, and they could not understand why the holy one should act in a way that would unavoidably scandalize and alienate those who believed in him. If he had indeed fathered the child, this was an act of adultery according to Jewish law, and his subsequent denial may have served as a prototype for the sexual license practiced secretly by later radical sabbatian groups. His sexual behavior overall reflects a strange mixture of drives and inhibitions, which allowed him to indulge in perverse and erotic fantasies on the one hand, yet forbade normal sexual expression on the other — a composition well-suited to his brand of erotic mysticism.

In 1676, in an extraordinary fit of illumination, he led a procession into the Turkish quarter of the city and, at midnight, ascended the minaret of the mosque singing his songs and hymns. The Turks were infuriated. He had decided that the time of redemption had come, and followed this performance with letters and royal proclamations. These writings contain allusions to his divinity, quoting the book of Daniel and Isaiah as referring to his ascension to the heavenly kingdom. A few months after, on September 17, 1676, Sabbatai died, shortly after his 50th birthday and almost exactly 10 years after his apostasy on September 16, 1666.

But the apotheosis of the messiah continued even after his death. The idea that Sabbatai's death was merely an "occultation" was probably coined by Nathan. The taunts of unbelievers were answered by the claim that the messiah was only concealed for a time, and that in due time he would return in triumph. The parallels to the Christian expectations of the second coming of Christ are obvious.

So it was with the messiah! What of Nathan, his prophet? The same rabbis, who were outraged at Sabbatai's peculiarities, remained respectful toward Nathan. Even though Nathan continued to actively advocate the sabbatian faith, the rabbis were careful to exclude him from their excommunications. They tried to prevent any contact between Nathan and the believers, hoping that they could avoid a further explosion of messianic fervor. In the years following the apostasy, Nathan left Gaza, never returning to Palestine, but led the life of a fugitive and vagabond until his death in 1680. Sabbatian sympathizers offered him shelter, but the rabbinic authorities exercised their power in order to limit his influence. After 1668, he was more or less ignored, probably because the authorities felt that he was no longer dangerous. Nonetheless, he continued to exercise considerable influence and was instrumental in the continuing process of evolving the heretical theology of sabbatianism.

The rabbis of Adrianople seemed to have particular animus toward Nathan, whom they excommunicated. They were determined to destroy his reputation and influence, particularly after the rabbis of Constantinople had sent a pastoral letter directing all Jewish communities to prevent Nathan from joining his messiah. It may have been that the rabbis of Adrianople were beginning to appreciate that the sabbatian movement was stronger than they had imagined. In fact, early sabbatianism was yet to develop into a radically antinomian sect, and its members were basically pious and orthodox Jews who behaved no differently than their fellow Jews, except in their belief in the imminent messianic redemption. However, Nathan's continued preaching of the messianic faith must have been a threat to the authority of the rabbis.

Early in 1668, Nathan arrived on Corfu, where he prepared for a journey into Italy. For unexplained reasons, he headed toward Venice where the majority of the rabbis were known to be against him. During his sojourn on Corfu, he began to adopt the double-faced behavior that his messiah had previously demonstrated. With his fellow Jews he preached the messianic mission, but to the gentiles he denied it. Subsequently, this duplicity became a characteristic of the sabbatian movement. After Sabbatai's death, the prophet of Gaza fell into bitterness and despondency. His bitterness and depression came to an end in Sofia, where he fell ill and died on January 11, 1680.

The influence of the sabbatian movement did not come to an end with the deaths of the messiah and his prophet. The reverberations have echoed through Jewish mystical traditions into modern times. Sabbatai's adherents continued to suffer persecution at the hands of more traditional Jewish groups well into the 18th century. The sect was viewed as a revolutionary sect which, as Scholem (1941) says, "kindled the flames of a destructive conflagration and which sometimes, if only darkly and abstrusely, proclaimed a new conception of Judaism." (p. 300) Sabbatian literature was destroyed, and every effort was made to destroy and minimize the movement, as though its impact was minor or insignificant. The reality was quite different. Scholem (1941) continues:

> There were, for instance, various moderate forms of Sabbatianism in which orthodox piety and Sabbatian belief existed side by side, and the number of more or less outstanding rabbis who were secret adherents of the new sectarian mysticism was far larger than orthodox apologists have ever been willing to admit. That there should be so much confusion regarding its strength is partly ac-

counted for by the fact that Sabbatianism as a movement was long identified with its more extreme, antinomian and nihilistic aspects. (p. 300)

CHAPTER 10

Hasidism and Frankism

Introduction

The echoes of Sabbatai's messianism were slow to fade away. The notion of the messiah as an incarnate God became another point of controversy between the "radicals" and the "moderates" among Sabbatai's followers. The belief centered at first on Sabbatai himself as "the holy king," but soon evolved into a view of God as incarnating himself in the person of the messiah to restore the world and nullify the Torah. Among Sephardic converts to Islam, the belief emerged that the leaders in every age were reincarnations of Sabbatai.

The sabbatian creed rose to a crescendo again in the 18th century in the Frankist movement in the Jewish communities in Poland. Sabbatai's apostasy had alienated him from a good many of his followers, but a hard core of faithful believers continued to believe in his mission. The sabbatian cult took a more mystical turn during the 17th century and became more of a secret sectarian cult. The expectations of the messianic revolution remained alive and led to the discarding of many traditional laws and customs. Sensuality and sexual liberality were practiced in often unbridled fashion after the pattern set by Sabbatai. The Jewish community was fragmented by these rebellious elements, and efforts of the Polish rabbis to exterminate this heresy, as at the Assembly of Lemberg in 1722, were only partially successful.

Hasidism

One offshoot of sabbatianism was the Jewish mystical sect known as the Hasidim.[1] The earlier pietistic movement was particularly important among German Ashkenazi Jewry. Its origins antedate the sabbatian movement: it can be traced back to the 12th century, but its influence spanned several centuries. As Scholem (1941) observes:

> The rise of Hasidism was the decisive event in the religious development of German Jewry. Of all the factors determining the deeper religion of that community, it was the greatest until the change which took place in the seventeenth century under the influence of the later Kabbalism, which originated at Safed in Palestine. . . . Its importance lies in the fact that it succeeded already during the Middle Ages in bringing about the triumph of new religious ideals and values which were acknowledged by the mass of the people; in Germany and for the German Jewish community, at any rate, the victory was complete. Where the thirteenth century Kabbalism of Spain failed — for it became a real historical factor only much later, after the expulsion of the Jews from Spain and after Safed had become the new center — German Hasidism succeeded. (p. 81)

The Hasidim rejected apocalyptic speculation and calculations concerning the coming of the messiah. Their emphasis fell on the contemplation of the divine unity and the practice of piety. The Hasidic masters, in contrast to Spanish kabbalists, addressed their teaching to the common people. They sought serenity of spirit and purity of life. Religious life for them was a matter of prayer, asceticism, and the love of God (Eliade 1985).

Modern Hasidism is the successor to the progression through Lurianic kabbalism and sabbatianism, and eventually would gain the adherence of many Eastern European Jews. Lurianism based its appeal on the messianic element that echoed the yearning for deliverance of the masses. This urge for redemption led to aberrations in sabbatianism that finally failed because of its extravagant appeal to paradox. Hasidism represents a further attempt to transform or reinterpret the world of *kabbalah* in more accessible and human terms. It tried to strip the messianism of the *kabbalah* of its mystical and apocalyptic excesses and to move the redemptive vision from the center of relig-

---

1. The earlier Hasidic movement in Germany should be distinguished from the later Slavic Hasidism based on the work of Israel Baal Shem Tov in the 18th century. See Scholem (1941).

ious life and thought, as had been the case in Lurianism and sabbatian messianism, to a more modest perspective. Not all of the mystical elements of ecstatic kabbalism were abandoned; as Idel (1988) observes, ". . . *devekut* understood as *unio mystica*, inspiration and revelation, the need for seclusion and equanimity for concentration, the psychological understanding of theosophy, and a unique interest in linguistic mysticism formed the basic structure of Hasidic mysticism." (p. xvii) Observance of the commandments was seen as essential to mystical life. If Hasidism was in some sense a reaction to sabbatianism and Frankism, it was also an extension of the effort of the kabbalists of Safed to restructure Jewish mysticism in terms of a better balance between the ecstatic and the theurgical-theosophical components of *kabbalah*.

The Hasidic movement sought to combine the individualistic emphasis of ecstatic *kabbalah* with theosophical *kabbalah* — the former stressing *devekut* and the latter the keeping of the commandments as the vehicle to unitive experience. Thus Hasidic mysticism sought to integrate a shared religious ritual in the social group with a residue of transcendence that underlies the uniquely individual experience of divine union. This included a retreat from kabbalistic symbolism, especially referents to the *sefiroth* or the divine configurations, in favor of metaphors of union and incorporation (Idel 1988). The Hasidim rejected the kabbalistic doctrine of the evilness of matter. If God was good, matter was also necessarily good and holy.

But paradoxically they also maintained the earlier gnostic persuasion that the fallen sparks of holiness had to be restored to God. The paradox required a revision of the creation myth such that the fullness of divine light was of such intensity that it had to be weakening in order for any creaturely existence to be possible. God thus diminished the fallen light so that the world could exist. This diminished light could also be seen as the revelation of the *Ein Sof* to the world of men. This meant that evil could be traced back to God as its origin, but it was seen as a temporary effect of the weakening of the divine light. Restoration of the fallen sparks of light to God would reconstitute the original goodness.

The result was confrontation with evil rather than avoidance so that it could be seized and restored to the *Ein Sof*. We can hear some of the echoes of sabbatianism, but the Hasidim never went to the extremes of the sabbatians in the actual practice of evil deeds. For the Hasidim, evil could be restored by seizing it mentally and thinking about it, as recognition and acceptance of "strange thoughts" — thoughts rather than the strange actions of Sabbatai. Sexual fantasies that occurred during prayer, for example, were to be repaired and elevated, and thus restored (*tikkun*) to the divine. As Scholem (1991) comments:

> One can virtually detoxify and transform sin and evil by contemplative absorption. By means of this contemplation one transforms ('sweetens') them at their very roots — albeit not by living them out in actuality, as was done by the Sabbatians, but by binding them to their root in holiness. (p. 129)

Scholem (1971) put forth the argument that modern Hasidism had equivalently "neutralized" the radical and moderate strains of sabbatian messianism. The argument was aimed against those who argued that Hasidism had completely abandoned any notion of a messiah (e.g., Martin Buber) on the one hand, and against the opposite view that Hasidism had retained the messianic vision of sabbatianism without significant alteration. In Scholem's analysis, Hasidism had substituted a form of individual and mystical redemption for the traditional belief in a historical and communal messianic redemption[2] — this Hasidic view took the form of the doctrine of *devekut*.[3]

In the early stages of kabbalism, ecstatic experience held a more central position in mystical lore that was decidedly gnostic in character. With the further evolution of kabbalism, these aspects tended to fade into the background, and a more spiritualized form of mystical contemplation came to the fore. The implication that ecstasy signifies a form of union with God is rare; even in the extremes of such ecstasy there is retained a sense of distance between the Creator and creature. Union leading to fusion and identity is out of the question. The goal of mystical perfection is *devekut* — the state of being joined to the divinity, of intimate union and conformity of the human will to the divine — yet always with a sense of difference and distance. Scholem (1971) observed:

> The school of Lurianism made every Jew a protagonist in the great Messianic struggle; it did not *allegorize* Messianism into a state of personal life. Hasidism in its most vigorous stages took precisely this step. The one and unique great act of final redemption, "the real thing," if I may say so, was thrown out, i.e., was removed from the sphere of man's immediate responsibility and

---

2. Not unlike the intellectualized doctrine of allegorical messianism advanced by Philo of Alexandria — see Hecht (1987).

3. See Scholem's discussion of the role of *devekut* in the chapter on "*Devekut*, or communion with God" in Scholem (1971).

thrown back into God's inscrutable counsels. But let us face the
fact: once this has been done. . . then Messianism as an actual
historic force is liquidated, it has lost its apocalyptic fire, its sense
of imminent catastrophe. (pp. 201-202)

Hasidic mysticism tried to merge the competing traditions of ecstasy and theurgy, or anthropocentrism and theocentrism, into a synthesis that moderated the theurgical while propagating ecstatic values.
Classical Spanish and Lurianic *kabbalah* were recast in ecstatic terms,
providing an emphasis on individual mystical experience that negated
or countered the strains of nationalistic messianism in Hasidism (Idel
1988). However, it seems that the final word on the relationship between *kabbalah* and Ashkenazic Hasidism has yet to be spoken. In all
probability, the Ashkenazi hasidim did not know the *kabbalah* in the
same sense as the sages of Provence; particularly they did not know the
kabbalistic-gnostic element, even when quasi-kabbalistic or proto-kab-
balistic sources were available (Idel 1988). In short, Ashkenazic Hasidism as a speculative movement and the *kabbalah* seemed to have remained separate and independent movements, at least until the middle
of the 13th century. To which, Idel (1988) adds:

These clearcut assessments . . . remain, for the time being, *le
dernier cri* on the question of the influence of Hasidic thought
upon the early Kabbalah. It seems to me that the entire question
must be reopened on the ground of the existence of additional
'Gnostic' motifs in Hasidic texts." (p. 15)

Frankism

Jacob Frank was born in 1726 in Podolia. His father was a rabbi,
but fell under suspicion of sabbatianism and was expelled from his
community. The family settled in Wallachia, and little Jacob grew up
surrounded by mystical fantasies, messianic dreams and sexual license.
By the time he left home at 13 to work for a wealthy Polish Jew in
Bucharest, he had already established a reputation for lying and deceit.
His work took him to Turkey, where he lived in Salonika and Smyrna,
active centers of the Sabbatian sect. He became obsessed with the idea
of returning to Poland as a prophet and messianic leader of the oppressed and underprivileged. He believed that the various messiahs
were incarnations of a single messianic soul that merely assumed different bodily expressions — as, for example, in Mohammed or Sabbatai Sevi. Frank saw no reason why he himself could not be such an
incarnation of the messianic soul. He incorporated the Sephardic

teaching to suit his own personality, and was understood by his disciples to be the incarnation of the living God once again on earth.

Apparently the time was ripe. Frank had acquired some wealth as a result of his shrewd trading, and in 1752 decided to marry a 14-year-old girl from Nicopolis; Frank himself was 26. They had two sons and a daughter. By 1755 Frank was back in Podolia, ready to carry out his mission. He joined forces with the remnants of the Sabbatian movement there, and began teaching his own brand of Turkish doctrine. The doctrine centered on a Sabbatian trinity composed of God, the messiah, and the *shekhinah*. Frank came to be regarded as the second person of this trinity and as a reincarnation of Sabbatai, and was designated as "the Holy Lord." Sabbatai was the messiah and the embodiment of "the Ancient Holy One," and was thus part of the Godhead, could perform miracles (positively vouched for by devoted followers), and was addressed prayers drawn from the mystical language of the *Zohar*. The last part of the trinity, the *shekhinah*, was equivalent to a female messiah who was to complete the work of redemption — reflecting the influence of certain mystical Christian sects active in eastern Europe that also believed in a triad of saviors and a feminine incarnation of the Sophia (Holy Spirit). Thus the three hypostases of this trinity were each separately incarnated in a corresponding messiah (Scholem, 1971).

Frank himself seems to cut far less the figure of an ideal religious leader than a corrupt and degenerate psychopath. Scholem (1971) describes him in disparaging terms, and comments:

> . . . just as the [Sabbatian] "believers" had deliberately chosen to follow that dangerous path along which nothing is impossible, so it was perhaps precisely this that attracted them to Frank, for here was a man who was not afraid to push on to the very end, to take the final step into the abyss, to drain the cup of desolation and destruction to the lees until the last bit of holiness has been made into a mockery. His admirers, who themselves fell far short of him in respect of this ability, were won over by his intrepidness, which neither the fear of God nor the terrors of the bottomless pit were able to daunt, and saw in him the type of the true saint, a new Sabbatai Zevi and an incarnate God. (p. 127)

The sect that formed around him called themselves the Frankists.

He taught and justified the acquisition of wealth by deceitful ways, and glorified the lust for power. For his followers, his personality exercised a peculiar fascination and demonic grandiosity. The sect declared war on the Talmud, asserting that the *Zohar* alone contained the true law of Moses. They publicly flaunted and violated all the laws and prohibitions of rabbinical Judaism, especially laws pertaining to sexuality and marriage. Their mystical rituals and services seemed to take the form of licentious orgies, whipping themselves into a frenzy of ecstasy and dancing around a nude woman who presumably represented the *shekhinah*. The sabbatian doctrine of *tikkun* had given evil acts redemptive value, and led to a doctrine in which evil acts were themselves a form of mystical experience; in these terms the most degraded and taboo form of sin was transformed into a cleansing of the world in preparation for the messianic advent. His ideas constituted a "religious myth of nihilism" (Scholem 1941).

This nihilistic myth was in no sense the product of rational discussion and argument. Rather it was the product of a mind steeped in the fantastic and mythological. We can hear the echoes of ancient gnostic themes. Scholem (1971) observes:

> Indeed, to anyone familiar with the history of religion it might seem far more likely that he was dealing here with an antinomian myth from the second century composed by such nihilistic gnostics as Carpocrates and his followers than that all this was actually taught and believed by Polish Jews living on the eve of the French Revolution, among whom neither the "master" nor his "disciples" had the slightest inkling that they were engaged in resuscitating an ancient tradition! Not only the general train of thought, but even some of the symbols and terms are the same! (pp. 132-133)

The gnostics of old had also utilized a biblical framework for their doctrines, but in the process completely inverted the biblical values. Their creator became an evil and pernicious demiurge who sought the deception and destruction of men. The serpent became their guide and the symbol of freedom from the rule of the evil demiurge, teaching them to disobey and destroy his laws and institutions. This new way imposed on them also the obligation to commit "strange acts" in direct contradiction to the law of Moses, promulgated by the hateful creator (Scholem 1971).[4]

The Polish authorities stepped in to stop this disruptive force in their midst, and Frank was banished to Turkey. The followers were turned over to the rabbis who collected accounts of subversion of the law, various violations of morality and chastity, sexual excesses and

---

4. The view of the creator-god as an evil demiurge is a common theme in gnostic sources. See the discussion of gnosticism in Meissner (in process).

improprieties including nudity, adultery and incest that were justified and rationalized by Frank's doctrine. The sect was forthwith excommunicated by the rabbis in several communities, and any participation in the Jewish community life was forbidden. Even reading of the *kabbalah* or the *Zohar* was prohibited to anyone under 30 years of age. As a further punishment, the Frankists were handed over to the Inquisition. There they declared themselves for all practical purposes Christians, since they rejected the Talmud and believed in a holy trinity. They were finally released from prison and allowed to practice their new faith. The result was that they shifted ground from being the persecuted to becoming the persecutors.

Their attack was directed against the Talmudists among the Jews. Their claim was that their trinity was based on the Bible and the *Zohar*, and that the Talmud was an abomination that even proclaimed the murder of Christians to be a sacred duty. In some manner, they were able to enlist the bishop in their cause; Frank passed sentence on the Talmudists and had the police search throughout the diocese for any copies of the Talmud. Over a thousand copies were thrown into a pit and burned.

In 1757, the death of the bishop brought about a change of affairs that resulted in a turning of the forces of persecution against the Frankists. Frank returned from Turkey and laid his plans to rid himself and his movement of all opposition. He insisted on his exalted mission and on the divine revelations that commanded him to follow in the footsteps of Sabbatai Sevi. Just as Sabbatai had been forced to adopt Islamism, Frank and his followers were forced to accept the Christian religion as a stepping stone to the realization of the true faith of the messiah. Frank advanced several of his followers to accept Christian baptism. Finally, a grand spectacle was arranged in which, at Frank's command and insistence, nearly a thousand of his followers were baptized in his presence. Frank arrived in great pomp and ceremony, clad in rich Turkish costume, seated in a splendid carriage drawn by six horses and surrounded by guardsmen. Frank himself accepted only a preliminary baptism, declaring that he would complete the ceremony with greater solemnity in Warsaw with the king as his godfather. This he did in 1759.

The newspapers of the day were full of accounts of the daily baptisms of many Jews and of the many noble lords and ladies who volunteered to act as godparents. Nonetheless, religious authorities were wary and suspicious, realizing that Frank was no better than an impostor using these events for his own grandiose aims and purposes. Several of his adherents questioned his objectives and methods and finally betrayed him. They informed the church authorities that the show of accepting Christianity was a fraud and that Frank himself continued to be worshipped as messiah, lord and god. In fact, most of Frank's followers remained in close contact with sabbatian extremists and regarded their apostasy as merely extrinsic (Scholem 1941).

Frank himself was arrested, brought to trial before the Inquisition and imprisoned in the Fortress of Czestochowa in 1760. He was saved from burning at the stake by reason of the fact that the king was his godfather. His followers were either imprisoned or dispersed. Frank remained in this prison from 1760 until 1772 — a total of 13 years — but the Catholic authorities could not break the ties between Frank and his followers. They regarded him as the Holy Lord, who now became in their eyes the personification of the suffering messiah. Many settled around the town, some even penetrating within the fortress itself. They saw Frank's imprisonment as a repetition of the messianic destiny of Sabbatai Sevi, who had also been kept prisoner by the Turks. Frank continued to dispense a strange amalgam of Christian and sabbatian ideas in his mystical discourses and epistles — a variety of antinomian myth or nihilistic gnosticism, a world of mythological entities that might have emerged from somewhere in the 2nd century. His religious perspective was without religious laws or morality, reflecting his earlier dictum, "I have come to rid the world of all the laws and statutes which have been in existence hitherto" (GAP 1976).

The partition of Poland in 1772 ended Frank's imprisonment; he was released by the commander of the Russians forces. He reestablished connections with the sectarians, but then left Poland for Moravia in 1773. He continued to live there until 1786, surrounded by many of his followers and visited frequently by pilgrims from Poland. The advent of the French Revolution brought the sabbatian and Frankist subversion of all morality and religion into new perspective. Some of the Frankists were active in revolutionary circles in Paris and Strasbourg. The revolution seemed to corroborate the nihilist confession as the pillars of the old regime were shaken and destroyed. The "believers" saw these developments as signs of divine intervention on their behalf, especially in the undermining of all established spiritual and secular authority. The spirits of religious nihilism and anticlericalism found and embraced each other.

Frank continued to proselytize in Western Europe, assuming the role of a Christian missionary to the Jews. He found some success in Austria for a time, but when his past exploits became known, he was invited to leave. He settled at Offenbach in Germany, dubbed himself the "Baron of Offenbach," and continued to lead a life of ease and luxury, supported by his faithful Polish and Moravian adherents. After his death in 1791, the movement gradually lost steam and began to dissolve. Some of his followers who remained in Poland lived outwardly as Catholics, but inwardly remained loyal to him until his death. Gradually they were absorbed into the Polish church and lost all identity as a sect. The messianic seeds that had been sown in sabbatianism seem to have ended in the renunciation of Judaism.

Section V

Millennarianism

Christian Millennarianism

Origins in Jewish Tradition

Millennarianism has a long and busy history that stretches at least as far back in time as the more ancient civilizations. Chinese history from the earliest times was pervaded by a yearning for paradise, a reenactment through ecstasy of a primordial context in which men could still encounter the gods face to face (Eliade 1982). In the Judeo-Christian tradition, we can trace the millennial vision back to the period of Jewish apocalyptic thinking that played such a central role in the genesis of these religious traditions. The phenomenon of millennarian movements has a broad reach — spanning the globe, arising in many different cultural settings, and recurring throughout the course of human history.

For the most part, the millennial vision seems to have come into being and to have sustained itself in conjunction with messianic expectations. Not only does its origins seem to have been entwined with the messianic vision, but nearly every occurrence of the millennial themes has been associated with some form of messianic conviction and expectation. As Worsley (1968) observes, "The history of apocalyptic religions and of messianism is of special interest to people whose culture has included a central belief in One whom they believe to be *the* Messiah, who died for mankind and with whom they hoped to be reunited in Paradise." (p. 221) The millennium partakes in the glorious fulfillment of the reign of the returned messiah who brings with him the fulfillment of all messianic hopes and triumphs. The actual terms of the messianic return may vary; it is not always explicitly patterned after the model of the messiah of Jewish eschatological hopes. But even that model is not clearly and unequivocally articulated: the patterns are multiple and various even in the context of Jewish apocalyptic. Even so the millennial vision seems to carry with it its own burden of anticipation and its own distinctive characteristics — enough to justify our consideration of it separately from the messianic context. Nonetheless, in their varying and analogous articulations throughout the course of history, both messianism and millennarianism weave a fascinating pattern of intersection and divergence — all expressing, as I hope to show, the underlying dynamics of the cultic process.

Characteristics

The millennarian vision envisions a future salvation that incorporates certain characteristics. Cohn (1970b) summarizes these as follows:

"millennarian sects or movements always picture salvation as

(a) collective, in the sense that it is to be enjoyed by the faithful as a collectivity;

(b) terrestrial, in the sense that it is to be realized on this earth and not in some other-worldly heaven;

(c) imminent, in the sense that it is to come both soon and suddenly;

(d) total, in the sense that it is utterly to transform life on earth, so that the new dispensation will be no mere improvement on the present but perfection itself;

(e) miraculous, in the sense that it is to be accomplished by, or with the help of, supernatural agencies." (p. 15)

Additional features might include:

(f) remembrance of a golden age from earlier in the history of the race. The descriptions of the golden age may differ considerably from culture to culture, but it is consistently described in terms of unalloyed happiness, pleasure that is both physical and spiritual, without suffering, sorrow or death. The genesis story of the garden of Eden, Paradise, and its loss through Adam's sin resulting in man's fall, is perhaps the best known of such myths. The golden age may represent a folk-memory of an earlier epoch, now transformed and idealized into a future vision. In more advanced forms, these wishes may merge with dreams of a secular utopia or a version of a classless society. The millennarian vision looks to the restoration of this mythic paradise by the overthrow of the hated oppressors and release from the misery and oppression of the present age. Millennial beliefs have a special and powerful appeal throughout history to those who have suffered failure, oppression, disappointments, dispossession, disinheritance, severe loss and humiliation. They flourish in a context in which the oppressed and deprived classes refuse to accept the domination of their oppressors or rulers, especially when they are representatives of a foreign power. Worsley (1968) comments:

> The anti-authoritarian attitude is expressed not only in the form of direct political resistance, but also through the rejection of the ideology of the ruling authority. The lower orders reject the dominant values, beliefs, philosophy, religion, etc., of those they are struggling against, as well as their material, economic and political domination. It is therefore natural that millennarian doctrines often become openly revolutionary and lead to violent conflict between rulers and ruled. Because of this revolutionary potential, millennarian movements are usually treated with the utmost suspicion by Church and State and have often been proscribed and persecuted. (p. 225-226)

(g) Revivalism, i.e., renewed interest in traditional beliefs with great enthusiasm and excitement in the aftermath of a period of religious decline or indifference. Revivalism represents an effort to restore the conditions of the lost golden age; other cultural and social institutions may be restored along with the religious. The upsurge of religious enthusiasm may be accompanied by visions, ecstasies, trances, and other hysterical manifestations, such as glossolalia.

(h) Nativism, a return to selected aspects of the pristine culture and rejection of elements acquired from the dominating culture. The rebellion against foreign domination arises from a deep-seated resentment within the populace as a result of changes in their way of life and attempts to destroy or corrupt their traditional values. Their present humiliation and degradation and suffering was imposed on them by the conquering or dominating foreigners by forcing or inducing them to abandon the old ways of living, believing and behaving. The movement is thus often strongly rooted in the indigenous culture and looks to its ancient gods for its inspiration and protection. The messianic leader or leaders receive their power and authority from the divine patrons of the community, and it is through the intervention of these propitious gods that the promise of the millennium will be realized.

(i) Syncretism, in the sense of the indiscriminate adoption of cultural traits from the dominant culture. This tendency runs counter to the nativist current. In certain cultures, it represents an effort to gain the power and superiority of the foreign oppressors by identification and mimicry. These new behaviors and attitudes are grafted on to old patterns. Where meaningful integration is possible, the outcome may be productive, but more often, especially in backward communities, the abandonment of old customs leads to social deterioration and discord, while the acquisitions from the alien culture are more destructive than otherwise, often simple-minded in execution, illogical, contradictory, and applied without understanding or context. We should not overlook the constructive dimension of such millennial cults insofar as they represent efforts to adjust to the new level of demands and pressures that arise from the interaction of two divergent cultures, rather than simply regressions into the past in the face of overwhelming conflicts and despair.

(j) Eschatologism, that is, the expectation of a world-wide revolution and catastrophe to be followed by a world of messianic fulfillment. The catastrophe is seen as required for the destruction of the present order; out of the ruins of the old order, the seed of the new reign of peace and justice will sprout.

(k) Millennarianism or chiliasm, referring to a paradise on earth that is to last literally 1,000 years, or figuratively for a very long time. The paradise is the return of the golden age, usually attributed to the return of the promised messiah who will establish his reign over the earth (Fuchs 1965).

Jewish Apocalyptic

Millennial ideas derive from Old Testament eschatology in which the definitive salvation was cast in terrestrial terms. The messianic reign was to be unending, but was marked by quite specific nationalistic characteristics. The messianic vision of the *eschaton* tended to diversify in the first centuries, one current contending that the world was essentially corrupt and could not be the place for the promised messianic kingdom. This view would require a completely new world that would come into being after the universal judgment. Another maintained a messianic reign that was to be national and terrestrial, but limited to a specific period of time, e.g., 7,000 years. This would serve as an intermediary period between the present age and the final eternal reign of God — the so-called *millennium*. This intermediate reign would be followed by the universal judgment and the destruction of the world.

The themes that dominated Old Testament apocalyptic were extensions and elaborations of motifs that can be found in the prophetic literature in less developed forms. Pivotal figures in the prophetic movement were Jeremiah and Ezekiel. Jeremiah's style was quite different from the standard apocalyptic mode. In Jeremiah there was a strong current of the subjective and personal. The apocalyptic writers eschew any inkling of the personal, even using fictitious names and stereotyped style to insure that their message remained faceless and opaque. Jeremiah addressed specific persons and situations; an apocalyptist wrote grandiose visions that involved casts of thousands and took place on a world stage (Dn 7: 9-10). Other striking differences have been noted between the prophetic and apocalyptic styles, but there are also threads of continuity in the tapestry. Yet Jeremiah opened the way to apocalyptic by his stress on the cosmic significance of Israel's sins (Jer 2: 12) and his vision of chaos strewn over the land of Judah, laying everything in waste and desolation (Jer 4: 7). Israel became identified with the cosmos (Jer 4: 23-36; 5: 22-23; 10: 10-13; 27: 5-6). He introduced a note of universalism by his proclamation of a new creation (Jer 31: 22) and a new covenant (Jer 31: 31-34).

The same themes were continued in Ezekiel, but in a style that drew another step closer to apocalyptic. In his writing, the elements of apocalyptic style coalesced into a model that influenced writers in several centuries to follow. In many sections he writes more as an apocalyptist than prophet. As Stuhlmueller (1968) observes:

> We are baffled by many features of Ezekiel's style: the enigmatic vagueness of his approach; the weird signs and symbols heaped one upon another; the necessity of angelic mediators to explain the visions; the great reversals from total destruction to complete renewal. In these details we can identify the essential elements of apocalyptic style. Even if a later editor, as we readily admit, rearranged the Prophet's message, Ezekiel remains an outstanding example of prophet-become-apocalyptist. (p. 339)

He expressed his prophetic visions in the form of symbolic actions as well as his preaching and writing. This style of apocalyptic action spilled over into his writing. His own ecstatic experiences were a major source of his apocalyptic inspiration. His imagery appealed to ancient and sacred traditions — examples include cherubim, references to ancestral figures (e.g., Noah, Job), the creation story (Ez 28: 11-19), prophecies against Gog of Magog, etc. His practice of telling the story with stage effects from the past will be followed with greater effect by later apocalyptists.

Ezekiel's priestly role also weighed in heavily in accounting for his later influence on the evolution of Judaic society in the direction of a priestly theocracy. The priestly emphasis had a profound influence on post-exilic apocalyptic writing: a prominent feature of ancient liturgies as well as late apocalyptic is the concentration on the war between Yahweh and his enemies. Yahweh's final victory over all other nations and gods proclaimed in the Psalms. In the apocalyptic genre, the struggle was an eschatological confrontation between the forces of good and the forces of evil, the final victory taking place in Jerusalem. The cosmic connotations of this eschatological battle were abetted by his mythological language and his references to mythological features, such as the cherubim (Ez 1-3), the paradise motif (Ez 28: 11-19), and primeval giants (Ez 38-39).

There is an important eschatological text in Ezekiel 37: 1-14 — the vision of the dry bones coming to life again. The text is cast in the imagery of corporal resurrection, but its message is one of the return of Israel to its native land where the people will be brought back to life by the power of Yahweh. The text is redolent with messianic and millennarian hopes and expectations cast in the context of the Babylonian exile.

The post-exilic prophets introduced a new strain into the understanding of the kingdom to come and the salvation it promised. As Stanley (1968a) noted:

> It was only after the Exile, when Israel's national aspirations were recognized as doomed to failure, that salvation was related to the individual and became more spiritual. The great prophets of the Exile, Jeremiah (Jer 31: 29-31) and Ezekiel (Ez 18: 1-32; 34: 2-20), adopt the individualist viewpoint. In the book of Isaiah there is mention of the universal (Is 2: 2-4) and eschatological (Is 25: 8; 45: 8; 51: 6; 61: 10) character of Yahweh's salvation. (pp. 23-24)

Another important figure in the prophetic foreshadowing of apocalyptic is the prophet known as Deutero-Isaiah, the unknown author of Is 40-55. His writing contains many of the features of later apocalyptic. According to his account, the secrets of the eschatological age are enunciated first in the divine assembly of Yahweh and his angels, and only then are they spoken to the prophet on earth. Yahweh appears in his majesty, glory and wisdom (Is 40: 10, 12-24; 41: 13-14, 29; 42: 8), possessing the fullness of being and knowing the secrets of everything earthly. He is responsible for both the chaos of the exile and the magnificence of the new creation that is to come (Is 41: 4-5, 21ff; 42: 9; 43: 9-13; 51: 9-11). The new creation is described in mythological language telling of the final struggle between Yahweh and the evil gods who are reduced to helpless impotence (Is 44: 9-20; 46: 1-2). The apocalyptic features are summed up by Stuhlmueller (1968):

> . . . the day of the Lord motif, with its terror and hopes, involving Gentiles as well as Jews; the vision of a new covenant that will fulfill and even surpass the Mosaic covenant; the actualization of history, found in the deuteronomic tradition; the deuteronomic revolt against the exclusive demands of the Jerusalem priests and their Torah; Deutero-Isaiah's vision of battle among the gods, with Yahweh supreme in his new creation, accomplished through the omnipotent word falling upon earth from the secret, heavenly council; and finally the overwhelming influence of Ezekiel, priest and prophet — the man of signs who stylized his words in the form of visions and symbols, and the man of the book, who became responsible for the dominant liturgical spirit of Judaism and its intense loyalty to the P tradition. (p. 340)

These elements were all identifiable in the preceding prophetic tradition but were brought into conjunction in unique combination in the apocalyptic writings. The emphasis on symbols, cosmic implications, unearthly implications and renewed forms of antiquity, and the imminence of eschatological age are the hallmarks of apocalyptic.

The age of the prophets came to an end, probably in the preaching of Malachi — but even then his preaching was subordinate to the priests and the temple worship. Preaching in the post-exilic age turned from themes of personal goodness and social justice to the functioning of the liturgy. Prophecy was no longer the highly individual mission to pass judgment on the nation and on the priests — it now was judged by the priests and subjected to the Torah. In place of prophecy there arose the sapiential literature, in which the utterances of the man of wisdom became the extension of prophetic inspiration. The prophets had deteriorated into apocalyptic dreamers. By the time of Joel, the prophetic message was concerned with fasting, sacrifices, oblations and prayers. His proclamation takes place in a temple setting and is addressed to the elders and priests. He appeals to the eschatological vision of the day of the Lord — cosmic eschatology and liturgical correctness have superseded reform and repentance.

The mythical and eschatological quality of religious thinking at this period is expressed in the so-called "eschatological psalms," particularly Ps 95-98. In these psalms, cosmic imagery reaches beyond the limits of known reality in the effort to communicate a sense of divine mystery and transcendence. The influence of Deutero-Isaiah and the priestly liturgy are evident, and the emphasis falls on the final eruption of the power and glory of Yahweh in his ultimate victory over evil and the establishing of his rule over the world. Prophecy is now dead, even though the apocalyptic writers have not been able to out-grow the influence of Ezekiel. The prevailing belief was that liturgical rigor and the faithful observance of the Law would bring about the intervention of Yahweh in the miseries of post-exilic Judaism and create a new order in which Yahweh would reign as king, Jerusalem would become the capital of the new dispensation, and Yahweh would pour out his spirit and fulfill all the ancient promises. History would have to wait another century and a half for the apocalyptic impulse to thrust beyond Ezekiel to become a medium of transcendent and ebullient symbolism.

It is in the *Book of Daniel* that we find the efflorescence of the apocalyptic style. The imagery transcends the limits of earthly experience; heavenly secrets are explained by angelic powers; the battle between the superhuman forces of good and evil rages; the glorious breakthrough of divine power and majesty are expected in the imminent future; the divine kingdom manifests; authorship is attributed to Daniel of the Babylonian exile, who lived several centuries previously — all marks of the apocalyptic spirit in the full flower of its expression. It was not long after the appearance of Daniel that the apocalyptic literature began to appear — the *Book of Enoch*, soon after the Maccabean revolt came the *Book of Jubilees*, to be followed by the *Testaments of the Twelve Patriarchs* and the *Psalms of Solomon*.

The millennarian theme can be found in apocryphal Jewish writings, for example, 4 Esdras, but the distinction between the messianic kingdom and millennial hopes is not clearly maintained. Allusions to the millennium are frequent in other apocryphal books, as for example the books of *Enoch*, *2 Esdras*, the *Ascension of Isaiah*, and the *Apocalypse of Peter*. References are made especially to the millennial kingdom, a paradise in which the saved remnant will be ruled by the messianic savior — a new Eden that will come into being after the cosmic holocaust in which Yahweh wages war on the forces of evil. His coming will inaugurate a 1,000-year reign of peace and prosperity. Such eschatological prophesies, as in the *Books of David*, were written during the Maccabean crisis and looked for a messiah who would rule not only Israel, but would extend his power to the whole world. As we have seen, these apocalyptic desires were intensified under the Roman boot-and-heel, and rose to a crescendo in the Palestinian revolt of AD 66-72.[1] There was a tendency to replace the Davidic messiah with a more explicitly military warrior king, especially in the *Apocalypse* of Baruch and Ezra (AD 1st century). The messiah of *Ezra* consumes the worst of the evil empires — represented by the Roman eagle — and the Son of Man annihilates the heathen and gathers the tribes into a reunited kingdom of peace and glory in Palestine. In *Baruch*, evil and suffering must reach a peak, and only then will the great warrior messiah appear to lead the conquest of the enemies of Israel, especially the Romans, and thus establish his kingdom that will last until the end of the world. This warrior messiah had his day in the revolt under Simon bar Kochba in AD 131.

Perhaps the primary source in the Old Testament literature for millennial ideas is the book of *Daniel*, the archetypal apocalyptic work of the Judeo-Christian tradition, in fact the only such work included in the Old Testament canon. Most of the apocryphal works owe much of their inspiration and style to *Daniel*. Besides its relation to the prophetic tradition, *Daniel* may also contain material derived from Iranian sources, e.g., Zoroastrian notions of a last judgment, the struggle between the forces of good and evil, and a fiery punishment for evildoers. *Daniel* was written in the religious and political crisis of the hellenizing rule of Antiochus IV Epiphanes, probably circa 165 BC. Its purpose was to give support to the Maccabean rebels and to reassure them that God was with them and that a new and glorious age was dawning.

In its prophetic vision, after the kingdoms of this world have been destroyed, the Son of Man would come to establish a new, righteous, just and eternal kingdom of justice and prosperity. The establishment of the golden age was to be accomplished by divine intervention, the violent overthrow and reversal of all worldly expectations. And this cataclysmic change was to be wrought in the imminent future. The vision was cast in terms of a complex array of symbolic numbers, metaphors, mythological figures and formulations, and an elaborate angelology that proved to be a ripe source for gnostic speculation,[2] as well as for the rehearsal of apocalyptic themes throughout the ensuing history. As Cohn (1970b) comments:

---

1. See chapter 4.
2. For discussion of this development, see Meissner (in process).

Already here one can recognize the paradigm of what was to become and to remain the central fantasy of revolutionary eschatology. The world is dominated by an evil, tyrannous power of boundless destructiveness — a power moreover which is imagined not as simply human but as demonic. The tyranny of that power will become more and more outrageous, the sufferings of its victims more and more intolerable — until suddenly the hour will strike when the Saints of God are able to rise up and overthrow it. The Saints themselves, the chosen, holy people who hitherto have groaned under the oppressor's heel, shall in their turn inherit dominion over the whole earth. This will be the culmination of history; the Kingdom of the Saints will not only surpass in glory all previous kingdoms, it will have no successors. It was thanks to this fantasy that Jewish apocalyptic exercised, through its derivatives, such a fascination upon the discontented and frustrated of later ages — and continued to do so long after the Jews themselves had forgotten its very existence. (p. 21)

The book is a powerful expression of the conviction of the Jewish people that they were the chosen people of Yahweh, who was the Lord of history and who determined the fate of kings and nations. Under the desperate strain of a cruel foreign domination and the desecration of their religious values and worship, the Jewish mind resorted to fantasies of the ultimate triumph of Judaism and of a reign of glorious prosperity and peace guaranteed by the power of Yahweh. The punishment and degradation they suffered in the present was but a prelude to the Day of Yahweh, the Day of Wrath, when Israel's enemies would be destroyed, and only the faithful remnant of true believers would survive to enjoy the kingdom of God. Yahweh will rule from the New Jerusalem which will become the spiritual center of the world. Disease, sorrow, and deprivation will be banished, and peace and justice will reign over all the earth. Eliade's (1982) summary comment is to the point:

In Judaism, as in other traditions, apocalyptic visions strengthened defenses against the terror of history. The instructed could decipher a comforting opresage in contemporary catastrophes. The worse the situation of the Jewish people became, the more the certainty increased that the present eon was nearing its end. In short, the worsening of the terror announced the imminence of salvation. In future, the religious valorization of the sufferings brought on by historical events will be reiterated time and again, and not only by the Jews and the Christians. (p. 272)

Early Christianity

In many respects early Christianity, absorbing many of its perspectives and religious orientations from the Judaic milieu in which it arose, had many of the characteristics of a millennarian sect (Gager 1975). Characteristic of such millennarian movements, the group that followed in Jesus' footsteps anticipated the imminent overthrow of the present world order; they looked forward to the fulfillment of the promise of a heaven realized here on earth; their message appealed largely to the impoverished, the disenfranchised, the oppressed and alienated from the established social order and the centers of power. In such movements, the charismatic prophet plays the role of a catalyst in bringing to a focus the discontent and frustration of the marginal and oppressed groups in the society, and offers them hope and release from their sufferings through a new doctrine that promises the dawn of a new era. In this view, Jesus was the charismatic prophet of a revolutionary millennarian cult.

When the prophet, who was hailed as the messiah and the leader who would guide his followers to a new and better kingdom, was arrested, tried, convicted, and crucified, the fervent hopes for messianic fulfillment were crushed. The prospects for realization of these frustrated desires were extinguished, or at least severely dimmed. But the movement did not die out — it found new life and conviction based on the resurrection and the faith in the risen Christ who, by his resurrection, was proven to be both Lord and messiah. Rather than defeat, the death of the savior was turned into a saving doctrine and the forces of survival and apostolic fervor were directed to the wider world of Roman civilization.[3]

The millennarian movement transformed itself into a recognizable religious movement that was able to define itself over against the prevailing Judaism extant in Palestine. Gager (1975) applies Weber's (1947) analysis of routinization of charisma to this transformation. He views charismatic authority as playing a vital role in the stages of the evolution of religious institutions, and argues that such charismatic authority and the rise of institutional structures are not antithetical but complementary. Harrington (1982) summarizes the argument:

---

3. The capacity for these early Christians to snatch victory from the jaws of defeat has been analyzed in terms of Festinger's (1957; Festinger et al. 1956) theory of cognitive dissonance. See Jackson (1975), Wernik (1975), and Gager (1975).

For the first two hundred years of its existence, Christianity was essentially a movement among the disprivileged (economically or socially) within the Roman empire. It incorporated the characteristics of the religion of the disprivileged: a strong tendency toward congregational units, a reliance on future-oriented compensation (salvation), and a rational system of ethics. Why did Christianity succeed? The existence of Hellenistic Judaism in the Diaspora and the peaceful conditions in the Roman empire were the most powerful external factors. The most prominent internal factor was the radical sense of community — open to all, insistent on absolute and exclusive loyalty, and concerned with every aspect of the believers' life.[4] (p. 153)

The political and socioeconomic and religious crisis that afflicted Palestinian society at the turn of the millennium provided a context that was ripe for the surge in millennarian expectations. The various sects in Greco-Roman Palestine of the time contended over the issue of access to and control over the redemptive media, namely the temple worship and the Mosaic Law (Isenberg 1974). The sects in which millennarian elements came into play with special emphasis, the Essenes and Christians and later the Zealots, felt excluded and alienated from the traditional sources of religious connection. These groups followed a common path, each with its characteristic divergences, toward a millennarian resolution. The common steps were: (a) feelings of deprivation and oppression, (b) the appearance of a millennarian prophet who provoked the expression and testing of a set of new beliefs and assumptions about power and religious relevance, and (c) a final phase of consolidation of the movement or dissolution. Within this frame of reference, the Essene Teacher of Righteousness, Jesus and Paul would all qualify as millennarian prophets. All three claimed religious authority outside of the usual and traditional channels of legitimate religious power in the social structure of Palestine; the claimed access to a higher source of power and truth as the guarantee of the validity of

---

4. Gager's approach has been criticized, largely on methodological grounds. Bartlett (1978) raises questions about the use of sociological models, the use of unclear categories, the tendency to homogenize the data about early Christianity, disparities between evidence and theory, and failure to adequately consider religious aspects. Smith (1978) objects to Gager's failure to take into account historical particularities and their consequences, to consider the context of the models he employs, and to take methodological issues seriously. Tracy (1978) would like to see more fundamental theology included in the discussion and more attention paid to internal (presumably psychological) factors in the analysis of early Christianity. The criticisms are well taken but do not add up to a refutation of the theory or the approach.

their new revelation; and finally they gathered around them disciples who responded to the new hope and promise contained in the revelation that seemed to answer to their underlying frustration and suffering (Isenberg 1974).

New Testament

The primary locus for millennial thinking in the New Testament is the *Book of the Apocalypse*. It is well to remember that, like the book of Daniel, the Apocalypse was written, probably in the last decade of the 1st century, in the face of the vicious persecutions started under Nero (AD 37-68) who is cast as the Antichrist. The classic texts are the following:

> Then I saw an angel come down from heaven with the key of the Abyss in his hand and an enormous chain. He overpowered the dragon, that primeval serpent which is the devil and Satan, and chained him up for a thousand years. He threw him into the Abyss, and shut the entrance and sealed it over him, to make sure he would not deceive the nations again until the thousand years had passed. At the end of that time he must be released, but only for a short while.
>
> Then I saw some thrones, and I saw those who are given the power to be judges take their seats on them. I saw the souls of all who had been beheaded for having witnessed for Jesus and for having preached God's word, and those who refused to worship the beast or his statue and would not have the brand-mark on their foreheads or hands; they came to life, and reigned with Christ for a thousand years. This is the first resurrection; the rest of the dead did not come to life until the thousand years were over. Happy and blessed are those who share in the first resurrection; the second death cannot affect them, but they will be priests of God and of Christ and reign with him for a thousand years. (20: 1-10)
>
> Then I saw a new heaven and a new earth; the first heaven and the first earth had disappeared now, and there was no longer any sea. I saw the holy city, and the new Jerusalem, coming down from God out of heaven, as beautiful as a bride all dressed for her husband. Then I heard a loud voice call from the throne, "You see this city? Here God lives among men. He will make his home among them; they shall be his people, and he will be their God; his name is God-with-them. He will wipe away all tears from their eyes; there will be no more death, and no more mourning or sadness. The world of the past has gone."

Then the One sitting on the throne spoke: "Now I am making the whole of creation new," he said. "Write this: that what I am saying is sure and will come true." And then he said, "It is already done. I am the Alpha and the Omega, the Beginning and the End. I will give water from the well of life free to anybody who is thirsty; it is the rightful inheritance of the one who proves victorious; and I will be his God and he a son to me. But the legacy for cowards, for those who break their word, or worship obscenities, for murders and fornicators, and for fortune-tellers, idolaters or any other sort of liars, is the second death in the burning lakes of sulphur." (21: 1-8)

The *Apocalypse* was accepted in early Christian circles as authentic revelation, recording the prophetic visions of the last of the apostles, the beloved disciple John, who was presumed to be the author of the fourth gospel. But in the 3rd century, particularly in the East, there was a reaction that cast doubt on these origins — presumably as a result of the use to which these millennial passages were being put to support the millennarian heresy. Denis of Alexandria reopened the question of the apostolic origin of the work; without challenging its traditional position as inspired and canonical, he questioned whether it was authored by the same person who had authored the gospel, basically on linguistic and stylistic grounds. Eusebius in the 4th century could not decide whether it was authentic or spurious, and other Eastern Fathers did not include it among the canonical books. Doubts about its canonicity persisted, although its authority remained unchallenged among the Latin Fathers of the West. Denis' doubts about authorship have been sustained by subsequent scholarship. Erasmus reopened the debate in the 16th century. Current opinion is divided regarding the unity of authorship of both the gospel and the *Apocalypse*. One face-saving solution is that both works may have derived from the Johannine community, possibly under the guidance of the apostle, but that the works might have undergone different redactions by different groups of disciples.

These passages look forward to a messianic future in two forms: the "days of the messiah" looked to the national restoration of the Jews, while the "end of days" referred to the universal consummation at the of the world. The messianic vision was to be realized by direct divine intervention, the cosmic manifestation of divine power and glory. Speculation about when the consummation was to take place was rife, but one of the more prominent was that the span of the world was measured in seven periods of 1,000 years each, the last (the millennium) to be inaugurated by the coming of the messiah and the founding of his 1,000 years reign of joy and peace. Then the martyrs and the just will come to life in the first resurrection, to reign with Christ. At the end of the millennium, at the end of days, the souls of the just would pass on to the heavenly kingdom. Satan is to be held captive during the millennium, while the faithful live and reign with Christ. When he is released, the final battle will take place leading to the ultimate victory of Christ and his angels and the damnation to eternal fire of Satan and his brood. Then the sinners will be resurrected to be condemned to eternal fire, and the just will enter the bliss of heaven.

In Christian lore, the days of the messiah were translated into the second coming of Christ. The linkage between Christ and Daniel's Son of Man is maintained. The work represents an assimilation of Jewish apocalyptic: numerological and symbolic expressions are repeated, the basic dualism is revived in the antithesis of good vs. evil, Christ vs. Antichrist, and there is the promise of divine assistance imminently expected coming to the aid of beleaguered and desperate believers to relieve their pain and misery. Orthodox interpretation tends to see these texts in symbolic terms, although it seems clear that Paul's own apocalyptic views had a more literal cast.[5] For example, the first resurrection is taken to refer to baptism, the millennium is taken to mean the reign of the Church here on earth, spanning the period from the resurrection of Christ to the Last Judgment. In the end, Satan, or the Antichrist, will be defeated once and for all, and the faithful will be revivified in a general resurrection. In contrast, heretical views have tended to use these passages in literal, nonsymbolic, and non-metaphorical senses.

The Fathers

In the early centuries of the Christian era, millennarianism was espoused by some of the Church fathers — Papias of Hieropolis and Justin Martyr, for example. They held that only after the return of the just Christ to establish his 1,000-year kingdom would there be a last judgment. Even Irenaeus in his *Adversus Haereses* argued that divine

---

5. Paul's views regarding the second coming of the Lord, the Parousia, as for example in 1 Thess 4:13-15:11 and Thess 1:3-2:12, were cast in terms of his expectation of the imminence of the parousia. These texts speak to the profound impact on early Christian thinking of Jewish apocalypticism. See also Mk 13.

justice demanded that the chiliastic vision be realized. Lactantius portrayed the demonic figure of the Antichrist and his ultimate defeat at the second coming. Similar views were taught by heretics such as the gnostic Cerinthus and the Ebionites. One of the great minds of the West, Tertullian, embraced the millennarian perspective and gave it considerable prestige. He at least partially endorsed the Montanist heresy.

Origen in the 3rd century was perhaps one of the earliest to attack the literal and radical form of chiliasm, arguing that eschatological change took place in the soul and not in nature. Augustine, a century or more later, when Christianity had become an accepted religion in the empire, put his stamp on the view that would remain in force until the Reformation. In his *The City of God*, he argued that the City of the World was ruled by Satan, and that he and all his followers would be plunged into eternal hellfire. In contrast, the City of God, the Church, was destined by God for salvation and eternal joy. Augustine's view was apocalyptic and pessimistic about the fate of the world and any prospects for progress in it. After his conversion he turned to an ascetic and world-denying spirituality that rejected carnal desires and any enjoyment of the material world. Augustine's rejection of the world was almost gnostic or manichean in flavor; for him the world could not be redeemed, and true happiness was to be found only in heaven. He interpreted the visions of the Apocalypse allegorically — for him the millennium became a spiritual state into which the Church had been inaugurated at Pentecost when the Holy Spirit came to dwell in the Church. Unlike the true millennarians, he expected no imminent supernatural intervention that would transform the world. His eschatology was in this sense "realized" — the battle had already been fought and won, God had won, and Satan was condemned to serve as Lord of this world. Eventually that, too, would be taken from him, and the reign of God will be eternally supreme.

Augustine's view became a major influence on orthodox acceptance and understanding of the Apocalypse. The more orthodox interpretation saw the visions of the Apocalypse as symbolic and metaphorical. The millennium was intended metaphorically; the first resurrection meant baptism, by which the newly minted Christian shared in the resurrection of Christ. All the faithful were to share in the 1,000-year reign of Christ, that is, the duration of the life of the Church extending from Christ's resurrection until the Last Judgment. Then the faithful will enter the bliss of heaven, and the unfaithful will suffer the "second death" of eternal punishment. For the early Christians, the beast of the Apocalypse or the Antichrist was identified with the oppressive and persecuting power of Rome that would be vanquished and dissolved at the second coming of Christ.

Montanism

Perhaps the leading apocalyptic heresy of the 2nd century was Montanism. Montanus was a Phrygian by birth, and probably a pagan priest before his conversion to Christianity. According to Epiphanius, Montanus began his preaching mission in AD 156, declaring himself the prophet of the new age of the Holy Spirit, and actually identifying himself as the incarnation of the Holy Spirit, the Spirit of Truth predicted by the gospel of John, through whom the voice of God the Father spoke (Dodds 1965). It was not long before the voice began to speak through two female devotees, Priscilla and Maximilla — their utterances were recorded as a Third Testament to surpass the Old and New Testaments.

Montanus quickly gathered around him a band of mystics and ecstatics who believed that their visionary experiences were of divine origin. Phrygia became the center of the ecstatic and ascetic movement, proclaiming the new prophecy that had been received by way of divine inspiration by the "Spirit of Truth." He announced that the New Jerusalem would descend near Pepuza in Phrygia. He and his followers looked for the imminent outpouring of the Spirit on the Church. He urged his followers and all Christians to gather at Pepuza and there to await the second coming of Christ in prayer and fasting. The arrival of the New Jerusalem would inaugurate the thousand-year reign of Christ on earth.

Montanism was an intensely ascetical movement that idealized suffering and sought martyrdom, for it was especially the martyrs whom the Apocalypse singled out for resurrection and enjoyment of the millennium. It was a doctrine admirably suited to an age of persecution. Montanus' teaching, especially the rigid asceticism, took hold rapidly and won many adherents. Among its many proscriptions: second marriages were forbidden, strict laws of fasting were imposed, and flight from persecution was outlawed. Apparently the rigor of this sect appealed to Tertullian, who condemned the penitential discipline in force at Rome as entirely too lax and regarded Christians as "psychic" (in the Valentinian sense) in contrast to the Montanists who were "pneumatics."

One view of the Montanist movement saw it as a return to the inspiration and enthusiasm of primitive Christianity, especially in its emphasis on the role of prophecy, in opposition to the increasing institutionalization and secularization of the Church. As it spread through the Roman empire, the strength of their conviction in the imminent coming of the New Jerusalem remained unabated. Even Tertullian wrote of the portent of the vision of a walled city appearing in the sky — a certain omen of the instant descent of the Heavenly Jerusalem. The failure of the appointment at Pepuza and the hostility of Roman bishops could not stay its course. But it probably represents one of the early apocalyptic movements that recur frequently in the course of Christian history. The flood of visions and ecstatic experiences continued.

The orthodox Church was not slow to attack the heretical visions of the Montanists. Denis of Alexandria attacked the Montanist doctrine at its roots by challenging the apostolic origins of the Apocalypse. The movement was finally condemned by Pope Zephyrinus (Cross 1957), a circumstance that put a damper on the appeal of millennial speculation for Christians. Even after the triumph of Constantine, the millennial fervor seemed to cool, but pockets of Montanist enthusiasm persisted. It was not until the time of Justinian that the last of the breed locked themselves in their churches and suffered death by fire rather than turning themselves over to their fellow Christians. With the demise of Montanism, the spirit of prophecy seemed to recede from the Church, not to resurface again until the appearance of chiliastic manias in the Middle Ages (Dodds 1965).

CHAPTER 12

The Kingdom of God

The Notion of the Kingdom

As the eschatological dreams and apocalyptic visions entered the mainstream of orthodox Christian belief, they were significantly modified in terms of the historical experience of the Christian community as it struggled to absorb the legacy of Jesus' message and mission and groped its way forward in the jungle of conflicting pressures — social and cultural — that composed the world in which it came into existence. These eschatological hopes and expectations came to center around the concept of the kingdom, one of the dominant themes of the gospel message. The theme is enunciated most distinctly by the synoptics, less so in the rest of the New Testament literature. The idea of the "kingdom of God" is found prominently in Mark and Luke; Matthew prefers the equivalent expression "kingdom of heaven."

God in these instances is God the Father whom Jesus preached — the loving Father in heaven who is also our father. The place of the Christian as adopted sons of this father is effected through connection with the Son of God, through whom God becomes our father. The Christian life thus becomes one of sonship to the Father (Mt 5: 45). It is this sonship and connection with the Father that is expressed in the kingdom of God — existing primarily in heaven but communicated through the Son to men on earth. Christians belonged to the kingdom by reason of their relationship with Christ.

The objective, then, of the Son of Man was to establish the kingdom; he proclaimed the kingdom from the beginning of his ministry (Mk 1: 15) and declared his message to be the gospel of the kingdom (Mt 24: 14). The "kingdom of God" must imply that God is king, a theme that reverberates with Old Testament usage and religious ideals but enunciates an entirely new and revolutionary concept. It implies a new covenant between God and men that carried with it certain promises and hopes. Jesus' disciples would gradually modify the concept as they adapted to the new order and increasingly made it their own. Jesus gave no definition of the kingdom, but he clearly had in mind a spiritual kingdom. But was it one that was already existing and only gradually evolving into something more, or was it something that would come suddenly and dramatically as the result of an eschatological revolution that would shake the world to its foundations?

> The idea of the kingdom can be given a somewhat loose definition: it is a system of salvation which begins with Jesus, but continues the order of the Old Covenant. It assumes several aspects: it is a doctrine, a mystery, which only the faithful can assimilate; it is also a society in the form of an organism developing continually in accordance with the laws of its being. It exists on earth, incarnate to some extent in the Church, a militant and imperfect state. It is to come into full existence only in the kingdom of God, the final state from which the worthless elements have been eliminated, where the divine blessings are received without any hindrance or reservation. It is in fact the type (and, as it were, the sum total) of all the supernatural benefits which are granted to us even on this earth, but only appear in all their glory in heaven. (Bonsirven 1963, cited in Fortmann 1966, pp. 31-32)

The notion of the kingdom was inexorably linked to that of salvation, and both underwent significant evolution. As Stanley (1968a) has noted:

> It was only in the post-exilic period of Israel's history that salvation acquired those spiritual, transcendent, and individual (as opposed to collective) qualities which in the Christian dispensation came to be associated with the term. In earlier ages, the Israelite thought of salvation merely as a deliverance from present, national, terrestrial calamities. Security and happiness in this life were the essence of salvation. (pp. 22-23)

Old Testament

While the theme of God's kingdom came more into focus in the New Testament, the idea of the kingdom of Yahweh also had its place in earlier Judaic writings, especially in the apocalyptic literature. Scattered references occur in the Pentateuch: "Who among the gods is your like, Yahweh?"

> Who is your like, majestic in holiness,
> terrible in deeds of prowess, worker of wonders?
> You stretched your right hand out, the earth swallowed them!
> By your grace you led the people you redeemed,
> by your strength you guided them to your holy house. . . .
> You will bring them and plant them on the mountain
> that is your own,
> the place you have made your dwelling, Yahweh,
> the sanctuary, Yahweh, prepared by your own hands.
> Yahweh will be king for ever and ever. (Ex 15: 11-13, 17-18)

In Numbers, he is the mighty ruler who humbles his enemies and against whom no one can stand (Num 24: 8). In Deuteronomy he is the king who joins the tribes together into a people of God (Deut 33: 5), a theme that echoes through the prophets (Mich 6: 4; Jer 2: 6ff; Is 63:11-14) and psalms (Ps 77: 12-21; 78: 3-29). Schnackenburg (1963) comments on these and similar texts:

> These texts show us that Israel experienced Yahweh's kingship in the historical action of its God. This is no "kingdom" and no "sphere of dominion" but a kingly leadership and reign which develops from Yahweh's absolute power and shows itself in the guidance of Israel. The original meaning, namely that Yahweh as king actively "rules," must be kept in mind through the whole growth of the *basileia* theme. God's kingship in the Bible is characterized not by latent authority but by the exercise of power, not by an office but a function; it is not a title but a deed. Israel was conscious that Yahweh was its king, king of the chosen people of the covenant. (p. 13)

Similarly, in Judges Yahweh was regarded as the ruler of Israel (Judges 8: 23) and in Kings Samuel rales against desires for an earthly king (1 Kings 8: 7; 10: 19; 12: 12). David's kingdom was established by God's favor (2 Kings 7: 12-16) so that the throne in Jerusalem became the "throne of the kingdom of the Lord over Israel" (1 Chron 28: 5; 29: 23; 2 Chron 9: 8). To the Israelite mind, Yahweh was truly king, and the human king only ruled in His name. A similar connection of royalty and divinity played a decisive role in the liturgical cycle of ancient Babylonian and Egyptian fertility cults in which the renewal of life was celebrated at the beginning of each year. In these rites the king represented the people and the dying and resurrecting god; residues of these ancient cultic practices had found root in Canaanite soil. But this ideology played no such role in the idea of kingship in Israel; neither in Israel nor Judah nor in Jerusalem was there any hint of divinity in the monarchy. God was king, but the king was not God.

God's throne was the ark of the covenant, a notion that survived the years in the desert (Num 10: 35ff), the shrine at Silo (1 Kings 4: 4), and the temple of Solomon (3 Kings 8: 6ff; 4 Kings 19: 14ff). The "tabernacle of the covenant" was a sort of royal residence, the place of God's dwelling among His people (Exod 25: 8; 40: 34-38; Num 14: 10). When David brought the ark to Jerusalem and ensconced it in the Holy of Holies, this "throne of Yahweh" within the temple stirred fantasies of the heavenly throne and court. As Schnackenburg (1963) comments:

> This is so peculiar and early a concept that we must regard it as an important and independent root of the many-branched concept of the *basileia*. In his great vision of his call to the prophetic office, Isaiah beholds the Lord "upon a throne high and elevated." Seraphim move unceasingly around him and chant: "Holy, holy, holy, the Lord God of hosts (*Yahweh Sabaoth*); all the earth is full of his glory." That is for him a vision of a king. "I have seen with my eyes the king, the Lord of hosts" (Is 6: 3, 5). Even if the prophet describes the heavenly sanctuary in terms of the earthly temple of Solomon, the expression "*Yahweh Sabaoth*" and the presence of the celestial beings suggest older conceptions. (pp. 17-18)

We are treated to a cosmic vision of the Lord on His heavenly throne and His dominion extending to the four corners of the globe. The prophet Micah appeals to a vision of the heavenly court when he prophecies the defeat of Israel to Ahab (1 Kings 22: 19). The heavenly court appears again in Job (1: 6; 2: 1), and in the hymn to the Lord of the storm, the psalmist proclaims, "The God of glory thunders. In his palace everything cries, "Glory!" Yahweh sat enthroned for the Flood, Yahweh sits enthroned as a king for ever" (Ps 29). And again in Ps 103, "Yahweh has fixed his throne in the heavens, his empire is over all" (103: 19). The kingship of Yahweh is universal and transcendent (Schnackenburg 1963). Ps 145 is a hymn of praise to Yahweh, the king, whose dominion stretches throughout the world and history. Yahweh is the king of kings who reigns over all

(1 Chron 29: 10ff) and brings salvation to his people (Ps 74: 12); he is both king and God (Ps 5: 2; 44: 4; 68: 24; 84: 3; 145: 1). The "throne ascent" psalms (Pss 47, 93, 96, 99) are liturgical paeans of joyful celebration of the majesty and glory of Yahweh, the king, who governs in heaven and comes to judge the world with mercy and justice, whose sovereignty is without limit.[1]

The same cosmic note is sounded in the annihilation of the armies of Gog in Ezekiel, where the wrath of God envelops the earth (Ezek 38: 18-23; 39: 1-7): "I will set my glory among the nations, and all nations shall see my judgment" (39: 21). In the Isaian Apocalypse (Is 24-27), God's earth-shaking judgment and final victory over all creation recognizes no limit to the divine hegemony. And in Daniel, the kingdoms of this world are to be replaced by the universal and eternal kingdom of God. As Schnackenburg (1963) comments on the Isaian Apocalypse:

> This prophetic vision contains all the fundamental elements that are crystallized to form the *basileia* concept of Jesus: the glad tidings of the dawn of God's kingly reign, its orientation towards eschatological salvation, a completely new era, in which God reigns to the delight of the redeemed; but also its universal scope which does not exclude the gentiles, the glad honour given to God by all and their free subjection to his holy will. This is a wholly pure, wholly religious notion of the kingdom of God that is not toned down or thinned out in mere images. It is God's eschatological reign that is to have absolute sway over mankind and creation. (p. 38)

Furthermore, adumbrations of later formulations can be identified in the prophetic literature as well. In Jeremiah, for example, despite his marked personalism and his recognition of personal worth and responsibility, we find the idea that it was not enough merely to be an Israelite to be included in God's kingdom; gentiles may also find a place in God's final kingdom. Yahweh is king not only of Israel, but of all the nations (Jer 10: 7, 10). Jeremiah proclaimed a profound individualism (Jer 31: 29-30), but almost in the same breath he proclaimed a new creation (Jer 31: 22) and a new covenant between God and men (Jer 31: 31-34). The same mingling of the strains of individualism and universalism are found in Ezekiel (Ez 18:2; 36: 26; 37: 26). In fact the trail of such thinking can be traced from the pre-exilic prophets through Jeremiah and Ezekiel to the apocalyptists. The universalist

---

1. See also Pss 2, 20, 24, 45, 48, 68, 72, 84, 87, 122, 132.

motif in Jeremiah may have influenced later apocalyptic writers quite directly (Stuhlmueller 1968).

Even though the expression "reign of Yahweh" does not occur frequently in the Old Testament, it served as a designation for the salvation that was expected at the end of time. It implies the acceptance of the will of Yahweh by all men, something that is impossible without knowledge of Him and acceptance of His revelation. The knowledge of Yahweh would bring about a radical change in mankind. Since men will not accept the will of Yahweh — any more than did Israel — all men will have to pass through a process of judgment which will be the ultimate saving act of Yahweh. This belief was at the root of the Israelite hope for salvation, so that further concepts of material plenitude and political hegemony must be subsumed under it.

The mind of Old Testament Israelites was fixed on this world and the hopes for material prosperity. The spiritual dimension was underemphasized, if not ignored. It is nonetheless clear that salvation involves a high degree of spiritual achievement, i.e., the total submission to the will of God. But the virtuous life was less convincing than the concrete changes that attended submission to Yahweh, namely the removal of obstacles to achievement of the good life — the danger of war and drought — dangers well-known to the inhabitants of Palestine. Once these threats to security were removed, salvation was assured. With the addition of freedom from debt, slavery, and oppression, the Israelite could rest content with life. Without the promise of an afterlife, the Israelite could not conceive of blessings in any but material terms, especially in terms that made sense to him in his basically agrarian experience.

The ideal of the good life also found expression in political terms. The only concept of a well-ordered society that the Israelite knew was that of a monarchy administered with wisdom and justice — the Solomonic model. Salvation meant the optimal form of social life that offered the maximal possibilities for security and well-being. The failure of monarchy because of the incompetence or venality of the rulers does not argue to the elimination of monarchical rule, but to the restoration of righteous and wise rulers. In the apocalyptic vision, Israel's rule was extended over the other nations of the world. Thus the reign of peace and justice would be extended to the entire world, but also such a circumstance would guarantee the safety and security of Israel herself who had long and bitterly suffered at the hands of rapacious and oppressive conquests by her more powerful neighbors. In the end, Yahweh will only reveal Himself to the nations through the mediation of Israel. Salvation was the salvation of Israel and, through her, of the other nations. As Schnackenburg (1963) comments:

> Although the idea of God's kingship may have various roots, these had grown together in the peak period of the Old Testament religion and formed a unified pattern. God rules over creation, over Israel and the nations, in varying degrees and in different ways. Full royal honours are his due but his power is not acknowledged everywhere or in equal degree. The rise and fall of history is a mirror which shows how individuals and peoples stand in relation to God's kingship. God may employ heathen monarchs such as Cyrus to realize his designs but he is always the Lord holding the reins by which he administers the world and directs the history of salvation (Is 44: 24-28; 45: 1-6). Its own destiny and the power of foreign kings and kingdoms compelled Israel to reflect continually on God's kingship. And all the time new branches were springing from the root stem of ancient beliefs. (p. 21)

In the *Book of Daniel*, particularly Dn 7, the prophecy foretells an eternal kingdom of God. The beneficiary of this promised kingdom will be first of all the Son of man, "coming on the clouds of heaven" (Dn 7: 13), on whom all the blessings of majesty and power are bestowed: "On him was conferred sovereignty, glory and kingship, and men of all peoples, nations and languages became his servants. His sovereignty is an eternal sovereignty which shall never pass away, nor will his empire ever be destroyed" (Dn 7: 14). But secondly, the blessings of the kingdom are received by the people of Israel: "And sovereignty and kingship and the splendors of all the kingdoms under heaven will be given to the people of the saints of the Most High" (Dn 7: 27). The intersection of the idea of the individual and the collectivity was a theme not only of Judaic messianism,[2] but would find its later expression in Christian thinking as well. As Cerfaux (1959) remarks on these texts: "Here we find already, in an extremely remarkable way, one of the characteristics which were to become dominant and even decisive in the Christian idea of the kingdom and the Church — the real identity of one and all: all is already one, all belongs to one, and yet all is realized in a collectivity, and all belongs to one people." (p. 284)

---

2. See the discussion of Jewish messianic ideas, particularly the theme of the Suffering Servant, in section II above.

Many of these expectations of the messianic kingdom were still extent in the time of Christ. As Schnackenburg (1963) notes:

> The old "national" eschatology represents the thoughts and senti-
> ments of the broad mass of the Jewish people in the two centuries
> prior to Christ and in the time of Jesus and the early Church. The
> idea that predominated, the usual and ordinary idea, was that God
> would send the Messiah-king, the "son of David," and through
> him restore the kingdom of Israel, with the ancient glory of the
> reunited tribes, liberated from foreign occupation and poverty but
> at the same time restored to a true service of God and a holy
> fulfillment of the Law. (pp. 41-42)

This belief was a passion for the Zealots, whose yearning for the coming of the kingship of God over Israel prompted them to armed insurrection against Israel's oppressors. The same expectations are found in the gospels, which reflect the Jewish background from which they arose. Similar sentiments are found in the apocryphal literature of the period: in the *Book of Jubilees*, the *Testaments of the Twelve Patriarchs*, the *Sybilline Books*, the *Syriac Apocalypse of Baruch*, and the *Fourth Book of Esdras*. And echoes of the same theme are contained in the Qumran literature, reflecting no doubt the aspirations of the Maccabean revolt and later the eschatological visions of the triumph of the sons of light over the sons of darkness.

The Kingdom in the Gospels

References to the kingdom or the kingdom of God occur primarily in the synoptics, to a certain extent in Paul, but only incidentally elsewhere. The expression plays no role in Acts, except for examples of the Pauline kerygma (Acts 14: 22; 19: 8; 28: 23). In the synoptics, Matthew tends to use the more Hebraic phrase, "kingdom of heaven," as equivalent to the "kingdom of God." The announcement in Mk 1: 15 that the kingdom of God is at hand is a statement of the essential message in Jesus' preaching and that the notion of the kingdom was a central concept in that message (Bonsirven 1963; Küng 1967).

The synoptic redactions present Jesus as announcing an imminent coming of the kingdom of God from the very beginning of his preaching mission (Mk 1: 15; Mt 4: 17; Lk 4: 43). There was a sense of urgency: "But as for that day or hour, nobody knows it, neither the angels of heaven, nor the Son; no one but the Father. Be on your guard, stay awake. because you never know when the time will come" (Mk 13: 32-33). In the baptismal scenario on the banks of the Jordan,

Jesus is declared to be the Lord's anointed, the one who is charged with bringing the kingdom to fulfillment. It is a statement of his unique vocation vis-à-vis the kingdom. The impression is reinforced by the accounts of the temptations, in which he rebuffs current messianic expectations (Mt 4: 1-11; Mk 1: 12-13; Lk 4: 1-13) and declares war on the kingdom of Satan. Through his mission the kingdom of God had become a present reality. But the present reality is compounded with adumbrations of a future fulfillment (Stanley 1968b). The choice of the title "Son of man" may have come from the original message and reflects the idea that Jesus has a unique role to play in the coming of the future kingdom of God. The title harkens back to Dn 7: 13-18 and indicates an awareness that there was to be a future phase to the kingdom, in addition to whatever present realization was achieved. His mission, in brief, was to establish a new order that would embody the religious ideals propounded on the pages of the Old Testament (Bonsirven 1963). This tension between the present and future embodiments of the promised kingdom pervade the New Testament considerations of the kingdom. Küng (1967) comments on this dual perspective:

> This perspective of a reign of God which has begun, but nevertheless belongs to the future, is not something that must be abandoned along with a mythological world-view; it is a *decisive perspective of the New Testament kerygma itself.* Just as we must distinguish between the protological myth and the protological event of the creation, so also we must distinguish between the eschatological myth and the eschatological event of consummation; for just as the Old Testament links its protological myths to history, so the New Testament links its eschatological myths to history. Not only Jesus' own message, but the whole of the New Testament, while concentrating on the idea of a reign of God which has already begun and on the necessity for decision here and now, maintains the perspective of future fulfillment and futurist eschatology — not just unreflectively, but in full consciousness of the significance of this perspective. (pp. 64-65)

Indeed, the force of these convictions may have powerfully shaped the Christian kerygma in stating the claim that with Jesus, God himself had entered human history in a unique and dramatic way. This conviction may underlie the various miracle stories. Thus not only Jesus' miracles, but also the miracles his disciples worked in his name attest to the continuing power of the reign of God that had been inaugurated by Christ.

Küng (1967) summarizes the salient points about the reign of God as it appears in the gospels in the following points:

(a) "The 'reign of God' to which Jesus refers does not mean the constant universal reign of God, which is a consequence of the creation and which Jesus in his message takes for granted on the basis of the Old Testament. It means the eschatological, that is fully realized, *final and absolute reign of God at the end of time, which as an event is now 'at hand'* (Mk 1: 15)" (pp. 47-48).[3]

(b) "The 'reign of God' is not in the preaching of Jesus, as it was in that of several rabbis — something that could be brought about or achieved by faithful adherence to the law; it appears as a powerful *sovereign act of God himself.*" (p. 48)

(c) "The 'reign of God' is not for Jesus — as it was for certain groups of the people, especially the zealots, who fought against the enemies of God in order to free their people from Roman domination — an earthly, national and religio-political theocracy. It is rather a purely religious kingdom" (p. 49).

(d) "The 'reign of God' is not for Jesus — as it was for many of his contemporaries, including the communities of Qumran — a judgment of vengeance on sinners and godless men: it is rather a *saving event for sinners.* Jesus' call to repentance does not invoke, as John the Baptist's did, God's anger, but God's mercy. The message of the reign of God is not one of threats and coming disaster, but of salvation, peace, joy." (p. 51)

(e) "Jesus' proclamation of the 'reign of God' does not involve a demand for men to follow a new, improved moral code. It demands rather a *radical decision for God.* The choice is clear: either God and his reign or the world and its reign." (p. 52)

In Mark, the idea of the kingdom is that of a heavenly reality that somehow enters human history. In a mysterious manner, it is already present in Jesus during his public life, but it will be established more definitively as a result of Christ's death and resurrection (Mk 9: 1). The fullness of its glorious realization remains for heaven (Mk 14: 25). In Mark's rendition, the secret of the kingdom is a kind of gnosis, revealed to the disciples but offered to outsiders only in parables (Mk 4: 11). The allegories for the kingdom are seeds (Mk 4: 26), the mus-

---

3. See also Schnackenburg (1963): "It must be insisted emphatically that the idea of God's reign in his [Jesus'] mouth referred always to God's eschatological kingship, though he was familiar with the notion of God's continuous government of the universe and took it for granted." (p. 81)

tard seed (Mk 4: 30-31), images of growth of that which is both present yet full of the promise of future fulfillment. The kingdom is equated with life (Mk 9: 43) or salvation (Mk 10: 26). The rendition here is also not without its eschatological emphases (Mk 12: 34; 14: 25).

In Matthew besides the shift to the "kingdom of heaven" phrase drawn from rabbinical usage, the evangelist's preoccupation is with describing the partial realization in an earthly reality of the kingdom in the form of the Christian community. There is also a distinction between the "kingdom of the Father" (Mt 13: 43; 26: 29) and the "kingdom of the Son of Man" (Mt 13: 41; 16: 28; 20: 21), identified with the church. The appeal to the return of the glorified Christ, inspired no doubt by Dn 7, suggests the linkage of the kingdom to the return of the messiah-son of man to the redeemed and faithful remnant of Israel. Matthew alone of the evangelists has John the Baptist proclaim the imminence of the kingdom (Mt 3: 2) and describes Jesus' message as the "good news of the Kingdom" (Mt 4: 23; 9: 35; 24: 14).

The substance of Matthew is in the five great discourses which formulate the realization of the kingdom of heaven in the earthly reality of the church. Stanley and Brown (1968) describe these discourses:

> The *first* of these, the Sermon on the Mount, presents Christianity as the perfect flowering of the OT [Old Testament] religious spirit: It might be entitled the Foundations of the Kingdom (Mt 5: 1 - 7: 29). The phrase "the Kingdom of heaven" occurs in Jesus' descriptions of the Christian ideal (Mt 5: 10, 19, 20; 7: 21). The *second* sermon, the Missionary Discourse (Mt 10: 5-42), depicting the dynamic character of the Church as the Kingdom on earth, represents the Twelve as proclaiming the imminence of the Kingdom of heaven, just as John and Jesus have done (Mt 10: 7). The mystery of the Church is the theme of Jesus' *third* instruction, a collection of his parables in which the phrase recurs like a litany (Mt 13: 11, 24, 31, 33, 44, 45, 47, 52). The Community Discourse (Mt 18: 1-35), the *fourth* sermon, is given in response to the disciples' query regarding "the greatest in the Kingdom of heaven" (Mt 18: 1), in which Jesus employs a little child as a living parable of the Christian spirit (Mt 18: 3, 4). The *fifth* and last instruction, Jesus' prophecy of the triumph of the Risen Christ upon the ruins of the Temple, concludes with three parables that discuss the various categories of membership in the Church. (p. 784)

The reign of God is clearly identified with the community of disciples, who achieve their connection with the kingdom through their attachment to Christ. Matthew does not think in terms of a Pauline mystical body or even of the imagery of the vine and its branches, but Jesus is present in his church even to the final consummation of the eschatological last day.

When we come to Luke, the influence of a divine reality in contemporary reality is a given. The theme is preached by Jesus (Lk 4: 43; 8: 1; 9: 11; 16: 16) and echoed by his disciples (Lk 9: 2, 60; 10: 9, 11). The kingdom theme applies to the nascent church: the eschatological utterances at the Last Supper ("I shall not eat this meat . . ." [Lk 22: 16] and "I shall not drink of the fruit of the vine . . ." [Lk 22: 18]) are connected to the coming of the kingdom of God, which seems associated in Luke's mind with the reality of the church (Stanley and Brown 1968). The eschatological and the realized motifs seem to stand side-by-side in Luke's rendition of the kingdom. This dual motif, the eschatological and the realized, are present in the fourth gospel as well, even though the importance of the theme recedes in John's perspective.

The emphasis on a realized eschatology dominates John's thinking. The idea of the coming of the Spirit in Jewish thought was a purely eschatological notion, but for John the outpouring of the Spirit has already occurred through the mission of Jesus, and salvation is now rather than in some far-off eschatological time. The expectations of an imminent parousia and the return of the conquering Christ pervaded New Testament thought from the primitive kerygma voiced in Acts (Acts 3: 12-26) until some of the latest New Testament writings (2 Pet 3: 1-13). In this John is no exception, but he seems to have followed that aspect of Paul's teaching that emphasized the mystery of salvation as present rather than as a matter of eschatological expectation. While the balance in John is tilted toward a realized eschatology, the futurist strain persists. As Küng notes: "In the fourth gospel, presentist eschatology is clearly much more important than elsewhere in the New Testament, and presentist and futurist eschatology is not combined in the same organic way as in Paul. . . . In John too . . . there are sayings which unequivocally point to the future and announce a final event to come on the "last day" . . . . But it is not so much an analysis of these passages in isolation as a view of the fourth gospel as a whole which provides the important evidence." (p. 65-66)

The Kingdom in Paul

Paul has been classified as a 1st century Jewish apocalypticist. In 1st-century Judaism, apocalyptic was intermingled with mystical strains, and Jewish mysticism was apocalyptic in its meditations on the meaning of the universe and in its anticipation of God's imminent judgment. The mystical and the apocalyptic were wedded in Paul; in fact, he is the only early Jewish mystic and apocalyptic writer whose works have come down to us (Segal 1990).

In Paul's view the kingdom is essentially the reign of the Father which is handed over to the Son until the final stage, when he will return it to the Father. Paul's perspective tends to be heavily eschatological (Phil 1: 1-11); the meaning of Christian life is cast in specifically eschatological terms — the destiny of Christian life in the Church is to triumph with Christ in the parousia. The kingdom of the Son (Col 1: 13) or of Christ (Eph 5: 5) tends to have a presentist emphasis, and the kingdom of the Father a more eschatological tone. Paul even refers once to the "kingdom of Christ and God" (Eph 5: 5), suggesting that they were synonymous or at least closely connected in his mind, since ultimately the Son would bring all things to the Father (1 Cor 15: 22-28). The kingdom is ultimately connected with the glory that is to come (Rom 1: 23; 1 Cor 15: 24). Sharing in the blessings of the kingdom meant entering into communion with God at the parousia. The faithful, the saved saints, will even come to share in God's power of judgment, even over the angels (1 Cor 6: 1-3). But already here on earth God has joined Christians to the kingdom of His beloved Son, and so conferred the promise of sharing in the inheritance of the saints who will join God in the triumph of light over darkness in the last days (Col 1: 12-13). Thus the kingdom of God is equivalent in meaning to eternal life (Rom 5: 21). But the kingdom of the Son is none other than the Church, since it alone possesses the sanctifying power of Christ (Cerfaux 1959).

All this is reminiscent of the kerygma of the church of Jerusalem, with the additional emphasis on the presence of the Spirit. The presence of the Spirit opens the way to eschatological expectations of the rewards of the kingdom and the realization of messianic promises. The seal of the Spirit is the pledge of Christian inheritance (Eph 1: 13-14; Gal 3: 14; 2 Cor 5: 5). The call to the kingdom requires a life of holiness in Christians as the appropriate response: ". . . appealing to you to live a life worthy of God, who is calling you to share the glory of his kingdom" (1 Thess 2: 13; see also 2 Thess 1: 11; 1 Thess 4: 7; 2 Thess 2: 13). Paul would even proclaim that the Christian had already entered into the earthly kingdom (1 Cor 4: 8). Paul even expected to be alive when the Lord returned (1 Thess 4: 13-18), fully expecting that the day was at hand (Rom 13: 11-12). But, as Schnackenburg

(1963) reminds us, ". . . the heavenly transcendent kingdom of Christ is not at the center of New Testament thinking and, when it does emerge, it continues to receive all its light, its colours and its strength from the awaited eschatological kingdom of Christ and God." (p. 321)

The apocalyptic themes have a strong place in Paul's thinking and writing. Paul's ecstatic and mystical experience links up with apocalyptic themes in the literature of Qumran. The recently recovered Angelic Liturgy, a pre-Christian treatise from no later than the 1st century, anticipates many of the features of later merkabah mysticism, even as it reflects characteristics of Jewish mysticism in the context of an apocalyptic community of the 1st century. As Segal (1990) notes, "In this general atmosphere, Paul is an important witness to the kind of experience that apocalyptic Jews were reporting and an important predecessor of merkabah mysticism." (p. 40)

Paul's apocalyptic leanings and his millennarian attitudes come most clearly to the fore in his letters to the church in Thessalonia — possibly the earliest of his epistles. He wrote, probably to gentile converts,

> We want you to be quite certain, brothers, about those who have died, to make sure that you do not grieve about them, like the other people who have no hope. We believe that Jesus died and rose again, and that it will be the same for those who have died in Jesus; God will bring them with him. We can tell you this from the Lord's own teaching, that any of us who are left alive until the Lord's coming will not have any advantage over those who have died. At the trumpet of God, the voice of the archangel will call out the command and the Lord himself will come down from heaven; those who have died in Christ will be the first to rise, and then those of us who are still alive will be taken up in the clouds, together with them, to meet the Lord in the air. So we shall stay with the Lord for ever. With such thoughts as these you should comfort one another. (1 Thess 4: 13-18)

The context for this vision was the opposition between the gentile mission preached by Paul and the Judaizing factions in the church. The Thessalonians were in danger from persecution by their neighbors, and the threat of death sets the stage for the martyrdom of the saints. These holy ones, who were faithful observers of God's commandments, will have their reward at the last trumpet when they shall rise again from the dead. The tradition is essentially Jewish (Dan 12: 2; 2 Macc 7) and appeals to traditional Jewish apocalyptic views. Those who had been their friends and even relatives would, after their conversion, become their enemies.

The apocalyptic imagery is drawn into the service of defining the new community of believers. The themes are vindication of the oppressed and persecuted Christians and condemnation of their persecutors and enemies (1 Thess 1: 7-10). Paul offers the promise and hope of salvation and heavenly reward for their suffering and martyrdom. The message carries with it the instillation of community values in the face of their alienation and isolation. The Christian belief system was subversive to both Judaic and pagan religious institutions: a small group of millennarian fanatics can pose a threat to the structure and integration of a society. This posed a focus of tension and conflict throughout the early history of Christianity (Segal 1990).

The Thessalonian community seems to have been a radical apocalyptic movement committed to the expectation of an imminent parousia and isolated from the surrounding world by hostility and suspicion. The Corinthian converts had been ostracized over the issue of eating meat sacrificed to idols, but the separation in Thessalonia was even more severe. The strains of Jewish apocalyptic belief came, no doubt, from Paul who refers to his fellow Christians as "the sons of light" and predicts the destruction of the sons of darkness (1 Thess 5: 1-5).

By the time of 2 Thessalonians, the persecutions have increased, so that Paul or one of his disciples can interpret the suffering of the community as the first indication that the wrath of God is about to fall upon the persecutors. But at the same time he cautions against false claims that the day of the Lord is at hand. This may well have been a reaction against millennarian beliefs that prophesied the imminent arrival of the final day. The writer of the letter insists on continuing the ordinary pattern of life, since only God knows the day of judgment. Segal (1990) offers a summary overview of these apocalyptic developments:

> The whole Thessalonian correspondence shows how originally Jewish apocalyptic ideas could be transmitted to a gentile Christian community. Apocalypticism, like the European millennialism it spawned, operates like social revolution, except that it concentrates on reforming the religious symbols of the society rather than the political order (insofar as they can be distinguished). The potential converts must first be disposed to interpret their lives in religious terms and then must feel that commitment to the new religious movement remedies some lack in their own lives or gives them some benefit that they do not already have. Otherwise, they will simply foment political rebellion. Apocalypticism

was endemic to Roman occupation, in Jewish as well as gentile lands. Jewish apocalypticism appealed to the disadvantaged members of gentile society and, as Paul clarifies in Corinthians and Romans, taught them to despise the conventional civic rites of the establishment in their town as idolatry. Active rebellion did not break out, but even passive resistance became dangerous when the Roman emperors of the second and third centuries demanded for themselves public civic rites as immortal gods on earth. . . . The persecutions that followed the failure of Christians and Jews to respect imperial wishes often evinced apocalyptic notions, pointing to an underlying broad dissatisfaction among the potential converts to Christianity and Judaism. (p. 165)

For Paul, then, the new people of God, the Christians, the church, became one body attached to Christ in a mystical union that brought with it spiritual gifts that were the foretaste and harbinger of the glory to come. These first fruits of the kingdom did not prevent the people of God from awaiting the glories of the parousia and hoping for the return of the messianic king. Cerfaux (1959) captures this tension in the Pauline vision:

> If the church at Jerusalem, the messianic community chosen by Jesus, had concentrated entirely on eschatology, and if Paul had suddenly plunged himself, and the whole Church with him, into the depths of Greek mysticism, there would have been a great disruption in the concepts of the Church. Paul would have renounced the idea which he had received from the primitive community. But on this subject the Jerusalem Christians, still bound up with the destiny of the first Israel, had their feet firmly on the ground and did not concentrate entirely on the end of time. Before Saint Paul, and much more vividly than he, they had seen in the resurrection of Christ and in the descent of the Holy Spirit, which was foretold for "the last days," the beginnings of the kingdom of God. For them, as for Paul, the divine gifts had come down upon the earth, and the kingdom of God was present in the power of the Spirit. Paul had only to build up the theory of a present participation in the divine gifts "in Christ Jesus." There was no need for him to borrow a pagan mysticism from the Greek world, for instance from Corinth, and to bring it into Christianity as a heterogeneous element breaking with the past. (pp. 208-209)

The Apocalypse

The *Apocalypse*, in its turn, presents an explicitly eschatological vision of the church. It is addressed to the church under the lash of persecution — the first oracle deals with the persecution from the Jews (Apoc 4: 1 - 11: 19), the second oracle then takes up the persecution under the Romans (Apoc 12: 1 - 21: 8). These are followed by the final eschatological and apocalyptic vision (Apoc 21: 9 - 22: 5). The final vision depicts the triumphant and glorious church under the imagery of the holy city, the new Jerusalem that descends from the heavens, the bride adorned for her wedding. The great assembly of the saints proclaiming the glory of God and the Lamb is the church in its final and glorious form (Dulles 1974). The two visions of the church — one imperfect and struggling in this world, the other glorious and triumphant in heaven — has crystallized in medieval theology into the distinction of the "church militant" and the "church triumphant."

The Apocalypse thus takes the form of the prophetic fulfillment of the ancient promises, but unlike Isaiah, Jeremiah and Ezekiel, who received their call from Yahweh, the writer of the Apocalypse receives his call from the glorious and risen Christ. It addresses a church undergoing a terrible affliction and ordeal (Feuillet 1968). But it offers no palliatives, no illusions of solace — rather a tale of endless suffering and mistreatment at the hands of the world. But if the diabolical beast slaughters Christians, it is not by force of arms that the armies of Christ will conquer but by following Christ's example who won the victory over Satan and his hordes by suffering and martyrdom.

Like apocalyptic writers of the past, the author of the Apocalypse will explain the present by an appeal to the future, specifically to the final vision that will make the present order understandable and give it meaning. The young church is threatened with extinction by the forces of evil, but the prophet declares that the suffering under the oppression of a totalitarian state fits into God's plan, leading to a final outcome in which good will triumph over evil. But that day of triumph lies in the distant future. Much will transpire before the day of triumph. As Feuillet (1968) comments,

> For that matter, all the events of chapters 12-20 (introduced by chapter 10), i.e., the persecution brought on by the Dragon and set in motion by the Beast come out of the sea, the plagues of the bowls, the punishment of Babylon, the victory of the Word of God over the Beast, the reign of Christ and of his witnesses throughout the symbolic thousand years, the final attack of Gog and Magog against the Church, — all this must come to pass before the blast of the last trumpet. (pp. 114-115)

Thus, in the ambiguity between a futurist and a realized eschatology, the writer of the Apocalypse states the futurist case, probably countering the denial of the parousia that would have followed in the wake of the destruction of Jerusalem. Christians of the time would have anticipated the onset of the messianic triumph after the day of wrath. But the prophet would have understood, better than others of his time, that the dawning of the parousia and the second coming of the Savior was a theological datum having nothing to do with chronology (Feuillet 1968).

While the second coming is envisioned by Paul in terms of the overthrow of cosmic spiritual powers, John puts the accent on the domination of worldly powers and kings by the risen and glorified Christ — the Christ of the parousia conquers the forces of Satan and the Antichrist, and his standard bears the title "King of Kings and Lord of Lords" (Apoc 19: 16). Schnackenburg (1963) comments:

> The prominence given to the earthly-political powers reflects the cruel experience of early Christianity which had come into contact with the pagan State, with Rome and its vassal kingdoms, a State which in emperor-worship assumed divine honours and became an enemy of God. Christian faith defies this to its face: Jesus is the ruler of all rulers, and so the final consequences of Christ's rule are drawn even for the political realm. But these Christians, persecuted for their faith and exposed to further persecutions are conscious of their dignity; they know they are loved and redeemed by their Lord, who still exercises his rule of the world in a hidden way in heaven; and even more, that they have been elevated to the rank of kings and priests (Apoc 1: 5ff). (p. 330)

The Kingdom and the Church

The progressive evolution of thinking about the kingdom of God gradually distilled the eschatological dreams and apocalyptic visions into a doctrine of the nature of the Christian church and its place in the divine economy of salvation. The doctrine of ecclesiology forms the final transformation of these ideas into a conception of the church, its nature, function, and final destiny. A brief review of some of these views of the church will fill out the picture of the evolution and metamorphosis of the originating eschatological and apocalyptic perspectives.

One view of the church makes a strong distinction between the kingdom of God in its terrestrial form and the kingdom of God as an eschatological reality. Küng (1967) argues that the church is not the kingdom of God, nor does it build the kingdom or work toward its realization. It is only the herald of the reign of God. Its mission is to spread the word of God — the rest is up to God. But like Barth, the discontinuity may be overstated, and the understanding of the church too narrow (Dulles 1974). As Dulles (1974) notes regarding the models of the church:

> In the institutional models, the official Church teaches, sanctifies, and rules with the authority of Christ. In the communion models, the Church is viewed as God's People or Christ's Body, growing into the final perfection of the Kingdom. In the sacramental ecclesiologies, the Church is understood as the visible manifestation of the grace of Christ in human community. Finally, in the herald models, the Church takes on an authoritarian role, proclaiming the gospel as a divine message to which the world must humbly listen. (p. 83)

The church may also have a role to play in the betterment of mankind. This would involve the model of the church as servant. The church in this view exists not for its own sake, but for the sake of the kingdom; its purpose is to prepare the world for the coming of the kingdom. In Küng's view, the church belongs to the present, whereas the kingdom belongs to the eschatological future. The former is the work of man, the latter of God. Pannenberg (1969) likewise argues that the church merely points to the kingdom which lies beyond it. But Dulles counters that to set the church over against the kingdom and to separate them so decisively obscures and distorts the biblical concept of both church and kingdom (Dulles 1974).

The servant motif would seem to fix the church in a this-worldly setting, but Moltmann (1967), for example, articulates this theme in an eschatological perspective. He writes:

> The Christian Church is not to serve mankind in order that this world may remain what it is, or may be preserved in the state in which it is, but in order that it may transform itself and become what it is promised to be. For this reason, "Church for the world" can mean nothing else but "Church for the kingdom of God" and the renewing of the world. This means in practice that Christianity takes up mankind — or to put it concretely, the Church takes up the society with which it lives — into its own horizon of expectation of the eschatological fulfillment of justice, life, humanity, and sociability, and communicates in its own decisions in history its openness and readiness for this future and its elasticity towards it. (pp. 327-328)

The viewpoints on the presence of the kingdom in the present, and therefore in the church, as opposed to a more eschatological perspective, run the gamut as varied as in the biblical sources. Some approaches focus their emphasis on a single-time perspective — present or future. In Schweitzer's (1914) "consistent eschatology," Jesus thought he was the messiah and was convinced that the realization of the kingdom was close at hand in the immediate future. He viewed it as a universal catastrophe as dictated by Jewish apocalyptic.[4] Similarly, Bultmann's (1963) "existential eschatology" makes Jesus only the proclaimer of the kingdom that lies beyond human power. The eschatological and apocalyptic expectations must be expunged ("demythologized"), meaning that the reign of God be understood as an existential moment in the future eschatological time brought about by divine action in each individual. Then again, as the prime example of the present timeframe, the "realized eschatology" proposed by Dodd (1935), writing in opposition to the views of Weiss and Schweitzer, would mean that in Jesus the *eschaton* had entered history so that the kingdom of God had become a present reality — for Jesus, as also for Christians of all ages.[5] Stanley and Brown (1968) summarize this view as follows:

> The Messiah has come, the Kingdom of God is present in history, the Day of the Lord is henceforth an actuality. Since eschatology has been realized by the advent of Jesus, nothing more is to be looked for in history. Christ the Light, through his death and resurrection, confronts each individual, provoking a judgment (*krisis*), the only judgment in any proper sense. It is carried to successive generations by the Church's preaching and by the Eucharist, which evokes a personal experience of Jesus' coming in humility and glory. In Dodd's opinion, the final judgment and the parousia constitute "the least inadequate myth of the goal of history." For while Jesus himself preached a realized eschatology, the transition from time to eternity was not as natural for his followers as for Jesus himself; consequently they misunderstood his meaning, envisaging the Kingdom as incomplete at present, and hence for the most part still to come in the future. This literalistic interpretation of what was merely symbolic in Jesus' doc-

---

4. Other theologians espousing similar views include Johannes Weiss (1892), Rosemary Ruether (1972), and Jürgen Moltmann (1967). Moltmann refers to a "transcendental eschatology."

5. J.A.T. Robinson (1958) would hold a similar view, but he dubs it an "inaugurated eschatology" rather than "realized."

trine was gradually corrected by Paul and John, who introduced realized eschatology into NT [New Testament] theology. John's work is the supreme achievement of this development, since he has adopted the correct perspective, that of Jesus himself. (p. 778)

Other exegetes, both Protestant (Cullman 1964) and Catholic (Schnackenburg 1963), have proposed a "salvation-historical eschatology" that holds a middle ground according to which the kingdom indeed came with Jesus but still awaits its eschatological fulfillment.

Needless to say, all these positions can be supported by many and weighty biblical texts. What seems to emerge from the debate is the conclusion that it is not possible to sustain any one position to the exclusion of others. The uncertainty and ambiguity lie in the texts themselves. Küng (1967) offers a summary of the complexity in the original kerygma preached by Jesus:

> His preaching is therefore not merely a variant on later Judaic apocalyptics, pointing forward to future events at the end of time. On the other hand, as we have seen, it is not just one way of interpreting the present time, completely separate from any of the contemporary apocalyptic ideas, proclaiming simply the present fulfillment of apocalyptic expectations. Jesus' preaching is situated between the two poles of "not yet" and "but already," and represents therefore a futurist-presentist eschatology. At the same time, these two poles should not be confused with two *periods* of preaching (first presentist and then futurist or *vice versa*), for the texts show no development in Jesus' eschatological thinking. On the contrary, many passages combine presentist and futurist perspectives (Mk 8: 38; Mt 19: 28; Lk 12: 31: man decides now, God judges then). The reign of God is a future which confronts us as present. Jesus' preaching of the reign of God is at once an expectation of the future and a proclamation of the present. (p. 59)

In the face of this welter of theological opinions regarding the nature and eschatological relevance of the church, one is left with multiple perspectives that present varicolored refractions of the eschatological light that shines behind them. Dulles (1974) brings these threads together from the study of disparate models of the church and so provides an accessible formulation of contemporary theology on this question. He writes:

> Having studied these various schools of thought, the reader will no doubt wish to form some opinion as to how the Church really is related to the eschaton, the ultimate Kingdom of God. For my part, I do not feel compelled to choose among the answers suggested by each of our five models. One can accept certain points

from each of them. From the first model [church as institution] I would appropriate the idea that the Church should help its own members work out their salvation by giving them guidance, admonition, comfort, and every kind of pastoral and sacramental assistance. From the second model [church as mystical communion], I would take over the idea that the Church is not a mere means of grace, but a place where grace is realized and lived even here on earth. The community of grace is an anticipation of the final Kingdom. From the third model [church as sacrament], I would adopt the view that the Church is to be, here on earth, a sign or representative of the salvation to which we look forward — a sign that is admittedly somewhat ambiguous in this earthly life, but one that promises to become clear and unequivocal when the final Kingdom arrives. From the fourth model [church as herald] I would derive the ideas that the Church proclaims the coming of the Kingdom in Christ, and that the proclamation itself is an eschatological event, in which God's saving and judging power is already at work. From the fifth model [church as servant], finally, I would accept the thesis that the Church has the task of introducing the values of the Kingdom into the whole of human society, and thus of preparing the world, insofar as human effort can, for the final transformation when God will establish the new heavens and the new earth.

The final coming of the Kingdom, I believe, will be the work of God, dependent on his initiative. But it seems likely that, as Rahner suggests, the parousia will not occur until human effort "has gone to its very limits and so is burst open by salvation from above by developing its own powers." The coming of the Kingdom will not be the destruction but the fulfillment of the Church. More than this, it will be the future of the world, insofar as God's gracious power is at work far beyond the horizons of the institutional Church. The final consummation will transcend the dichotomy between Church and world. The glorious, triumphant Church will be indivisibly united with the renewed cosmos, "the new heavens and the new earth" foreseen by the prophets. And the triumph will not be that of a Church resting on its own laurels, but that of Christ who triumphs in his Church in spite of the weakness and sinfulness of men. (pp. 113-114)

Evolution of the Millennarian Kingdom

The notion of the kingdom of God is intertwined with the parallel concepts of the messiah and the millennarian dream. The above discussion traces the evolution of the idea from its place in Hebrew lore regarding the kingdom associated with the house of David. The messianic expectations and the millennarian visions were cast around the hope that Israel would one day see the restoration of the Davidic monarchy in all its worldly glory and power — but magnified, enhanced, glorified and idealized as a result of the terrifying and powerful intervention of Yahweh in human history, destroying his enemies — who were also the enemies of Israel — and erecting his definitive and final kingdom that was to be sustained by his divine power and benevolence. That vision was gradually tempered in the fires of defeat, oppression and seemingly endless suffering and hardship. The strains of spiritual transformation gradually entered the picture and opened the possibility that the promised kingdom was not simply one of worldly power and magnificence, but that it might take place beyond this world and beyond the limits of human history.

The thrust of this dynamic came to fruition in the revolution started by the preaching of Jesus, who announced that the kingdom was *now*. The kingdom of God was no longer to be sought in some unknown and remote future eschatological realm, but it was to be lived and experienced in the present moment. But this good news, this gospel, was seed cast on reluctant ground. Those who heard this word of the Lord were steeped in the ancient traditions of Judaic belief and especially in the attitudes and expectations centering on the kingdom of God that was to come. The subsequent evolution of the doctrine of the kingdom was shaped by the post-resurrection faith of the early church which was increasingly influenced by religious and philosophical currents extant in the Mediterranean culture of the time. The doctrinal tensions that arose between the Judaic forces in the church and the hellenizing influences that came from the widened cultural matrix in which the growing church found itself set off a dialectic within the church that profoundly modified the understanding of the nature of the church as well as a more profound view of Christ and his role in relation to the kingdom. This involved the struggle over the higher christology that found its most telling expression in the Johannine community and tradition, and its contention with the lower christology that found acceptance in much of the rest of the church (Meissner, in process). These in-house debates came near to tearing the fabric of the newly spun Christian robe apart. Compounding the difficulties, but also in time providing a common enemy against which the contending forces in the church could align themselves, there were the numerous heretical sects and cultic expressions that arose on the periphery of the orthodox church and gradually separated from the body of the church to become oppositional forces. The history of the rise and evolution of gnosticism is an important part of this story.

The notion of the kingdom at the same time underwent a modification that drew it away from its Judaic roots, but not completely. Parallel to the development and clarification of the idea of a spiritual messiah who was raised to the level of the divine, particularly after his resurrection and ascension, the idea of the kingdom became spiritualized. He himself had clearly stated that his kingdom was not of this world. It was at this juncture, then, that the eschatological dynamic reasserted itself. If the kingdom was not of this world, and if the hoped-for parousia was not to take place in any imminent time, the only resort was a return to the eschatological vision — but now displaced beyond time and beyond this world to a heavenly kingdom beyond death. But this displacement could not easily shake itself loose from its Judaic roots. As the understanding of the kingdom had evolved, the suggestions that the kingdom was in some sense present and active in the lives and hearts of men could not be dispelled. It was inherent in some sense in the preaching of Christ himself as preserved in the traditions and gospels. The eschatological resolution could carry the full weight of the revelation.

Schnackenburg (1963) summarizes this development in the following terms:

> This idea of the rule of Christ and God is expressed differently by the other theologians of the early Church. They speak at times of the heavenly, that is transcendent, kingdom of Christ, without, however, losing their eschatological vision. The future kingdom of glory is represented in various images and awaited with varying degrees of vigour and urgency. Frequently the presence of Christ comes to the fore, in which all salvation consists and in which his gifts and saving graces are received, as in John's theology. At other times, the emphasis is rather on yearning for his Parousia and the perfect kingdom. Yet the early Church is always conscious that beneath Christ's gracious rule it is still on the way, that it is the pilgrim people of God (Hebrews), "strangers and sojourners" in this world (1 Peter), still oppressed and persecuted, yet certain of its hope (Apocalypse). It is highly probable that the Apocalypse, the prophetic work of the New Testament, does not envisage an interim eschatological kingdom (the "kingdom of a thousand years," Apoc. 20: 1-6), similar to the Messianic kingdom which according to some Jews was to precede the future aeon. The forms in which the idea is expressed vary but the basic notion remains the same: it is now the era of Christ's hidden rule which

in its turn is to prepare the way for and bring about the manifestation of the perfect cosmic kingdom of God. (pp. 352-353)

The solution, then, came in the emerging doctrine of the church which came to be seen as the worldly manifestation of the kingdom here on earth. If the church in this world did not satisfy the glorious expectations of the apocalyptic visions of future glory, it was a harbinger of that future triumph, so that by faithful membership in the church believers were assured of a share in the promised eschatological glory. The apostles and the theologians who have followed in their wake have evolved a rich and profound doctrine on the nature of the church and its place in the economy of salvation. My purpose in tracing this evolution in doctrine is to argue that inherent in the whole process, from beginning to end, there is an underlying stratum of desire, wish, fantasy, and hopeful expectation that taps in on the deepest levels of human motivation and dynamic power. In this sense, the sophisticated and highly abstract superstructure of the Christian theology of the church is embedded in and draws its motivational power from the same rudimentary foundation as the most ancient visions of eschatological fulfillment and apocalyptic triumph. The "dreams and visions" to which Peter appealed on the day of Pentecost have not left us, but persist with the same intensity of desire and hope as on that day.

Medieval Millennarianism

Introduction

The millennial vision gradually came into disrepute as the process of theological reflection came to view the apocalyptic utterances of the Book of Revelation more in allegorical and metaphorical terms. The allegorical millennialism of Augustine became the standard view, and apocalyptic interpretations were pushed to the background; the Augustinian view remained dominant until the Reformation. But that more sensible and reasonable assessment could not long withstand the impulses to millennial fulfillment that seem somehow endemic to the human condition. In the medieval period, these insatiable desires seem to have risen to a new crescendo, largely in the form of radical or dissident movements, possibly impelled by socioeconomic and cultural forces that drove men to look for the fulfillment of profound desires in the face of deprivation, hopelessness, and death. As Eliade (1985) notes, it was "also the age of an exceptional proliferation of ascetic and eschatological movements, for the most part on the margins of orthodoxy, or frankly heterodoxy." (p. 97)

The approach of the year 1000 became a focus of millennarian hopes. The belief was popular and fairly widespread that the millennium would be inaugurated in that year and was to be followed by the glorious reign of Christ. The threats to European civilization from the Huns, Saracens, and Turks undoubtedly fed basic anxieties and hopes. In the heavily populated regions of northern France, the Low Countries and the valley of the Rhine, problems attendant on overpopulation, the rise of mercantile capitalism, and developments in the technology of agriculture led to the emergence of a class of unskilled laborers who had neither the skill nor the training to find a place in an increasingly competitive society. And not to be underestimated among the devastating influences of the age, the Black Death played out its inexorable role on the stage of history. The smell of death permeated every corner of these troubled centuries and added to the burden of desperation.

As their economic and existential conditions worsened and became more desperate, these people became ever more susceptible to the eschatological fantasies and blandishments of millennarian prophets claiming to be divinely inspired saviors and promising instant or imminent gratification of chiliastic expectations. As Cohn (1970b) observes:

> The world of millennarian exaltation and the world of social unrest, then, did not coincide but did overlap. It often happened that certain segments of the poor were captured by some millennarian prophet. Then the usual desire of the poor to improve the material conditions of their lives became transfused with fantasies of a world reborn into innocence through a final, apocalyptic massacre. The evil ones — variously identified with the Jews, the clergy or the rich — were to be exterminated; after which the Saints — i.e., the poor in question — would set up their kingdom, a realm without suffering or sin. Inspired by such fantasies, numbers of poor folk embarked on enterprises which were quite different from the usual revolts of peasants or artisans, with local, limited aims. (pp. 14-15)

The central fantasy of revolutionary eschatology is of a world dominated by evil forces of demonic and unlimited destructiveness. These forces will inflict untold suffering on innocent victims until the breaking point of tolerance is reached and the Saints of God will rise up against them and overthrow them. Then the oppressed will inherit the earth and establish their own dominion of the world, a kingdom superseding all others and having no successors.

Millennial Visions

It was not long before the prophets of the millennium began to appear on the medieval stage. One of the earliest expressions of this dynamic came in the form of Crusades to liberate the Holy Land from the Turks, especially those involving the common people. Preachers of the crusades played on the popular substratum of belief that the poor and dispossessed had a special divinely sanctioned mission to set Palestine free from the grip of the infidel as a reflection of the role of the elect in the millennium. As Thrupp (1970) notes: " . . . some surviving elements of older Christian millennialism had drawn new life from association with the Sybilline prophetic tradition. Prophecy could cast a messianic aura about any figure — king, emperor, or self-appointed leader" (p. 20).

The 12th century saw the appearance of urban millennial sects, at first in the cities of France and Italy. Many of these doctrines carried a gnostic cast, possibly reintroduced to the West in the 12th century, that transformed the millennial vision into a belief in the perfectibility of man. Other millennial inspirations took a more militant and revolutionary turn. Among these can be counted the advent of Tanchelm, who appeared in Antwerp to announce that he was God. He quickly developed a rabid following, and only after a series of massacres was he apprehended and executed. Within a generation, another millennarian prophet, Budo de Stella, arose in Brittany and rallied large numbers of peasants to his cause by representing himself as the Son of God who had come to judge the living and the dead. Both these prophets of the age-to-come found the Church an implacable adversary to their millennial dreams, and so the Church became the Antichrist.

Joachim di Fiore

In this period also came one Joachim di Fiore, who brought the montanist vision of the third age of the spirit[1] to life in all its millennial glory — a vision that has had its reverberations through subsequent history, even so far as to extend its mythology to the Communist ideal of a classless society and to the Nazi fantasy of a glorious Third Reich that was to endure for a thousand years (Manuel and Manuel 1979). The good abbot claimed to have received a special revelation on Mt. Tabor in the Holy Land, in which the secret meaning of the Old and New Testaments had been granted him, especially the interpretation of the cryptic and mysterious Apocalypse.

The new prophet's message fell on fertile ground. Joachim had forecast the dawning of a third and last age of the world, the age of the Holy Spirit, an era of peace and love that was to occur in 1260.. The first age had been that of the Old Testament and the Father, extending from Adam to Christ, and marked by fear and the authority of the law;

---

1. For discussion of montanism, see chapter 11 above.

the second era, governed by the Son, belonged to the New Testament and the Church sanctified in faith and grace, covering the period from the time of Christ till the present. The third new age, under the guidance of the Holy Spirit, would abrogate and surpass the old Christian dispensation, much as the Christian era had replaced the Old Testament. This would inaugurate the millennium in which Jews, Moslems, and all the heathen would be converted to Christianity. To prepare for the new age, the clergy of the present Church would have to be massacred. 1260 came and went, and the date for the millennial transformation had to be postponed repeatedly. The Joachite doctrine lived on, nonetheless, profoundly influencing subsequent millennarian movements — the Fratricelli, the Beghards and Beguines — and even extending to the Reformation and beyond (Cohn 1970b; Eliade 1985).

The Emperor of the Last Days

The 13th century weighed in with the legend of the "Emperor of the Last Days" that had arisen in Sibylline prophecies. There was a series of royal claimants to this exalted title, not the least of whom was Frederick II Hohenstaufen, who never in fact denied his claim to divinity. Frederick would have known Joachim as a boy, since the aged abbot had been his mother's confessor. The mantle of messianic expectation fell on his handsome head and broad shoulders. When he assumed the role of emperor, he had vowed to lead a crusade to deliver the Holy Land from the infidels. Various popes had urged, scolded and threatened him to fulfill this obligation. His second wife brought with her the crown of Jerusalem as a dowry, and nothing less would do than he set his face toward the east and lead the promised crusade. This he did in 1227 — an ill-fated escapade that was doomed by the ravaging plague. The great fleet he had assembled never reached the Holy Land; and for his failure to fulfill his promise, Pope Gregory IX excommunicated him.

But Frederick was determined to complete his mission, and again sailed for the Holy Land. But rather than bathe the country in infidel blood, he entered into friendly negotiations with the Sultan and came away with his right to claim the kingship of Jerusalem intact. In the Church of the Holy Sepulcher he placed the crown on his own head, a shattering of centuries-long precedent that equivalently claimed that he was subordinate to God alone, and not to the Pope. Pope Gregory's efforts to overthrow the imperial power, in the absence of the emperor, were thwarted by the emperor's triumphant return, a return most welcome to the principalities that squirmed under the irksome papal power, especially in Germany, Frederick's own preserve (Chamberlin 1975).

When Frederick died in 1250, all Europe was thrown into turmoil. Joachim had prophesied a long reign during which the papacy would be reduced to humble status. But the emperor's death was far too soon, and the Pope was triumphant. The Joachites had seen Frederick as the instrument for realization of the predicted last age, and so had to resort to juggling the dates for the great dispensation. It was not long before they stumbled on the legend that he was not dead, but only absent as he had been before, and would return as the conquering messiah to establish the millennial kingdom and the last age of the spirit proclaimed by Joachim (Chamberlin, 1975) — another rendition of the theme of the "occultation of the messiah" or the second coming.

Flagellants

As the 14th century dawned, new millennarian visions came into view. Prominent among these were the Flagellants, a new group of chiliastic enthusiasts that arose originally in the 13th century in the form of bands of men marching in procession through the towns of Italy. There was a particularly dramatic upsurge in this penitential exercise in 1260, the apocalyptic year of Joachite prophecy. This was followed quickly by ecclesiastical condemnation. The movement resurfaced again about 1348 in the face of the ravages of the Black Death in parts of Germany. Konrad Schmid declared himself to be the messiah of eschatological prophecies, and preached that the end of the world was imminent and that self-flagellation was required to prepare for the millennium. He required of his followers total submission to himself as the one true messiah, and taught that only by complete dependence and subservience to him could they achieve salvation. Thus would they become the bearers of a new dispensation, one higher and holier than the Christian dispensation.

The longing among the German masses for the millennial kingdom of the saints was intense. The minds of these Flagellants were filled with millennarian fantasies and desires. All existing orders of monks and friars would be done away with, to be replaced by a new order of unique holiness — namely themselves. The element of identification with Christ played a powerful role: they called themselves the Brethren of the Cross, and some even claimed that Christ had appeared to them to order them to go forth and scourge themselves, and even further that their suffering had the same redemptive value as the torments of the Savior (Cohn 1970b).

The German sects were virulently anticlerical and rejected the authority of Rome. In time the movement turned into a mass messianic delusion that cast itself in implacable opposition to the Church. The flagellant view was that they could achieve salvation by their own merits without benefit of church or clergy, since participation in their scourging orgies itself absolved them of all sin. They denied all ecclesiastic authority, denied that the Eucharist had any value or meaning and refused to reverence it. They thought themselves superior to church and clergy because they had been taught directly by the Holy Spirit. Any priest who dared contradict them should be dragged from the pulpit and burnt at the stake. Interestingly, the Jews shared with the Roman clergy the odium of these cultists, because they were thought to be responsible for the plague deaths. Large scale massacres of Jews took place in 1348-9, until only a few scattered Jews remained in Germany or the Low Countries (Cohn 1970b). These Germanic versions of the sect were also duly condemned by papal bull in 1349, a move prompted both by the threat to the Church authority and by the Flagellants flaunting of secular authority. These secular authorities lost no time in suppressing the movement and exterminating its members with considerable vigor.

The Free Spirit

The Flagellant movement was associated with the heretical Brethren of the Free Spirit, a neoplatonic cult originated in the 13th century by a theologian at the University of Paris, one Amaury, although its mystical and heretical roots may reach further back to the 11th century. They rested their claims on nothing more than their own subjective experience, rejecting the Church and its teachings as an obstacle to salvation. In a sense they resurrected the Joachite vision of the third age of man that looked forward to a community of perfect men who lived in complete satisfaction and harmony under the guidance of the Holy Spirit — and so had no need of church or state. They saw themselves as possessed of a higher degree of perfection that allowed them to reject all authority and all moral norms. The perfected men of the Joachites were ascetics, but for the Free Spirit they became moral anarchists. This gave them the privilege and right to disregard all norms and to do whatever they might forbid. The result was flagrant antinomianism and promiscuity in principle. Eroticism and free love became the hallmarks of spiritual emancipation. As Cohn (1970b) comments, "What distinguished the adepts of the Free Spirit from all other medieval sectarians was, precisely, their total amoralism. For them the proof of salvation was to know nothing of conscience or remorse." (p. 177) The doctrine carries a familiar ring that could be heard in many of the gnostic heresies of the 2nd and 3rd centuries.[2] The Amaurians thought themselves to be the reincarnated Christ whose mission it was to preach the coming of the millennium in which they would realize the fullness of the Holy Spirit.

The doctrine of the Free Spirit had strong pantheistic overtones. They espoused a Plotinian view that God was in all created things, and that the aim of human existence was to reunite the divine in man with the divine source of all being so that ultimately all would be in God and God in all. The echoes of gnostic themes are heard throughout. As Cohn (1970b) observes:

> To have the Holy Spirit incarnated in oneself and to receive the revelation which that brought — that was to rise from the dead and to possess heaven. A man who had knowledge of the God within himself carried his own heaven about with him. One had only to recognize one's own divinity and one was resurrected as a Spiritual, a denizen of heaven on earth. To be ignorant of one's own divinity, on the other hand, was mortal sin, indeed it was the only sin. That was the meaning of hell; and that too was something which one carried with one in this life. (p. 173)

The highest privileges were reserved for themselves. Humanity was divided between the "crude" and the "subtle" in spirit — the crude were absorbed into God only after death, but the subtle (i.e., the Brethren) were already absorbed into God in this life. Cohn (1970a) comments on the social consequences of the Free Spirit movement:

> But it was certain adepts of the Free Spirit who, towards the end of the fourteenth century, first tried to call the egalitarian State of Nature out of the depths of the past and to present it as an attainable ideal. In doing so they provided the basis for a new form of millennarianism. The Millennium could now be imagined as a recreation of that lost Golden Age which had known nothing of social classes or of private property. During the great social upheavals which accompanied the close of the Middle Ages, various extremist groups were inspired by the conviction that at any mo-

---

2. See the discussion of gnosticism and associated attitudes toward morality and particularly sexuality in Meissner (in process).

ment the egalitarian, communistic Millennium would be established by the direct intervention of God. (p. 37)

And a further comment can be added from Chamberlin (1975):

The old pattern of faith was breaking up in Europe, and some of its fragments were being used to form most bizarre mosaics. The new beliefs were unconsciously based on social protest, but it was impossible to shake off overnight the habits of thought formed over generations, and protest continued to take religious form. Belief in a specific Antichrist or Messiah might be on the wane, but belief in the Millennium and an earthly paradise grew correspondingly stronger as the passionate desire spread for a reformed society. As the Empire itself began to pass into history and the continent broke down into its racial components, so nationalism arose and took on the prevalent religious covering. (p. 60)

By the dawn of the 14th century, the movement had become less conspicuous but continued to flourish in the shadows. As Cohn (1970b) observed, "The Millennium of the Free Spirit had become an invisible empire, held together by the emotional bonds — which of course were often erotic bonds — between men and women." (p. 162)

The Alumbrados

Echoes of the doctrine of the Free Spirit would be heard through several more centuries. One interesting derivative of the ideology of the Free Spirit was the recurrence of the same themes in the *Alumbrados* of Spain in the 15th century.[3] These ideas probably found their way onto the Spanish peninsula by way of contacts with the Netherlands and Italy. Among the Dutch, strongly pietistic strains of spirituality had developed, stressing prayer and mystical experience as opposed to external and ceremonial expressions of devotion. In Florence, Savonarola's visionary and apocalyptic message caught the fancy of some of the Spanish Franciscans who listened to his preaching. Both strains found their sympathetic adherents in Spain, especially among devout women (*beatas*) and Franciscans of *converso* backgrounds.[4]

---

3. It was this heretical movement that gave Ignatius of Loyola such difficulty as he strove to promote his own spiritual views in the *Spiritual Exercises*. See Dudon (1949), Dalmases (1985), Bangert (1986), and Meissner (1992a).

4. The *conversos* were converted Jews who had adopted the Christian religion in the face of threatened persecution and expulsion — also known as *marranos*. The role of the *marranos* in the development of kabbalism is discussed in section IV above.

By the 16th century, the movement had begun to take shape. The Franciscan nun Isabel de la Cruz took the lead in organizing centers of devotion in various cities, including Alcala and Toledo. The *Alumbrados* gradually abandoned the visionary emphasis of Savonarola in favor of a more mystical passivism, emphasizing direct communion of the soul with God by a process of inner purification and complete subjection to the will of God. The rapid spread of this brand of mysticism came to attention of the Inquisition, then enjoying new vigor under the protection of Cardinal Cisneros, the Inquisitor General and Regent of Castile. Nor was the Inquisition slow to exercise its newfound powers. The *Alumbrados* were cast under the same veil of suspicion as Lutherans. The charge was false, but was apparently based on the Lutheran emphasis on faith without works (Kagan 1990).

Despite protests regarding the abuse of power by the Inquisition, the Lutheran peril was enough to persuade Charles V to leave the Holy Office intact. Ideas as to what Lutheranism was or who might be a Lutheran were none too clear in the minds of the Inquisitors, but this only made them more zealous to carry out their mission. Isabel was arrested for heresy in 1524 and, in the following years, 48 of the Illuminist propositions were formally condemned as heretical. The Inquisition cast a wide net of suspicion, wide enough to catch the then-wandering pilgrim-preacher Iñigo de Loyola in its coils in 1526 and again in 1527. The movement was thus effectively suppressed, at least in Spain (Elliott 1977).

Beghards and Beguines

By the end of the 13th century, the movement of the Free Spirit began to spread rapidly, largely through the efforts of the Beghards and Beguines. These were groups of mendicants, counterparts of the mendicant orders who arose in northern regions (Flanders, the Netherlands, Germany) and ranged through the towns begging for alms for the poor. Their spirituality emphasized Christlike poverty and humility, and they led lives of harsh asceticism and evangelical poverty reminiscent of the religious ideal of the Waldensians (Eliade 1985). When the neophyte had achieved a sufficient level of spiritual discipline and self-mortification, he advanced to a level of spiritual liberty in which he became one with God. This spiritual freedom released him from all restraints, rules, and obligations, freeing him to indulge all impulses: he could steal or have intercourse with anyone as he wished (Kaminsky 1970). These holy beggars were contemptuous of monks and friars, frequently disrupted church services, preached without authorization, and resisted ecclesiastical discipline. Their numbers included many of the Brethren of the Free Spirit.

The movement included many women known as Beguines, corresponding to their masculine counterparts the Beghards. The appeal to unmarried and widowed women of the upper classes is noteworthy. The numbers of such women were considerable and they were often prey for extreme religious experiences: severe mortifications, extreme penances, intense prayer experiences and mystical ecstasies, and for the most part with little clerical supervision. They were often from well-to-do families, and devoted themselves to a religious life while still living in the world. Many formed unofficial religious communities, living together in small groups. Soon these millennarian communities attracted the suspicions of ecclesiastical authorities and were variously threatened with condemnation and excommunication. The Council of Vienna finally condemned the Beghards in 1311. Kaminsky (1970) recounts the council's view of the sect:

> The sect, we are told, believed (1) "that man in his present life can acquire such a degree of perfection as to render him wholly sinless"; (2) that in this condition "a man can freely grant his body whatever he likes"; (3) that "those who are in this degree of perfection and in this spirit of liberty are not subject to human obedience . . . for, as they assert, where the spirit of the Lord is, there is liberty" [II Cor iii, 17]; (4) that man can attain the same perfection of beatitude in the present as he will obtain in the blessed life to come; (5) that "every intelligent nature is naturally blessed in itself"; (6) that the perfect soul does not need to practice acts of virtue; (7) that "the carnal act is not a sin, since nature inclines one to it"; (8) that the members of the sect "should not stand up when the Body of Jesus Christ is elevated, nor show reverence to it," for "it would be a mark of imperfection in them if from the purity and loftiness of their contemplation they descended so far as to occupy their minds with the sacrament of the Eucharist or the passion of Christ's humanity." (pp. 166-167)

But that was hardly the end of it. In 16th-century Spain, the visionary Lucrecia de León, whose prophetic dreams had considerable influence in political and royal circles, was thought to be a *beata*, a beguine who was pledged to chastity and poverty but belonged to no religious order. As Kagan (1990) comments:

> An important aspect of lay piety during the later Middle Ages, the beguine movement in northern Europe peaked in the fifteenth century, although in Spain, as in Italy, it flourished for another two

hundred years. During the sixteenth century most Spanish cities continued to support a large number of beatas, living singly as well as in groups, often in special dwellings — *beaterías* — annexed to regular convents. Toledo, an important religious center, had eight such communities in 1575; Madrid nearly as many. Individual *beatas,* moreover, frequently became famous for their piety and acts of charity." (p. 18)

Thus the inspiration of the Free Spirit seems to have lived on well into later medieval times, even to the threshold of the modern era.

Revolutionary Millennarian Movements

Taborites and Hussites

The 15th century saw another virulent outburst of revolutionary millennarianism during the Hussite rebellion in Bohemia in the form of the massive Taborite attack against clerical interests and a provocative proclamation of the imminence of the coming of Christ. The Taborites were a more revolutionary splinter group within the Hussite movement, who espoused the chiliastic expectations of the Free Spirit, attacked the Pope and his minions as the Antichrist, and lived in constant preparation for the expected coming of the Lord. Not only did they proclaim the imminent destruction of the world and the inauguration of the millennium — set for February 1420 — but they added a savage and brutal exclusiveness: outsiders would not merely miss out on salvation, but where they could be found they were to be summarily slaughtered (Chamberlin 1975).

After the death of John Hus (d. 1415) and then King Wenceslaus (d. 1419), the Taborites began to spread their doctrine of the Kingdom of God by armed force. A combination of the cult leader Zizka's military skills and the fanaticism of the followers enabled them to repel superior military forces sent to control them. Only after Zizka's death were they finally defeated and dispersed.

The Taborites scorned church and theology. They had no churches, celebrated no religious feasts, and rejected the doctrine of transubstantiation in the Eucharist. Their priests wore no distinguishing garb and they reduced the liturgical functions to the simplest terms. Their social doctrine was extreme: they demanded the abolition of oaths, elimination of all courts of justice, removal of all worldly dignities and positions. To reinforce their views, they resorted to the grossest cruelties and inhumanities. Needless to say, Bohemia was the right place for such a draconian reform movement. The Church was excessively wealthy, owning more than half of the land; clerics and especially prelates lived worldly and affluent lives. Antipathy to the clergy was rife. In addition, many of the higher clergy were German and deeply resented by the Czechs.

Consequently when John Milic, an ascetic reformer, launched his millennial preaching, it was logically aimed at the Antichrist in their midst, the Church. The Antichrist would have to be overthrown and destroyed before the last days could be realized. The preaching of Milic and his disciple Matthew of Janov were taken up by Wyclif and later, at the turn of the century, by Hus. In Hus' hands, the movement grew to become a reform of universal scope. His favorite theme was the worldliness and corruption of the clergy. Interestingly, a major focus of antagonism and rebellion against Rome was the sale of indulgences, a *cause célèbre* that became a central issue in the reform movement launched by Martin Luther a century later. Hus was excommunicated in 1412 and commanded to appear before the Council of Constance to account for himself. His intent was to preach reform to the Council, but he was summarily seized and condemned to be burnt at the stake. His heresy was to claim that the papacy was a human institution, and that Christ rather than the Pope was head of the Church. Ironically the Council had just deposed the illegitimate Pope John XXIII.

The result was to create a movement of national reformation in Bohemia, with king, barons and people lined up against the authority of the Church. But when the king, under pressure from the emperor and the pope, withdrew his support from the Hussite cause and removed all Hussite councilors from office, the populace rebelled violently. The movement became more radical, and developed into a movement of the lower strata of society and the laboring classes. The rebellion was also in part prompted by the fact that these workers had no say in city administration that remained in the hands of patricians, most of them German to boot. In the insurrection, the guilds seized power, expelled many wealthy Catholics, appropriating their properties and emptying the monasteries of their wealth. As the movement moved toward a radical extreme, it was increasingly dominated, not by skilled workers, but by the unskilled, downtrodden, propertyless beggars and criminals, of whom there were a large number in Prague. The movement was nourished by this proletarian matrix (Cohn 1970b).

During the 14th century, royal protection had in some measure safeguarded the rights of peasants against the power of lords and landowners. But by the beginning of the 15th century, a reaction had set in among disgruntled nobility, seeking to deprive peasants of their traditional rights, and by increasing the burden of debt and infringing on the rights of inheritance depriving them of all property as well. As Cohn (1970b) observes:

> It seems that by the time of the Hussite upheaval the Bohemian peasantry was uneasily aware that its position was threatened. Moreover in the countryside too there existed a stratum with nothing to lose: landless labourers, farm hands and many members of that surplus population which could be accommodated neither in towns nor on the land. All these people were more than ready to support any movement which seemed likely to bring succour and relief. (p. 209)

Gradually small congregations gathered around radical priests to form settlements in which communion under both species was observed and efforts made to live according to the ideals of evangelical poverty and moral purity in the early church of the New Testament. These communities recognized no external authority, civil or ecclesiastical, observed no moral or legal conditions in dealing with the outside world, and few restraints over their own behavior with each other. The most prominent of these was renamed "Mount Tabor," recalling the place where Christ had foretold his second coming and where he was thought to reappear in glory. Originally religious in inspiration, the shift to a movement of national reform brought with it violent persecution. There was little recourse but revolution, fanned by intense millennial fervor that derived from the doctrines of the Free Spirit (Kaminsky 1970). The radical Hussites became known as Taborites, and their program called for nothing less than a total break with Rome. They met with great opposition from Hussite nobles, who were intent on putting Wenceslaus' brother, the Emperor Sigismund, on the throne of Bohemia. The intensification of the persecution had its effect in the recrudescence of apocalyptic and millennarian fantasies. The final struggle against the Antichrist and his hosts was at hand. As Cohn (1970b) recounts: "In the very afflictions descending on them the millennarians recognized the long-expected `messianic woes'; and the conviction gave them a new militancy. No longer content to await the destruction of the godless by a miracle, the preachers called upon the faithful to carry out the necessary purification of the earth themselves." (p. 212)

The ruthless logic of "If not with me, against me" held sway. In the eyes of these radical Taborites, anyone who opposed them was an enemy of Christ and had to be exterminated. When the Catholic forces invaded Bohemia, the military genius of Zizka staved off defeat after defeat, his followers transported in the illusion that they were suffering through the last days that would terminate in the dawn of the millennium.

And the vision of the millennium was fairly specific. All authority would be abolished, all property would belong to the people in a kind of classless society. There would be no division of rich vs. poor, noble vs. commoner, no laws, rules or taxes. This gave them the power to steal, rob, pillage and murder, especially anything belonging to the enemies of God — particularly the privileged classes of nobility and clergy. Prague, the stronghold of Sigismund's supporters, was declared to be Babylon, the home of the Antichrist. Once the Antichrist had been exterminated and Babylon destroyed, so that all Bohemia was in their power, then the rest of the earth must be subdued and brought under Taborite rule. The Taborite rule came to an inglorious end in the total annihilation of the battle of Lipan in 1434.

False Prophets

Even after the debacle of Lipan, the Taborites managed to retain a remnant in the so-called Moravian Brethren, a rather pacifist and nonpolitical group, but in addition a strain of militant millennarianism seems to have persisted in Bohemia. In the middle of the 15th century, another Anointed Savior arose to inaugurate the last age. He was the true and only messiah whose mission it was to save not only mankind but God himself. The task could only be accomplished by violence and bloodshed, starting with the destruction of the Antichrist himself, the Pope, and after him all his followers, bishops and clergy. Only the mendicant orders were preserved: an interesting touch, since the Anointed One seems to have been a Franciscan friar who had wandered from his community and fallen into this delusional conviction.

While the prospects for Taborite doctrine waned in Bohemia, fertile ground offered itself in neighboring Germany. The imperial dignity had lost its luster and the principalities were in disarray. Frederick III, who ruled in the latter half of the century, was an ineffectual monarch. The millennial expectations that had attached to his name were replaced by anticipations of a future Frederick who would accomplish the messianic mission. Eschatological ferment persisted in the form of old cultic expressions, mass pilgrimages, flagellant processions, and the begging of wandering Beghards. This atmosphere provided fertile soil for Taborite ideas, fed by the dissolute condition of the clergy whose drinking, gambling, and wenching did little to sustain the good name of the priesthood and the authority of religion.

In the little village of Nicklashausen, a new messiah arose in 1476, a shepherd, Hans Bohm by name, who received a vision from the Virgin Mary who instructed him to save the world by preaching the devotion to her statue in the church of Nicklashausen. Soon the newly crowned prophet began to claim miraculous powers. His message was repentance at first, but soon turned against the vices of the clergy with virulence and violence. Massive pilgrimages came to hear him preach his doctrine of social and religious revolution. Finally the ecclesiastical and civil authorities felt severely threatened and mobilized to seize and deal with the wayward prophet. The Bishop of Wurzburg moved to have him seized and held.

The followers of the messiah were outraged that their hero had been snatched from under their noses. A throng of peasants surged toward Wurzburg, armed and bent on violence if their master were not returned to them. The standoff discouraged some, but many persisted. Finally Bohm was condemned by an ecclesiastical court and burned at the stake. The simple shepherd may have been the unknowing tool of political adversaries of the Bishop who saw the opportunity to embarrass him and gain advantage from these uprisings. Bohm himself was a simple shepherd, perhaps even half-witted, who was seized by his inspired enthusiasm for preaching the Virgin's message. He was also the willing tool of a more shadowy figure, a hermit who may have been a Beghard or Hussite, but who manipulated, prompted and influenced Bohm so that the religious pilgrimage became in time a militant and virulent revolutionary movement.

These millennial uprisings continued well into the period of the Reformation. In the early part of the 16th century, Luther vigorously opposed the enthusiastic prophets of the millennial age and the second coming. As the Reformation was picking up steam, a doctrine sprang up called the Spiritual Liberty that was essentially the same as the old Free Spirit. When emissaries from Antwerp came to Luther, he was sufficiently disturbed to warn his followers in Antwerp of the false prophets in their midst. These warnings did not seem to impede the growth of the sect, which drew to it large numbers of peasants, thieves, prostitutes and beggars. But there were also wealthy adherents who contributed large funds. The sect flourished until 1544, when its prophet was finally condemned and burned to death and his chief followers beheaded (Cohn 1970b).

Müntzer

In the meanwhile, Luther was caught up with the famous German Peasants' War that took place in 1525. The German peasants as a class were reasonably well-off and constituted a socially and economically rising class. As their influence and power grew, they were increasingly intent on removing the obstacles to further progress. Their purposes were political and economic, and not at all eschatological. Tough bargaining had gained them a greater degree of autonomy and freedom. But with the collapse of royal power and the fragmentation of political authorities, the way of life and rights of the peasantry were increasingly threatened by the emerging absolutist principalities. The peasant uprising gave the princes their chance to consolidate their power, and this they did by way of massive massacres of peasants by the thousands.

The insurrection was led by one Thomas Müntzer, a university graduate and priest who was both learned and intellectual. He broke away from the Church to become a follower of Luther, but soon after formed his own doctrine that bade him turn away from Luther, too. His faith became the militant and bloodthirsty millennialism he absorbed from Nicholas Storch, who professed the old Taborite doctrines: that the last days were at hand, that the godless must be annihilated, that the elect would rise up and destroy the Antichrist so that Christ could come in glory to inaugurate the millennium: echoes of the vision of Joachim di Fiore (Manuel and Manuel 1979). Müntzer was imbued with the literal sense of the prophecies in the Apocalypse, with a lust for blood that amounted to sheer raving. In his view, those destined to live in the millennial kingdom were the poor and dispossessed, since they alone had not been corrupted by riches and greed. The mission he preached was one of violent overthrow and annihilation of those who possessed wealth, both ecclesiastical and secular (Cohn 1970b). Müntzer's influence in the rest of Germany was minimal, but in Thuringia the uprising took a violent and destructive turn. Monasteries, convents and churches were looted and burned. Revolutionary fervor ran high. Müntzer himself was steeped in apocalyptic fantasies: the struggles of the "day of wrath" would be followed by the glories of the second coming and the messianic kingdom.

In the meanwhile, Luther was busily at work composing his pamphlet, "Against the thievish, murderous gangs of the peasants," that roused the German princes to oppose the revolt. Müntzer, who had taken to calling himself the "sword of Gideon," pulled together a ragtag army of peasants who took the field against the greatly superior army of the princes. The outcome was a foregone conclusion. The princes offered to spare the peasants' lives if they were to hand Müntzer and his immediate followers over to them. Müntzer then made an impassioned speech in which he declared that the power of the Lord was on their side, that he could work miracles to defeat the enemy, and that God would perform a miracle to save their lives and grant them the victory. Having received no reply, the princes' artillery fired a salvo. The big guns struck terror in the hearts of these naive peasants, and they turned and fled in panic. The enemy cavalry descended on them and wrought a slaughter against which the peasants were defenseless. Müntzer had fled the battle, but was soon apprehended, tortured and beheaded. He became a heroic and prophetic figure to the Anabaptist movement in the years following the Peasants' War, and even became a heroic figure to Communist historians as a symbolic hero in the history of class warfare.

Münster

When the Reformation struck Catholic Europe, the stabilizing influence of the Church was disrupted, and the resources of the Lutheran reform were not able to substitute for it. Additional factors — economic difficulties creating distress and poverty among artisans and tradesmen, inflationary price increases, and another outbreak of the plague — contributed to the unrest and dissatisfaction. The result, along with the sense of liberation, was a sense of confusion and disorientation that brought with them widespread anxieties. The disenchantment of the common people with both Catholicism and Lutheranism made room for another movement that came to be known as Anabaptism. The movement was a loose organization of many disparate sects, each with its own divinely inspired prophet. They discounted theological speculation and cultivated the study of the Bible. They generally sought a return to the ways of the primitive church: an ideal of brotherly love, common sharing of goods and possessions, and following the ethical principles of Christ.

The respective groups tended to be exclusive, reflecting suspicion and rejection of the outside world. Within the group itself, there tended to be intense solidarity and an attitude of suspicion of civil and ecclesiastical authorities. The civil government was suspect, regarded as perhaps a necessity for sinners, but not for the true believers. They complied with civil regulations, but only for the sake of order, and allowed no interference with religion or conscience. They regarded themselves as the elect and avoided all dealings with the pernicious and evil world around them. They were obsessed with separation from the unredeemed sinners of the world. After the Peasants' War, the movement spread rapidly throughout Switzerland and Germany. They were by and large peaceful folk, not intent on social upheaval or revolution. Because of the many peasants in their ranks, however, the Anabaptists continued to be persecuted and killed by the thousands. The persecution tended to create the monster it sought to destroy. The Anabaptists grew more hardened in their hatred of the established order, but also began to see their sufferings in apocalyptic terms as the last great struggle of Satan and the Antichrist against the saints — the woes of the last days that would introduce the millennium. The preoccupations with the day of reckoning, when they would rise up and overthrow the mighty to establish the millennial kingdom under the guidance of a new prophet, became nearly universal obsessions. While the majority of Anabaptists followed the honored Waldensian tradition of peaceful dissent, there gradually grew up a more radical group for whom the tradition of militant millennialism and violent revolution became ever more dominant.

One of the saddest spectacles in this catalogue of millennial disasters is the story of the Anabaptist movement in the city of Münster in Westphalia. As the town came to be an important commercial center of the Hanseatic League, the power of the guilds grew accordingly. Stimulated by the revolutionary fervor of the Peasants' War, the guilds launched an attack against a competing monastery and demanded restriction of clerical privileges. The concessions were short-lived, since as soon as the peasants had been crushed, the town chapter regained its power and withdrew any previous concessions. Punitive measures were even more repressive, so that resentment against the clergy and nobility among the guilds was more intense than before. The situation was complicated by a fresh outbreak of the Black Death in Westphalia in 1529, as well as a failure of the crops. Chamberlin (1975) comments on this gothic nightmare:

> By their nature, the millennial cults were foredoomed to failure, for their members either became disillusioned and so fell away, or were destroyed as dangerous rebels and heretics. But each contributed something to the common stock of belief, a heritage upon which successive leaders drew, consciously or unconsciously. Until the sixteenth century all continued to place the earthly paradise at some point, near or distant, in the future. In 1534 a confident young Dutchman, Jan van Leiden, introduced a startling new variant: The Millennium had commenced in the small Westphalian

town of Münster, for Münster and the New Jerusalem were one. (p. 61)

The Münster saga developed quickly. Into this explosive situation of economic, social and plague-ridden disaster stepped two preachers, Melchior Hoffmann and Bernt Rothmann. Rothmann arrived in 1531 and launched a campaign to bring Münster within the Lutheran fold. But in the course of 1532-33, increasing numbers of Anabaptists came to the city seeking refuge. Among them was one Melchior Hoffmann, a visionary in the mold of the itinerant prophets of the Middle Ages, who devoted himself to preaching the second coming and the millennium. Convinced that he alone possessed the vision of the truth, Hoffman declared himself another Elijah and prophesied the imminent day of judgment. The millennial fantasy that Hoffmann and his followers brought with them quickly took hold and became the dominant obsession among the poorer classes of the city. Rothmann soon abandoned his Lutheran faith and joined forces with Hoffmann.

This mass movement of reform posed a threat to town authorities. Lutherans and Catholics closed ranks and tried to have Rothmann expelled. The struggles between Lutherans and Anabaptists surged back and forth, with ever-increasing tension. Hoffmann was arrested and his place taken by one Jan Matthys. While Hoffmann was a visionary, he remained a man of peace who sought to avoid violence. Matthys was a revolutionary who taught that violence was the only way to prepare the way for the millennium. He and his followers were called on by God to cleanse the earth of the unrighteous by the edge of the sword. He sent two of his emissaries to Münster, where Rothmann and the other Anabaptist ministers were rebaptized. These apostles were followed by other witnesses whose mission was to announce the arrival of the second coming. One of these was Jan Bockelson, otherwise known as John of Leyden, a tailor, tavernkeeper, writer of obscene ballads, and a close disciple of Matthys, who came to Münster to preach the millennial vision of the New Jerusalem. As Cohn (1970b) comments: "It was Bockelson, at first together with his master and later alone, who was to give to Anabaptism in Münster a fierce militancy such as it possessed nowhere else and who was to stimulate an outbreak of revolutionary millennarianism even more startling than that at Tabor a century before." (p. 261)

During the early months of 1534, apocalyptic fervor seized hold of Münster. John preached his fiery sermons, whipping up eschatological enthusiasm to a fever pitch. Rothmann's followers were swept up in the flood of hysteria, especially the women, whose numbers were swollen by nuns who had left their convents, donned secular garb and been rebaptized. Visions and hysterical seizures were the order of the day. Finally the Anabaptists, although still a minority, staged an armed uprising that succeeded only because the Lutherans did little or nothing to oppose it. This was a signal for many well-to-do Lutherans to get out of town. The Anabaptists had taken control, and the call went out over the countryside for Anabaptists to gather at Münster: the day of the Lord was coming before that Easter, and the world was to be destroyed; only Münster would be saved to become the New Jerusalem. Only those who dwelt in the city were leading lives worthy of salvation, and all the rest of the world was to perish in the imminent parousia.

Anabaptists flocked to the town and set up the two prophets, Matthys and Bockelson, as rulers of the city. They sought to turn the city into a prototype of the New Jerusalem, and instituted a theocracy in which every aspect of life was rigidly controlled. Unbelievers, Catholics and Lutherans, were driven out of the city without food or possessions. The rest were forced to submit to rebaptism.

This militant turn called forth the forces of opposition. The Bishop of Münster organized a siege of the town, supported by mercenary forces from neighboring princes. What ensued within the embattled city was a gruesome tragedy that was horrible to contemplate, a prototypical example of the extremes to which misguided religious beliefs can carry men, to the most inhumane and vicious behaviors that bring down starvation, torture, murder, illness and death on the heads of countless numbers. Caught up in his delusional conviction that he was another Enoch who could not die, Matthys led an attack against the imperial forces and was killed. The way was clear for Bockelson to declare himself the true prophet and the elect of God. He set himself up as "King of the World" and set about implementing a reign of terror, intimidation and murderous destruction rarely paralleled in human annals. After Matthys' death, Bockelson assumed full control of this absolute dictatorship, and intensified the terror even further. He regarded himself as the messiah of the last days, king of the world, who possessed absolute authority and power. This delusion was supported by lavish displays and public celebrations in which the entire population was forced to show him obeisance and worship. While the population starved to death, he and his entourage lived richly and enjoyed lavish feasts and entertainments.

Every imaginable measure that would ensure the repression and subjugation of the population and would strengthen and sustain Bockelson's impossible position was taken and brutally enforced. Murder and death reigned supreme and the population was decimated in horrible fashion. When the siege was tightened to achieve a total blockade, starvation became universal with all of its deadly consequences. But Bockelson would not budge; he was determined to hold out even if every person in the city would starve to death. The siege was mercifully brought to a close by a successful breach in the defenses that allowed the besiegers to enter the doomed city on the night of June 24, 1535. A ruthless massacre ensued in which every Anabaptist was put to the sword. John of Leyden was taken captive and was condemned to be led about the countryside on a chain to be exhibited to the people. In January 1536, he was brought back to Münster to be tortured to death with red-hot irons.[5]

---

5. The torture cages still hang on the facade of St. Lambert's Church, grim reminders of the savage vengeance wrought in the name of religion — also a tourist attraction. The original church and cages were destroyed in World War II, but have been replaced by authentic replicas.

CHAPTER 14

The Millennial Kingdom in the New World

The Augustinian view of the millennium in allegorical and ecclesiastical terms dominated more orthodox understandings of the visions of the Apocalypse throughout the middle ages. The more heretical militant and revolutionary millennial movements of those centuries, however, interpreted the apocalyptic visions in literal and immediate terms. The revolutionary ferment behind these fanatical expressions was driven by combinations of social, economic and psychic forces. In the wake of the Reformation, the eschatological vision seemed to lose its literal fascination, and the understanding of Christ's coming became more spiritualized. Many of the more orthodox theologians seemed to turn back toward the traditional Augustinian view in which the apocalyptic visions were interpreted in a figurative and symbolic sense, rather than as literal predictions of events to come in this world (Harrison 1984).

But other forces and processes were at work bringing about profound changes in the way men experienced and understood their world. If the millennarian visions of the late middle ages laid the groundwork and prepared the way for the Reformation, the onset of the scientific world view and the development of natural scientific paradigms for coming to grips with natural phenomena changed the intellectual orientation of Western civilization. Allegorical interpretations and the medieval way of understanding the world fell into disrepute. The effects were felt in the arena of millennial thinking as well, leading to a new era of millennial thinking that is referred to as "progressive millennialism."

My purpose in this chapter is to round out the story of millennial thinking and to point to some of the influences of millennial views as they continued to express themselves in cultic and religious contexts. While the place of millennial thinking in religion and other human endeavors has become more diversified, it continues to exercise a fatal fascination to the human mind. Perhaps a look at some of these more diversified samples will help our overall understanding of the phenomenon and its relation to the cultic process.

Early Progressive Millennarianism

Progressive millennarian thinking originated in the 17th century. One of the early figures was Joseph Mead, an Anglican biblical scholar, who carefully studied the text of the Apocalypse, and firmly rejected the traditional allegorical sense. He finally concluded that the promise of a kingdom of God was to be interpreted literally, and that the work of redemption of the world would be accomplished within the span of human history. Mead's views led to further speculations as to whether the account in the Book of Revelation was meant as having historical reference and where in the prophetic timetable to locate the present era.

This way of reading Revelation had similarities with the apocalyptic millennialism in the early Church. The progressive view, however, did not see the coming of the millennium as resulting from some sudden and dramatic reversal of the historical process or a miraculous divine intervention, nor did they necessarily believe that the second coming of Christ was necessary to save believers from destruction. The fundamental apocalyptic assumptions — that of a final cataclysmic struggle and defeat of the forces of Satan, and a miraculous deliverance from the jaws of defeat by the hand of God — were jettisoned and replaced by a more reasoned understanding, better in keeping with the enlightenment understanding of the scriptural texts. In contrast, they viewed history as a record of continuing progress in which the kingdom of God came ever closer to realization. Its final achievement in this world would arrive, perhaps not without struggle, but certainly as a result of the same processes that had sustained its progressive approximation in the past.

As the eighteenth century dawned, these understandings of progressive millennial thought assumed a dominant position in Protestant theological thinking. The Anglican commentator Daniel Whitby added his support to the position. The result was that the progressive millennial view came to exercise a powerful influence, especially in Calvinist and Puritan circles. This understanding of Revelation flourished among English divines, but in time was transplanted to the American colonies, where it took vigorous root.[1]

Calvinism

The goal of the Calvinist effort was the achievement of the good society here on earth. The accomplishment of that state of perfection would assure the collective happiness of mankind. At the dawn of the millennium, the complete harmony among the members of Christ's body, joyous in their mutual society and communion, united in a holy union of natural love, would be realized. This was God's purpose in creating the world, and as many believed, was to be the harbinger of a yet more perfect and sublime union with God himself. For others, the work of progressive realization of the millennium was never to end. As Heimert (1966) observed:

> . . . by the 1770's, Calvinist spokesmen were all but announcing that the "glory and pleasures" of the good society on earth could provide the full equivalent, in terms of "pure felicity, and exalted beauty," of the Deity. Even in the previous thirty years, the God of Calvinism (or, more accurately, the Christ) had been, in effect, the "*Paradise* of Beauty and Pleasure" into which the Spirit was expected to change "this disordered Earth." (pp. 102-103)

---

1. It is one of the ironies of history that the visionary Columbus, discoverer of the New World, was inspired by his millennarian vision. Eliade (1985) writes: "But Christopher Columbus was already impressed by the eschatological character of his voyage. In 'marvelous circumstances' (of which we know nothing), 'God had shown his hand.' Columbus considered his voyage as 'an evident miracle.' For it was not just a matter of the discovery of the 'Indies,' but of a transfigured world. 'It is I whom God had chosen for his messenger, showing me on which side were to be found the new heaven and new earth of which the Lord had spoken through the mouth of Saint John in his Apocalypse, and of which Isaiah had made previous mention.' According to Columbus's calculations, the end of the world was due to occur in 155 years. But in the intervening years, thanks to the gold brought back from the 'Indies,' Jerusalem would be reconquered and the 'Holy House' could be made 'into the Holy Church.' (p. 237) The millennial seed would take root in this new soil of the "Indies."

The beatific vision for those who aspired to such deliverance was not to be found in the face of God, but in a perfect and harmonious society. The Calvinist pursuit of happiness was synonymous with a seeking for the perfect community among men. "These radical Puritan 'saints' see their chosenness as a mandate for change. The destruction of evil and the perfection of society lie in their own hands. They must methodically and systematically transform the world and, however much their activities may conform to the requirements of a Divine Plan or the necessities of History, the actual constructive effort must be their own" (Barkun 1974, p. 25). For many the imagery was not mere pious rhetoric, but a conviction of the very nature of things. The die had been cast and the divine purposes had been set in motion: God's people were destined to establish a more perfect society. And in the minds of some, that society would arise in the New World.

The evangelical churches found great inspiration in a millennial dream of a world at peace and without any stain of sinfulness. The apocalyptic message of the Book of Revelation had received new life in the course of the Protestant Reformation. Believers looked forward to the coming of the New Jerusalem that would descend from the heavens after a period of tribulation, and thus inaugurate a period of earthly utopia in which the righteous would reign for a thousand years of peace and prosperity. These millennial themes had arisen with renewed force in the English Puritan Revolution, and had formed a core element in the preaching of the Great Awakening in New England.

The seeds of millennial expectation took hold in the soil of pre-Revolutionary America. As the work of redemption moved forward, the children of the light would be more decisively separated from the children of darkness, a separation that would be finalized in the last great judgment in which an everlasting division would be made between the saints and the wicked. At the dawn of the millennium the true character of men would become clear, and the increasing segregation between these classes was to be taken as a sign of the approaching millennium. As the battle lines were more clearly drawn, the divergence between saints and sinners would provide the basis for advancing the approach of the kingdom. The effort to clarify the ranks of the saints and the sinners was a powerful current among Calvinist divines in the mid-18th-century colonies.

The Great Awakening

The religious spirit in this pre-revolution setting found expression in the Great Awakening. To the preachers and converts of this mid-century revival, it seemed that they were experiencing a great outpouring of God's grace that would transform their hearts and souls, and prepare them to fulfill a great destiny that was envisioned in millennarian terms (Strout 1974). The religious revival centered in New England, spurred largely by the preaching of Jonathan Edwards and others. It was an experiment to demonstrate that a godly people, joined together in a common weal, could begin the process of drawing the Kingdom of Christ closer to full realization. The messianic hope of ancient Israel had found new growth in the New World, especially in New England (Johannesen 1984).

The stress fell on the visible expressions of conversion, and if any erstwhile soul did not manifest these signs of inner grace, they were to be openly denounced as unregenerate sinners. The movement was marked by "a spirit of contentious bickering, bigoted, censorious accusations, open hostility, and warfare" (McNearney 1984, p. 42). The eminent Charles Chauncy remarked that one of the marks of the awakening "was that it makes Men spiritually proud and conceited beyond Measure, infinitely censorious and uncharitable, to Neighbors, to Relations, even the nearest and dearest; to Ministers in an especial Manner; yea, to all Mankind, who are not as they are, and don't think and act as they do."[2] (p. 42) The result was, to the consternation of many, deep divisions among the faithful and the splitting of churches. As Strout (1974) notes:

> The Awakening shattered the standing order of churches in schisms and withdrawals, but it also reinstituted community control and conformity — the repressive side of the story that has been largely omitted from accounts bent on drawing a straight line from the Awakening to the American Revolution. . . . But it was not freedom from law or society so much as conformity to the censorious pressure of the brethren that followed conversion: "Every church member considered himself his brother's keeper. The most trivial derelictions from duty were noted and reported, and espionage and tale-bearing encouraged as if they were cardinal virtues. . . . Every man was at the mercy of the "inward actings" of his neighbor's soul.[3] (pp. 43-44)

---

2. The quote is taken from Lovejoy (1969), p. 79.
3. The quotation is from Goen (1962), p. 167.

The Awakening, spurred on by millennial optimism, arose as a means for restoring clerical prestige and renewing the constraints of the Protestant ethic. But the restlessness in the younger generation could not be so easily quelled. The effort to reimpose Puritan restraints only led to greater resentment and resistance. Strout (1974) offers a summary judgment on this movement:

> The Awakening was enmeshed in a net of historical ambiguities. By stressing the necessity for a religion of the heart that was truly experienced and not merely intellectually understood or morally practiced, the revivalists had made an issue out of sincerity that inevitably fostered schisms, contention, and eventual doubts about the authenticity of their own mass influxes to the churches. Devoted to social peace, family government, and stricter moral control over the young, they found themselves forced to challenge public laws that were passed to restrict their own movement. Skeptical of the learned institutions for their harboring of Arminian tendencies[4] and their emphasis on institutional credentials, they were compelled to build their own colleges to produce pietistically oriented ministers. Tending to exalt individual congregations as gathered brethren of true believers, they were led by the technique of itinerancy and by fear of their enemies to organize in denominational associations to foster the influence of their own pietist faith. The Awakening was caught in an irony of history that turned all their original intentions to the service of purposes they had not originally contemplated and only temporarily fulfilled what they had intended. (p. 45)

But the role of the Great Awakening, with its millennial dimension, in the spiritual opening of the colonies to the American adventure should not be underestimated. McNearney's (1984) summary statement conveys this import:

> Historians of colonial American culture have been too often and too easily stymied by the sectarian, defensive, and self-righteous categories which characterize the Great Awakening. Consequently

---

4. Arminianism was the bugaboo of Calvinist divines. The theological teachings of Arminius (1560-1609) derived from the Dutch Reform tradition and strongly opposed the classical Calvinist convictions. In contradistinction to Calvinism, the so-called Arminians held that there was no incompatibility between divine power and free will in man, that Christ died for all men and not merely the elect, and that predestination of any sort could not be defended in the Bible. They represented a more liberal school of theology than strict Calvinism, and exercised a powerful influence on Protestant theology. The Laudian revival in 17th-century England and the Methodist movement instituted by John Wesley were regarded as Arminian by their Calvinist opponents (Cross 1957).

they have tended to view the Awakening as excessive, narrow, fanatical, and as not contributing in any significant way to the development of religious and civil liberties culminating in the Declaration of Independence. What they fail to recognize is that Whitefield and his followers inherited these old categories of sectarian religion and emptied them of their traditional meanings through apocalyptic imagery so that they could be employed to establish the legitimacy of a new ethos and social structure more compatible with their new experiences and aspirations. The boundaries of this new community were as expansive as America itself, and all could aspire to full membership in it who forsook the dead structures of the corrupt old world and glimpsed the visionary promise of the new one which was coming to be in their new birth. (p. 65)

As resentment against British stewardship grew apace and revolutionary fervor mounted, the clergy found a new focus for their energies by riding the current of popular resentment. Sermons from the pulpits, especially of New England, grew more fiery and militant in tone. The defense of American liberties was tempered by a persistent stress on respect for legitimate authority and an emphasis on seeking the common good. They believed in good government as essential to the public weal as much as they inveighed against the evils of tyranny. As Strout (1974) writes:

> No rebels have been more saturated with respect for traditional morality and civic order, yet without calling for dictatorship or terror; and no enthusiasts for the millennial prospects of the revolutionary future can ever have been as troubled as the Americans were by the special guilts of those who considered themselves a chosen people, addicted to declaring occasions for public fasts and national humiliation. Calvinism, originally elitist and authoritarian, offered themes of constitutional limitations and collective redemption that could be redefined in a post-Puritan world of greater toleration and wider popular participation in government so as to lend the energy of moral passion to the republican cause. (p. 54)

By the close of the Revolution, the Calvinist vision of imminent prospects included both spiritual glories but also blessings of a more tangible order. Men would indeed receive the just fruits of their labor, each in due measure. But there would be no room for avarice or selfish acquisition. In the face of economic divergence and difference, the millennial spirit called for the active pursuit of the general welfare rather than personal gain or pleasure.

Jonathan Edwards

One of the guiding lights of the Great Awakening was Jonathan Edwards (1703-1758), a Calvinist minister who carried on a vigorous campaign to stem the tide of Arminianism in the colonies. His preaching and writing stimulated a religious revival along strict Calvinist lines that would exclude all of the unconverted from the communion of the saints. The rigidity of his views led to the loss of his post at Northhampton and the continuation of his mission at Stockbridge, where most of his influential works were written. Edwards espoused a millennial vision of the New World as the place where the kingdom of Christ would be established.

The notion of the imminent millennium captured the imagination of American colonists in the wake of the Great Awakening. Evangelical preaching was filled with the expectation of millennial fulfillment: the glorious prosperity of Christ's kingdom was approaching and was soon to be realized. The work of Edwards, more than any others, proclaimed that the work of God was progressing and would be continued until the messianic kingdom of holiness, purity, peace and love was fulfilled. Heimert (1966) observes:

> The explosion of millennarianism in the Great Awakening was one of the symptoms of some Americans' dissatisfaction with the conditions of eighteenth century life. Edwards described the world in which he lived as "for the most part a scene of trouble and sorrow," and, whatever the judgment of others, apocalyptic speculations persisted throughout the sixty years of American history after the Awakening. Yet the revival of the 1740s also brought hope: the Great Awakening, like the revivals of 1800-1801, was preceded as well as accompanied by popular speculations and prophecies concerning "when Christ would appear and set up his true kingdom." (pp. 59-60)

Similar themes were sounded by the Mathers earlier in the century, whose millennial visions included great sufferings and destructions as part of the general judgment they presumed would inaugurate the millennium. But many more preferred to displace the cataclysm to beyond the millennium, along with the threat of final judgment.

The American disposition against premillennarianism thus took hold early; it was, no doubt, part of the American illusion that peace and prosperity need not be purchased at the cost of sorrow or pain. The themes were articulated in splendid fashion in Edwards' *History of the Work of Redemption*, a work that "sustained several American generations in a belief that the millennium was not a mere possibility but an imminent and attainable reality" (Heimert 1966, pp. 60-61), as well as enunciating a post-millennial view that not only rejected the premillennial orientation of earlier years but insisted on a form of noncataclysmic and progressive achievement of the millennial kingdom. The revivalist impulse stimulated wishful visions of millennial fulfillment that translated the colonial experience into millennial terms. The New Jerusalem was not coming at some uncertain time in the future — it was already on the way. Although Edwards had to retract some of his enthusiastic utterances, he continued to insist that the revivals were signs of the approaching millennium.

This view of history and the world was optimistic, to say the least, and based on a vision of the spirit at work in regenerating the earth in order to create the messianic kingdom. The good society did not need a cataclysmic divine intervention, but could be achieved by the good works of religious men. But in Edwards' view, the true redemption and the earthly kingdom were to be sought, not in the material world, but in the minds and hearts of men, in the regeneration of the domain of virtue through the work of the Spirit. The inscrutable God of Calvinist theology acted as the ultimate guarantor of this process, ensuring the ultimate end of divine action in the restoration of all the saints to a state of unification with the Godhead. Edwards' major contribution was to purge Calvinist millennarianism of its traditional elements of despair and punitive retribution of divine wrath that would chasten a refractory and sinful humankind. Heimert (1966) comments:

> The heart and soul of Calvinism was not doctrine but an implicit faith that God intended to establish this earthly Kingdom — and to do so within the eighteenth century. The awakening had brought history to a critical juncture, a discernible confluence which disposed the Calvinist mind to "look for the beginnings" of the millennium "from year to year." And the faith of the 1740s sustained the Calvinists through dispensations of Providence which other Americans, less confident than they that Edwards had read God's plan aright, found both dark and bewildering. (pp. 66-67)

Joseph Bellamy

The pathways opened by Edwards' millennial speculations were pursued further by his disciple, Joseph Bellamy. Edwards had laid the specter of Armageddon to rest; for him the slaying of the enemies of Christ had been accomplished in the struggles of the Reformation so that the downfall of the papal Antichrist could be dated from the time of Luther and Calvin. The Seven Years' War provided Calvinist attitudes a fresh opportunity to envision the conflictual crisis between God's people and the enemies of Christ in the character of the French king, the Pope and the devil. Some felt that the outcome of the struggle would give the signal whether the time had arrived for the beginning of the millennium. But the message of the Great Awakening had been that the agenda for America was cast in terms of the vision of millennial grandeur and the mission of God's people in the New World to bring it to realization.

It remained for Bellamy to lay the axe to the remnants of pre-Awakening Calvinism. In his sermon on the millennium, delivered in 1758, the year of Edwards' death, he rejected the idea that the course of history was to be determined by the conflict between Protestants and Catholics, and spurned out of hand the numerological speculations and efforts to fix the dates of the beginning or ending of Christ's reign on earth. The work of redemption lay closer to home in the triumph over enemies at hand.

But Bellamy's Connecticut parishioners were not entirely convinced that the earth as they knew it could sustain the wondrous abundance of the millennium. Providing themselves with food and clothing was trouble enough, but the added burdens of supporting the array of civil and ecclesiastical establishments required for sustaining harmonious community life seemed beyond reach. They were bothered, too, by the seeming prosperity of the wicked, who seemed to be doing very nicely in the expanding economy of colonial America. There were doubts about the millennial assurances of Edwards and about his program for attaining the benefits of the kingdom. Was the Calvinist God up to overcoming the sinful dispositions of humans? While their Arminian counterparts were making good profits and living well, the Calvinist efforts at self-denial and spiritual dedication were not sitting well. How was it that more liberal-minded men could deviate from the path of spiritual rigor without suffering divine retribution and punishment?

Bellamy's answer was to extend Edwards' inspiration and, in the process, proclaim the necessity for a civil war to take place in America before the millennium could be possible. As had Edwards, Bellamy insisted that spiritual progress, the work of redemption, could take place only in the face of man's natural dispositions to sinfulness, and only as the result of the continuing gracious influx of divine power that would exercise its effects in the overcoming of sinful opposition to progress. If this were to be seen as a gradual program of preparation for the Kingdom, the millennial promises would nonetheless be fulfilled in a moment of glorious triumph of the forces of good over the forces of evil. For him, it was inconceivable that the Creator of the world would have from the beginning intended victory for his enemies and the dominance and prosperity of Satan. The spiritual man could look forward in hope and confidence to the certain conclusion of the final victory of Christ over all his enemies. The link between millennarian hopes and the revolutionary spirit were being forged. Sweet (1979) has commented on this linkage:

> In an earthly sense, of course, millennialism is anti-authoritative. The advent of the highest authority is blessed and beckoned. Thus millennialism is often the study of change, instability, social protest, subversion, political expression, and radical resistance . . . . Indeed, Ernst Block and others have been so struck by this overwhelming evidence of a linkage between millennialism and revolution that they have theorized that millennialism served as an ideological ancestor of the revolutionary tradition in the modern West. The envisioning of the millennium's onset in terms "not of graves burst open but of institutions broke down" . . . helped to sire Western revolutionary traditions. (p. 525)

Regardless of millennial visions and hopes, the march of events proceeded on its inexorable course. Increasing anti-British sentiment and resentment brought a scene of chaos and confusion that Bellamy and his confreres had neither anticipated nor intended. Bellamy sought to prevent the spread of what he called "Connecticut's civil war" by an appeal to Christian charity, addressed to rich and poor and Arminians and Calvinists — but especially the rich and Arminian. This and other efforts at religious revival went unanswered, so that "by 1773 they were once again convinced that the saints, and the saints alone, would have to be marshaled under the banner of the coming Kingdom" (Heimert 1966, p. 347). Even if the elect had not been gathered together as yet, the glorious day of God's kingdom was not far away. Those who wished to join the number of the elect had best serve notice of their intention by signing up with the Church Militant. In Connecticut, saintly mobs joined together and went about harassing Arminians, but it was not long before their animus was directed towards a more suitable target. If Arminianism and sin were suitable enemies, they were cast into an oblivious background by a more profound and dramatic evil — British tyranny. The Church Militant became a military force: when the British fired on Boston, and Israel Putnam called for armed men to march on Boston, Bellamy took his place at the head of a glorious army of 40,000 ready to do battle for God's kingdom. The time for the final battle with the Antichrist was rapidly approaching.

The conviction grew that the divine plan had singled out America to be the place where the glorious kingdom of Christ would be erected. The favorite text of Revelation 12: 6-14, dealing with the flight into the wilderness, was taken to refer to the escape from European tyranny and the establishment of the kingdom in the wilderness. As the Revolution wound down, the triumph of the true religion of Christ was envisioned as the overthrow of all religious establishments and any semblance of state religion; absolute and complete religious freedom was a necessity for the millennium to begin in America (Heimert 1966). If Edwards had provided a millennarian vision that fed the imaginations of pre-Revolutionary Americans, Bellamy and his followers helped to extend that vision beyond the Revolution to a new set of millennial expectations and hopes.

The New Millennial Kingdom

The emergence of the United States in the wake of the Revolution provided a focus and a stimulus for the millennial aspirations of Protestant divines that fueled a volatile spirit of nationalism and the idea of a Manifest Destiny — an idealized vision that stemmed from colonial times that saw America as the new world promised in the Apocalypse, free of the contaminating heresies of the old world and opening the way to almost unlimited optimism and belief in progress (Shepperson 1970a). The dawn of a new era was seen by many as the occasion, if not the initial fulfillment, of the long-promised millennium. Religious aspirations rose to the occasion by increasing dedication to the project of realizing the kingdom in the here-and-now of the new nation, and continued its crusade toward national perfection in the later Social Gospel. The belief in the progressive realization of the millennium, particularly as formulated by the powerful religious rhetoric of Jonathan Edwards in prerevolutionary days, contributed to the belief of Americans for several generations that the promised millennium was within their grasp. For many, the Revolution was seen as the last great battle against the Antichrist, and the victory against the forces of evil and tyranny was a harbinger of the dawning of the millennium in America. The work of redemption was at last to be completed.

And the flow of events gave some support and substance to these dreams. The formation of the union and its charter of liberties and rights gave good reason to think that the social goals inspired by the Great Awakening were in process of achievement. The union of Christians under the Bill of Rights and the Constitution was a palpable and momentous step toward the millennial vision of all men united in peace and prosperity under the rule of God. As Heimert (1966) comments, "The revival and the evangelical impulse pressed to the goal of a more beautiful social order — which meant, in the New World, a union of Americans, freed from the covenant relationships of the parochial past and united by the love which God's American children bore for one another." (p. 95)

The optimistic millennialists saw the work of redemption as constantly progressing, and, guided as it was by the providential hand of God, they had every reason to sense the rightness and ultimate triumph of their cause and the ultimate victory over evil and the forces of darkness. The strain of progressive optimism was matched by a countermovement of pessimism. As Shepperson (1970a) comments: "And yet, paradoxically, this optimistic millennialism coexisted and coexists — not always peacefully — with the fundamental pessimism of the premillennial groups of America, by far the most common form of American millennarians. This paradox runs throughout the history of the pursuit of the Millennium in America." (p. 51)

The Grapes of Wrath

In the first half of the 19th century, the stage was set for the emergence of a multitude of revolutionary religious movements. As Ahlstrom (1972) comments:

> Tumultuous population growth and the westward movement transformed the map and makeup of the country. Social and geographical mobility took on new meaning. Canals, railroads, textile mills, and the cotton gin led to or symbolized other transformations. Voluntarism, freedom, and personal initiative brought the individual and collective aspirations of Americans to a new order of magnitude. The nation was on the make. Yet there were frustrations of equal magnitude for those who were displaced by the new egalitarian order, and more drastically for those left behind in the race. Immigration, exploitation, dislocation, loneliness — and, very significantly, the financial panic of 1837 — darkened the dream. Modern thought and the newer science, meanwhile, seemed to controvert one traditional belief after an-

other. All these factors served to ripen the sectarian harvest. (p. 475)

The dominant religious movement to arise from this cauldron was evangelical revivalism. It laid the way open for new channels of disruption and innovation, challenging the more traditional religious views. Among the emphases of revivalist thought, the millennarian vision held no small place, rousing believers to prepare themselves for the imminent second coming of Christ and the declaration of God's kingdom (Ahlstrom 1972; Jamison 1961). As Jamison (1961) observes, "Christian history has been sprinkled with sincere zealots who have wished to enter the Kingdom without delay, and with the rise of the revivalist spirit, America acquired its share of similar zealots. All put great emphasis on the direct and immediate work of the Holy Spirit in the regenerated incline toward perfectionism." (p. 203) In addition, the impact of millennial perfectionism was of such an order that fervent converts were wont to regard any who opposed or doubted them as apostate or bound for perdition.

A powerful strain of such millennial fervor came to the fore in the crisis over slavery and abolition that led to the Civil War (Barkun 1974). Shining millennial hopes were gradually dimmed by the apprehension that the abolition of slavery could only be achieved through a cataclysmic struggle. As Strout (1974) observes:

> As the spiral of violence mounted, it persuaded some reformist abolitionists that only war could end slavery, while it taught the revolutionist Garrison to become more reformist in relation to the political process for the same reason. In either case Biblical Christianity had eloquent texts for rationalizing violence as well as for turning the other cheek. Toqueville was largely right that Christianity for most Americans was a conservative influence, but the coming convulsion of American society would bring many to see what a Nat Turner or a John Brown knew in their bones: that the Bible tells some terrifying millennial stories. (p. 172)

The evil of slavery, born and sustained in violence, was a blight on the American landscape that contradicted the millennial images of peace and harmony among Christians. As the tensions mounted and the prospects of war grew closer, the religious imagination found powerful and persuasive imagery in the apocalyptic and millennial visions. The apocalyptic rhetoric of the Bible came readily to mind for abolitionists from Nat Turner to Abe Lincoln. Harriet Beecher Stowe, in her epochal *Uncle Tom's Cabin*, constantly invoked the millennial vision that the revivalists of the day had inherited from Jonathan

Edwards. Themes of the millennial era when all men would live in freedom and justice and equality were enunciated over and over, along with the menace of an apocalyptic crisis of a day of vengeance when the Lord would visit his wrath on the unjust; the dark shadow of the looming war was already cast over the optimistic hopes of American Protestantism. As Strout (1974) comments, ". . . her millennialism . . . was at the blazing center of the furnace of abolitionism." (p. 184) The millennial flag became a crusading banner in Julia Ward Howe's "Battle Hymn of the Republic," spurring the armies of the North on to a war of righteousness and justice in which God's truth was marching on to "the glory of the Coming of the Lord." And Lincoln's second inaugural connected slavery with human sinfulness and invoked the power of God to save the Union from the consequences of national guilt.

Premillennial Eschatology

After the Civil War, the prevailing post-millennial American Protestantism gave way to a premillennial eschatology; and in the same way the abolitionist fervor gave way to radical temperance and anti-prostitution movements. The Social Gospel became a powerful current within liberal Protestantism that was called to face the often-appalling conditions of rapid urbanization and the intolerable conditions of city ghettos, industrialization and the evils of the sweat shops and inhumane working conditions, and the specter of mass poverty. The premillennial orientation that things will only get worse until Christ comes to set them right has been accused of a pessimism that lacks social concern. But active social concern seems to have been no less under the influence of premillennialism than it had under the post-millennial era (Rausch 1984). The evangelical emphasis in such groups may have run the risk of emphasizing the spiritual restoration of the poor and destitute to the detriment of their physical needs and struggles; the drive to save all men for Christ's kingdom and the conviction that sin was at the root of mankind's problems drew evangelical efforts to try to correct the evil and sin-inducing conditions of life.

The premillennial Social Gospel conviction that change in the environment would bring about individual change and abolition of sin might have been naive, but the problems created by the Depression brought increased awareness of the complexities of the economic system. If profitmaking could not be done away with, it was at least the role of the responsible Christian to try to make the system operate fairly and equitably. If premillennialists generally could accept the Social Gospel idea of a Christian responsibility to care for the poor, they could not so easily accept the assumption that the world is good or man basically Christian. The premillennialists faced a dilemma between the wish to ease the burdens of the poor and the conviction poverty could never be abolished by mere human actions. These conflicts were exacerbated by the Depression. And the conflicts continued between the Social Gospel view that changes in society will bring about the desired changes in individual members of the society, and the premillennial view that change can only begin in individual men and thus lead to social change (Rausch 1984).

American Millennial Religious Movements

The millennial spirit not only found fertile soil in the national aspirations and the optimistic ideologies of Americans, but has found its way into the lifeblood of the American scene in the form of religious sects, in which the millennial impulse has flourished in various forms. My intention in describing these religious expressions of the millennial themes is not to provide an exhaustive catalogue, but to merely scan the field of millennial movements to provide some sense of the persistence and character of these recurrent manifestations of an ancient theme.

Adventists

In the modern era, Adventist sects of various descriptions have maintained a premillennarian view, proclaiming the imminence of the second coming of Christ and that his appearance would announce the inauguration of the millennium (Jamison, 1961). Such premillennarian preoccupations can be identified in the teachings of Seventh Day Adventists, Jehovah's Witnesses, Southern Baptists, and Mormons, and certain forms of conservative fundamentalism among others. These movements were in part stimulated by the rising hopes and expectations that followed in the wake of the Revolution, and were presumably reinforced by the social consequences and effects of the increasing pace of industrialization. The appeal of millennarian themes seemed to rise to a crescendo at times of national crisis and in times of war, especially the world wars of the present century.

The details of the millennial vision varied, but they were generated out of the sense of optimism, expectancy and Christian hope that came to life in the new soil of liberty and opportunity in early 19th-century America. Evangelists of all stripes turned their faces in anticipation to the millennial dawn. As Handy (1984) comments:

> Some interpretations of the millennial hope were clearly literalistic, apocalyptic, and intensely otherworldly in emphasis. They affirmed that only the miraculous second coming of Christ could save the world from despair and inaugurate the glorious reign of God beyond history. But other interpretations — and these came to be more frequently expressed by the leadership of the major evangelical churches — saw the millennium coming as the climax of the Christianization of civilization, fulfilling history. (p. 30)

Various groups, sharing the label of Adventists, share the common belief that the second coming of Christ is due in some immediate future. One of the earliest expressions of the Adventist faith came from William Miller, who immersed himself in the Book of Daniel and its apocalyptic symbolism, and finally began to proclaim in 1831 the imminence of the second coming. His conclusion from study of the Old Testament texts was that the date for the Lord's arrival fell in the year 1843-4. His message had widespread appeal, and he drew many to his cause. His prophecy was a literal premillennarian pronouncement of a widely accepted belief. The so-called Millerite movement maintained contacts with English Adventists, and combined their millennarian convictions with anti-slavery attitudes and abolitionist commitments (Strout 1974).

The passage of the fatal year without incident put something of a damper on the exuberance of Miller's followers, but efforts to recalculate the date continued. Miller remained firm in his conviction that the coming was imminent, but was less inclined to pronounce the promised date as time went on. If the failure of prophecy was a disillusionment for some (Handy 1984), for the hard-core believers the "great disappointment" was more of a challenge, an obstacle to be overcome. The debates about the speculated dates brought about schisms, one of which has persisted as the Seventh Day Adventists. They split off from the Miller group after the debacle of 1844. The cause was carried on by Ellen Harmon and her husband, James White. Soon after the failure of the Millerite movement, she began to experience the first of many visions and transports. As her following increased, she and White set up headquarters in Battle Creek in 1855 and presided over the continuing growth of the Adventist church. They took the sabbath as the prescribed day of rest, rather than the traditional Sunday. They adhere stoutly to the scriptures as the unerring guide to faith and morals, and

remain convinced of the imminent return of Christ. Members are subjected to a strict code of temperance (no alcohol, tobacco, and even in
some groups, tea and coffee).

Jehovah's Witnesses

The Jehovah's Witnesses, founded by Charles Russell, seemed to
act as a magnet, drawing many of the millennial strains on the American
scene together: elements of the Shakers, the Millerites, the Mormons,
Christadelphians, Seventh Day Adventists and others found their way
into his teachings. Russell began publishing his *Zion's Watch Tower* in
1879, that in the following century has become *The Watchtower*, whose
distribution spans the globe. Its distributors contribute their efforts to
bear witness to the imminent coming of the millennium. Russell himself had been inspired by an Adventist meeting that drew its teaching
from the heritage of the Millerites (Chamberlin 1975). Their doctrine is
intransigently biblical, believing that Christ returned invisibly and spiritually in 1914 to inaugurate the final cosmic drama. For those who
know the truth, the kingdom already exists, and they await the inevitable Armageddon in which all human institutions will be overthrown
(Jamison 1961). Many of these revivalist movements declaring the perfectibility of man took on an aspect of urgency and militancy when
joined to the idea of the imminent conquest of the earth by the returning
Christ. In the wake of the Millerite disappointment of 1844, the reaction of fervent post-millennialism marched on without breaking stride
towards the post-Civil War social gospel (Shepperson 1970a).

Mormons

The millennial themes make their appearance in Mormon doctrine
as well. The Mormons, or the Church of Jesus Christ of Latter-Day
Saints, was founded by Joseph Smith in 1830, whose revelation was
continued in the Book of Mormon, the church's bible. The early history of the sect was marked by persecution and violence; Smith himself
was killed by a mob in 1844. His successor, Brigham Young, moved
the headquarters of the sect to Utah, where it remains. The book of
revelations was delivered to Smith by the angel Moroni, and contained
prophecies of the coming of the messiah and the New Jerusalem.
Strout (1974) summarizes as follows:

> Like the early Puritans' works, the Book of Mormon in its histori-
> cal sections links the fate of believers with the Jews and provides
> a covenant for a New Jerusalem; like the revivalists of Smith's

period, it stresses free will, the perfectibility of man, judgment according to one's works, and potential salvation for all, with the exception of apostates and persecutors of the Saints. It adds some appealing novelties of its own in its theory of the material perpetuity of the world; its tritheistic conception of a deity who is yet of the same race as mankind, needs them, and develops by his own efforts as they do; and it finds a place for the Indians by defining them as apostate Jews, descendants of the lost tribes of Israel, who will one day be reconverted into friendly whites. Mormons restored as well the mystical practices of visions, faith healing, and exercise of the gift of tongues, and they drew upon the deep-seated adventist expectations of American Protestantism to forecast a Second Coming of Christ who would preside over an American Zion in the West. (p. 131)

The millennial dream since the 18th century had a powerful appeal for small rural communities that arose in the east and spread west. The conservative Puritan core of their belief was all too prone to fanaticism and extremism. As they developed isolated communities, whose members were drawn from unsophisticated and poorly educated peasant immigrants, the potentiality for controlled conformity and a penchant for the miraculous were reinforced. It was ripe soil for the ravings of a prophet, the more extreme the better. Some imported cults managed to find a quiet niche in the American landscape. Some Anabaptists tried to cast Boston as the New Jerusalem in the 17th century, but in time evolved into more settled nonconformist sects, such as the Amish and the Mennonites.

Shakers

Another millennial import came with Ann Lee Stanley, who arrived from England in 1774 to found the movement that came to be known as the Shakers, from the tremblings and gyrations that accompanied the visitations of the Spirit in their prayer meetings. They provide an extraordinary example of communitarian ideals founded solidly on perfectionist and millennarian ideas (Jamison, 1961). As Ahlstrom (1972) comments:

Ann Lee seems to have outdone all others in the intensity of her piety; and after some years, during which she suffered much distress and gave birth to four very short-lived children, her trances and visions convinced others and then herself that Christ's Second Coming would be in the form of a woman, and that she was that woman. She had also become convinced that sexual relations, ever since Adam and Eve, had been the root of all sin. (p. 492)

For her followers Miss Lee was regarded as the second incarnation of Christ, "a curious reappearance of that long dead Montanist teaching that Christ had returned to his prophetess Priscilla in the guise of a woman" (Chamberlin 1975, p. 142).

Quakers

The Quakers, or the Society of Friends, trace their roots back to the 17th century, when George Fox founded the movement in protest against Puritanism. Their millennial hopes were deep-seated and motivated their early participation in the Puritan Revolution. But they became disenchanted with Cromwell's leadership and declared themselves pacifists, refused to pay taxes, cut themselves off from the body politic as a nonconformist group that set itself apart by special forms of speech and dress. Persecution from the Puritan majority followed, and led to the transplantation of the sect to William Penn's newly opened colony in America in 1682. Penn's own vision of the role of government in the new colony was as an aspect of religion whose purpose was not merely to punish evildoers, but to facilitate kindness, goodness and charity. The ideology that inspired the new colony was based on a millennial vision that sought as its ideal and objective a millennium that was to be ushered in by the coming of the second Adam, the Lord Himself descending from heaven to plant the blessings of the millennium in the New World, specifically in the Quaker community of Penn's Woods (Strout 1974).

Premillennial Vision

The premillennial vision has not seen its last: it has played an important, if limited, part in the revival of conservative religious views in the 1980s, particularly among fundamentalists who tend to view the doctrine as a test of orthodoxy. Many a Baptist church regards itself as fundamental and premillennial, although any essential connection between fundamentalism and premillennialism would be debated by many. Even so, as Harrell (1984) observes: "At the same time, once again as in the 1920s, premillennial theory today spills over beyond the boundaries of organized fundamentalism. Most pentecostals are premillennialists, as are many southern Baptists. A sizable portion of the moderate evangelical community is premillennial, including the theory's most important biblical defenders." (p. 11)

And along the same line of thinking, Bettis (1984) renders a cautionary note on the potential power of newly minted millennial thrusts:

> During the past two decades, millennialism has returned. The resurgence of evangelical Christianity, as well as the emergence of new religions, has been accompanied by a new interest in historical transformation. This interest has been considerably abetted by the heightened awareness of the proximity of nuclear holocaust. Any attempt to introduce millennial ideas into the contemporary theological debate must understand the theological force of apocalyptic symbolism and the political power of millennial thought run wild. The effort to avoid nuclear destruction cannot justify genocidal totalitarianism. Better a resigned pessimism about the future of human history than a repeat of the tragic European experiment in millennialism. (pp. 153-154)

This survey, however cursory, has focused on some of the millennial currents in the religious life of Protestant America. Needless to say, the reach of millennial aspirations was to enjoy a much more generous scope than that. Enough has been said to underline the impression that millennarian motivations underlie and give dynamic focus to religious inspirations of many kinds. Moreover, to bring this discussion closer to the central theme of this study, it offers a basis to support the view that the millennial impulse serves as an important ideational and motivational substratum for the workings of the mechanisms of the cultic process. In reviewing recent studies of American millennialism, Sweet (1979) commented: "They are sensitive to the importance of eschatological symbols and apocalyptic rhetoric. They marvel at the endurance, flexibility, and tenacity of the myth of America as the "New Israel" and the arena for the future. . . Finally, the paranoid and polarizing tendencies in millennialism are confronted without the conclusion that millennialism is the product of mental aberration and psycho-social disorder." (p. 512)

The American experience underlines the fact that millennial visions do not necessarily arise from deprivation or oppression, nor is it necessarily the preserve of rampant psychopathology, even when its powerful lava pours itself in a consuming torrent into the power and passion of revolutionary religious movements. To this extent it shares the vicissitudes of the cultic process with its roots in the paranoid process: it can become a force for good, for constructive religious expression and for the seeking of surcease for profoundly human needs; it can also be diverted into destructive and catastrophic channels that lead to religious distortion, despair, and even death.

Section VI

Psychoanalytic Perspectives

Psychoanalysis and Cult Dynamics

The Cultic and the Paranoid Process

Eschatological and apocalyptic themes demonstrate a unique vitality and persistence in man's religious experience, and can take root in a broad variety of cultic contexts (Meissner 1984a, in process). Cultic groups differ in lifestyle, ideology, and modes of existence. For some, preoccupations with apocalyptic renewal and salvation predominate; others emphasize personal psychological growth (Cushman 1986).

Despite the countless variations on these themes throughout religious history, the genesis of religious movements follows a fairly consistent process, in which they assume a characteristic form, run their historical course, and finally undergo transformation or dispersal, only to be replaced by other religious constellations that express the same compositional elements with new emphases and nuances. Behind or beneath these historical and more or less sociological dynamics involved in the coming-to-be, evolution, and dispersal of religious groups lies the cultic process in its manifold articulations that contribute to the evolving pattern of religious group experience. It is the cultic process that gives rise to the splits, divisions, and partitions that adorn the chronicle of religious history.

The focus of the present study is on the interplay between structural aspects of the organization of religious movements, as depicted in terms of the cultic process and the internal, dynamic processes generated intrapsychically by the mechanisms of the paranoid process (Meissner 1978). As has become evident from the preceding chapters, the cultic process enjoys a particular functional role in each of the various contexts within which it finds expression. Religious groups comprise a heterogeneous spectrum of widely varying forms of organization and integration, and in each of these the cultic process finds its variant expression conditioned by the context within which it operates.

In phenomonological terms, the cultic process expresses a general tendency to factionalization in human religious experience and in the organization of religious groups. The cultic process is active and finds expression in all forms of religious experience, thriving on the tendency to form factions or subgroupings, to set up divergent or deviant elements of belief at variance with, or even in opposition to, more generally accepted belief systems of a given religious organization or organizations. At the same time, religious beliefs and practices always are contaminated by a highly individual, personal, and idiosyncratic dimension. Not only is the inherent variation of individual patterns of belief within a shared belief system part of the problem, but there are also almost completely idiosyncratic, even delusional, belief systems that by reason of their religious quality and emphasis can reasonably be regarded as religious phenomena. Consequently, while the consideration of religious phenomena as expressions of group processes has a certain utility, other forms of nongroup-related or nongroup-involved religious expression continue to play a vital role.

The cultic process, then, takes place within specifically religious contexts. As an aspect of religious experience, it shares in the diversity, complexity, and uniqueness of religious phenomena. Although the cultic process can be regarded as a specifically religious expression and process, it does not take place without a complex array of influences that can be described in both psychological and sociological terms. The psychological factor — the mechanisms, motives, and processes in the inner world of the believer — are continually and inexorably influenced by aspects of the environment. These factors can be variously described in terms of social, cultural, economic, and political factors.

Relation to the Paranoid Process

The cultic process is an aspect of the group process that draws its dynamic power from underlying psychological and motivational dynamics of the paranoid process (Meissner 1978).[1] The dynamic forces that drive the powerful wishes and fantasies embedded in all forms of eschatological and apocalyptic expectation are part of the motivational structure of the paranoid process (Meissner 1978).

My objective is to link these aspects of religious organizations and movements to operations of the paranoid process as a means of articulating some of the basic psychological mechanisms inherent in the cultic process. The paranoid process was defined originally in clinical terms (Meissner 1978), but finds its natural extension in the dynamics of the cultic process (Meissner 1984b). The clinical understanding of the paranoid process is rooted in the internal, drive-dependent, defensively motivated psychic structural configurations drawn from relationships with significant others during the course of development and life experience. When these internal configurations (introjects) are pathologically derived, they provide a core formation of pathogenic structures around which one's inner world and pathological sense of self becomes organized. These formations are organized in terms of aggressive and narcissistic polarities: the aggressive themes tend to be cast in terms of aggressive (victimizing) and victim (victimized) configurations, and the narcissistic dimensions take the form of superior and inferior configurations. To the extent that one or another of these configurations comes to dominate the subject's internal world, the self is experienced as aggressive, hostile, and destructive; vulnerable, weak, impotent, and helpless; special, entitled, omnipotent, even grandiose or, alternatively, inadequate, inferior, worthless, and shameful (Meissner 1978, 1986b). The combinations and interactions of these components of the self-system are the basis for the pathology of the self and for its variant characterological and symptomatic expressions.

---

1. A word of clarification may be useful here. The term "paranoid" does not refer to a form of psychopathology, nor does it refer to a form of personality structure. I have developed the rationale behind the concept of the paranoid process at length elsewhere (Meissner 1978, 1986b), but the potential for confusion must be continually addressed. The paranoid process is a general process of complex internalizations-cum-externalizations that come into play in the structuring of the personality (both normal and abnormal) and play an important role in social and cultural expressions. The cultic process is one such. The implications of the term "paranoid" are that these otherwise normal and adaptive processes carry within them the potential for paranoid distortion and, under specific eliciting conditions, can take a pathological turn. The recognition of such a potential would not justify the conclusion that the cultic process or any similar group process was in itself pathological, or that the individual personalities involved in the group process were all of the same personality structure (i.e., paranoid personalities).

The significance of such self-configurations for our present consideration is that they provide the foundation for defensive patterns of projection that can color and otherwise shape the subject's experience of his environment. The interaction of projection and such internalized self-configurations influences the experience of the relationship between the self and outside objects from very early on in the infant's career, and they continue to play a role in all subsequent phases of development and life experience. Any aspect of the self-organization can serve as the basis for projection; but usually when one polarity becomes the dominant focus of self-organization, the opposite polarity is projected. For example, if a patient experiences himself predominantly as weak, vulnerable, and victimized, his tendency is to project the opposite configuration outside himself so that he experiences certain key figures in his environment as powerful, threatening, or even persecuting. These vicissitudes play a powerful and central role in the development of transferences, not only in the psychoanalytic setting, but in a variety of life circumstances.

Such projective propensities, common as they are to the human condition, are inherently unstable and precarious, particularly where they may come into contradiction with or fail to find adequate sustaining confirmation in the external world. They require a framework, a sustaining organization of conceptual integration, to allow them to take on further meaning and relevance. This construction is provided by the paranoid construction, that is, a cognitive elaboration that justifies and sustains the patterns of projection and lends them a context of purposeful intention and meaningful connection. Such paranoid constructions, while they may take the form of conspiratorial hypotheses in their pathological renditions, more usually in the common run of human experience find expression in various forms of ideology or belief systems. Religious belief systems are obviously primary expressions of this process, but similar constructions, often serving similar functions, can be found articulated in political, social, and even cultural terms. The paranoid construction not only provides a sense of cognitive integration and purposeful organization intrapsychically, but it also serves to connect the ideology to a given group structure and reinforces the sense of belonging, of common commitment and participation that goes along with adherence to a group context and its related group culture. This dynamic is seen with dramatic clarity in the adherence to religious groups and their doctrinal ideologies.

My basic hypothesis is that social processes provide appropriate contexts within which the paranoid process can come into play, to preserve certain specific adaptive functions within society. Achievement of these goals is intimately linked to the sustaining of a sense of identity in the individual. Integration of the self, along with the sense of meaningful identity and the social participation and embeddedness of the self, are intimately intertwined and connected (Erikson 1959). Society provides structures and contexts within which the personal self finds appropriate involvements and commitments that allow the basic mechanisms of the paranoid process to be turned to adaptive and useful purposes.

The argument I will develop inevitably suffers from all the drawbacks of psychohistorical research. We cannot investigate the psychic processes of living subjects — only the dark and opaque residues of history. We can proceed only in the shadow of uncertainty and doubt regarding how much of the ancient events have been conveyed to us by the surviving texts, how much is selected and distorted by the processes of preservation and redaction, how much the sources are biased by the vicissitudes of the historical process, how much dictated by the ideological needs and belief systems of extant witnesses and their respective traditions, and so on. We can lean only on slender reeds and can lay claim to no more than conjectural plausibility to sustain our conclusions.

Moreover, when we deal with subjects of religious tradition and belief, we run the risks of reduction and the substitution of social or psychological plausibility for religious truth. I can only claim that the sociopsychological analysis of religiously relevant events and movements is unavoidably reductive, since it looks at the phenomena only through its own social or psychological lens and can say little or nothing about the religious significance or meaning of the events in question. Obviously that does not imply that the analysis need by that reason be reductionistic, as though the social or psychological analysis exhausted the meaning and relevance of the events or deprived them of their inherent religious significance. The concern here arises from the suspicion of the role of social sciences in the investigation of religious phenomena. The fear may be diminished by the realization that there are inherent limitations and cultural biases in any theological or philosophical method. More than a matter of bias, it is a question of what aspect of reality we choose to serve as the medium for analyzing the complexity of the problem we are exploring. In this sense, any interpretive paradigm runs the risk of becoming reductionistic (Osiek 1989). As far as psychoanalysis is concerned, Ricoeur (1970) has already made the case: "My working hypothesis . . . is that psychoanalysis is necessarily iconoclastic, regardless of the faith or nonfaith of the psychoanalyst, and that this 'destruction' of religion can be the counterpart of a faith purified of all idolatry. Psychoanalysis as such cannot go beyond the necessity of iconoclasm. This necessity is open to a double possibility, that of faith and that of nonfaith, but the decision about these two possibilities does not rest with psychoanalysis." (p. 230) Thus the linkage of religious phenomena and cultic processes with surrounding social and underlying psychodynamic processes has its iconoclastic and reductive dimension, but it does not distort and need not destroy the religious meaning and validity of the same events. Particularly, the connection of cultic events and belief systems with dimensions of the paranoid process does not deprive them of their religious relevance.

When we inquire into a causal context out of which paranoid pathology arises, we are unavoidably led to consider the relevance of this potentially paranoid matrix which permeates the whole of our social fabric and which serves adaptively to sustain both social and intrapsychic objectives. This point of view implies, then, that the process by which the paranoid disposition is formed takes its origins in part and is influenced by other social and group processes that can contribute important influences to the shaping of the paranoid disposition in a given pathologically affected individual. Basic to this argument is the idea that the emergence and persistence of messianic dreams and millennarian visions are based on the operation of the paranoid process, and that the paranoid process is the intrapsychic process for the channeling and expression of both narcissistic and aggressive dynamics as they come into play both internally, in the mind of the individual believer, and externally, in the development of the cult or religious movement. It is these psychodynamic elements that influence the persistence and vitality of these beliefs.

Social Prejudice

Social structures take multiple forms which provide the varied contexts within which the individual articulates his social sense of self. These multiple group forms embrace a wide spectrum of differences, each of which can serve as the rationale for group formation and for the division and opposition between groups. A given individual, living within this social ambience, may affiliate himself in varying degrees with many such reference groups, most of which have a degree of non-exclusiveness, but among which certain tensions are possible. If many such reference groups are not mutually exclusive, others are.

In discussing such paranoid manifestations, the question is not one of the reality of the situation as opposed to, let us say, a fanciful distortion. The question is rather of the ways and extent to which the paranoid mechanisms are brought into play. In many situations of social prejudice, the underlying issues have to do with the competition between subgroups. While the threat inherent in the competition can be seen at one level, for example, as an economic one, in the basic sense of competition for available jobs, the threat may also be posed at an intrapsychic level in terms of a threat to narcissism. It is not surprising, then, that paranoid mechanisms can be mobilized to defend against this potential threat. From clinical experience, we are familiar with the propensity for threatened or injured narcissism to think in terms of extreme alternatives, to blur realistic distinctions, to conceptualize in terms of stereotypical categories, and to seize upon any identifiable differences as the basis for drawing the line between that to which one affiliates oneself and that to which one is opposed — to draw the line, that is, between those who belong and those who do not, between those who are members of the "in" group and those who must be regarded as enemies.

The formation of such extreme and radical groupings provides a context within which the paranoid resources of members can be mobilized to sustain a significant sense of self and a context within which purposeful striving and belonging can be realized. The provision of such a matrix provides an important source of sustenance and support for an emergent sense of identity that otherwise is in danger of being undermined and overwhelmed. As Volkan (1988) comments:

> A sense of self is the impression one has of how his emotional, intellectual, and physical components respond together to the world about him and to pressures arising within himself. . . . The obstacles encountered along the way contribute to the developing concept of the enemy, partly through their coalescence with issues pertaining to the sense of self. Finally, as adults equipped with their own value system and the values belonging to their culture, they know whom they like and dislike and who is safe and who is not. (p. 4)

The danger, of course, is the same danger that is always inherent in the mobilization of such paranoid resources. It runs the risk of verifying its own projections, and eliciting a mutually responsive paranoid rejoinder from the larger community within which it functions. To the extent that paranoia elicits and generates a reciprocal paranoid response, the process becomes mutually destructive and pathological.

On both sides of the dividing line between the subjective group and the outside world, there grows up a mythology which builds on the history of significant episodes in which essentially paranoid distortions were apparently realized and verified. What is noteworthy here, as in so many other areas in which the paranoid process plays itself out, is not only that the paranoid mechanisms have a propensity for eliciting their own verification, but that the paranoid construction tends to generate a mythology which may be based on a small number of verifiable incidents, but which it uses as the basis for a general ideology expressing both the victimization of one's own group and the malicious and untrustworthy evil of the other. In such contexts we can clearly see the mythopoeic potentiality of the paranoid process, as an aspect of the mechanism of the paranoid construction, coming into clear elaboration.

In instances of this sort, society brings the paranoid process into play and so organizes a variety of groupings and structures based on and organized around discriminable differences between groups. The paranoid process not only defines and consolidates such groupings, but provides the basic psychic conditions in terms of which the group processes work themselves out and through which the interaction between groups on various levels is determined and qualified. Thus the functioning of the paranoid process in its various manifestations becomes an essential dimension in the organization and maintenance of such social groupings.

Group participation often offers the basis for a degree of inner healing and restitution. Embracing the group ideology and commitment to the belief system carries with it the potential for a meaningful degree of self-integration and consolidation of a sense of identity. In many cases, the fragile narcissism of the member is the locus of this restitution. This narcissistic restitution is accomplished through the integration of ego and ego ideal. As Chasseguet-Smirgel (1985) observes:

> Groups often offer a much shorter route to the longstanding wish for the union of ego and ideal. Such groups are based upon an ideology which may be defined, psychoanalytically, as a system that appears to have a more or less rational basis, corresponding to the outward appearance of dreams and to secondary elaboration. An ideology always contains within it a fantasy of narcissistic assumption linked to a return to a state of primary fusion,

which equally excludes conflict and castration and thus operates within the order of illusion. (p. 193)

If such social organization serves the interests of sustaining and integrating individual identities, we must also not lose sight of the fact that such groupings and the working through of social processes have an important role to play in the maintaining of social order and in the working out of social adaptations. Social processes are by no means fixed or static in nature. They are rather processes of dynamic tension and change, in which progressive social adaptations and structural modifications are continually being elaborated and worked through by means of the oppositional tension created between social groupings. In the contexts of a dynamic and changing social structure, a reasonable and manageable degree of confrontation and social struggle is not only unavoidable, but is indeed a necessary and optimal condition for the adaptive integration of social processes. The paranoid process, functioning within such a social system, provides the dynamic underpinning and motivating force maintaining social processes in a state of continual tension and dynamic opposition.

The paranoid potential of these processes can at times reach explosive and inflammatory proportions. These dynamics are unmistakable, for example, in revolutionary millennarian movements, but are by no means restricted to these more flagrant and dramatically explosive expressions of the cultic process (Barkun 1974; Cohn 1970a; Worsley 1968). In one degree or other, and in one manner or other, these observations are pertinent for the origins and evolution of all religious movements.

The Paranoid Style

The discussion of the dynamics of the emergence and shaping of religious cults and sects aims at focusing aspects of the cultic process as sociocultural and religious phenomena and explicating their connection with the paranoid process. The general hypothesis that provides the basic framework for this discussion is that in the clinical manifestations of the paranoid process — that is, in their specifically pathological forms — we see only the tip of the paranoid iceberg. We can find identifiable paranoid mechanisms operating not only in a broad spectrum of psychopathologies, but also at large in the general population, manifested in more commonly experienced emotional states of envy, jealousy, prejudice, etc., that are not in themselves pathological but share a close affinity with pathological states. Large segments of the population are afflicted with such basically paranoid-like attitudes without ever coming to clinical attention. In fact, our social fabric is such that we entertain a high degree of tolerance of such attitudes without feeling it necessary to regard them or react to them as forms of pathology (Meissner 1978).

Thus the paranoid iceberg is definable not merely in terms of realms of identifiable pathology which remain within the limits of the socially acceptable and nonclinical, but it also has relevance to the areas of not merely socially acceptable, but constructive and adaptive processes that serve to sustain the functioning of human personality on one level, but which on another level make significant contributions to the development and functioning of social processes and institutions.

In emphasizing the paranoid propensities within social and specifically religious structures, the paranoid dimensions carry a somewhat different cast from that found in frank clinical paranoia. In discussing the paranoid style in political contexts, Hofstadter (1967) offers the following description:

> In the paranoid style, as I conceive it, the feeling of persecution is central, and it is indeed systematized in grandiose theories of conspiracy. But there is a vital difference between the paranoid spokesman in politics and the clinical paranoiac: although they both tend to be overheated, over-suspicious, over-aggressive, grandiose, and apocalyptic in expression, the clinical paranoid sees the hostile and conspiratorial world in which he feels himself to be living as directed specifically *against him*; whereas the spokesman of the paranoid style finds it directed against a nation, a culture, a way of life whose fate affects not himself alone but millions of others. Insofar as he does not usually see himself singled out as the individual victim of a personal conspiracy, he is somewhat more rational and much more disinterested. His sense that his political passions are unselfish and patriotic, in fact, goes far to intensify his feeling of righteousness and his moral indignation. (p. 4)

The description applies analogously to cultic movements, especially millennarian or salvationist cults, that engage in the demonization of out-groups and divide the world into the good and the bad, the saved and the damned. The common fears and anxieties of the cult group are discharged by projection onto stereotypical objects that threaten the security of the group. Evil may be personified in the form of Satan, the Antichrist, the Pope or any symbolic representative of the hated and feared out-group. And the relation of persecuted and persecutor becomes reciprocal; as Trevor-Roper (1969) wrote of the witch-craze in medieval Europe, "just as psychopathic individuals, in those years, centered their separate fantasies . . . on the Devil, and thus gave an apparent objective identity to their subjective experiences, so societies in fear articulated their collective neuroses about the same obsessive figure, and found a scapegoat for their fears in his agents, the witches." (pp. 165-166)

Developmental Issues

In developmental terms, the influence of paranoid mechanisms in the oedipal period plays a central role in the shaping of the individual's capacity for social engagement. The oedipal involvement provides the initial point for the young child of a more complex level of social involvement than had previously been in question on the more pregenital levels of one-to-one interaction. The child's involvement in the oedipal situation forces him to begin to grapple with the intricacies of relating to others in more complex social relationships. Paranoid mechanisms are called into play in the service of resolving the inherent ambivalence of such involvements (Meissner 1986a).

This view of the essentially paranoid dynamics in the developmental sequence is expressed in Pinderhughes' (1986) differential bonding hypothesis. He argues that group behavior is characterized by affiliation and attachment to group structures, ideals, values, belief systems, religions, schools of thought, principles, etc. Such affiliative or bonding behavior is either positive or negative, similar to the way in which the child affiliatively idealizes one parent and aggressively competes with the other in the oedipal alignment. Men are thus both social and antisocial creatures. There are affectionate and affiliative bonds to friends and loved ones, but also aggressive, hostile, and disaffiliative bonds to our enemies, the objects of our hatred and aversion. Bonding behavior involves both approach-affiliative-affectionate behavior on one hand and avoidance-differentiative-aggressive behavior on the other. Acknowledged aspects of the self are associated with affiliative bonds; the renounced and rejected aspects correspondingly are associated with differentiative bonds. The object of affiliative bonding is idealized and aggrandized, the object of differentiative bonding devalued through the operation of the paranoid process. Affiliative bonding takes place between the members of the in-group, differentiative-aggressive bonding to certain out-groups. Illusive beliefs are maintained regarding the in-group and devaluing illusions regarding the out-group or enemies.

Differential-aggressive bonding involves projective and paranoid processes that we tend to deny. The more adversarial and aggressive our interaction, the stronger the paranoia and projection onto the enemy. The extremes of such differentiative bonding result in devaluation and dehumanization of the enemy, the process of pseudo-speciation described by Erikson (1966) which makes the adversary something inhuman or less than human. Such a tactic is evident in the treatment of concentration camp inmates, POWs, the treatment of enemies in war, in forms of racial and ethnic prejudice, in religious conflicts and controversies, and so on. Erikson (1975) pondered whether mankind was ". . . destined to remained divided into 'pseudo-species' forever playing out one (necessarily incomplete) version of mankind against all the others until, in the dubious glory of the nuclear age, one version will have the power and the luck to destroy all the others just moments before it perishes itself?" (p. 47)

The oedipal situation itself is an expression of such mechanisms and is to that extent brought into being by the the mechanisms of introjection and projection. (Meissner 1978, 1986a) The need to resolve ambivalence and the manner of its accomplishment suggest that the loved object can only be protected from destructive impulses by the diversion of such impulses to alternate objects which are then assigned a negative status. The conflict inherent in all ambivalence, namely the impulse to destroy that which one also loves and wishes to preserve, can be resolved only to the extent that the conflicting impulses can be distributed between different objects. Thus the use of the familiar mechanisms of splitting and projection to resolve ambivalence leads to a situation in which the loved object is preserved by projecting destructive impulses to a relatively devalued object, thus leaving the preserved object relatively idealized. Where the object of the displaced destructive impulses is a part of one's self, the outcome is potentially toxic and self-destructive. This is the course that is followed in many forms of depressive illness, in which the value of the ambivalently held object is sustained by means of the devaluation of the self (Rochlin 1965). Clinically depression is one alternative to a paranoid resolution.

However, as Pinderhughes (1970, 1971) points out, the destructive impulses are ultimately a part of the self and can only successfully be gotten rid of and projected insofar as they are linked associatively with those components of one's own person which lend themselves readily to devaluation and expulsion. Thus the object of destructive impulses must be linked to representations of expendable body parts or products so that it can be successfully utilized as an object for projection. A variety of processes of riddance of devalued body products can be employed as symbolic equivalents of the projective displacement of negative and destructive attitudes. The most striking and powerful such bodily process of devaluation and riddance is obviously the anal one. Pinderhughes (1971) comments:

> Mental representations associated with excreted body products are invested with a denigrating false belief system as they are ejected, projected upon, and attacked. Mental representations of persons or groups may be invested with denigrating false belief systems, often by linkages with excreted body products through relationships in the body image. Idealized persons, groups, and body parts are invested with an aggrandizing false belief system. Both patterns are employed normally and consistently in the resolution of ambivalence by a non-pathological but nevertheless paranoid mechanism which projects negative components of ambivalent feelings toward a renounced outside object, and positive components toward an object one associates with oneself. Each individual achieves thereby an outward expression of destructive aggression without endangering any acknowledged parts of the self. (pp. 680-681)

In the context of oedipal relationships, the ambivalence in the relationship with each parent is reduced by distributing ambivalent feelings between them. Classically, in the positive resolution of the oedipal constellation, it is the opposite-sex parent who is consciously idealized and sought after, while the same-sex parent becomes the object of aggressive and negative impulses. However in the negative resolution of the oedipal configuration, the opposite tendency obtains: namely, that the same-sex parent becomes the object of positive and idealized strivings while the opposite-sex parent becomes the recipient of negative projections. Thus the libidinal bond with the one parent and the aggressive bond with the other serves to protect from the threat of psychic loss of these significant objects which is involved in the destructive components of the underlying ambivalence. The protection from the threat of loss and separation is dependent on the success with which this process can be worked through and the paranoid mechanisms successfully employed in the interests of diverting destructive feelings and resolving ambivalence. They accomplish this by the use of displacements, projections, introjections, and the institution of a form of false belief system in which one object is relatively idealized and the other devalued (the paranoid construction).

CHAPTER 16

Beliefs and the Paranoid Process

Relation to Belief Systems

The eschatological and apocalyptic belief systems are expressions of the cultic process which, in turn, touches on and reflects several aspects of the psychological components of the paranoid process. One aspect of the cultic process is the formation of and commitment to a specific belief system; a second is the tendency to sectarian divisiveness and exclusivity. The belief system or ideology (Erikson 1959; Barratt 1986) of any religious group is equivalent to a form of paranoid construction (Meissner 1978), a cognitive system or elaboration providing a context of meaning that supports and makes sense of particular projections or systems of projections, and lends credibility, justification, and purposefulness to individual commitments based wholly or in part on such projective components.[1] I will argue that messianic and millennarian beliefs are equivalent to paranoid constructions that sustain the hopes and expectations invested in these belief systems. Insofar as the projective elements derive from subjective self-configurations in the individual's inner world, the consolidation and coherence of

---

1. See the discussion of the relation between projections and the paranoid construction in the previous chapter.

these elements through the paranoid construction serve the further function of sustaining a coherent sense of self and identity.

In the religious context, then, commitment to the belief system brings with it a sense of meaning and purpose to one's human existence and suffering; it conveys a sense of significance and purpose in death; it confirms the believer in sharing in the life of a community of believers that form the in-group, and it indicates an ethic of salvation, a code of morality and ritualized praxis pointing the way toward right living and the ultimate fulfillment of human destiny. From a psychological perspective, the belief system serves the same function as the paranoid construction, namely it provides a meaningful context within which the believer's sense of identity and self-integrity can find consolidation and confirmation. This makes it understandable why belief systems come to play such a discriminative role and suggests why such ideological constructions can easily become divisive and exclusive.

The resolution of ambivalence and the avoidance of loss are cardinal motives for the use of paranoid mechanisms on the level of group processes and cultural dynamics. In the organization of groups and the working out of group behavior, protection from the sense of loss and separation is accomplished by idealizing and libidinizing the values, attitudes and beliefs of one's own group while, at the same time, devaluing, rejecting and opposing the values and attitudes of what does not belong to one's own group. Many aspects of these forms of group-related paranoid mechanisms insure that group members will direct positive feelings towards one another and towards their own group and negative feelings towards outsiders. The process serves to resolve the inherent ambivalence in any such group relationship and provides a greater constancy and stability of psychic relationships. It is a form of normal illusion formation which serves to aggrandize one object or set of objects and conversely denigrates and devalues other objects.

Thus the operation of paranoid mechanisms can be seen to serve highly adaptive functions. Where the levels of ambivalence are not excessively intense, and where the susceptibility to loss is not catastrophic or overwhelming, and where sufficient ego resources have been allowed to emerge by way of significantly constructive introjections and internalizations, there will be a sufficient capacity for trust to enable an individual to form social bonds with other individuals and to align their paranoid responses with those of others to permit the development of such nonpathological and group-related paranoid systems. In becoming members of an in-group, they share a certain set of values, attitudes, positions, belief systems or ideologies, etc., with other like-minded individuals.

Such individuals are able to respond to and satisfy the needs which underlie the paranoid process and, by this means, achieve a sense of belonging and acceptance which mitigates the basic ambivalence threatening both their sense of self internally and their sense of participation and belonging extrinsically. However, where individuals are unable to muster a sufficient degree of trust to allow such participation and are unable to form such social bonds, they become vulnerable to increasingly idiosyncratic belief systems, and the workings of the paranoid process must then begin to verge toward the pathological. The same dynamics are observable in religious movements that become so isolated and embattled that the paranoid mechanisms involved take a pathological turn — as, for example, in the Zealots of ancient Palestine, the messianic revolt of bar Kochba, and certain revolutionary millennarian sects.

Group Formation

Social processes find their most basic expression in the formation of groups. The forming of social groupings is in part a shaping of an in-group, to which are aggregated the aspects of value and belonging which provide the matrix of support for individual identities. A basic aspect of the process of identity formation has to do with the delineation and affiliation with such specific in-groups, within which the individual can define himself as a participating member with a sense of belonging and purposive participation. However, the defining of the in-group is in part accomplished by setting it apart from and in opposite to the variety of out-groups that embrace divergent or oppositional sets of values and beliefs to those adhered to by the in-group.

Pinderhughes' (1971) hypothesis is quite congruent with the point of view of the present study:

> One relates by introjection to representatives of groups of which one feels a part, and one relates by projection to representatives of groups which one perceives as different from one's own. Thus, a group or its constituents are perceived and related to as if they were a single object. One is inclined to join or leave, to swallow or spit out, to accept or reject, and to associate pleasure or discomfort with social groups insofar as they are perceived as similar to one own or different from one's own. (p. 685)

Consequently the nonpathological group-related paranoias tend to idealize by introjection the groups with which an individual affiliates himself and with which he identifies, and correspondingly to denigrate by means of projection the groups from which the individual disassociates himself. Thus the forming of such groups can provide a buffer against the loss of significant relationships and belonging within one's own group, but at the same time it provides a potent source for intergroup conflict.

Reciprocally, of course, the group process provides a support and context within which the individual paranoia can assert and sustain itself. Given the mutual support and reinforcement for the false belief system shared by the group, the belief system then becomes for the group a matter of principle, an ideology, or a dogma, for which group members are willing to contend, fight, and even in certain extreme situations surrender their lives. In reflecting on the paranoid process, consequently, it is important to remember that the system of delusional belief which characterizes the paranoid distortion is driven by strong internal defensive and adaptive needs. It is motivated by the need to resolve intolerable ambivalence and to avoid the pain of loss — most poignantly and pressingly the pain of narcissistic loss and deprivation. Thus the individual psyche resorts to any devices which offer it the promise of sustaining narcissistic impairment and integrating a sense of self and identity, which is both internally consistent and coherent and articulated within a context of social acceptance and belonging. It is precisely this aspect of the pressure toward identity which the group formation responds to most acutely.

Where the level of ambivalence is too intense, or the sensitivity to narcissistic loss and compromise too powerful for the individual to be able to sustain an adequate sense of self in interaction with such a social matrix, the powerful pressures continue to operate in such a way that the individual must resolve the defensive needs by resorting to a more idiosyncratic and divergent paranoid system. Where the processes are operating in such a fashion as to reinforce and capitalize on such personal pathology in a subject who has the potentiality and capacity for charismatic leadership, the explosive potential is created for destructive, apocalyptic leadership to which the paranoid propensities of the group members respond, so as to bring to realization a group paranoia of powerful and irresistible dimensions.

Need for the Enemy

There is another aspect of group formation, on which we have touched briefly, and which often plays a telling part in the dynamics of religious group formation and the workings of the cultic process. Sustaining the integrity and strength of the group may require that it set itself over against an enemy. This is specifically where the paranoid mechanisms come into play. In a sense the group needs an enemy in order to bolster its own inner resources and to maintain its own inner sense of value and purposiveness. We see frequently in paranoid patients the need to sustain a meaningful sense, of self by putting down and devaluing others around them. A similar mechanism operates at the group level. The group sustains itself by idealizing its own values and setting them over against and in conflict with the lesser and denigrated values of other groups. Furthermore, the dynamics of the situation will not tolerate a mere appraisal in terms of greater-or-lesser or more-or-less, the narcissistic basis on which the process operates demands a logic of extremes, in which there is a tendency for all value to be inherent in the in-group and no value or negative value to be inherent elsewhere. The natural extension of this logic is to set the respective value systems in opposition and to regard them as mutually exclusive and destructive. What is in question here is not merely differences in degree but the narcissistically derived need for enemies.

The paranoid construction, in a sense, rationalizes the pattern of projections so that adherents to the belief system and members of the in-group are viewed as bearers of truth and goodness, while those who reject or oppose the belief system or belong to deviant out-groups are regarded as the agents of falsehood, error, even evil. This projective necessity requires the existence of an enemy[2] who becomes the target and bearer of projections; the projections themselves do not stand alone, but require a sustaining matrix within which they can find confirmation and rationalization.

The need for an enemy arises out of the developmental context, in which the child's developing personalization requires the projection of bad elements to outside objects. These bad elements, primarily aggressive and destructive, are externalized and thus allow a more cohesive integration of the child's self with less conflicted and ambivalent

---

2. The motif of the need for enemies has been proposed by a number of authors (Boyer 1986; Meissner 1978; Pinderhughes 1970, 1979, 1982, 1986; Volkan 1985, 1988) and unquestionably plays a central role in the paranoid process.

internalizations (Meissner 1978). But as the aggressivized projections develop, the enemy is painted in increasingly dehumanized and demonic colors, so that he easily becomes a monstrous, destructive and evil entity seen as posing a dire threat to the integrity, purpose, and beliefs of the in-group. In religious movements, the enemy becomes the unbeliever, the infidel, who is colored with the dark shadows of deceit, evil intent, and demonic characteristics that earn him the label of Satan, the Devil, the Antichrist.

In some sense, the finding or creating of an enemy is integral to the consolidation and reinforcement of in-group dynamics. This inference derives from the basic hypothesis regarding the role of paranoid mechanisms in the constitution and sustaining of social groups, articulated here in terms of the paranoid process. The process, however, requires that suitable targets for such externalization be selected as safe and durable containers for such bad self- and object-images. The designation of such suitable targets is a function of the child's internalization and introjection of group norms and values, and a separation and distancing from other less desirable and alien groups. Where such suitable targets for externalization (projection) are not established as part of the child's development within the group and part of his assimilation of the group culture, an important component of his emerging identity and sense of self may be lacking and have dire developmental consequences. The subsequent separation, devaluation, and hostile rejection of the targets of projection lay the basis for the later emergence of a concept of an enemy (Volkan 1986, 1988).

The existence of the enemy and the threat he poses can have an indirect but beneficial effect within the in-group. The threat posed by the enemy forces the members of the in-group to value all the more intently and fanatically what the in-group stands for and to commit themselves all the more convincingly to the purposes, beliefs and values to which the group directs itself. Thus the more strongly the enemy confronts and attempts to undermine the group, the more powerful is the inner impulse to defend, cherish and adhere to what the group represents. Once we are in a position to grasp the significance of the sustaining of the values and perspectives of the in-group, we can also begin to appreciate the important dynamics which are brought into the service of such needs, particularly in terms of the need for an enemy in sustaining and reinforcing the integrity and cohesiveness of the group.

One can suggest that participation in communal paranoid undertakings, such as involved in membership in religious groups, has an important function in terms of the adjustment capacity for such individuals. The commitment to and investment in the religious group and its ideology seems to absorb significant amounts of paranoid potentiality, so that instead of resorting to deviant forms of antisocial behavior, the group members are enabled to share in a communal effort in the defense of shared values and convictions. These individuals are thus accepted into a transient grouping, which provides them with a context of usefulness and meaningful belonging and participation which serves to sustain and consolidate their fragile or potentially fragmented sense of identity.

It is clear that the parameters of the paranoid process play a central and significant role in such manifestations. They serve to undercut the element of self-devaluation and self-rejection which play such a central role in psychosocial deviance (Kaplan 1972). At the same time, they provide the context of meaningful participation and group belonging which contributes powerfully to the maintenance of self-esteem. It seems that more accurately than the need to have enemies, there is the need to have enemies to hate and a need to be able to hate our enemies (Stein 1986) as an important contributing and stabilizing force for the maintenance of both group and individual identity (Meissner 1978). The mechanisms are no different in the context of belonging to religious cultic movements, and in large measure tend to bring about similar results and effects on individual psychic functioning.

Thus, the definition of one's self and particularly of one's self as a participant in the group to which he attaches and with which he identifies is in part defined by contrasts with the other groups to which the individual does not belong and against which he defines his own sense of self. For these purposes, some enemies are better than others; the best enemy is the one who can optimally mirror and embody the negative identity of the group, the one that can best come to represent the disowned and projected aspects of the self (Stein 1986). The paradox often is that the more we strive to differentiate ourselves and our group from the enemy, the greater the resemblance seems to be on an unconscious level. As Volkan (1988) comments:

> Of the two principles that seem to dominate preoccupation with an enemy, the first deals in a paradoxical way with a sameness between ourselves and the enemy. Because the enemy, whatever realistic considerations may be involved, is a reservoir of our unwanted self- and object- representations with which elements of our projections are condensed, there should be some unconscious perception of a likeness, a reverse correspondence that binds us together while alienating us. However, the externalizations and

projections we have given our enemy are repugnant to us, so we disavow them and do not want to acknowledge this connection consciously. We feel ourselves obliged to see huge and important differences between us that support our sense of self and of membership 'in our own group. (p. 99)

The process leads in the direction of the development of increasingly aggressive and threatening stereotypes that bypass any positive characteristics or qualities of the enemy, but serve to increase a sense of psychological distance and differentiation between ourselves and them.

The relationship to the enemy is a complex psychological phenomenon. From one perspective, it is necessary to maintain a sense of separation, difference, and distance from the enemy — Volkan's (1988) second principle. From another perspective, the aggression directed to the enemy binds us to him. It becomes necessary to control the psychological gap, maintaining simultaneously a sense of difference and connection (Volkan 1986). The gap serves to maintain a sense of unconscious connection through the unconsciously shared derivatives of aggression (Volkan 1986, 1987).

Sense of Self

The added step in the process concerns the motivation behind the projections. The paranoid process perspective suggests that the projections become necessary to preserve the integrity of the self-system of the individual believer. The organization of the self embraces a configuration of introjects as the core constituents. Whatever aspects of this core configuration which cannot be meaningfully integrated in the functional self must either be repressed or projected. These elements may be hostile or destructive; they may involve weakness or vulnerability; they may involve elements of shame and inferiority; or they may have the cast of omnipotence or grandiosity. The projection serves the stability of the self by internal denial and repression and by attribution of such conflictual qualities to the external objects. The overall function of the paranoid system, then, is to achieve and preserve the integrity and meaningful existence of the self. This likewise is the basis of its motivation (Meissner 1978).

These powerful motives would have been at work in the drama of contending religious forces in the early history of Christianity. The Palestinian origins took place in the context of the struggle of an oppressed people against Roman domination and of the destruction of Jerusalem. For the Jews, this meant profound humiliation and desperation. Jewish Christians sought refuge in an adherence to the mosaic law and a reaffirmation of messianic hopes. Hellenistic Christians, for a variety of reasons (Meissner 1988), sought to dissociate themselves from judaizing influences and associations. Their common lot was persecution.

Where the sense of self is more profoundly threatened by unresolved ambivalences, the need for an enemy becomes a predominant influence in the shaping and sustaining of a sense of self (Kets de Vries 1977; Meissner 1978). We can recognize in this aspect of the process the workings of unresolved narcissistic needs. Primitive and unresolved narcissism, with its tendency to unremitting and exclusive demands, leaves little room for sharing or alliance, and sees external objects as generally threatening to its need for omnipotence and omnivorous possessiveness. Such pathogenic narcissism carries within itself the potentiality and the need for enemies. As long as the individual sense of self remains congruent and adaptive in the functioning social matrix, we do not tend to regard the sense of self as pathological. Where the individual's relationships to the group are pervaded by a sense of conformity, we may recognize a certain impairment of the individuality of that identity and may be able to recognize the lineaments of what is essentially a false self; but we nonetheless regard this as falling within the relatively normal range of socially acceptable adaptation. Where the individual cannot join himself to these forms of group-related paranoia and where the internal pressures override the resources of these processes to absorb the intensity of destructive and ambivalent impulses, the individual must resort to a delusional system within which the false sense of self overwhelms the intrapsychic configuration, and in which that false sense of self seeks its pathological relatedness to a persecutory environment.

Paranoid Mechanisms

The burden of these conclusions is obvious, since it points us in the direction of resolving broad areas of social and religious conflict in terms of the underlying paranoid mechanisms. As Pinderhughes (1970), in a lucid discussion of these issues, has observed:

> Nonpathological paranoia well might be viewed as a pervasive, even universal, process stimulated by and dealing with conflicting psychic impulses. Such a concept is consistent with the vast scale on which we find conflict, exploitation, discrimination, and destruction taking place between human beings. One of the reasons

why we have made so little progress in curbing and eliminating discrimination, exploitation, violence and war lies in our refusal to recognize and acknowledge that all human beings depend heavily upon paranoid processes throughout their lives. Most persons are too narcissistic to conceptualize themselves as primitive or irrational in thinking and behavior. They prefer instead to view themselves as intelligent and rational, while failing to observe that their intelligence and reason are impaired in the service of paranoid processes which aggrandize those with whom they identify and denigrate those they project upon. Intellect and reason are employed unconsciously to maintain and advance the position, benefits, and comforts of some persons at the expense of others. (p. 608)

Groups tend to exaggerate their distinguishing differences from other groups in ways which denigrate the others and enhance their own status as "special." As the GAP report (1987) comments,

Tragically, as groups "discover" themselves to be special and superior to others, they behave as though they are unaware that all groups engage in this kind of assessment — and for the same reason. All draw attention to their culture and direct it away from the vulnerable identity core they use culture to defend. What a paradox — the insistence on uniqueness is universal; only the cultural trimmings differ, and the core — the core purpose — of identity remains the same. (pp. 22-23)

Erikson (1966) pointed to the role of ritualization in this process, particularly in its function of deflecting feelings of unworthiness onto outside objects. In adolescence certain rituals of confirmation serve to integrate earlier childhood identifications and introjections into ideological beliefs to which one gives allegiance and to the crystallization of foreign belief systems, wishes, fantasies and images that have become alien and undesirable. The assignment of these alien ideological elements to the outside group serve to consolidate the boundaries between the in-group and the out-group. Thus ritualization has as its purpose the overcoming or at least tolerance of ambivalence within the group by projection of negative aspects to the outside objects in a process of pseudospeciation. The assimilation of these cultural norms are the mark of the individual's participation in the culture of the group, an aspect of his group belonging, and of his integration of his own sense of self and identity in social and cultural terms.

It may be worth noting the quality of the thinking which attends such processes. There is clearly a logic of all-or-nothing, either-or, black-and-white, which pervades the propaganda characteristic of such situations. One side is right and the other is wrong — completely and more or less absolutely. All virtue and truth and goodness is aggregated to one side of the controversy, while evil, wrongdoing, destructiveness, error and falsehood are attributed to the other side. The capacity for discrimination seems to be obfuscated and impoverished, with the result that thinking takes place in terms of stereotypes. And even further, the stereotypes tend to run in terms of desperate extremes. Passions run high, and the individuals involved seem to be impervious to reason or to evidence.

These are all familiar expressions of the paranoid process. The distortions that we have been discussing are in fact quite consistent with the understanding of the paranoid process that we have been elaborating in these pages. We can recognize that the attitudes and feelings and points of view which characterize these situations are driven by inner need rather than by external realities or available evidences. We can recognize that on both sides of these situations of confrontation and conflict, there is at work a pervasive fear and an impending sense of vulnerability and threatened loss. We can also recognize the characteristic paranoid mechanisms — the paranoid construction which organizes and rationalizes the perceptions of reality and the available data into a framework, which supports and justifies the underlying projections; the sense of vulnerability and narcissistic fragility found in all situations of paranoid defense. We can also detect the intolerance of ambivalence which seeks to resolve itself by resorting to paranoid mechanisms.

While the paranoid aspects of these situations are relatively transparent and easily identifiable, we want to keep in focus the adaptive aspects which also serve in important ways to sustain these processes. One of the salient rewards, which accrue to the individual by reason of his affiliation to the group, is a sense of acceptance and belonging; there is an affiliation to a certain set of values which are esteemed and accorded regard within the community. By assimilating and adopting as well as internalizing these values, therefore, the individual aggregates himself to the community and thus assimilates to himself some of the esteem and sense of value that is derived from and inherent in the community.

In conclusion, the various aspects of the cultic process can be seen to have an intrinsic connection with the underlying dynamic forces of the paranoid process. The emotional power and intensity of religious beliefs and commitments derive in some degree from unconscious forces of libidinal, narcissistic, and even aggressive drive components that are embedded in and shaped by the mechanisms of the paranoid process. It is through these mechanisms that these derivatives find their way into communal expression in a variety of social, cultural and religious settings. It is through the interpenetration of these dynamic components with other factors, operating at more conscious and group-oriented levels of action and interaction, that a deeper and more comprehensive understanding of the impact of religious beliefs and movements becomes available. The effort to bring some aspects of the history of the development and evolution of messianic and millennarian belief systems and their relations with religious cultic movements into focus, in terms of the integral interplay of the cultic and paranoid processes, adds another dimension to the understanding of man's religious experience and its psychic meaning.

CHAPTER 17

Messianism and the Cultic
Process

The preceding discussion of messianism,[1] has explored various aspects of the messianic vision as it emerged from the ancient prophetic tradition and evolved within the Judeo-Christian tradition. Within that religious context or series of contexts, the messianic idea evolved and took on a variety of forms and expressions that were more or less congruent with the historical conditions of the time and place. While the messianic metaphor may have taken its origin within the framework of Judaic eschatological expectations and apocalyptic hopes, the messianic phenomenon was by no means constrained to that religious context. While the most important and historically meaningful transformation of the messianic visions of the Judaic tradition came in the emergence of Christianity, as a heterodox sectarian divergence from more central Jewish beliefs, further anthropological research has demonstrated that the messianic emphasis has an almost universal appeal, so that messianic groups and dynamics have found their way into countless religious traditions in the course of subsequent history. Rather than a specific culturally bound form of religious doctrine, messianism has taken on the character of an almost universal form of religious response.

---

1. See sections II, III, and IV above.

I would like to turn at this point to a more theoretical account of the role and dynamics of the messianic phenomenon as exemplified in the above sections, and to bring into clearer focus the relevance of this material for an understanding of the cultic process.

Aspects of the Messianic Ideal

Messianic religious movements reveal certain general, identifiable characteristics that are analogously relevant to the development of messianic traditions within Judaism and later Christianity. Generally speaking, faith in a savior who is to come at the end of time is by no means alien to many religious systems, whether primitive or more culturally evolved. Its origin and persistence must rest on powerful and persistent underlying psychological motives, as well as on a variety of external conditions involving social and economic forces, along with cultural determinants — especially the prevailing religious beliefs of a given culture or nation. The desire for perfection and unalloyed happiness is constantly threatened and denied by the forces of harsh reality, but this chronic disappointment can be balanced by a twofold illusion — that of a golden age somewhere in the distant past, and by a future-oriented hope for a return to that golden age or something like it. As Fuchs (1965) observes:

> The conviction that mankind or, more precisely, a particular tribe or people, has changed in the course of time from a state of perfect happiness and prosperity in the past to the unsatisfactory and unhappy present state, suggests a basically pessimistic attitude of the human mind. This pessimistic outlook, however, assuming a deterioration of the world and of mankind, has not been able to wholly extinguish human hope for a return to the Golden Age. If a divine or semi-divine benefactor could create a paradise in the early days of mankind, it can be recreated, and the perfect human happiness lost long ago through human wickedness or stupidity can be restored by the same benevolent superhuman agency or by another divine or semi-divine benefactor. (p. ix)

It can also be argued that, whatever the other ideological and motivational sources of such beliefs, messianic movements seem to arise in contexts of particular economic and social tension and distress. The typical situation is one of domination and oppression by an alien power and culture. This was clearly the case for the rise of messianic hopes in ancient Israel and in the circumstances of Judaic life around the turn of the millennium. The less developed and essentially agrarian culture

of Israel was swallowed up by the power, wealth and philosophic so-
phistication of the Roman Empire. Thrust within the sphere of first
Seleucid, then Ptolemaic, and finally Roman influence, Israelite culture
was in no position to withstand the cultural assimilation and erosion
these powerful political entities brought with them; yet the Israelite
spirit was not about to yield to the forces of paganism and hellenistic
thought, and easily assimilate or adopt the new ways of thinking and
living. The more the oppressors tried to force these changes on the
people of Israel, the stronger the resistances grew and the deeper the
resentments.

Coupled with severe economic exploitation and harsh oppression,
the psychological consequences for the individual Israelite had to be
severe, if not catastrophic. They were unable to endure life under such
depressing conditions, but also unable to find surcease or escape from
the predicament. The frustration of sporadic efforts at flight or rebellion left them little alternative but to turn their hopes to a charismatic
figure or leader who would save them from their pain and rage — if
not in the present, at least in some future earthly paradise or heavenly
kingdom. And he would do this by no ordinary means, such as those
that had been tried and failed, but by a miraculous and supernatural
intervention that would call into play the infinite power of God.

The Messianic Belief System

The messianic idea or ideas that lie so close to the core of both
the Judaic and the Christian belief systems can be characterized by the
following points:[2]

(1) The messianic movement arises in a society marked by intense dissatisfaction with social and economic conditions it is forced to accept
by an external oppressor.

The dissatisfaction is the result of cultural conflict between a superior and an inferior culture. The inferior culture provides little opportunity for relief or socioeconomic progress. Before the confrontation with the higher culture, members of the lower culture would have
been relatively satisfied and would have had little desire for anything
better. But confronted with the advanced, different, and often unattain-

---

2. These points are based on the analysis of messianic movements in India by Stephen
Fuchs (1965). Fuchs bases his analysis on Indian cults, but the relevant characteristics have
general application.

able lifestyle of the higher culture, dissatisfaction rears its head. The typical context for such culture clash is in colonies that are economically underdeveloped, isolated, without a strong central government, and generally passively accepting foreign domination and rule.

These conditions obtained in Judea under Seleucid power. Not only was Palestine relatively economically impoverished, but under the increasing exploitation and oppression of the Seleucids, conditions worsened so that large segments of the populace began to feel the pinch of poverty and the pangs of hunger. Powerful emotions were stirred: jealousy, hatred of the alien oppressors, rage at the fundamental injustices wrought on them by the humiliating and punitive practices of rulers and their military agents. The avenues of escape were limited. The ruling classes of the powerful and the priestly aristocracy solved the problem by accommodation and collusion with their oppressors. That course led the poor and the marginal groups of farmers and artisans down the path to destruction. They could not abandon their religious convictions which were the only bastion of stability and hope in a torn and tormented world. Powerful intrapsychic forces were set at work to find a resolution to these impossible dilemmas.

(2) In such a society, powerful psychological forces are set in motion that contribute to profound anxiety, depression, and narcissistic disequilibrium.

The emotional disequilibrium results from several causes. Economic pressures were telling, especially in circumstances in which the rulers were intent on finding new and increasingly burdensome ways of extorting money from the lower classes, and depriving them of all economic solvency. The consequences were dire. Property owners were driven first into debt, then as the debt mounted and could not be paid, confiscation of property and abject poverty, at times even death. The demands and regulations imposed on them were severe and uncompromising; there was no leniency, no room for exceptions or humanitarian easement, only harsh rule and judgment, reinforced by brutal violence and abusive military might. All avenues of redressment or alleviation of the increasing burdens and difficulties were denied. Political rights and freedom were abrogated and ignored. The Palestinian Israelites were a totally conquered and oppressed people.

These conditions were especially distressing for the Jewish people since they had counted on the power of their God to protect and save them. They were confronted by a clash of fundamental values. They were forced to accept regulations and social forms that flew in the face of their traditional values. Not only were the most humiliating and oppressive conditions imposed on them, but the sustaining hopes and beliefs that had enabled them to live through alien assaults and conquests so often in the past were being undermined. Even the collusion between the priests and the Romans deprived them of the traditional sources of leadership and guidance. Once more, ethical values were challenged and put to the test. Observance of traditional practices and ethical standards were punished and rejected by the rulers and alien judges. The mythology, the system of traditional beliefs, that sustained and gave the very breath of life to their social fabric was ridiculed, insulted, treated as erroneous, primitive, and foolish.

The psychological consequences can only be reconstructed hypothetically. I would argue that these conditions brought about a situation in which the psychic cost could be counted in terms of severe narcissistic injury, a state of mental regression, a crisis in self-esteem regulation, and with it varying degrees of self-fragmentation and threats to the maintenance of a sense of identity. In the face of these dire crises, defensive and countervailing psychic forces would have been thrown in gear. One component of these countermeasures was aggression. The desperate situation of profound and pervasive victimization could be balanced by the mobilization of aggressive resources. To the degree that aggression can be called on effectively, the position of victimization can be alleviated and modified. To many who were immured in the quicksand of victimization, the solution was to turn to aggressive and violent courses of action. These were the elements of the population that were caught up in the spiral of violence (Horsley 1987) that led to outright rebellion and ultimately bloody warfare.

Another component of this reaction was narcissistic. The continual humiliations, the erosion of values both social and religious, the assaults on self-respect and personal integrity inflicted a condition of narcissistic depletion and disequilibrium. Redressment became a psychological necessity. The dynamics here are similar to those of the loss-restitution complex (Rochlin 1965). The narcissistic imbalance had to be compensated. The messianic vision with its attendant hopes and expectations served the purpose: it provided a vehicle by which the meaning and purpose of Jewish life and the adherence to traditional religious values once again took on significance and restored the sense of the Jewish people as chosen, as the children of Abraham, the people on whom Yahweh had put his stamp, whom He would never abandon, and whom He would restore to their position of primacy and hegemony over all other nations, including their present oppressors. By identification with this projected and fantasied salvation and with the power of Yahweh that guaranteed and effected it, narcissistic equilibrium and identity were stabilized and restored.

(3) The charismatic leader. Some charismatic leaders are born, some are made. Some leaders are made by the forces at work in the religious movement — often in the service of political purposes. The movement in this sense finds a prophet to lead it. But in other cases it seems that a leader arises who brings together a coterie of followers and thus inaugurates the movement. In other cases, leader and followers arise more or less independently and manage to find each other. Often the charismatic leader or prophet is killed early in the game, as was the case in Christianity, so that selected followers must take up the mantle of leadership and continue the mission of the prophet.

(4) The demand of the leader for implicit faith and obedience. This is a universal characteristic in messianic movements and an indispensable requirement for admission to membership. The demand is a corollary of the leader's conviction of his superhuman position or of the divine guidance and inspiration he follows. There is no room for opposition or doubt. The inspiration and decision-making of the messiah must be accepted without question. Recruitment must therefore be selective: only those who believe and surrender their own opinions can be admitted as followers, certainly in the beginning of the movement. As the movement evolves, these disciples assume positions of importance and influence and thus bind themselves to the leader and his cause with additional ties of devotion and submission. This in turn tends to inflate the self-assurance and grandiosity of the leader and shrouds him in an aura of exaltation and a highly narcissistically colored mystique, as was very likely the case for Sabbatai Sevi and, subsequently, Jacob Frank.

Rigid adherence to the cause and to the leader becomes mandatory, not only as a requirement imposed by the narcissistic need of the leader, but also as a dynamic to reinforce the solidarity and cohesion within the group. Such groups often have a revolutionary cast that sets them off from and in opposition to the surrounding social structure. Some of the roots of the in-group-out-group dynamic that is so characteristic of the cultic process come into view here (Meissner, in process). Goodness and truth, and the means for achieving salvation, are contained within the in-group. Evil, ignorance, and the conditions of damnation are maintained beyond the group boundary. This sets up a pattern of isolation, separation, withdrawal and rejection that allows the in-group to set itself apart from its social and religious environment and grant itself the special privileges of the elect. These hopes are concentrated and contained in the figure of the leader, the messiah who brings with him the promise of restitution and salvation.

In Palestine of the first two centuries, these aspects of the designation of the messiah and the adherence to his cause came to forceful expression, but were doomed to disappointment and failure by the failure of the messianic movements and their destruction by force of arms. The earlier messianic movement centered around the person of Jesus of Nazareth also came to ignominious grief. But this messiah, whether as a matter of his own determination or as the result of the selective reporting and reconstructing by his disciples after his death, turned away from violent means of establishing his kingdom, denied that his kingdom was political at all, but rather spiritual and ultimately not of this world. The messianic message was muted and transformed into a doctrine of spiritual leadership and divine inspiration. If his messiahship was revolutionary, it was cast in a mold of spiritual renewal and the regeneration of values. Even so, the same demands for faith and obedience played their part. The nascent Christian in-group had to close ranks and present a solid phalanx to the outside world. Faith in Jesus was the touchstone of membership, even to the point of enduring painful persecution and death. We can presume that the same dynamic need for acceptance and adherence to a core of doctrinal positions synonymous with the in-group was one of the driving forces behind the centuries-long debate with gnosticism.[3]

(5) This unquestioning faith and obedience results in a radical change of life or a wholesale dispossession of property. The messianic leader provides a program that will lead his followers to fulfill their revolutionary aims — usually involving a radical departure from former ways of living. The inner circle is called to a full-time dedication to the work of the mission. They are called on to abandon former life commitments and to devote themselves wholly to the movement. They have to give up their occupations or careers, sometimes even their possessions, homes, and families. This was certainly the case of the twelve disciples in Jesus' inner circle: they gave up everything to attach themselves to him and follow him on the dusty roads of Palestine.

---

3. The tension and oppositional dialogue between nascent Christianity and gnosticism is traced in Meissner (in process).

The demand placed on other followers is not so stringent, but may reach a climax when the movement confronts a crisis. Then they are expected to rally behind the leader and make whatever sacrifices are necessary to preserve the movement and realize its goals. The traditional theme of giving up attachments to riches, pleasures, and the things of this world in order to follow in Christ's footsteps is one of the great cadences of Christian spirituality that has not lost its power even in our own day.

An added component of this turning from one's past and its entanglements is the conviction that the movement inaugurates a new era in which all things will be transformed and made different. Where the messianic movement carries with it a millennial or eschatological conviction, the believer could look forward to a renewal of ancient glories or a new golden age in which all needs would be supplied, an age of plenty and fulfillment. Clinging to the past and the things of the past would run counter to this expectation, as though the doubtful follower did not really believe it. Giving up all independent resources becomes a test of the sincerity and total acceptance by the believer. The disciple must turn his back on the past in order to face the future. Giving up one's property and attachments was a declaration of faith in the leader and in his messianic mission. If the expectations took the form of a great eschatological catastrophe, what was the point of providing for the future? This attitude may well have undergirded the personal and communal sacrifices of the early Christian communities.

There was little room for compromise in the message Luke put in the mouth of Jesus:

> Then to all he said, 'If anyone wants to be a follower of mine, let him renounce himself and take up his cross every day and follow me. For anyone who wants to save his life will lose it; but anyone who loses his life for my sake, that man will save it. What gain, then, is it for a man to have won the whole world and to have lost or ruined his very self? For if anyone is ashamed of me and of my words, of him the Son of Man will be ashamed when he comes in his own glory and in the glory of the Father and the holy angels.' (Luke 9: 23-26)

(6) Messianic movements tend to be characterized by antinomian attitudes expressed in a tendency to reject established authority and to rebel against it: in the first instance, religious authority, and at times also political authority.

Messianic movements share in the divisive dynamic of the cultic process (Meissner, in process). New movements must split off from the main body of established religious affiliation and thus create a situation of antithesis. Such a development tends to bring in its wake contentiousness, opposition, recrimination, confrontation, divisive attacks and counterattacks, tension and confusion in the mass of believers, and at times even persecution and physical violence. Change does not come about easily at best, but when the established social structures have become rigid and consolidated in their position of power and influence, they do not yield any of that power willingly or readily. Messianic movements come into being for the purpose of change and to overthrow the existing order, to force the established authorities to abrogate their privileges and resign their power. Violent overthrow of the established power is not excluded.

Where the movement takes a political turn and resorts to forceful and violent means to secure its ends, the challenge may be met with counterviolence — as was the case in the messianic revolts attempted by Palestinian Jews in AD 66 and again in AD 135. Rome flexed its muscles and crushed the revolts and with them the messianic hopes that gave rise to them. The Roman Empire and the governance of Palestine was a powerful and well-organized structure against which the messianic upsurge would have had little chance for success. There are occasions, however, when the social structure is loose or weakly organized, that such messianic movements have an easier time of it and can enjoy greater success in transforming the social structure. Such movements usually tend to become more political than simply religious. Fuchs (1965) writes in this regard:

> Messianic movements, being in their very essence revolutionary, become provocative and dangerous to the established government if the leaders are strong and militant. The established government often reacts violently to such provocation and suppresses the movement with great severity. If this is done when the movement is still in its initial stage, and when the government succeeds in eliminating the ringleaders, such a movement can be completely suppressed. But once the movement has gained momentum and spread over a wide area and attracted many followers, even the removal of the leader is abortive. New leaders rise in place of the old one, and often they are more violent and extreme, more efficient and more capable of leadership than their predecessor. (p. 10)

If we think of the Christian movement, removal of the messiah did not do much to abort the movement. The early Christians seem to have gone underground, and then resurfaced with a new group of leaders, the apostles, including Paul. How much the change of leadership changed the nature and direction of the movement is an open question, but they were certainly capable of assuming leadership roles in the nascent Church and developed the movement in the direction of a more widely spread and universal religious movement. There may also have been a shift away from political involvement toward the more specifically religious and spiritual. This was reflected in the spiritualization of the messianic idea, abandoning the political and this-worldly implications of Jewish aspirations, and disengaging the work of the Church from political objectives. We might wonder to what extent the political overtones of Jesus' supposedly messianic mission and its disastrous outcome may have taught the disciples a lesson and encouraged their dissociation from Jewish political aspirations and their potential reverberations in Rome.

It seems safe to say that the one motivating force behind the persecutions of the Christians in the early centuries was the uncertainty of their political role and the threat they posed to Roman power. The same confusion was at work in the suppression of messianic movements among the Jews of Palestine. The lines between religious renovation and political rebellion were not clearly drawn in either context. Fuchs' (1965) comment is to the point:

> Where the dominating culture [Rome] which causes the confusion and despair in the inferior community [Palestine, Church] is at the same time the established authority and government (often indeed a self-imposed authority which the subjects have never really accepted), opposition to the domination of the superior community appears also as rebellion against the established authority and government. A messianic movement, born out of the clash of two vastly different cultures and supported by the inner rejection and smoldering hatred of the subject community against its masters, is essentially a revolutionary movement. A religious revolution will in such a predicament always turn into a political revolution. (p. 10)

The Jewish messianic movements that we know of, presumably because of the this-worldly and therefore inescapably political nature of the messianic vision, ran afoul of this problem. By the same token, this was the problem that Christianity sought to escape by its disavowal of this worldly ambitions and by projecting the kingdom of Christ beyond the present world into the next.

(7) Threats of severe punishments or attacks against opponents of the movement, or against members who betray or abandon the movement in one or other form.

This aspect brings more clearly into focus the in-group-out-group dynamic of the cultic process. The dictate is that those who are not with us are against us. The mechanisms operate in such a way as to focus all good, truth, validity, and the promise of salvation within the movement; outside of the movement there is nothing but the opposite: evil, deception, invalidity, and loss of the means to salvation. The movement is presumed to be inspired by God, and exclusively so; no other movement can be tolerated as having a similar stamp of divine approbation. Opposition to the cause is therefore equivalent to opposition to God; it is blasphemy and sacrilege. The structure of the movement requires a closing of ranks in the face of such opposition, and to the extent that the dynamics are dominated by the cultic process, the closure must be total, secure and allow for no exceptions. The ideology thus becomes a closed belief-system (Meissner, 1991).

Preservation of the movement under these circumstances requires relatively strict discipline, both in matters of praxis and doctrinal orthodoxy. Loosening of the ties weakens the movement and impairs its effectiveness. The threat posed by the Jesus movement unleashed the repressive efforts of the Scribes and Pharisees, particularly the work of the Sanhedrin in bringing Jesus to trial. The threat posed by heretical movements pushed the Church and her defenders into repressive and at times persecutory actions. It also served as an important stimulus for the Church to get its disciplinary and doctrinal act together. The threat posed by the nascent Church and its challenge to Roman belief and authority called forth repressive and at times violent persecutions by imperial power.

There are other dimensions of the messianic phenomenon worthy of discussion, particularly the millennial, revivalist, and eschatological aspects, that will be treated more extensively under the heading of millennialism.[4] But the particular elements underlined here — the origin of messianic movements within contexts of oppression and crisis, the critical role of the messianic leader as drawing together and focusing the dynamic forces that drive the movement, the pattern of opposition that arises between the messianic movement and other religious (and at

---

4. See section V above and chapters 19 and 21 below.

times also political) movements, are all aspects of the cultic process at work in these diverse historical and religious contexts.

Messianism and the Paranoid Process

The pattern of messianic expectation and hopes that carried over from the Jewish and Palestinian traditions into the New Testament shared in substantially the same dynamic forces of motivation and purpose. The Christian messianic outlook accepted and took its direction from the preexisting messianic tradition of 1st-century Judaism. The gospels pronounce Jesus as the promised messiah, the one who is anointed and blessed by God to announce and bring into being the new kingdom in which the reign of Yahweh is to be established on earth. The New Testament reconstruction, then, of Christ's messianic mission takes up the multiple and at times contradictory strains of the earlier messianic vision and tries to establish the continuity between various strata of that tradition and the Christian kerygma.

The Christian vision saw the messianic promises as being fulfilled and realized in the person of Jesus Christ. As the story of the public ministry unfolds in the gospels, this awareness seems to emerge only gradually, haltingly, and fragmentedly, largely due to Christ's own reticence, suggesting a degree of uncertainty, ambivalence, and ambiguity. It is only in the light of the post-resurrection faith that the terms of Jesus' messianic mission are brought into clarified articulation. As that doctrine emerged, the different emphases and points of contrast between the Christian message and the traditional viewpoint became more decisively etched into the Christian consciousness. Jesus was the messiah of the ancient tradition, but he was not the messiah of Jewish expectation. His mission was spiritual and his messianic kingdom was of another and higher world. And Jesus himself was not merely the chosen instrument of God's purposes, the anointed messenger of divine intentions, but he was himself divine, sharing in God's essence and nature; he was the divine word that came from the mouth of God, son of God and Lord.

The effect of this clarification was to drive a wedge between preexisting religious perspectives and the Christian orientation. The oppositional trends that had characterized Christ's public life now extended themselves to the messianic realm. The Christian messiah was a different messiah, just as the Christian religious outlook and life was different and opposed to the prevailing Jewish tenets. This difference brought into play the in-group-out-group dynamics that have become familiar as aspects of the paranoid process. Faith in Jesus and adherence to his divine and messianic role became the touchstone of adherence to the Christian Church. Opposing religious groups, including the other religious sects that populated the Palestinian landscape and the pagan cults that flourished in the Roman empire of the period, became the enemies of the Church.

For some centuries, this opposition was more than ideological: it took the form of persecution in which martyrdom became the way of Christian life. The paranoid dynamics were unleashed in savage and unmitigated form. To be a Christian was synonymous with leading the life of a victim, persecuted and constantly under the shadow of the threat of death. Projective distortions were rampant, both within the Christian community and in the eschalons of Roman society that organized, directed and implemented the persecutions. And, as is typically the case, these paranoid dynamics came to play a reinforcing and sustaining role for both sides. As always, paranoia feeds on paranoia.

It is interesting that the traditional Jewish view of the messiah was that he would come in power and glory and wage war against the enemies of Israel. Israel would triumph in this messianic conquest and would assume a position of hegemony over all the nations of the earth. This aspect of the messianic doctrine was part and parcel of the nationalistic form of the messianic vision. The Jewish mind could not divorce national power and victory over other nations from their view of redemption. This element is entirely lacking from the Christian perspective. Not only do the gospel accounts eschew violence and armed conflict, but Christ is portrayed as the man of peace. He orders his followers to put up their swords in the garden of Gethsemane, and in reply to Pilate he says that if he wanted to defend himself he could summon armies of angels to his cause.

But this is not his purpose. The Christian messianic conquest is not to be by force of arms, but by spiritual means. We can infer that Christ and the 1st-century Christians were anxious to dissociate themselves from the adventist implications of the Zealot movement that had largely been responsible for the Jewish revolt and the destruction of the temple. Rather than the armed revolution and overthrow of the Roman empire that was the primary tenet of Zealot ambitions, the Christians sought for the establishment of a new order of spiritual values and belief. The war against the beast of the Apocalypse was not to be a war of swords and chariots, but a struggle for the spiritual lives and the hearts of men.

Freud (1923) had observed in his discussion of the superego dynamics that in proportion as aggression failed to find direct expression to the outside, it was turned against the self. The superego was the intrapsychic structure that carried the burden of aggression directed against the self. We can suggest that not only was the Christian ethic caught in an internal conflict over the role of aggression, but that paranoid processes were brought into play to reinforce the sense of victimization in Christian beliefs and to consolidate the sense of persecution and attack from external persecutors. Martyrdom became the glory of Christian existence: one who was martyred for the faith was assured of a heavenly crown. Better to be a victim and martyred for the faith than to become a conquering aggressor and deviate from the creed of the in-group. Better to be a victim than run the gauntlet of conflicts over aggressive impulses and wishes.

Christian messianism, like its traditional predecessor, built on a powerful narcissistic foundation. The Christian faith did not have very auspicious origins. Its charismatic leader was a simple carpenter's son born in the backwoods of a nondescript Judean town and raised in the hick town of Nazareth in Galilee, who came to no good end: hanged on the infamous gibbet like a common criminal. Its early members counted no one of importance or influence — simple fishermen and common folk. There was nothing in all this to elevate the enterprise to a level of lofty inspiration and commitment. The messianic doctrine came to the rescue. Not only was the message and ministry of this man of the people the fulfillment of messianic hopes, but it was a mission blessed by God and carried out by God's own son. This gave the Christian vision a power, a conviction, a purpose and direction that was immense. This belief system generated a framework of conviction and purpose that drew the members of the nascent church together with a sense of mission and shared direction. To each member who shared in this vision, there came a sense of belonging, of identity, of communion with the idealized and powerful king, prophet and priest of the messianic hopes. They were united in purpose and spirit not only among themselves, but with the Son of God.

In gnostic sects, the secret and mystical ideology plays a central role in unifying the sect and providing it with special status, not only internally but in setting it off in opposition and contrast with competing belief systems. The special gnosis of the sect gives the believers a superior religious status to those who do not believe. The ideology in such contexts serves an important function of narcissistic enhancement. It is reinforced by adherence to the charismatic leader, who is usually invested with powerful narcissistic and idealizing cathexis (Meissner, in process). The early Christian faith was founded unequivocally on the adherence to the person of Christ and the belief in his divinity. Whatever else can be said of this conviction, it seems clearly to fit the pattern of narcissistic enhancement determined by the paranoid process. One could not find a more grandiosely sublime leader than God Himself, and in the context of Judaic belief, one could find no better enhancing ideology than that provided by the messianic themes.

We can conclude that the form of expression of the messianic expectations in the Christian kerygma of the early centuries reveals the underlying dynamics and patterns of the workings of the paranoid process. The paranoid process deals primarily with the intrapsychic integration of the structuralized derivatives of both aggressive and narcissistic drives. The pattern that these structuralizing components took in the shaping of early Christian belief systems was to split both narcissistic and aggressive derivatives. The aspect of the aggressive configuration that we associate with the victim introject took expression in the commitment to passivity and victimhood that emerges so clearly from the gospel accounts and early adaptations of the Christian community to opposition and persecution. The Christian way of life was almost equivalent to the pattern of victimization required by living out the victim introject. The corresponding projections both brought into being and reinforced the persecutory forces of the pagan world that sought to crush the new religious movement.

On the narcissistic side, the special doctrine of following Christ, the messiah, and belief in and adherence to the cause of the Son of God provided a sense of religious superiority and privilege, along with a devaluation and contempt for the misguided beliefs of other religious groups. The narcissistic superiority was retained and served to support and reinforce the internal narcissistic introjective configuration in the minds and hearts of believers, and cast the unbelievers in the position of misguided inferiority and spiritual blindness. Whatever other forces may have been at work in propelling these momentous historical events, one might wonder whether the intersection of these narcissistic and aggressive dynamics may not have provided sufficient ground for fueling the wave of persecutions that played such a significant role in the early life of the Christian church.

The Dynamics of Messianic Leadership

The Messianic Leader

An additional dimension of the problem of religious and charismatic leadership is the association between leadership functions and the paranoid process. The effective religious leader is one who expresses and is responsive to the inner needs that play themselves out in the paranoid process (Meissner 1978, 1988, 1990a, in process). The most effective leader, then, is one who best embodies, gives form and shape to, and is responsive to those beliefs, values, attitudes and ideologies which best express the interests and intents of the community of believers. The leader or prophet, therefore, serves as an appropriate figure to receive the idealized projections from the members of the group and thus sustains the values and beliefs that are vital to the inner life of the group.

The effective leader, then, serves as a unifying and consolidating force vis-à-vis the group, which allows the group to sustain a sense of cohesion and purposeful implementation. The effective political leader, for example, is able to mobilize these resources of the group and to direct them in a way that provides the members of the group with a sense of utility and purposeful action. It is specifically in these terms that the notion of "charism" takes on psychological meaning.

The messianic mythology centers around the figure of the messiah, the idealized leader who will come in some distant eschatological time or, in the fantasy of a more realized eschatology, will emerge in the present time to bring surcease and salvation to those who believe in him and follow him. There is something numinous about such personalities, something uncanny that evokes a feeling of awe and the otherworldly (Otto 1917) — a quality LaBarre (1970) calls "phatic." The messianic leader, then, in fantasy or in reality becomes the cult leader, especially when the cult arises as a crisis cult, as is so frequently the situation in the origins of messianic cults, including Christianity. Christ fulfilled the role of a charismatic leader, one who is in contact with the Spirit and whose mission is to serve as a conduit between the power of the Spirit and the world of ordinary experience (Borg 1987). Such leaders invariably come to the fore as cultural heroes, bearing some inspiration or revelation responding to the crisis needs of the culture under stress (LaBarre 1970). Charismatic leaders tend to arise in conditions of cultural stress, and their inspiration tends to follow the pattern of crisis needs in the society.

The prophetic leader is ordinarily the one who fashions or enunciates the new doctrine or revelation that seeds the origin of the cult. In the case of the messianic leader, the complexities of the eschatological perspective and the impulse toward present realization compound the situation. The messiah is anticipated in the end-times, but in many instances the mantle of messiahship is placed on a contemporary figure. The circumstances of his appearance and of the acceptance of his doctrine demand explanation. His appearance in contexts of social unrest may be fortuitous or providential, but by the same token the appearance of such a prophet in stable and untroubled times might be ignored or treated as deviant and pathological. Then again, the conjunction of the appearance of the messiah at a point of elevated need and crisis may be neither accidental nor unrelated to the social conditions. Disaster creates situations in which the capacity of traditional authority to adapt and absorb is strained or the authority itself is even destroyed. The failure of traditional authority leaves a vacuum for new leaders and ideas to emerge. The scenario has been retold several times in the above pages. To meet their inner needs and anxieties, people turn to new sources of assurance and hope (Barkun 1974).

The first objective of the prophet-leader is to bring some meaningful response to the emotional needs of uncertain and threatened listeners. He conveys his message in words as well as in the personal image he casts before them. He takes the position of a role model who has mastered the anxieties, achieved a state of assured conviction and belief, has experienced the transformation offered by the new dispensation and realized, in some degree, its hoped-for effects. Without question, this is the portrait of Jesus painted by the evangelists. In order for this process to take place, the leader cannot become excessively deviant nor can he be regarded as essentially pathological or disturbed by potential followers. In certain cultural settings, aberrant characteristics may provide the basis for selection to fill religious leadership roles, e.g., the shaman (Eliade 1964). In such cases society finds a way to provide an acceptable niche that allows eccentricities and peculiarities of behavior to be enlisted in the service of the spiritual and even physical needs of the group. The leader then becomes the vehicle for the expression of unresolved inner conflicts; a certain number of such vatic figures are drawn from the ranks of manic and/or paranoid subjects. The prophet's message may be received as originating in the "other world" or coming from the supernatural. In naturalistic terms, the supernatural is nothing more than the prophet's own unconscious (LaBarre 1970). On the contrary, there is no evidence to suggest that the followers who are drawn to and participate in the mission of pathologically deviant leaders are in any sense socially or psychologically any different than the ordinary members of the larger community (Barkun 1974).

Rise of the Leader

The leader tends to arise from within the community, but even when he does not, he has an intimate knowledge of the larger community against which the messianic movement is aimed. He has usually been educated by them, or worked for them, or lived with them for a significant period of time. The messianic vocation results from an inner conversion and alienation from the foreign oppressors. They usually have spurned or rejected him in some fashion, setting the stage for motives of revenge as part of the prophetic impulse. Such leaders are poorly educated as a rule, often mistaken about their own capacities and abilities and about the power of the movement they lead. They may claim either a divine origin or reception of a divine revelation about the religious mission and its doctrines. They tend to be supremely confident of their mission, doctrine, convictions and decisions, and at times are accorded almost divine veneration. They often claim to possess magical powers of healing the sick, multiplying food, foretelling the future, and working miracles. Or, as we saw so strikingly in the case of Sabbatai Sevi, credulous followers were only too ready to attribute such powers to the messianic figure. The sense of authority and self-assured power that characterizes the delivery of their message exercises a profound influence on their hearers. As Fuchs (1965) writes:

> Guided by a divine inspiration, they inspire hope and confidence in their followers. They pretend to know the root and cause of the evils which beset the community and to know also the way out of the trouble. If success fails to follow their remedial intervention, they have an explanation and excuse ready. Generous assurance is given that all obstacles will presently be removed. Success is always just around the corner. This hope is infused into all new disciples of the movement; it inspires those interested in the cause to exert themselves and, in fact, stimulates unexpected energies and abilities. (p. 6)

We have seen these characteristics of the messianic leader fulfilled in varying degrees by the succession of messianic claimants. Closer to the pattern, as far as I can see, were the figures who played a significant role in leading rebellions against the foreign oppressors of Israel. The Maccabees were such, also Menahem and Simon bar Giora at the time of the revolt against the Romans and the destruction of the temple; and, perhaps more dramatically than any, bar Kochba with whom the messianic hopes of Israel seemed to burn out in a blaze of glory.

But the pattern comes to life again in much clearer detail and delineation in the career of Sabbatai Sevi. In each case, the so-called messiah arises out of a context of oppression and crisis. The unrest, resentment and rebellious stirrings among the Jews found their leader and crystallized their rebellion around his leadership. The Maccabees and bar Kochba are striking examples. Sabbatai provides a less dramatic instance. He was not chosen by a popular movement, but his own self-inspired revelation that he was the promised messiah coincided with a situation of crisis and need in the community that desperately required a figure to whom the messianic aspirations could be attached. His delusional grandiosity fit with the desperate situation of Jewish degradation and persecution like a key in the lock. A similar set of circumstances seems to have applied in the ascendancy of Jacob Frank as well.

But what of the messianic role of Christ? It seems safest to say that his messianic claims were at best uncertain. It seems clear that he was tried and convicted and condemned to death precisely as a messianic pretender.[1] But he himself did not seem to lay any forthright claim to that title (Léon-Dufour 1968). The amplification and clarification of his messianic title was largely the work of his disciples in the light of the post-resurrection faith. One can make a case in these circumstances for the operation of certain dynamics of loss-and-restitution: the loss of their prophet through crucifixion set off a profound mourning process in his disciples that found its resolution in the restoration of Jesus in messianic terms (Hummel 1975). His image took shape in their minds in elevated terms and took the form of the higher christology of Christian doctrine. If there was a messianic movement that he led, we know nothing about it, even if we could accept the efforts to grasp at a few tentative straws, e.g., the question of the cleansing of the Temple, or the implications of the entrance to Jerusalem on the feast of the Passover (Palm Sunday). Were these expressions of a messianic movement and an abortive attempt to overthrow the Temple authorities? However one casts the messianic mission of Jesus and the political implications of the Jesus movement, it has to have been a far cry from the Zealot revolt in the following generation and the revolt of bar Kochba in the next century. Ultimately, there is no way to transcend the barriers that separate us from these events. We cannot know to what extent the gospel accounts at our disposal are constructions motivated by a complex of interests and purposes that we can do little more than guess at, or to what extent they may be valid and reliable historical reconstructions. Certainly they cannot be taken simply at face value.

Charisma

As we have seen, when the mix of contributing elements is right, there arises a leader or prophet who acts as a catalyst to bring the cultic fantasies to an actualizing focus, be they millennarian, messianic, gnostic, salvific or whatever. To the marginal and desperate masses the messianic prophet announces his inspiration or revelation, for which he claims divine origin and authentication, and proclaims to his needy hearers a mission of lofty ideals and worldwide scope. The conviction of a divine mission, of being divinely appointed as the instrument of God to carry out this important role, conveys to the vulnerable and

---

1. See the discussion of these claims and their political and religious contexts in Meissner (in process).

credulous masses a sense of significance, hope, the fulfillment of deep-seated wishes and desires, a sense of elevation from the association and identification with God's messenger and God's purposes. They also become important, and their role in the world becomes defined in specific and divinely sanctioned terms. For the needy and impoverished, there was no better nor more appealing mission than the total transformation of the world from a place of sickness, pain and suffering to one of wealth, luxurious ease, and the surcease of all pain and suffering. Where they had been poor, they would become rich. Where they had suffered deprivation, they would find the satisfaction of all desires. Where they had been persecuted and oppressed, their enemies would be put to flight and crushed, and they themselves would become the inheritors of the earth and exercise dominion and power in the name of Christ.

In Weber's (1922) original formulation, charism referred to a type of personal authority based on "devotion to the specific sanctity, heroism or exemplary character of an individual person and of the normative patterns or order revealed or ordained by him." Despite the often contradictory usages, charismatic leadership seems to possess the following characteristics:

(1) The leader is perceived by his followers to possess superhuman capacities;

(2) The followers blindly accept and believe the leader's statements;

(3) They unconditionally comply with and obey the leader's directives for action or behavior;

(4) They give the leader unqualified emotional support and allegiance (Wilner 1984).

In more specifically Freudian terms, the charismatic relation can be described in libidinal terms as a special form of love relation based on a model of unconscious hysterical object love (Zaleznik 1974). The leader becomes a love object of sorts, giving rise to the peculiar devotion, intensity, and narcissistic enhancement of the leader (Volkan 1988). The love relation inherent in the charismatic relationship is analogous to analytic transference, and in fact may be compounded of the same elements (Hayley 1990). This emotional investment can become so powerful that it can result in the transformation of values and the overthrow of traditional and rational norms. Hummel (1975) concludes that "charisma" exists as the experience of a follower when there is "(1) a moment of distress/object-loss, (2) complete personal devotion to a leader/love projection, (3) experiencing the leader's qualities as extraordinary or supernatural/sense of the uncanny produced by unconscious nature of projection." (p. 760)

The Bond Between Leader and Led

Charism is only in one perspective simply an attribute or mystical quality in the personality of the leader; it is also a reflection of the social relationship in which certain attributions and projections are involved on the part of the led. The prophet cannot be charismatic unless he is recognized and honored as such. It is thus as valid to say that the leader creates the movement as that the movement creates the leader. Belief in the charism of the leader provides a degree of legitimation of the convictions of the led that is grounded in devotion and loyalty to the cause, embodied usually in the person of the leader, and identification with him (Barkun 1974). The leader is believed and followed because he embodies the values that are embraced or sought by the led. As LaBarre (1970) notes, "The culture hero's charisma, that uncanny authority and supernatural ascendance he seems to have over his fellows, is in purely naturalistic terms merely the phatic attractiveness of his teaching to others under the same stress, an attractiveness aiding its diffusion from individual to individual. Charisma is only shared unconscious wishes and symbiotic thought paradigms in leader and communicants." (p. 48)

Certain individuals seem to have a more marked propensity to be influenced by the charismatic attraction of the leader. They seem to have a certain need to submit themselves to some powerful personality, to be taken care of and to be guided by the knowledge and conviction of a powerful and idealized figure. In so doing, they find the strength to tolerate otherwise intolerable tensions and anxieties. The need to attach themselves to and remain subjected and obedient to the leader is based on basically narcissistic and erotic needs, often deriving from quite infantile levels of development. They see others as more powerful and superior and themselves as weak, vulnerable and inferior.

Despite the surrender of omnipotence in themselves, they preserve a sense of omnipotent potentiality, seeking magical powers and forces to guarantee some degree of narcissistic reconstitution and self-esteem. Idealized and power-invested objects are necessary in order to participate in his omnipotence; submission to him will gain the magic power that will salve the inner sense of insufficiency and impotence. Developmentally, this narcissistic fixation comes from a period in which infantile omnipotence has been lost and can only be regained by attachment to the projected omnipotence in outside objects — the idealized parental imago (Kohut 1971, 1977) — "the fantasized image of the all-powerful, all-knowing, all-giving, all-loving parent" (Post 1986, p. 678). Olden (1941) summarized this interaction in terms of the mutually reinforcing relation between the dominant (leader) and the dependent (follower) type of narcissism. She wrote:

> If the dependent type meets with the dominating type, they establish a complementary situation. The dominating type, being more or less narcissistic, either lives without object-relationships altogether, or uses the dependent's attitude as a confirmation of his omnipotence. The dependent type uses the omnipotent attitude of the dominating type for his need for protection. Both types have no capacity of full object-relationships, either because of disturbance in their development or by regression. The dependent type, who represents a relatively higher phase of development, has no real object-relationship either. His relationship to people signifies only: They can provide me with security and protection, therefore, I must make myself dependent on them; consequently, I am in fear of them and have to repress my tendency to get my supplies by aggressive force. (p. 354)

Post (1986) has offered a parallel analysis of the narcissistic dynamics of the leader-follower relationship in terms of the interplay between the propensities of the mirror-hungry personalities, which he attributes to the leaders, and the ideal-hungry personalities that characterize the followers. This interaction was also addressed by Kohut (1973) in the following terms:

> The great seducers of mankind have retained from their childhood an unshakable conviction of being all-powerful and all-knowing. It is this pervasive sense of infallibility which shapes their attitudes and forges their actions. Such personalities are prone to formulate certain simple and clearly depicted goals — whether in the realm of religion or of politics; whether as the prophets of a salvation through physical exercise or through the eating of herbs. Although these goals may be rational in appearance, they are, nevertheless, the manifestations of an archaic self which, in accordance with the solipsistic conceptions of early life, is still experienced as possessing absolute power and unlimited knowledge. It is this connection with the archaic self which lends dogmatic certainty to the opinions held by such individuals, and it explains the ruthlessness with which they are able to pursue their goals. These personalities, furthermore, exert a quasi-hypnotic effect on many people. Deeply rooted in our earliest childhood there remains in us a longing to merge with an all-powerful and all-knowing ideal

figure. This yearning finds an apparently irresistible fulfillment for many in their total submission to a Messianic leader and to his dogmatic beliefs. (pp. 16-17)

Beyond this, charismatic leaders convey a promise of a new reordering of life that constitutes a radical change from existing conditions. The reordering requires iconoclasm, the challenge to existing authority and the socioreligious order and the implication of connection with sacred powers revealed in miracles, healing, or revelations that bypass and go beyond traditional authorities (Stone 1982).

Interactional Model

More than any other type of leader, political or religious, the charismatic leader depends uniquely on the acceptance and support of his followers. He must be seen as a great man, narcissistically enhanced and idealized, or his program will not fall upon receptive ears (Bord 1975). The sources of his legitimate authority depend on the faith of his followers; but not on faith without proofs that provide some support for his claims. Realization to some degree of the consequences of charismatic belief in organizational or behavioral terms is essential to the maintenance of the belief. Worsley (1968) comments:

> Followers . . . do not follow simply because of some abstracted "mystical" quality: a leader is able to magnetize them because he evokes or plays upon some strand of intellectual or emotional predisposition, and because — more than this — he purports to offer the realization of certain values in action. But this promise has to be effected: an abstract programme is no lasting basis for a continuing and developing association-in-action. This is why "signs," 'proofs,' the behavioral acting out or demonstration of the abstract 'promise' are a *sine qua non* for the continuation of the movement. (p. xii-xiii)

Thus the model for charismatic authority can be viewed as interactional — the followers accept the leader to the extent that he embodies and articulates their aspirations. He transposes these aspirations into concrete goals and collective beliefs that can be translated into action. The prophet's message thus attains a central significance in the organization of the movement. With due recognition of the importance and role of the prophet in messianic movements, there are also circumstances in which the personal charism of the leader gives way to the central impact of the message. The balance and mix of the elements will vary from context to context and from time to time within any given context. Worsley (1968) summarizes this variability:

> The extent to which the movement depends upon the personal innovatory initiative of the prophet is, at the least, highly variable, and cannot be assumed to be a constant; it requires empirical investigation to see what actually is the case. In some movements, the prophet is merely a 'vessel,' channel, instrument, or bearer of a message which he himself does not create, formulate, or even modify, but merely transmits. But other charismatic leaders tie the movement and the message to their coattails: *they* define what the message is, and their personal declaration is everything. (p. xv)

The followers in their turn tend to accept the prophetic vision all too readily, and are quick to adopt the role of the chosen people, the holy people of God, the saints, who were called to unqualified submission to the will of the prophet and devotion to his cause. They are to share in his power and in the fruits of his crusade; they cannot fail or be disappointed because they are backed by the infinite and miraculous power of God. We can read the accounts of the early history of Christianity, as for example in the Acts of the Apostles, in this light. Their triumph was decreed from all eternity. But this inspiration can take a deviant turn; as Cohn (1970b) remarks with respect to revolutionary millennarian movements, ". . . and meanwhile their every deed, though it were robbery or rape or massacre, not only was guiltless but was a holy act." (p. 85) The message of the holy prophet offered them relief from the misery of their lives, but in addition the prospect of participating in a divinely ordained and world-shattering mission of the utmost importance. Under the spell of such a charismatic prophet, the followers often experience grandiose and exalted feelings (Kets de Vries and Miller 1985). As Cohn (1970b) comments:

> This phantasy performed a real function for them, both as an escape from their isolated and atomized condition and as an emotional compensation for their abject status; so it quickly came to enthrall them in their turn. And what emerged then was a new group — a restlessly dynamic and utterly ruthless group which, obsessed by the apocalyptic phantasy and filled with the conviction of its own infallibility, set itself infinitely above the rest of humanity and recognized no claims save that of its own supposed mission. And finally this group might — though it did not always — succeed in imposing its leadership on the great mass of the disoriented, the perplexed and the frightened. (p. 285)

In some situations the millennial impulse, for example, arises within the group, and at the critical juncture seizes on an appropriate available figure to play the role of the prophet and leader. The initiative comes from the community and imposes the leadership role. Often the leadership position is more symbolic than real, as seems to be the case when the leader is absent or is removed by death, imprisonment, or other more mysterious disappearance. In some cases, the emergence of the prophetic charism comes only after such a removal (Talmon 1962). Worsley (1968) summarizes this heterogeneity of leadership patterns:

> Far from being intensely focused on the person of the leader, then, we find movements which, empirically, are eminently millenarian, but in which the leader may be (a) absent; (b) not a single person at all, but with leadership divided amongst several people; (c) where the functions of prophet and organizer, at least, are separately embodied in two distinct persons; (d) where the leader is often one of a number of local leaders, rather than a single central figure (as Weber implies); (e) where the prophet is an insignificant person; (f) where the symbolic importance of the leader only becomes significant after his physical removal. Analytically, whatever the empirical case concerning the degree to which the component elements in the leadership syndrome are weighted, leadership still has to be comprehended as the meeting of social wants in potential followers in a given situation of unsatisfied aspirations. From this standpoint, all leadership, whatever the empirical facts, is primarily symbolic and relational, and only secondarily personal. (p. xvi-xvii)

In a word, charismatic movements do not arise at the whim, inspiration or bidding of any prophetic figure; they depend on a context, on a mix of determining influences, and on the psychological dispositions in the mass of potential followers who are receptive to the stimulation of the prophetic message and the charism of the prophet, or interact in such a way as to elicit the conditions for prophet expectation and actualization (GAP 1987).

Shared Fantasies

Such prophetic leaders seem to share in common an ability to stir primitive emotions in their followers and are masterful manipulators of certain symbols. Under the spell of charismatic leaders, the followers feel either powerfully grandiose or helplessly dependent. Leaders often induce regressive behavior in the group and are able to attune themselves to and exploit unconscious feelings and fantasies of their followers. The followers in turn seek to embrace an idealized, omnipotent image of the leader that answers to their dependency needs and helplessness. Narcissistic gratifications for both leader and led can take precedence over more realistic, task-related activity. At times and under certain conditions, such leadership capacities may become inspirational and lead to important transformative and constructive outcomes; but it also has the potentiality for destructive and negative results (Kets de Vries and Miller 1985).

The communication and sharing of regressive wishful fantasies is a central aspect of charismatic leader-led relations. As Deutsch (1938) noted, commenting on the analogy with folie-à-deux: "We also find the process as a mass phenomenon, where entire groups of physically healthy people are carried away by psychically diseased members of the group: world reformers and paranoids, for example. Indeed, great national and religious movements of history and social revolutions have had, in addition to their reality motives, psychological determinants which come very close to the psychological processes of folie-à-deux" (p. 307).

Narcissism

An important component of the personality organization of charismatic-prophetic (messianic) leaders is narcissism. Freud (1921) characterized such leaders as having a masterful nature, narcissistic, self-confident, independent and needing to love no one else but themselves. They tend to be self-centered, independent, difficult to intimidate, often fearlessly ready to spring to any action, counterphobic — strong personalities that step readily and willingly into the position of leadership (Freud 1931). They are the phallic narcissistic characters that Reich (1949) described as "self-confident, often arrogant, elastic, vigorous and often impressive. . . . The outspoken types tend to achieve leading positions in life and resent subordination." (p. 201) To this Kernberg (1979) adds, ". . . because narcissistic personalities are often driven by intense needs for power and prestige to assume positions of authority and leadership, individuals with such characteristics are found rather frequently in top leadership positions." (p. 33) Thus the leader's drive for leadership is rooted in his narcissism, a drive that compels him to take risks and undertake arduous tasks for the sake of winning a narcissistic prize and gaining a position of power and grandiose satisfaction.

Types of leaders can be described on the basis of their narcissistic style — patterns which find their reflections in messianic figures. To start with the most pathological form, reactive narcissism involves a sense of lingering inadequacy that defensively calls for a countering image of the self as special, an illusion of being unique and different, that requires masking of any discrepancy between wishes and reality and avoidance of any sense of limitation, loss or disappointment. Such leaders may have the capacity to ignore or minimize large segments of reality in the interest of preserving their narcissistic defenses and self-image. The vulnerability of the sense of self and the dependence on narcissistic defenses lends a strong paranoid bent to the leader's personality (Volkan 1988). The mystical messiah, Sabbatai Sevi, reflects many of these characteristics. Jacob Frank would meet the same requirements, as I am sure would John of Leyden. When paranoid mechanisms have been put into play in pathological terms, the leader becomes impervious to influence from outside sources and from realistic sources of information. The potential for directing the group down a path of self-destructive or self-defeating behavior can become unbridled and reversible only by drastic means (Kets de Vries 1977; Meissner 1978). We can wonder whether the messianic leaders of the Zealot revolt in AD 66 or the ill-starred destiny of bar Kochba were not cast in this mold.

Such reactive narcissism is usually the result of the failure of parents early in life to foster the child's management of narcissistic needs, both in terms of the omnipotence of the grandiose self and the idealizing illusion of the power and perfection of the parents. Such leaders are often severe and demanding of their followers, preferring subservience and unquestioning obedience from their subordinates. Ideas contrary to the leader's own tend to be ignored or rejected. Subordinates who do not fit the mold are eliminated or expelled from the group. The leader can be ruthless in exploiting and manipulating others to meet his needs and wishes. Empathy for others is minimal; what matters are his concerns and desires and nothing else. His failings often are the result of his disregard of reality and his grandiose conviction that he can control and manipulate reality to suit his needs. His grandiosity and omnipotence propel him to undertake daring and sometimes risky ventures, often on a grand scale that leads to inevitable failure. His undertakings are more often aimed at demonstrating his brilliance and mastery than at any meaningful accomplishment. This aspect, together with his inability to admit limitation or error, often sets him on a destructive course from which he cannot and will not deviate.

Self-deceptive narcissism has a somewhat different cast. Even though he may have many of the same qualities, they do not operate as dramatically in his leadership role. These leaders had parents who made them believe that they were unquestionably lovable and perfect, regardless of their limitations and shortcomings. As children they never learned to modulate their grandiose illusions and omnipotent fantasies. The self-delusory and unrealistic quality of the individual's self-image and ambitions runs afoul of more realistic limitations, imperfections, failures and disappointments. Both these forms of narcissism reveal pathological flaws and tend to employ relatively primitive defenses — predominantly those associated with borderline personality organization (Kernberg 1975; Meissner 1984a). These would include splitting that leads to oversimplification of cognitive and affective representations both of themselves and others.

These characteristics result in difficulties recognizing the complexities and ambiguities of human relationships and a tendency to polarize hatred, fear and aggression on one hand, and omnipotence and overidealization on the other. The latter qualities are retained in the self and one's group, while the former tend to be attributed to external groups and forces. It is vital to such religious leaders to see themselves as on the side of God, while the enemy is identified as Satan (Post 1986). Additional mechanisms include idealization and devaluation, leading to the creation of unrealistic and all-powerful representations of others as buffers for one's own sense of vulnerability and helplessness. This aspect of charismatic leaders has been described as a form of mirror-hungry personality, in which the seeking out of idealized sources of strength serves as a mask for inner doubt and weakness (Post 1986). The last important mechanism is projection, by which predominantly bad or undesirable aspects of the self are displaced onto external objects or groups. The pattern is easily discriminable in many messianic pretenders or in the equivalent forms of charismatic prophetic leadership.

Narcissism can also take a more constructive bent. Constructive narcissism is described as follows:

> The constructive narcissists do not behave in a reactive or self-deceptive manner. They do not feel the same need to distort reality to deal with life's frustrations. Nor are they so prone to anxiety. They make less frequent use of primitive defenses, and are less estranged from their feelings, wishes, or thoughts. In fact, they often generate a sense of positive vitality that derives from confidence about their personal worth. Such people have internalized

relatively stable and benign objects, which sustain them in the face of life's adversities. They are willing to express their wants and to stand behind their actions, irrespective of the reactions of others. When disappointed, they do not act spitefully, but are able to engage in reparative action. That is, they have the patience to wait, to search out the moment when their talents will be needed. Boldness in action, introspection, and thoughtfulness are common. (Kets de Vries and Miller 1985, p. 593)

Such leaders generally get on well with subordinates and can function well in task- and goal-oriented contexts. They wish to be admired, but have a better sense of their limitations and capacities. They can recognize, appreciate, and utilize competence in others. They can listen to subordinates, but take the ultimate responsibility for their own decisions. Their narcissistic needs at times can put them at risk of appearing to be arrogant or insensitive. Religious leaders, even prophetic figures, can and often do fit the mold of constructive narcissism. But when they do, they tend not to be charismatic, but fall more into the mold of conventional leadership in established religious groups. Religious leaders in general may fit into any one of these descriptive categories, but the charismatic leader, especially when he propounds a revelation that is markedly personal or that strains credibility or rationality, tends to follow the format of the more narcissistically pathological types.

Idealization

As Cohn (1970b) points out, the eschatological leader, as for example the returning Christ of the parousia, combines the images of the good father and the good son. Like the idealized father, he is wise, just, and powerful. And as the idealized son, his task is to transform the world, to establish the new heaven and the new earth. He stands above the masses, a colossal, almost superhuman figure, who is credited with supernatural powers, the emblem of the power of the Spirit that dwells within him. His miraculous powers guarantee that he will be inevitably triumphant and that he will be able to transform the world. The images were born of the fantasy system embedded in the hearts and minds of many and projected onto the prospective prophet.

And there were always those who were primed to accept and internalize the projection — who fell quite easily and unconflictedly into the role of infallible, wonder-working savior of the world. They were never distinguished by birth or merit, but rather by the force of their personalities — their eloquence, their commanding presence, their personal magnetism, their charism — qualities that stamp them as exceptional, perhaps as possessing supernatural powers or acting as the agent of transcendent intervention in human affairs (Wallis 1982a). Some were simply imposters, but many also saw themselves as incarnate gods, or as the special instruments of God's work, chosen out to perform the miraculous transformation of the millennial or messianic dream. The sense of inner conviction and strength was one of the primary elements in the power they exercised over their too-willing followers.

Cohn (1970ab) offers some generalizations about the figure of the *propheta*. They differed from the leaders of great popular uprisings in that they were usually petty nobles, sometimes imposters, often intellectuals of a sort — the fallen-away priest-turned-preacher was a common type in the medieval setting. They were often steeped in the lore of apocalyptic and millennarian prophecy, and their fanatical preoccupation with eschatological fantasies was part of their psychic world well before the call to social reform and spiritual transformation of the masses. They possessed a personal magnetism that was of great appeal to their followers.

Psychopathology

The question of psychopathology in the leader arises inevitably. In writing of the proponents of utopian visions, the Manuels (1979) comment:

> An ideal visionary type, the perfect utopian, would probably both hate his father and come from a disinherited class. A bit of schizophrenia, a dose of megalomania, obsessiveness, and compulsiveness fit neatly into the stereotype. But the utopian personality that is more than an item in a catalogue must also be gifted and stirred by a creative passion. . . . In the first instance the utopian is overwhelmed by the evil complexities of existence. The great utopians have all borne witness to their anger at the world, their disgust with society, their acute suffering as their sensibilities are assaulted from all sides. They withdraw from this world into a far simpler form of existence which they fantasy. . . . And their way back from utopia, their return to the real world they had abandoned, is often characterized by devotion to a fixed idea with which they become obsessed. They clutch frantically to this over-valued idea that at once explains all evil and offers the universal remedy, and they build an impregnable fortification

around it. The one idea becomes a fetish that they worship and defend with marvelous ingenuity. To outsiders they are monomaniacs. (p. 27)

Phenomenologically, this view of the leader comes close to the picture of the delusional paranoid. The omnipotence and grandiosity of such leaders reaches back to the omnipotence of infancy or to the identification with the fantasied omnipotence of the father. As Kets de Vries (1977) notes, "in addition to developing delusions of grandeur, these leaders possess the ever-present potential for developing delusions of persecution. Suspiciousness may become a way of life." (p. 354) When the male child cannot relinquish his omnipotence and cannot adopt a more realistic position of limited and contingent potency, he runs the risk of becoming fixed in a chronically paranoid position. Ego boundaries become permeable and precarious, so that the discrimination between the prophet and his god become doubtful, at times leading to adoption of an oracular function, at other times claiming the prerogatives of divinity. Omnipotence is purchased at the price of real and symbolic potency.

The leader's sense of complete certainty and unwavering conviction counteract any doubt and insecurity in the group, even as this stance serves to ward off the leader's own inner doubts. Kohut (1971) emphasizes the narcissistically fixated and even paranoid propensities in such charismatic figures. They are convinced that they are in the right and any who oppose them are in the wrong. They do not hesitate to hold themselves up as guides and leaders and as targets for the admiration and even reverence of others. They are capable of the extremes of moral righteousness. It is typical for them to disown and project to the outside world any unacceptable failing, imperfection or weakness that they cannot acknowledge within themselves. The shell of conviction and certainty must be maintained in order to prevent the inner doubts and vulnerabilities from showing through. In his paranoid rhetoric, aggression is projected to external objects and groups who then become identified as the enemy. By expelling and destroying the weakness within, the group can become the strong and chosen people of God. Leader and led are caught up in an intoxicating whirl of mutual narcissistic reinforcement: the followers feed on the narcissistic enhancement and omnipotence of the leader, and the leader is sustained and reinforced by the idealizing elevation of his followers' admiration and praise (Post 1986).

When the leader realizes the power to shape fantasies into realities, he is at risk of yielding to his wishes for omnipotence and megalomaniacal ambition. Reality and its limitations fade into the background to be replaced by paranoid fantasies and delusions. To the extent that his omnipotence elicits corresponding savior images in his followers, the result is a kind of manic enthusiasm and delusion that embraces the entire group. Attachment in the led and omnipotence in the leader are mutually reinforcing, so that the leader's narcissistic grandiosity becomes a self-fulfilling prophecy in which everything becomes possible and all limits are denied (Kets de Vries 1977).

In the case of Sabbatai, the erstwhile messiah, or even with that of Nathan his devoted prophet, or with the evident psychopathy of Jacob Frank, the point of interest is the intersection between the psychopathology of the cult leader and the dynamic forces operating within the cult members. The case study provided by the phenomenon of Sabbatai and the sabbatian movement is far from unique. Rather it would seem to provide a paradigm for many such pathological leader-follower interactions that are not only characteristic of the cultic process,[2] but also are identifiable in various other contexts — social and political.[3]

In the case of sabbatianism, the messianic teachings, held widely and firmly as matter of common belief, provided the matrix within which the movement came to life and the nourishing substratum that fed and sustained it throughout its course. The shift of emphasis from a temporal messiah-king to a more mystical and spiritual conception of the messiah opened the way for a messiah whose power and importance would not require the external trappings of worldly power and grandeur. The intensity of messianic expectations and wishes were raised to a high pitch by the level of suffering and persecutory torment of Jewry in the contemporary European scene.

It is worth noting that Sabbatianism bore certain characteristics that run parallel to aspects of the origins of Christianity (Davies 1976). The primary characteristics of such messianic movements would be first, a radical confrontation with the established social order, with its religious traditions, so that faith in the mission of the new messiah is

---

2. Dramatic contemporary examples might be found in the tragedy of the People's Temple and the catastrophe at Jonestown, or on a larger scale the fanatical following of the Ayatollah Khomeini among Moslem fundamentalists. The basic pattern is reflected in many other less-extreme religious contexts.

3. The extent to which these dynamics enter the political process varies in different contexts and is always modified by other factors. The elements involved in the cultic process may have considered relevance for understanding some aspects of more or less fanatical adherence to charismatic political leaders, often with catastrophic effects. The classic example is the leadership of Adolf Hitler in Nazi Germany.

essential, and second, the power of communicating the lived experience of redemption to a community of believers. Secondary characteristics would include religious enthusiasm, performance of miracles, the character and activity of the messiah (his hiddenness, power, origins, etc.), his capacity to overcome death, and the role of significant interpreters. My emphasis here is on the characteristics common to messianic movements. This emphasis does not gainsay important differences.[4]

It is no mystery, viewed in hindsight, that the messianic revelation should come to Sabbatai Sevi in the immediate wake of the Cossack insurrection, the ensuing persecutions, and the notorious Chmielnicki massacre, when the extant messianic hopes were so crudely and painfully dashed. The time was ripe for it. But the elevation of Sabbatai to messianic status was not new to him: he had accepted that accolade previously in his states of mystical exaltation. The only problem was the acceptance of his messianic role by the rest of the Jewish community, especially the rabbis.

Narcissistic Dynamics

Clearly the messianic role meshed exquisitely with Sabbatai's own pathology. His states of manic exaltation reflected the inherent narcissistic grandiosity of his personality organization. His self-engendered exaltation to messianic status, even to the extent that it involved quasi-divine transformation, articulated neatly with his own frustrated narcissistic needs for self-aggrandizement and fulfillment of the demands of the grandiose self. In this sense, his messianic exaltation was the external expression of the grandiosity of his narcissistic introject that lay at the root of his manic pathology.

The case was not much different for Frank. His pathology took a slightly different form, but the strains of unbridled and pathological narcissism dominate the picture of his personality organization. As Scholem (1971) observes:

> Frank was a nihilist, and his nihilism possessed a rare authenticity. Certainly its primitive ferocity is frightening to behold. Certainly too, Frank himself was not only an unlettered man, but

---

4. Harrington (1982) suggests two important differences between Sabbatianism and Christianity: "For all their similarities, Christianity and Sabbatianism are said to differ in two important aspects: (1) The conceptual background of early Christianity was far more complex and varied; (2) the constructive constraint of Jesus' ministry stands in marked contrast to the negative, distorting, and ultimately nihilistic influence of Sabbatai." (p. 157)

boasted continually of his own lack of culture. But in spite of all
this — and here is the significant point — we are confronted in
his person with the extraordinary spectacle of a powerful and tyrannical soul living in the middle of the eighteenth century and
yet immersed entirely in a mythological world of its own making.
Out of the ideas of Sabbatianism, a movement in which he was
apparently raised and educated, Frank was able to weave a complete myth of religious nihilism. (pp. 127-128)

The picture comes dangerously close to that of the delusional paranoid
with a highly developed and differentiated paranoid construction
(Meissner 1978).

In this sense, Sabbatai's psychopathology was beautifully adapted
to the extant cultural expectations and hopes that were embedded in the
messianic belief system. To some extent, the messianic belief served
to salvage the torn and battered narcissism of the Jewish mind and
soul. The fulfillment of messianic hopes and the restitution of narcissistic woundedness required not merely a wishful fantasy or a hope; it
required a real messiah, an actual figure in whom idealizing fantasies
could be invested and to whom specific messianic hopes could be attached. This investment in the putative figure of the messiah took
place by an idealizing projection by which the unresolved narcissistic
needs of the believer were in their own place salvaged and fulfilled.
The aggrandizing projection derives from the introjective configuration
in the internal world of the believer, the residues of the grandiose self
with its unsatisfied needs and wishes for narcissistic enhancement, so
that the cultic leader becomes the recipient and bearer of the believer's
idealized and grandiose narcissistic projections (Meissner 1978, 1988).[5]

The problem for Sabbatai, and later for Nathan, was to rationalize
or explain away the messiah's psychosis. The so-called "strange behavior" was no less than the expression and acting out of psychotic
delusional thought, resulting in psychotically motivated and organized

---

5. None of this is in itself necessarily pathological, but it does remain open to pathological
influences that can distort the basic belief system and shape it to fit pathological needs. A
central point of my argument regarding the paranoid process is that paranoid pathology is an
extreme expression of mechanisms that are at work in all human beings — for some, perhaps
most, they work in the direction of building an inner psychic world and a cohesive
self-system, but for others they can deviate into building a pathological self-organization.
Further, for all human beings, the potentiality remains inherent in their psychic structure for
regressive activation of explicitly paranoid (pathological) reactions. This argument, based on
clinical observations, is developed at length in Meissner (1978). In a word — messianism is
not pathological, but pathological messianism is. See my discussion of pathological beliefs in
Meissner (1991, in process).

behavior. The delusional quality was striking and was not missed by contemporary observers. The force and deranged quality of these episodes and the outright eruption of primary process material must have been stunning to observers — as well as a scandal to believers. Certainly the artful implementation of the doctrine of *tiqqun*, along with the ingenious theological elaboration and adaptation of it by Nathan, went a long way toward accomplishing this rationalization. One could argue that Sabbatai's inspiration and Nathan's rationalization may have struck a sympathetic chord that offered theological release to many faithful Jews who felt trapped in the centuries-long frustration and hopelessness of traditional rabbinical teaching. The delusional elaborations of the messiah brought a ray of hope and enthusiasm in the darkness.

Even so, many remained skeptical, and it does not seem that Sabbatai ever succeeded in convincing the more sober and theologically minded of the rabbis. But the argument had sufficient force to convince the naive and willing that Sabbatai's psychotic manifestations were not only not contraindications to his messianic status, but were to be taken as proofs of it. So powerful must have been the need to believe in the popular mind of vast numbers of European Jews, who gave fanatical support to this troublesome messiah even in the face of the objections of their traditional religious leaders and the evidence of their senses!

Narcissistic Pathology in the Believers

But the tenor of Sabbatai's reception by the faithful was remarkable. His self-proclaimed mission as messiah was embraced with enthusiasm, and he was widely regarded and proclaimed as the true promised messiah, as was also the case for Frank. How is this nearly universal acclaim and seemingly wholehearted acceptance by the multitudes to be understood? As Scholem (1971) observes:

> From the standpoint of sexual pathology it can hardly be doubted that Frank himself was a diseased individual, just as there can be no question that at the center and among the ranks of the Sabbatian movement (as in all radical movements that spring from certain particular tensions, some of which are not so far removed from those of "ordinary" life) it would be possible to find cases of marked mental aberrance. But what is the significance of all this? We are not, after all, so much concerned with this or that prominent Sabbatian personality as with the question of why such peo-

ple were able to attract the following that they did. . . . It is undoubtedly true that Jacob Frank was every bit the depraved and unscrupulous person he is supposed to have been, and yet the moment we seriously ponder his "teachings," or attempt to understand why masses of men should have regarded him as their leader and prophet, this same individual becomes highly problematic. Even more than the psychology of the leader, however, it is the psychology of the led that demands to be understood . . . . Whatever we may think of Sabbatai Sevi and Jacob Frank, the fact is: their followers . . . were sincere in their faith, and it is the nature of this faith, which penetrated to the hidden depths and abysses of the human spirit, that we wish to understand. (pp. 85-86)

I would advance an argument that, if it does not provide an adequate or encompassing explanation of this remarkable phenomenon, might at least provide a theoretical basis for such understanding. The argument is based on the paranoid process (Meissner 1978, 1988). It postulates a meshing and interaction between the narcissistic grandiosity of Sabbatai's psychosis and its messianic delusions on one hand, and the desperate need for narcissistic enhancement and the severe state of narcissistic depletion suffered in the souls of individual Jews throughout the diaspora. The circumstances of persecution and pogrom suffered by the Jewish people during this period left them in a state of embattled and deprived narcissistic disequilibrium and need. These traumatic effects were particularly acute in the wake of the disappointment of the messianic expectations of the year 1648.

How did these narcissistic deprivations affect the individual Jewish believer? Casting the analysis in terms of the paranoid process, the impact would have exercised its effects on the narcissistic aspects of the introjective configuration of each and every believer. External circumstances cast a dark shadow over the inner world, which tilted the balance of narcissistic forces toward the inferior narcissistic pole. This condition of narcissistic depletion would have been expressed in terms of a sense of inferiority, shame, humiliation and depression. The same dynamic would have increased the pressure for narcissistic redressment; the failure of messianic expectations that formed the centerpiece of the narcissistically impregnated hopes for redressment and restitution would have intensified the need to find the hoped-for messiah — the sooner the better. The exacerbation and intensification of the inferior narcissistic introject called for the projection of the countervailing elements of narcissistic superiority to whatever available and congruent object might have presented itself. The individual believer, in a sense, had the choice either of believing himself to be the promised messiah or of believing that someone else was. The former option was closed off due to the average believer's incapacity for delusional self-deception; but the latter option would have been available and viable for many. So the inherent need of many to find such narcissistic restitution meshed with the delusional conviction of Sabbatai that he was that messianic figure. Once the fit had been actuated, no reasonable objection, difficulty, or contrary evidence could stand in its way. It became, in fact, a kind of folie-à-plus — a form of mass paranoid delusion that Freud (1927) had in mind when he wrote of religious beliefs as mass delusions.

Millennarianism and the Cultic Process

Introduction

Over the centuries of its history, from the first glimmerings in apocalyptic fantasies of the ancient prophets of Israel to the modern imaginings of totalitarian regimes and religious cults, the millennial vision has exercised a peculiar and powerful fascination for the religious mind. Not only has its reverberations echoed through every phase of religious history, but its visionary stimulus has found expression in every corner of the globe and in a wide spectrum of cultures. In addition to the cultic variants discussed in preceding chapters, the millennial themes can be traced in a variety of African tribal and religious movements (Nyang 1984; Shepperson 1970b), in Indian religious sects (Fuchs 1965), and in a rich sampling of millennial religious cults in parts of South America, particularly Brazil (Ribeiro 1970), in the Pacific island nation of Indonesia (van der Kroef 1970), in the South Pacific (Guiart 1970), in the cargo cults of Melanesia (Worsley 1968; Eliade 1970), in Jamaica (Simpson 1970), and in politico-religious movements as varied as the Taiping rebellion (Boardman 1970; Barkun 1974) and the Ghost Dance movements in American Indian tribes (LaBarre 1970) in the 19th century. As the Manuels (1979) comment:

Anthropologists tell us that blessed isles and paradises are part of the dream-world of savages everywhere. The dogged wanderings of the Guarani tribe in search of a "Land-without-Evil" have been tracked over the length and breadth of Brazil, and the contemporary cargo-cults of Asia and Africa have been investigated for their marvelous syncretism of Christian and native paradises. Neither pictorial nor discursive philosophico-religious utopias are exclusive to the Western world. Taoism, Theravada Buddhism, and medieval Muslim philosophy are impregnated with utopian elements. There are treatises on ideal states and stories about imaginary havens of delight among the Chinese, the Japanese, the Hindus, and the Arabs, but the profusion of Western utopias has not been equaled in any other culture. Perhaps the Chinese have been too worldly and practical, the Hindus too transcendental to recognize a tension between the Two Kingdoms and to resolve it in that myth of a heaven-on-earth that lies at the heart of utopian fantasy. (p. 1)

Characteristics

In all these cases and more, these millennial and utopian fantasies have added a powerful motivational impetus to religious movements that have varied in their mix of contributing elements, but have brought the fanaticism of millions to the fever pitch of at times hysterical, at-times mystical, at-times revolutionary intensity. The delimitation of millennarian movements provided by Cohn (1970a) is as good as any; religious movements are millennarian that display these characteristics: "(a) collective, in the sense that it is to be enjoyed by the faithful as a group; (b) terrestrial, in the sense that it is to be realized on this earth and not in some other-worldly heaven; (c) imminent, in the sense that it is to come both soon and suddenly; (d) total, in the sense that it is utterly to transform life on earth, so that the new dispensation will be no mere improvement on the present but perfection itself; (e) accomplished by agencies which are consciously regarded as supernatural" (p. 31).

As Wallis (1982a) describes it:

Millennialism — a form of belief and its associated movement which anticipates a total and supernatural transformation of the physical world, with the elimination of its present evils and indignities and characteristically, the elevation of believers to the status of an elite — marks the sharpest conceivable break with the prevailing order; sharper even than secular revolution since it often

embraces all that this entails and a spiritual transformation as
well, a fusing of the natural and the supernatural realms." (p. 1)

And as Barkun (1974) adds, "It is the world of millennarian movements, those collective endeavors to anticipate, produce or enter a
realm of human perfection. Its hallmarks are nervous anticipation,
withdrawal from normal social commitments, and bitter renunciation of
the established order." (p. 1) As I have suggested,[1] this belief and the
underlying fantasy system that generates it might also have found its
displaced expression in the idea of the heavenly kingdom, especially to
the extent that it shares a common quality of wish-fulfillment and narcissistic gratification.

The idea of divine kingship appears early in the record of the Old
Testament, but does not achieve precise formulation until the time of
the monarchy. The concept is analogous, and in its various expressions
we find numerous additions and elaborations until its culminating articulation in the eschatological doctrine of Jesus and the New Testament. It is Yahweh alone who rules over his people — the kings of
Israel from Saul on are only his representatives. He is enthroned in
heaven as Lord and Creator whose dominion extends over the whole
world and all nations. His guidance of his chosen people is manifested
in his power and the promise of future salvation.

The preaching of Jesus takes its origin from the prophets who proclaimed that, in spite of Israel's recalcitrance and temporal punishments,
God would establish his eschatological reign and would thereby bring
salvation to Israel. This eschatological promise was expressed in the
"national" hope for the restoration of the ancient theocracy, the establishment of the messianic kingdom, and the cosmic renewal of the universe. These beliefs were combined in the expectations of a temporary
messianic reign that would culminate in the final salvific disposition.
This resolution can be found in the apocalyptic literature of the end of
the 1st century AD — the *Fourth Book of Esdras* and the *Syriac Apocalypse of Baruch,* for example. Only at the end of time would the full
realization of God's kingship be manifested in all its glory and joy
(Schnackenburg 1963).

The announcement of Jesus that the kingdom of God was at hand
brought with it a new revelation that repudiated any notion of a national and political kingdom and staked its claim to an apocalyptic vision of a universal cosmic reign inaugurated by the grace and power of

---

1. See particularly the discussion of the kingdom of God in chapter 12 above.

God. Pharisaic legalistic interpretations of the Law are rejected, along with any form of particularism. His is not a doctrine of the elite, but a call to all men, and especially sinners, to repent and believe. His message is that God's kingdom is not yet fully present, but that it has begun to insert itself in human history, and the fullness of its realization was to come in the near future. The divine eschatological reign was initiated in the teaching and mission of Jesus, and its perfection was to be realized in the glorious coming of the Lord in the parousia.

In the wake of the resurrection and the events of Pentecost, the messianic belief and the messianic promise took on a new form: in virtue of his resurrection and ascension, Jesus had become the Lord who was raised to his heavenly throne at God's right hand, from which he ruled his kingdom on earth, the Church, through the agency of the Holy Spirit. The promised kingship of God was being realized in the rule of Christ in his Church. As Schnackenburg (1963) comments, "We can understand how in the preaching of the early Church the accent moves from God's reign to the rule of Christ on high. Not that the Church forgets Jesus' gospel of the future kingdom of God: but the gospel of Jesus, Messiah and Lord, comes into the foreground." (pp. 351-352)

The basic belief system on which the millennial visions feed were first articulated on the tablets of recorded history in the utterances of the Hebrew prophets, but in the perspective under discussion in these pages, the sources lie more deeply embedded in the human heart and mind. The same millennial fantasies that surged to the lips of the prophets struck a resonant chord in the hearts and minds of religious believers throughout the centuries. The doctrine in its apocalyptic expression enunciates a theologized view of history cast in terms of a titanic and cosmic struggle between the forces of good and the forces of evil, between the power of Christ and the power of the Antichrist or Satan, to gain ascendancy over the earth and the souls of men. The vision of the triumph of Christ and the casting of Satan into a bottomless pit sets the stage for the millennial reign of Christ for the legendary 1,000 years. During this glorious reign of Christ, all yearnings and desires of the human heart for peace, justice, harmony and freedom from evil will be richly satisfied. The vision is one of earthly resolution of the problems attending a Christian eschatology, an effort to bring clarity and focus to concerns regarding the issues of death, immortality, the end of the world, the last judgment, the justification of the good and the damnation of evil. As has often been noted, the fantasy of reunion with lost loved ones is part of the unconscious motivation of beliefs in heaven, paradise, an afterlife: "The denial of death and mourning is accomplished through the belief in eternal life, transformed in space, and timeless" (Pollock 1989, p. 179).

The mythical 1,000 years has often been taken in various cultic contexts in a literal sense, but even this concrete expression of millennial hopes has undergone evolution. For many it applies in some figurative sense to a conception of some perfect age yet to come, of some attainable state of human perfection and happiness, sometimes thought of in terms of images of a former Golden Age that is to be restored or recaptured, or in terms of conditions and circumstances yet to be realized in future times. One of the dangers in millennial thinking is that it can easily become disengaged from its theological moorings, with disastrous results. The more traditional fathers of the Church and orthodox theologians have avoided this danger by containing the millennial impulse within the theological constraints of doctrines of creation, redemption and eschatology. Flinn (1984) sounds a cogent warning:

> When the teaching on the millennium becomes dislodged from this theological grammar, it is liable to all sorts of distortion. The Nazi doctrine of *da dritte Reich* [sic], for example, sundered the Last Things, which it envisioned as a bifurcated humanity of superior vs. inferior humans, from the doctrine of the First Things, i.e., the teaching that God created *one type* of humanity, all members of which equally bear the *imago Dei*. Millennial beliefs can be subject to lesser blandishments; for example, they can induce some into a kind of eschatological arrogance which separates the "we" (angels) from the "they" (devils), or which allows the ends to rule the means without realizing that means are ends in the making, or which stumbles into magical millennialism (catastrophism) of the naivist stripe, etc. Yet what is common to all types of disoriented millennialisms is that they mistakenly separate "heaven" from "earth" or transcendence from immanence by loosening the woof and warp of calm and serene theological discourse. (p. 6)

We cannot console ourselves that millennarian ideas have faded from the contemporary scene either. The primary vehicles in our times for millennarian impulses are totalitarian political movements (Cohn 1970b; Barkun 1974). The millennarian-totalitarian link weighed in heavily in the Bolshevik revolution, in the rise of Nazism, and in the emergence of Chinese Communism. Each was preceded by the classic form of disaster prologue that is typical of millennarian movements; each was carried along by preexisting millennarian expectations; each was centered around a charismatic leader-figure.

Typology

Millennial thought comes in various guises and can be distinguished along various dimensions. In historical terms, we can speak of the apocalyptic millennialism of Judaic and early Christian usage that was closely connected with the experience of oppression and persecution. In the established traditions, this was replaced by allegorical millennialism that dominated theological interpretation in the medieval Church and many of the leading figures in the Protestant Reformation. During this period, heretical instincts seemed to cling to the apocalyptic mode of earlier times. From the 17th century on, and particularly in the American scene, forms of progressive millennarianism came into being that tended to downplay the cataclysmic vision of apocalyptic disaster and subsequent millennium and to replace it with a sense of progressive realization that was more immanent than transcendent, more within the grasp of human agency than dependent on miraculous divine intervention.

While allegorical and progressive understandings fall more readily within the purview of traditional religious orientations, the apocalyptic vision seems to appeal more dramatically to heretical orientations and to draw new life from contexts of rebellion or dissent. Johannesen (1984) distinguishes the traditionally orthodox sense of millennial optimism from its more heretical expressions: "Millennialism in this sense is not to be confused with the ecstatic and confused visions of imminent apocalyptic fury that we sometimes refer to as millennary or chiliastic. Such visions are the opposite of the millennialist hope of Christian moral community, because they elevate the *gnosis* of the visionary over the collective moral experience of the community in time, and their myth of the future is designed to vindicate the living rather than to judge the living." (p. 214)

Millennial cults may also take a form of expression that is relatively passive or active. The activists are concerned with bringing about actual social change; the passivists assume a more theoretical position (Shepperson 1970a). The activist stance may take the form of a separatist movement, or a prophetic cult, usually in response to some social or cultural situation of distress. The progression in such movements is usually in the direction of a more secular and often revolutionary political movement or to some form of cultic resignation (Worsley 1968). The religious impulse in such politically active involvements can serve as a unifying force among potentially divisive political groups, depending on the degree of common cultural and religious ties. Worsley (1968) comments:

In a society split into numerous component units, jealous of each other but seeking to unite on a new basis, a political leader must avoid identification with any particular section of that society. He must avoid being seen as representative of the interests of any one group, particularly, of course, his own. He must therefore show that he seeks to establish his movement on the basis of a higher loyalty. By projecting his message on to the supernatural plane, he clearly demonstrates that his authority comes from a higher sphere, and that it transcends the narrow province of local gods and spirits associated with particular clans, tribes or villages. (p. 237)

Millennial movements may take a more passive turn and need not follow the path toward political revolution. They may choose to turn the final cataclysmic clash between the forces of good and evil over to the gods or, more mundanely, human progress. They will bring about the hoped-for transformation in their own good time. Such passivity may be the result of defeat or retreat from the confrontation with established institutions, or from the fact that the predictions of more active anticipation have been disappointed.

Revitalization Movements

Millennial cults fall under the rubric of revitalization movements (Wallace 1956, 1966) that share a number of messianic and utopian characteristics. These characteristics may be shared in some degree by similar cult movements, so that a sharp dividing line between millennarian and other similar prophetic cults is often difficult (Worsley 1968). There is a continuum of millennial movements involving value disparity and consensus in varying proportions, but the closer one moves toward millennarian revolution, the greater is the commitment to basic and total structural change of society (Barkun 1974). At the extreme this can turn into a "reign of terror and virtue." As Barkun comments, "The old evils must be extirpated and perfection instantly attained. All manner of surveillance, confession, ritual demonstrations, and punitive action are harnessed in the service of these twin aims." (p. 24) To which is added an observation by Brinton (1965): "What separates these revolutionaries from traditional Christianity is most obviously their insistence on having their heaven here, now, on earth, their impatient intent to conquer evil once and for all. Christianity in its traditional forms has long since, not by any means given up the moral struggle, but given up its chiliastic hopes — the hopes it too had when it was young and revolutionary, the hopes of the immediate Second Coming of Christ." (p. 197)

Millennial Thinking

As we have already seen, millennial views can be divided along a temporal dimension — the premillennialists holding that the coming of Christ will inaugurate the millennium, and the post-millennialists holding just the opposite, that Christ's coming will bring the millennium to a close (Shepperson 1970a). Those who interpret Apoc 20 figuratively have no expectations of any millennial kingdom and have been called amillennialists. The premillennial view usually holds that Christ's return will be preceded by a period of enlightenment and social reform that prepares the way for the messianic return in which the forces of evil in the world will be finally defeated. For some (historicists), the apocalyptic prophecies have been fulfilled symbolically in the Church; for others (futurists), these prophecies are yet to be fulfilled and are only to be fulfilled in the period immediately before the return of Christ. Other forms of premillennial thought have been described as dispensational because they divide the history of God's dealings with men into periods or dispensations. Such dispensational millennialism is the leading eschatology for modern conservative Protestantism, that maintains a balanced tension between the anticipation of an end that was near but uncertain and the moral fervor of reform to anticipate and promote the blessings of the promised kingdom (Harrell 1984).

The premillennial view usually reflects a degree of pessimism about the potentiality of human efforts to achieve meaningful change, and implies the necessity for cataclysmic upheaval in order to attain social transformation. In contrast, post-millennial thinking tends to see the coming of the millennium as the fruit of Christian forces now at work in the world, and that the second coming of Christ will take place when this process has reached its fulfillment. Consequently, the pre- and post-millennial positions have their secular counterparts in revolutionary and reformist approaches to social change — the post-millennial tending more toward reform, and the premillennial toward revolution. The dividing line between religious and political aspects of such movements is often obscured in more primitive social settings, but has greater validity in more advanced societies (Shepperson 1970a). In this sense the shift from a premillennial to a post-millennial emphasis and the acceptance of post-millennial views by Baptists and Presbyterians was probably one of the chief by-products of the failure of the Millerite movement (Handy 1984).

Millennarian Movements and the Cultic Process

My argument is that the characteristics of millennarian movements described in these pages reflects the dynamics of the cultic process. They arise as divergent elements within the larger and more traditional religious community, as splinter groups and/or in rebellion against preexisting and dominant religious orientations. As cultic formations, they fall within the category of adventist cults and reflect the characteristics of such cults.

In addition they reveal the elements of the cultic process as I have been developing it in these pages. Barkun (1974) summarizes some of these elements succinctly:

> Millennarianism, then, survives in areas with these characteristics: physical-cultural separateness; much communication within the area but little between it and other areas; relatively homogeneous population; preexisting salvationist ideas; potential charismatic leadership; and vulnerability to and frequent occurrence of environment-destroying disasters. Within this ecology of millennarianism, ideas that might be rapidly and effectively challenged elsewhere grow in a hothouse atmosphere of constant nourishment. Suspicion of dark forces outside and common interests and weaknesses within, well-articulated family structures and intermittent but unpredictable catastrophes — all serve to maintain adherence to ideas which in time of larger upheavals may spread rapidly outside. (pp. 96-97)

The in-group-out-group dynamics operate in these contexts with particular intensity and force. Similar to the gnostic movements, there is often clearly delineated in these cults an attitude of moral and spiritual superiority that serves to set the cult members off from ordinary mortals and declares the spiritual superiority of their beliefs and conduct. Selengut (1984) describes this attitude as follows:

> Millennarian movements are daring attempts at the creation of alternative realities and meaning systems. Millennarians claim to be in possession of a truer, more insightful understanding of the nature of reality than is available to those who acknowledge conventional reality. The millennarian says, in essence, "The rest of you are wrong; things are not what they appear to be. We have access to a source of truth (usually based on revelation of mysticism) which enables us to perceive the true nature of things. Oth-

ers haven't learned of this truth or as a consequence of 'sin,' 'bias' or accident of birth are not able to acknowledge this truth." Millennarian groups are so infused with the certainty and expectation of the coming transformation that they are enthusiastic proselytizers for this new reality and its healing powers for self, society and universe. (p. 167)

It is important not to miss the narcissistic underpinnings of such group processes. The narcissistic need to contain all truth and purity in association with oneself demands a manichean solution: all truth and good (the narcissistic ideal) is on my side, all error, falsehood, and evil on the other side. As Grunberger (1989) comments, " . . . we often find that the peculiar violence the narcissist projects on to his adversary is an expression of his serious but secret doubts as to the validity of his own system (as is the contempt he displays and the alienation he uses to maintain his contemptuous attitude)." (p. 23)

Schnackenburg (1963) comments on the presence of these elements in the apocalyptic literature of the intertestamental period:

All these elements: this dwelling on fantastic and fearsome pictures, this conscious stirring of anxiety and fear, the descent into a mood of complete defeatism, the boast of a special apocalyptic gnosis, this concealment from the people and revelation to the *illuminati "in whom flow the spring of insight, the source of wisdom and the stream of knowledge"* (4 Esdras 14: 47), the pride of the elect and their scorn for the *massa damnata*, their very spirit of revenge and their perverted joy in the annihilation of the wicked: all these are dark shadows on an otherwise bright picture of the fulfillment of the world and a blemish in the apocalyptic authors who composed them. However noble their conception of the kingship of God, it betrays a human pettiness and narrowness that are quite unbecoming in the "elect." Their apocalyptic excess of fervour and the way in which they calculate and reckon the advent of God's reign do serious damage to the genuine vision of transformation found in many places in their literature. (pp. 74-75)

The message and its sometimes fanatical expression are all too similar to clinically paranoid delusions. Such views inevitably run counter to the reality-oriented views of others. It is little wonder then that millennarian groups have been regarded as the product of mental disturbance, or have been labeled as politically subversive or religiously heretical. The response of the rest of the social organism to the initiatives of the cult is social ostracism and persecution. The cult is thus defined as socially marginal, as a form of suspect and rejected minority that is stigmatized on the basis of its beliefs. They are "cog-

314 \ *Thy Kingdom Come*

nitive minorities" that violate the moral norms and theological consensus of the dominant religious, and at times sociopolitical, environment (Selengut 1984).

Apocalyptic as Transitional

Apocalyptic Visions as Transitional Religious Phenomena

One problem that remains to be discussed is the question of how to conceptualize the eschatological dreams and the apocalyptic visions that we have been discussing in the above chapters. This looms as a particularly vexing and significant question in the context of an attempt to bring some degree of psychoanalytic understanding to these profoundly meaningful and nearly universal beliefs. The spectrum of manifestations runs the gamut from the pathological extreme of millennarian delusions in the most psychotic and unrealistic convictions of the fulfillment of messianic or millennarian expectations — as we might suspect in the manic exaltations of a Sabbatai or the millennarian delusions of a John of Leyden — all the way to the highly abstract and intellectualized formulations of sophisticated theological discussions of aspects of Christian eschatology and ecclesiology. I have argued to the connection of this entire spectrum of eschatological and apocalyptic mythology with an underlying unconscious fantasy system that entertains specific and deep-seated motivational roots in fundamental instinctual and narcissistic sources. The problem of how to understand these phenomena is not specific to these beliefs, but is inherent in all religious belief systems.

The options are threefold — such belief systems can be regarded within a restrictively subjective frame of reference, in an exclusively objective frame of reference, or lastly in the framework of transitional conceptualization. The first subjective perspective was favored by Freud. His views on religious illusions are sufficiently well-known that they do not need extensive elaboration here.[1] The critical distinction centers around the differentiation between illusions and delusions.

Freud's Approach

Freud cast himself more or less self-consciously in the role of the destroyer of illusions. In 1923 he wrote to Romain Rolland, "a great part of my life's work (I am ten years older than you) has been spent 'trying to' destroy illusions of my own and those of mankind" (E. Freud 1960, p. 341). If Rolland was a creator of illusions, particularly religious and mystical illusions, Freud would be their destroyer (Freud 1930, 1936). For him the strongest, and therefore the worst, illusions of all were those of religion. Religious illusions were a dragon to be slain with the hard steel of the sword of scientific reason. He saw religious beliefs as opposed to reality and providing one form of withdrawal from the pain of reality. His attack on religion was uncompromising. He (1927) wrote:

> It regards reality as the sole enemy and as the source of all suffering, with which it is impossible to live, so that one must break off all relations with it if one is to be in any way happy. The hermit turns his back on the world and will have no truck with it. But one can do more than that; one can try to recreate the world, to build up in its stead another world in which its most unbearable features are eliminated and replaced by others that are in conformity with one's wishes. But whoever, in desperate defiance, sets out upon this path to happiness will as a rule attain nothing. Reality is too strong for him. He becomes a madman, who for the most part finds no one to help him in carrying through his delusion. It is asserted, however, that each one of us behaves in some respect like a paranoic, corrects some aspect of the world which is unbearable to him by the construction of a wish and introduces this delusion into reality. A special importance attaches to the case in which this attempt to procure a certainty of happiness and a protection against suffering through a delusional remoulding of reality is made by a considerable number of people in common. The religions of mankind must be classed among the mass-delusions of this kind. No one, needless to say, who shares a delusion ever recognizes it as such. (p. 81)

---

1. See all my discussion of Freud's views on this topic in Meissner (1984c).

Freud here moves beyond the language of illusion to say that religious belief is, in fact, a delusion. As far as Freud was concerned, religious illusions were akin to psychosis. Freud was actually cognizant of a distinction between the terms "illusion" and "delusion." An illusion is not simply an error, even though it may be a false belief. The basic defining characteristic of illusions is that they derive from wishes. As such, illusions are neither necessarily false nor in contradiction to reality, but when they do contradict reality they become delusions. Freud (1927) wrote: "We call a belief an illusion when a wish-fulfillment is a prominent factor in its motivation, and in doing so we disregard its relation to reality, just as the illusion itself sets no store by verification." (p. 31) But it is also clear that Freud regarded religious beliefs as standing in contradiction to reality at a number of points, and to that extent they were for him unequivocally delusions.

One of the difficulties with the Freudian argument is precisely that he shifts the ground from considering religion as a form of illusion to that of delusion. The shift is subtle but nonetheless devastating. The mark of illusions is the quality of being generated by wishes so that they express a form of wish fulfillment. Wishes may be consistent with the demands of reality or not. Wishes that seek the possible are the basis of hope (Meissner 1973, 1987b, 1989); wishes that seek the impossible are unrealistic and sow the seeds of discontent, disappointment and frustration. In themselves, illusions are neither realistic nor unrealistic. Delusions, however, are characterized by their opposition to reality. The note of "opposition" is critical. We can be certain of the delusional status of any belief or idea only when we have contradictory evidence to belie it. When such evidence is lacking, the judgment regarding the status of the delusion cannot be rendered. In passing judgment on religious beliefs, Freud oversteps the bounds of logic. While religious beliefs qualify as illusions in one or other degree, the fact is that there is no evidence to contravene them, just as there is no evidence independent of the belief system to support them (Meissner in process). Freud mistakes the lack of supportive evidence for contradiction by reality.

Without doubt, Freud would decree that the eschatological and apocalyptic visions we have been discussing are flagrant examples of wish-fulfilling illusions; the further question is whether they would qualify as delusions. I suspect the Freudian verdict would be "guilty as charged." For Freud's mind-set, the claims of future glory and redemption could be no more than totally unsubstantiated figments of the imagination, without any correspondence or support in the real order.

In other words, the criterion adopted by Freud is completely subjective, that is, that the belief system expressed in the eschatological dreams of the messianic reign of the promised Davidic king, or of the heralded second coming of the triumphant savior Christ, or in the final establishment of the glorious kingdom of the millennial era, is entirely based on the imaginative elaborations of a fantasy system driven by infantile wish-fulfillments — and nothing more. There is no reality to correspond to these fantasies, so that they are in the end no more than delusions, no more real than the hallucinations or ravings of a deranged psychotic.

The Objective Perspective

To those who embrace the belief system, to those who accept and give credence to the fervent hopes and expectations of the coming of the messiah and to the glorious establishment of his kingdom in the final days, the Freudian perspective is quite alien. For them, the belief is no fairy tale, no exercise of idle imagination, no wishful fiction. For them it is real, and only to the extent that it is real does it have any meaning. The basis of their conviction lies not in some set of consensual evidences, but in traditions and beliefs that have a long history and that answer to certain basic psychological needs. The test of validity is not that of validation by correspondence to some determinable reality or set of data, but the degree to which the belief system responds to, answers, brings consolation, conviction, moral strength and hope to limited, painful and desperate lives.

The conviction of validity and the acceptance of the belief system as real and true are thus matters of faith rather than scientific proof. As Freud observed, the illusion sets no store by verification — in a scientific sense, that is. The belief, by the same token, is not merely a matter of imagination or fantasy. For the theologian who busies himself with the eschatology, ecclesiology, and apocalypticism of these beliefs, validity is a matter of the meaning of the revelation that is to be found in the sources of his religious belief: in the scriptures, traditions, writings of Church Fathers, other theologians, in the teachings of the Church and its leaders through the ages. His task is to explore and seek to understand the religious significance and levels of meaning embedded in the symbolic density of many religious expressions of these beliefs. This is not the reflection of wish-fulfillment or fantasy. Nor is it for the believing theologian an unreality. He works with the abiding conviction, born of faith, that whatever graspable truth or mystery is contained in these visions, behind them is the ultimate reality of an existing God who creates, loves, and reveals. The perspective is unequivocally objective. In this realm of obsessive devotion to the truth, of dedicated scholarship, and of scientific veracity, there is almost no room for fantasy — or at least it plays so little a role that it could well be discounted. Fantasy would have more to say when the same scholar goes to church or kneels to pray.

This is one kind of objectivity. Another might be the religious fanatic who remains convinced of the objectivity of his belief on an emotional or drive-determined basis, as only a response to the intensity of inner drives and needs. Such, I would think, were fanatical Zealots who rebelled against the Romans, or the followers of bar Kochba, or the more credulous Christians who stripped themselves of all worldly possessions in anticipation of the imminent parousia, or the enthusiastic followers of Sabbatai Sevi who sold all and gave to the poor in preparation for the messianic arrival, or even the all-too-believing Millerites who surrendered everything to await the day of the second coming. This is the brand of objectivism that spurns verification, that has no trust in reason, that turns faith into fanaticism. It is the kind of wishful credulity against which Freud directed his criticisms.

Religious Beliefs as Transitional

Winnicott's genial contributions have spawned a revolution in psychoanalytic thinking that has affected our ways of theorizing and has played a powerful role in determining our thinking about the psychoanalytic process. His ideas regarding transitional objects, transitional object relations, and transitional phenomena have also exercised a tremendous influence on our thinking about broader human concerns. One of the most important areas in which Winnicott's ideas have taken root and undergone significant evolution is in the psychoanalytic understanding of religious phenomena. In that particular area of applied psychoanalysis, his ideas regarding transitional experience and the area of illusion have found their most meaningful extension.

Transitional Objects. Winnicott approached the question of the understanding of illusion through his analysis of transitional objects as a childhood developmental phenomenon (Winnicott 1953). His contributions have stimulated a considerable literature on the vicissitudes of the infant's use of transitional objects and the development of transitional phenomena (Grolnick and Barkin 1978; Hong 1978). There are various forms of transitional objects and stages of the evolution of transitional phenomena in the infant's experience. In essence, the transitional object is the first real thing that the infant uses to establish contact with reality that is independent of the maternal object. As the child begins to grow out of his symbiotic attachment to the mother, he begins a process of separation that allows him to broaden his experience of the world around him. The first step is to find a substitute for the mother, or even more specifically, the mother's breast. He may choose for this purpose a teddy bear, a doll, a towel that he can suck on — anything that meets his need for seeking substitution in the context of maintaining his connection with the mother. That object becomes his transitional object, the first real object substitute for the mother. As he grows, the quality and nature of his use of transitional objects change as his engagement with the real world becomes more secure and extensive. To the extent that the process succeeds, he is able to negotiate the perils of separation and individuation and to gain a beachhead in toddlerhood.

Illusion. This developmental consideration served as the initial platform on which Winnicott based his ideas concerning developmental aspects of play and the transitional space within which the play phenomenon took place, and which gave way to the locus of later transitional phenomena. My interest here is in the contribution of the understanding of transitional phenomena to the area of illusion. Winnicott argues that illusion is an important aspect of human involvement in the world of experience, a capacity that expresses itself in the creative shaping of a humanly meaningful environment and in facilitating in psychic terms the interlocking processes of accommodation and assimilation. In his analysis of the developmental contexts of transitional object experience, Winnicott argues that in the optimal mother-child interaction, the "good-enough mother" is sufficiently attuned to the infant's needs so that she is available and responsive at the very point at which the need demands satisfaction. The conjunction of the infant's need and the response by the real object — mother — creates a situation of illusion in which, from the point of view of the child, he has the experience of creating the need-satisfying object. Thus, as Winnicott observes, to the eyes of the external observer the response comes from the outside, but not from the point of view of the baby. But at the same time it does not come exclusively from within, that is, it is not a hallucination. As Modell (1991) recently commented:

Within the illusion of the potential space the mother accepts and does not challenge the child's construction of reality; the question, whose reality is it?, does not arise. Winnicott generalized from the observation of infants to suggest that this potential space characterizes the mental process that underlies the shared illusions of aesthetic and cultural experiences. From the standpoint of an outside observer, this potential space is a space that belongs neither entirely to the subject's inner world nor to objective external reality; it represents the subject's creative transformation of the external world. (p. 234)

This area of the infant's experience is simultaneously subjective and objective. The formation of the transitional bond to the mother, or the use of the transitional object, does not take place without a real object. But the reality of the object is transformed into something else that is determined by the infant's psychological need and is thus created out of that need. Winnicott (1971) thus stakes out an important dimension of human experience, over and above involvement in interpersonal relationships and the inner realm of intrapsychic experience and functioning. He articulates an intermediate area that he designates as "experiencing," which lies at the intersection of psychic and external reality. He writes, "It is an area that is not challenged, because no claim is made on its behalf except that it shall exist as a resting-place for the individual engaged in the perpetual human task of keeping inner and outer reality separate yet interrelated." (p. 2)

In Winnicott's view, the claims of illusion and of this intermediate realm of experiencing reach far beyond the developmental context. He (1971) comments:

It is usual to refer to "reality-testing," and to make a clear distinction between apperception and perception. I am staking a claim for an intermediate state between a baby's inability and his growing ability to recognize and accept reality. I am therefore studying the substance of *illusion*, that which is allowed to the infant, and which in adult life is inherent in art and religion, and yet becomes the hallmark of madness when an adult puts too powerful a claim on the credulity of others, forcing them to acknowledge a sharing of illusion that is not their own. We can share a respect for *illusory experience*, and if we wish we may collect together and form a group on the basis of the similarity of our illusory experiences. This is a natural root of grouping among human beings. (p. 3)

In the course of development, the child's illusion of magical omnipotence and control over the transitional object gradually gives way to increasing degrees of disillusionment and optimal frustration, leading gradually toward accommodation to reality. This dialectic and tension between illusion and disillusion continues to elaborate throughout the whole of human life and experience. The process of gaining knowledge and acceptance of reality is never fully accomplished. Every human being is caught up in the tension and struggle of relating inner to outer reality. The relief and resolution of this interminable tension can be gained only within the intermediate area of illusory experience, which for the most part even in the life of the adult remains unchallenged, particularly as it finds expression in the arts and religion. Winnicott (1971) comments: "Should an adult make claims on us for our acceptance of the objectivity of his subjective phenomena, we discern or diagnose madness. If, however, the adult can manage to enjoy the personal intermediate area without making claims, then we can acknowledge our own corresponding intermediate areas, and are pleased to find a degree of overlapping, that is to say common experience between members of a group in art or religion or philosophy." (p. 14)

The capacity for illusory experience develops and evolves in the play of the child and later in the creative and cultural experience of the adult. Certain aspects of the playing experience reflect its illusory character. The area of playful illusion belongs neither to the child's psychic reality, nor to the external world. Into this transitional space the child gathers objects (toys) that he invests with meanings and feelings derived from his subjective world. Play has an inherent excitement that derives not from instinctual arousal but from the precarious interplay between the child's subjectivity and what is objectively perceived and received. Winnicott notes a direct development from the appearance of transitional phenomena to the capacity for play, from isolated play to shared playing, and from shared playing to the capacity for cultural experience. The child who plays well demonstrates a capacity for blending illusion and reality and reflects a relatively smooth integration of both libidinal and aggressive impulses. The capacity to utilize both libidinal and aggressive energy harmoniously is essential not only in the play of children but in more adult forms of creative activity (Winnicott 1971).

Transitional Conceptualization. The question in this consideration has to do with the extent to which Winnicott's understanding of transitional phenomena can serve as a meaningful model for the analysis of religious experience and ideation. The analysis of culture in terms of transitional experience and the value of illusion stands in stark opposition to Freud's views. For Freud, the purpose and value of culture was instinctual restraint and a matter of channeling intrapsychic conflict; for Winnicott, the cultural dynamisms originate in the mother-child dyad and continually evolve in other interpersonal and social contexts as a matter of establishing and maintaining a sense of self. For Freud, civilization and culture are necessary evils that result in neurotic adjustments; for Winnicott, they are indispensable sources of human psychic development and selfhood that keep the personality from slipping into schizoid isolation and despair. For Freud, religious beliefs were little more than vain wish-fulfillments; for Winnicott they were essential illusions answering to fundamental and ineradicable human needs.

It is not difficult to see the impact of Winnicott's notions of the transitional object and the transitional phenomenon as they extend into the realm of cultural experience. It is also important to recognize the extent to which Winnicott's approach differs from Freud's view of illusion. Freud's emphasis on the distortion or contradiction of reality in the service of wish-fulfillment is basic to his view of illusion. But what Freud sees as distortion and contradiction of reality, Winnicott sees as part of man's creative experience. What Freud sees as wish-fulfillment in accordance with the pleasure principle and in resistance to the reality principle, Winnicott views as an inherent aspect of human creativity.

In Winnicott's view, then, illusion plays a role in the developmental transition to reality: without the capacity to utilize transitional objects and to generate transitional forms of experience, the child's efforts to gain a foothold in reality will inevitably be frustrated. Further, without continuing access to and participation in illusory experience, human life becomes impoverished and withers, insofar as fundamental and vital human needs lack appropriate nourishment and support. Thus illusion is not an obstruction to experiencing reality but a means of gaining access to it. In the same sense, the symbolic dimension of human understanding represents an attempt to see beyond the immediate, the material, the merely sensual or perceptual, to a level of deeper meaning and human, if not spiritual, significance.

Winnicott's genial insights have been further elaborated by Pruyser (1979, 1983). His formulation calls for three distinct spheres of human experience: the sphere of transitional experience is separate and different from the more familiar spheres of subjective intrapsychic experience on one hand and external objective experience on the other. The transitional objects of childhood are neither the mental images produced within the mind nor objective images produced by the effects of the external world impinging on sense perception. They are certainly not hallucinatory or delusional objects. The transitional sphere of illusory experience embraces the religious, the sacred, the sacramental, the mysterious (Pruyser 1985).

The child's developmental experience involves the acceptance of certain beliefs and the rejection of unbeliefs as part of his emerging sense of identity (Pruyser 1974). As Pruyser (1979) observed:

> The child obtains training in illusionistic thinking and imagining and attains a sense of the values inherent in beliefs. But he also develops a sense of the un-values attached to the alternative beliefs which his parents reject or ridicule; he acquires some set of disbeliefs. His as well as his parents' beliefs and disbeliefs are building blocks of his growing sense of identity. . . . In a word, definite links are formed between the content or tenet of any belief or disbelief and the emotional tones inherent in his object relations, i.e., the feeling tones attached to his parents and to his own nascent self. His wishes and ideals become canalized to follow a certain direction and to assume a certain form which will subsequently influence many of his later ventures into belief and disbelief systems. (p. 165)

The three realms of experience have their separate claims, but the transitional sphere stakes its claim as the arena of belief, symbolic meaning, and culture generally. The transitional cannot be reduced to either the subjective or objective realms. The symbolic is neither an autistic creation of the inner world nor a sensory datum. The area of the "illusionistic world" is where man searches for meaning and beauty. "Illusion is neither hallucination or delusion (both of which are spawned by the autistic mind), nor is it straightforward sense perception (as produced by the external world of nature and the things man has made from natural resources). Illusion includes mystery: since it has a special object relationship endowed with many surplus values about whose legitimacy one cannot bicker in terms derived from either the subjective or the objective" (Pruyser 1979, p. 166).

The Problem in Religious Thinking

The problem arises in the interface between psychoanalytic and religious thinking. Each of these areas represents separate disciplines and ranges of discourse, each with its separate reference points, modes of conceptualization and symbolic connotation. Within the context of an accepted belief system and the record of revelation, religious thought addresses itself to a realm of conceptualization that it takes as having existential validity and substantial truth value.

On the opposite side of the conceptual chasm, psychoanalysis stakes its claim to an inner world of man's psychic experience that expresses itself in wishes and fantasies and is more or less rooted in the subjective polarity of man's experience. In addressing human religious experience and conceptualization, psychoanalysis makes no commitments to a framework of existent or objective realities but confines its focus and the implication of its arguments to the intrapsychic realm. It asserts no more than the subjective and the intrapsychic, and at least prescinds from the objective or extrapsychic implications of its formulations. The business of psychoanalysis is psychic reality and nothing beyond.

In its classic mode, as I have suggested, psychoanalytic formulations have included the added implication that any extrapsychic or objective existence is to be denied. If psychoanalysis speaks of God, it addresses itself to no more than a God-representation with all of the dynamic, wishful and fantasied concomitants of that central psychic representation. The question of any relation, connection or implication between the representational God in psychic reality and an existing living God in the realms of external reality is simply unaddressed or denied. When psychoanalysts speak of God and maintain that they can say no more than is found in the psychic reality and mental representations of their patients, they are on solid ground. When they go beyond those boundaries to assert that there is no reality to the patient's belief in God, they transgress. The fact that Freud committed the same transgression does not make the failure legitimate.

This brings into focus a most salient consideration that has particular application to the argument developed on these pages. The psychoanalytic perspective has nothing to say about the truth-value or validity of any of the beliefs we have been considering. Even in instances where frank psychopathology lies behind or is even expressed in the belief system, we can draw no conclusion as to the religious validity or verifiability of the beliefs in question (Meissner 1991). The point is important since I believe that it was at this critical juncture that Freud's understanding of religion derailed itself. Freud thought that if he could demonstrate the operation of psychological or even psychopathological processes in the genesis of religious beliefs, that would mean that such propositions had no real validity or truth-value and that they were restrictively psychological productions based on underlying infantile motivations. Unfortunately, the Freudian verdict was premature. The jury is still out.

The psychoanalytic method has nothing in its conceptual tool kit to enable it to render judgment on the truth-value of religious beliefs. It has no basis on which to either confirm them or reject them. In its more extreme forms, the psychoanalytic perspective has led many analysts to go beyond the limited purview of the intrapsychic to assert on the basis of psychoanalytic arguments that the existence of a God and, indeed, with him all the panoply of religious processes, entities and realities must be cast into doubt, or at least left in the realm of agnostic obscurity. In this perspective, then, the entire spectrum of religiously endorsed and theologically elaborated conceptualizations is put under attack. And this form of argument is not entirely misguided. Within the methodology and purview of psychoanalysis, no statement is possible about the existence or nonexistence of such a divinity. But the religious concept of the existence of God is not asserted within a psychoanalytic framework. The psychoanalyst may claim that the existential proposition has no meaning for psychoanalysis — and his claim would be valid. If the psychoanalyst carries his claim a step further, to declare that then any assertion of God's existence is false, he has crossed the boundaries of legitimacy and has made a psychoanalytically meaningless statement. This was Freud's error, which has become part of the heritage of psychoanalytic thinking in this area. Little wonder, then, that theologians or religious thinkers of any persuasion should approach psychoanalysis with suspicion and wariness. The conflict and tension between these respective perspectives is cast in terms of the dichotomies of the intrapsychic versus the extrapsychic, of psychic reality versus external reality, and of subjectivity versus objectivity.

In an effort to construct a conceptual bridge over this chasm between religious and psychoanalytic thinking, I have tried to extend Winnicott's genial formulations regarding transitional phenomena as pointing toward a useful and potential conceptual space that provided a medium for a dialectical resolution of these tensions between the subjective and the objective (Meissner 1978b, 1984c, 1990b, 1992b). This analysis takes Winnicott's ideas regarding transitional phenomena and the area of illusion and extends them to include a form of conceptualization that operates within the area of illusion; that, as such, is neither subjective nor objective and lies open simultaneously to both subjective and objective poles of meaning without violation or exclusion of either.

The Millennial Vision as Transitional

Religious symbolic systems are, at least in the Judeo-Christian tradition, derived from a twofold source that is at once subjective and objective. The subjective dimension comes from the dynamic constituents of human understanding and motivation, while the objective dimension is contributed by a revelation with the presumption of a divine presence and action behind it. Leavy (1986) articulates this dimension of religious belief systems as follows:

> Faith is by nature — human nature — presented symbolically, and religions are symbol systems. The believer, knowingly or not, owes his or her religious language to a revelation that is the spring of the tradition, coming from outside the believer's mind. The ultimate reference of faiths are not themselves products of regressive fantasies, but symbolic representations of ultimate truths." (p. 153)

It is within this dimension of religious experience that the psychological and the theological intersect, and it is likewise within this area of conceptualization that I have proposed the transitional form of understanding as providing the basis for bridging concepts that might facilitate a dialogue between the psychoanalytic perspective and the religious perspective (Meissner 1984c, 1990b).

In the case of the messianic and millennial dreams and visions, the transitional mode of conceptualization offers a way of understanding these beliefs that commits them neither to total subjectivity nor to total objectivity. If there is to be any possibility of a dialogue between psychoanalysis and theology or religious thinking, a common conceptual ground must be defined on which it can take place. Focusing the messianic and millennial systems in transitional terms allows the understanding of their meaning to be cast in terms that are neither subjective nor objective, but remain open to the possibilities of both subjective and objective interpretation. Thus, for example, the belief in the second coming of Christ can remain open to a subjectivist interpretation in terms of narcissistic needs and wish-fulfillments, and without contradiction leave open the possibility that some form of fulfillment in real terms guaranteed by divine prophecy and promise can be entertained. By the same token, commitment to a conviction of real fulfillment in the eschatological framework does not disavow underlying psychic determinants that have to do with drive derivatives and fundamental, even infantile, motivations. The bottom line is that psychoanalytic understanding and interpretation can enrich religious experience and commitment without violating its faith commitment and devotion.

Transitional versus Fetishistic Thought

As is the case with other forms of transitional experience, this process can be misdirected into infantile or pathological channels. Greenacre (1969, 1970) has provided a workable model of the relationship between the transitional object and the development of a fetish. A word of caution may be useful at this point regarding the use and implication of terms. Just as the realm of transitional experience and conceptualization is not synonymous with the transitional object, so the application of terms pertaining to the transitional realm or to fetishistic distortions is not synonymous with the infantile or pathological experience of either. The terms are used analogously to suggest modes of thinking that are in some respects similar, but in other respects different. If we speak of a fetishistic dimension in thinking about religious objects, this does not imply that the phenomenon is a piece of fetishistic pathology.

I would contend that, just as the transitional object of the child can degenerate into a fetish, transitional religious experience can be distorted into less authentic, relatively fetishistic directions that tend to contaminate and distort the more profoundly meaningful aspects of the religious experience. Greenacre (1969, 1970) describes the similarities and differences between these modes of relating, one relatively adaptive and serving the developmental process, the other pathological and serving neurotic and perverse needs. The fetish evolves as a necessary prop to the individual's capacity to function as an adult, particularly with regard to sexual involvement and expression. She describes the fetish " . . . as a patch for a flaw in the genital area of the body image." (p. 334) Both the transitional object and the fetish contribute to the maintenance of illusion, and both involve a degree of symbolic magic. The magic of the transitional object serves developmental needs and is gradually modified as those needs are diminished and otherwise fulfilled. The fetish involves a more complicated and need-driven magic, which does not easily abate. Greenacre emphasizes the gradations between them: "They are phenomena at two ends of a spectrum of predisposing and variously combining conditions, between which there is a series of gradations of intermediate forms with different qualities and intensities." (p. 341) Greenacre only hints at the application of these ideas to our subject, when she mentions " . . . the role of the transitional object in relation to illusion, symbolism, and to creativity in general. It is also important in the development of religious feeling and, with the fetish, plays a part in religious practices." (p. 342)

The model, derived from areas of development and psychopathology, can find analogous application to the understanding of religious experience. The transitional mode of experiencing and conceptualizing can be distorted by the excessive injection of subjective needs, needs which may be pathologically derived. The needs when pathological are not necessarily synonymous with the needs involved in the pathology of the fetish. They may reflect unresolved dependency needs, passivity, narcissism, conflicts over aggression, guilt, shame, inadequacy, identity conflicts, and so on. The religious object can become the vehicle for projective or transference processes which involve the object in a defensive or need-satisfying system. When such a defensive course is followed, religious objects or practices begin to take on a magical quality that perverts their authentic religious impulse and meaning. Religious objects, prayers, and rites become magical talismans in the service of magical expectations and infantile needs.

In this sense religious objects can be reduced to talismans, religious rites can become obsessional rituals, and religious faith can be corrupted into ideology. The ideology is drawn into the fetishistic dynamic — as Chasseguet-Smirgel (1985) observes, "An ideology always contains within it a phantasy of narcissistic assumption linked to a return to a state of primary fusion [with the mother], which equally excludes conflict and castration and thus operates within the order of Illusion." (p. 193) The more these "fetishistic" or otherwise defensive components pervade the individual believer's beliefs and the belief systems of the religious community, the more they might be presumed to veer toward Freud's vision of religious systems as delusional and as reflecting infantile wish-fulfillments. The entire panorama of messianic and millennarian beliefs we have discussed here can be evaluated from this perspective. To what extent was a balance of subjective and objective components attained and maintained as expressions of transitional experiencing in any one of the cult movements that embraced messianic or millennarian beliefs? It seems that the spectrum is broad and the range extensive.

The Dynamics of Millennarian Movements

Precipitating Conditions

The millennial vision has a persistence and recurrence that allows it to sprout afresh with renewed vigor again and again across the centuries. One important question has to do with the effort to understand what factors or what concatenation of influences provide the fertile soil in which these millennarian seeds find nourishment. My contention throughout this study is that the matrix within which the cultic process strikes its roots involves a mix of psychological, social, economical, environmental, and cultural elements. When the mix is right in any given historical context, the workings of the cultic process play themselves out. While the central focus in this study is on the psychic processes that underlie the cultic process, other influences cannot be ignored and may in many settings play a more telling and significant role than the psychic elements, and may often act in such a way as to shape and direct reactive psychic components.

Appeal to Underprivileged

Cohn (1970b) maintains that the millennial dreams had their major appeal to the lowest strata of society. He quotes Max Weber (1920):

A salvationist kind of religion can very well originate in socially privileged strata. The charisma of the prophet . . . is normally associated with a certain minimum of intellectual culture. . . . But it regularly changes its character . . . when it penetrates to under-privileged strata. . . . And one can point to at least one feature that normally accompanies this shift; one result of the unavoidable adaptation to the needs of the masses. This is the appearance of a *personal* saviour, whether wholly divine or a mixture of human and divine; and of the religious relationship to that saviour as the precondition for salvation. The further one descends the ladder of social stratification, the more radical the ways in which this need for a saviour is wont to express itself . . . (p. 51)

Among the ranks of these underprivileged in the medieval world of millennarian ferment were the unskilled workers, the journeymen, the unlanded peasants, the beggars and vagabonds, the unemployed, the many who could claim no recognizable place in society as their own — all those who lived in a state of chronic frustration and anxiety, the most unstable and impulse-prone elements of medieval social structure. Under any circumstances that induced social stress, these elements of society tended to react extremely and violently. The established peasants or artisans who were guild members might experience poverty or oppression, and they might respond by rebelling or submitting, but they were not likely to lunge to the support of a newly inspired prophet and his fanatical pursuit of the millennium (Cohn 1970b).

Deprivation and Insecurity

When such deprived people were threatened with previously unknown hazards, with the unfamiliar and strange, their disorientation and distress could be marked and their tendency to resort to demonological fantasies enhanced. If the threats were sufficiently intense and overwhelming, the outcome might well be a mass delusion that carried in it the seeds of explosive destructiveness. The insecure numbers who lived on the margins of society were the most vulnerable to threatening disasters and least able to cope with them. The tendency to turn to messiah-saviors to save them, and to see themselves as the chosen of God called to right the wrongs that surrounded them does not seem difficult to understand. Cohn (1970b) observes: "So it came about that multitudes of people acted out with fierce energy a shared phantasy which, though delusional, yet brought them such intense emotional relief that they could live only through it, and were perfectly willing both to kill and to die for it." (p. 88)

When the millennial idea surfaces, it can act as a catalyst to the frustrated, deprived and helpless, spurring them on to redress their wrongs and find satisfaction for their needs. In a sense the disparity between "cultural goals" and "institutionalized means" (Merton 1957) can produce an explosive and emotionally intense mixture. In this sense, deprivation remains relative and to a degree subjective. Only when the subjective sense of deprivation in a sufficient number of individuals reaches a critical mass is the matrix for millennial reaction set (Barkun 1974). In addition to the sheer facts of deprivation and impotence, there may be a sense of having been wronged, unjustly deprived and denied, and a righteous sense of entitlement that empowers the cult believers to utilize every means and to justify any and all actions, no matter how inhumane and destructive, that can be presumed to redress the wrongs and satisfy the deprived needs (Worsley 1968). Barkun (1974) comes close to this view in his disaster-based model, emphasizing the role of multiple disasters impinging on a homogeneous (usually rural) population and leading to reaction shaped by a charismatic leader.

The question remains unsettled as to what forms of deprivation are critical to the arousal of millennarian fantasies. Though deprivation remains a significant factor, the mere fact of deprivation and the assumption that the critically deprived are at the bottom of the social ladder does not adequately explain the phenomenon (Aberle 1970; Barkun 1974). As an example, one of the groups that Cohn (1970a) notes as vulnerable to emotional frustration in the medieval period is women of means and leisure. Such women are traditionally targets for revivalist movements, often resulting in the introduction of an erotic element into the antinomian spirit of the movement. The erotic millennarianism of the Brethren of the Free Spirit would be a case in point. Whatever the deprivations of such classes, they are not the deprivations of the poor and oppressed. The deprivation model has found its critics, but the fact remains that those who are vulnerable to forms of millennial and other cult beliefs are not the content and satisfied, but those who have suffered some form of deprivation or loss of meaning in their lives (Townsend 1984).

External Factors

The conditions of deprivation are often influenced by external factors. Revolutionary millennarianism has often arisen in areas of significant overpopulation. The rapid rise in population seems to have been a contributing factor in most of the cases of the rise of millennial cults in the Middle Ages (Cohn 1970b). An additional component is rapid social and economic changes, such as were occurring in the rapid urbanization and industrialization in Western societies, resulting in the disruption or weakening of traditional social bonds and the widening gap between the well-to-do and the poor, between the haves and the have-nots (Cohn 1970b; Thrupp 1970). The millennial vision serves as a rallying point for the uprooted and disadvantaged that provides hopeful expectations that can sustain them in the face of harsh realities and adversities and allow for the possibility of more advantageous social conditions (Thrupp 1970). Millennial movements also can arise when traditional social structures are destroyed or weakened by wars or oppression — as was the case in the original prophetic formulation of the millennial visions. The millennial myth proclaims that the oppressor can be overcome and even annihilated with the help of supernatural forces — particularly by the return of the avenging Christ who will right all wrongs and mete out due punishment to those who have persecuted or victimized his saints (Cohn 1970a).

Cohn (1970b) also points out that in the case of the anarcho-communistic millennarian groups that flourished toward the end of the medieval period, the cult movement arose in the context of a wider revolutionary situation — e.g., the English peasants' revolt of 1381, the early stages of the Hussite revolt in 1419-1421, Müntzer and the German peasants' revolt in 1525, and even in the Anabaptist crisis at Münster. As Cohn (1970b) comments: "In each of these instances the mass insurrection itself was directed towards limited and realistic aims — yet in each instance the climate of mass insurrection fostered a special kind of millenarian group. As social tensions mounted and the revolt became nationwide, there would appear, somewhere on the radical fringe, a *propheta* with his following of paupers, intent on turning this one particular upheaval into the apocalyptic battle, the final purification of the world." (p. 284)

In almost all cases, the rise of the cult takes place under circumstances of threat — the threat of deprivation, hardship, economic disaster, disruptive social changes, and even death. Catastrophe or the fear of catastrophe seem to play a central role in the provocation of the millennarian impulse (Cohn 1970a; Barkun 1974). The millennial movements of the Middle Ages flourished in the shadow of the Black Death, the omnipresent and virulent plague that swept through Western Europe and left a swath of corpses behind it. The terror and desperation took its toll. Cohn (1970b) writes:

But when a situation arose which was not only menacing but went altogether outside the normal run of experience, when people were confronted with hazards which were all the more frightening because they were unfamiliar — at such times a collective flight into the world of demonological phantasies could occur very easily. And if the threat was sufficiently overwhelming, the disorientation sufficiently widespread and acute, there could arise a mass delusion of the most explosive kind. Thus when the Black Death reached western Europe in 1348 it was at once concluded that some class of people must have introduced into the water supply a poison concocted of spiders, frogs and lizards — all of them symbols of earth, dirt and the Devil — or else maybe of basilisk-flesh. As the plague continued and people grew more and more bewildered and desperate, suspicion swung now here, now there, lighting successively on the lepers, the poor, the rich, the clergy, before it came finally to rest on the Jews, who thereupon were almost exterminated. (p. 87)

And again it was the lowest social strata of the poor and dispossessed that felt the heaviest burden of disaster and in whom the millennial fervor found its deepest and most sustained roots, and in whom the millennial expression took its most violent and destructive course.

Social Conditions

Social conditions obviously play a determinative role in the development of millennarian cults. Such religious expressions tend to arise in contexts of low social and political organization. Social structures that seem predisposed to millennarian expressions are characterized by a lack of technological and scientific knowledge. The lack of a basis for scientific understanding of natural phenomena, particularly threatening and disruptive occurrences, makes it impossible to predict or control natural disasters of whatever kind. This opens the way to animistic and fantastic supernatural explanations, and increases the appeal of magical or miraculous solutions to their difficulties. As Worsley (1968) comments: "The primitive peasant is thus disposed to the acceptance of supernaturalist interpretations of reality: the soil is ready tilled for the millenarian leader. As pragmatic social experience increases and as education spreads, the ground becomes less fertile for millenarism." (p. 239)

Values

One of the more poignant factors that is often more difficult to document, but may for all of that play a more salient role nonetheless, is the disruption, distortion, or changing patterns of value systems that override and govern social and psychological function within a given socioeconomic setting. As Cohn (1970b) points out, the most fertile soil for fanatical and revolutionary millennarianism is not merely among the poor and oppressed as such, but among such classes that have had their traditional way of life disrupted and have lost faith in the traditional values that have been the abiding and guiding norms for their social adaptation and their sense of personal identity and integrity. These were the conditions that could be found strikingly expressed in the emerging religious disease and disruption that arose in medieval Europe after the 11th century and that formed a tradition of religious dissent that finally culminated in the Reformation and gave rise to the messiahs and messianic movements of the poor.

The ethical vacuum must be filled, accompanied as it is with highly charged social, emotional and personal stress (Thrupp 1970). The erosion of values can often be precipitated or aggravated by external conditions of conquest, foreign oppression, or any form of confrontation with a more evolved or superior culture. Such was the case, for example, in the ancient setting of the oppressions of Palestine under the conqueror's heel, both Seleucid and Roman. Writing of the cargo cult phenomenon, Worsley (1968) comments:

> Those things which formerly brought a man high social status, such as being a polygamist, are now the objects of attack by missionaries and their followers. Men of low status are thrust into key political offices by Government, while aristocrats are ignored. The most sacred beliefs and rites are dubbed pagan superstition. Young men defy their fathers; they know more of the new life, and as labourers have greater access to the cash and knowledge which now count for so much. (p. 248)

A similar theme could have been applied in the ancient Hebrew context, and in many others I have discussed.

In the medieval context, one of the major social structures that provided social stability and the consistency and continuity of values was the Church. In addition to the other anxiogenic assaults that afflicted medieval society, the demise in the authority and authenticity of the Church as a vital spiritual force in the lives of medieval men played a decisive role in opening the way to the onrush of millennarian fantasies. All too often, when men looked to the Church for spiritual guidance and leadership they found worldliness and spiritual sloth. Instead of humility, there was pride and arrogance. Instead of love of the poor, there was greed and avarice. There was large scale disaffection among the laity, and a deep and deepening sense of alienation. We can hardly fail to be reminded of the growing sense of alienation and loss of faith in traditional religious leaders that held sway in ancient Palestine, when the priests of the temple aristocracy cast their lot with the Roman conquerors and exploited rather than sustained their people. Cohn (1970b) writes:

> But if these people were alienated from the Church, they also suffered from their alienation. How much they needed the Church is shown by the enthusiasm with which they welcomed every sign of ascetic reform and the eagerness with which they would accept, even adore, any genuine ascetic. To be uncertain of the consolation and guidance and mediation of the Church aggravated their sense of helplessness and increased their desperation. It is because of these emotional needs of the poor that the militant social movements we have considered were at the same time surrogates for the Church — salvationist groups led by miracle-working ascetics. (p. 283)

Cohn (1970a) offers a summary statement that brings this complex of determining factors into focus:

. . . the decisive causative factors are these:

1. Many traditional religious worldviews include a promise of a future age of bliss to be enjoyed by the faithful. This traditional promise provides the indispensible basis for a millennarian faith. It seems that in societies — such as that of ancient Greece — where the religious worldview has no place for such a fantasy, millennarianism cannot develop. Where, on the other hand, such a fantasy is familiar, it can sometimes be given the immediacy and particularity necessary to convert it into an effective millennarian ideology.

2. It is the prophet who carries out this adaptation of traditional lore and who becomes the bearer of the resulting ideology. If in addition the prophet possesses a suitable personality and is able to convey an impression of absolute conviction, he is likely in certain situations of emotional tension to become the nucleus of a millenarian movement.

3. It is perhaps possible to indicate how such situations of emotional tension arise. It seems that there is in many, perhaps in all, human psyches a latent yearning for total salvation from suffering; and that that yearning is greatly intensified by any frustration or anxiety or humiliation which is unaccustomed and which cannot be tackled either by taking thought or by any institutionalized routine. Where a particular frustration or anxiety or humiliation of this nature is experienced at the same time and in the same area by a number of indi-

viduals, the result is a collective emotional agitation which is peculiar not only in its intensity but also in the boundlessness of its aims.

4. Such a situation provides the perfect opportunity for a prophet
promising a collective salvation which is to be both immediate and
total. It is the discharge of accumulated emotional tension that gives
such energy to the resulting millennarian movement. (p. 42)

Revolutionary and Ascetical Trends

The degree of psychological intensity in millennarian cult movements tends to the fanatical and extreme. The outcome is often cast in
terms of outright revolution that tends to invade and disrupt the political sphere (Thrupp 1970), or in forms of ascetical extreme in more
specifically religious terms. Worsley (1968) comments on this phenomenon:

> Millennarian beliefs have recurred again and again throughout his-
> tory, despite failures, disappointments, and repression, precisely
> because they make such a strong appeal to the oppressed, the dis-
> inherited and the wretched. They therefore form an integral part
> of that stream of thought which refused to accept the rule of a
> superordinate class, or of a foreign power, or some combination
> of both, as in Taiping China. This anti-authoritarian attitude is
> expressed not only in the form of direct political resistance, but
> also through the rejection of the ideology of the ruling authority.
> The lower orders reject the dominant values, beliefs, philosophy,
> religion, etc., of those they are struggling against, as well as their
> material economic and political domination. It is therefore natural
> that millennarian doctrines often become openly revolutionary and
> lead to violent conflict between rulers and ruled. Because of this
> revolutionary potential, millennarian movements are usually
> treated with the utmost suspicion by Church and State and have
> often been proscribed and persecuted. (pp. 225-226)

This does not mean that the drive and direction of the revolutionary impulse is irrational or counterproductive; it may serve as a creative expression of the underlying need to undo an impossible or burdensome condition and to reshape the political life of the community in
more optimistic terms. The religious myth may serve as a catalyst to
seek a better form of life that gives way to a political transformation
that achieves more restrictively political goals. This would require that
the unconscious fantasy system yield to political and economic and social realities in order to find meaningful expression. Where the fantasy

retains its fanatical form, the outcome is doomed to illusory and possibly destructive resolution. As McNearney (1984) comments:

> The most important difficulty inherent in the use of language of apocalyptic metaphor is its tendency to encourage a sense of persecution and concomitant sectarian defensiveness that is often destructive of the larger community. The price one must usually pay in order to affirm the cosmic and apocalyptic importance of an individual or a group is the radical break with all former communal ties and traditional bonds both cognitive and social. (p. 56)

By the same token, there is a marked tendency within millennarian movements toward the totalitarian and toward the rigid exercise of moral control over its members (Eby 1984).

The same revolutionary and antinomian strain affects the forms of libidinal license and lack of moral restraint that come into being in many of these cult movements. The overthrow of traditional values and unconstrained behavior represents a casting off of the bonds of the past in the process of creating a new world, a new morality, and new context of values and norms adapted to the renewed order of the millennial kingdom. In many millennarian revolutions, the overthrow of the old order can take the form of either moral and sexual promiscuity or the opposite, the adoption of a severe moral code and a rigid and harsh ascetical discipline. Both alternatives are driven by the rejection and rebellion against old codes and values — two sides of the same coin. The renovation and transformation of the social order can be achieved in either way.

Central Fantasy

Perhaps more than any other cult belief system — with the possible exception of the messianic movements — the millennarian cults reflect the influence of a central fantasy that in varying degrees lies at the root of all forms of millennarian conviction. There is at work here an unconscious fantasy system that derives from deepseated unconscious desires and wishes based on and expressing fundamental human drives and aspirations. The yearning for peace, for the release from pain, suffering and death, the wish for the fulfillment of all desires and needs, for peace, harmony, tranquillity, and love — all this to be accomplished under the all-powerful dominion of a loving and protecting God. All vulnerability and weakness is to be banished, and men can once and for all live in peace and good will. As the Manuels (1979) note: "The conception of a heaven on earth that underlies Western utopian thought presupposes an idea of perfection in another sphere, and at the same time a measure of confidence in human capacity to fashion on earth what is recognized as a transient mortal state into a simulacrum of the transcendental." (p. 17)

The instinctual roots of this wishful fantasy lie in the narcissistic sector of the psyche, insofar as the millennial culmination answers to every dimension of the narcissistic need of the human soul. God himself comes to the aid of men and provides for them the fulfillment of their fondest hopes and wishes. The saints become the special and precious remnant who become the recipients of divine love and care. Even in the Melanesian cargo cults, a prophet announces the imminent and cataclysmic destruction of the world, after which the ancestors, or some other divine and liberating power, will bring all the goods (the "cargo") that are desired, and thus usher in the reign of eternal and unlimited happiness. The response among the simple and wishful natives is to form a cult, start building storehouses to receive and store the cherished cargo, and often in the process let their gardens go to seed, killing off their livestock, consuming the rest of their food, and throwing their money away (Worsley 1968; Meissner 1984b). The element of wish-fulfillment that is so dramatically expressed carries within it the seeds of grandiosity, exclusivism, exceptionality, and specialness. The narcissism is central and essential to the millennarian fantasy.

Roots in Infantile Narcissism

The narcissistic need that underlies these fantasies is rooted in the early helplessness of the infant as he emerges from the symbiotic union with the mother to face the frustrations and limitations of reality. The infant is forced to surrender his infantile omnipotence — a surrender that he struggles to undo for the rest of life. His first effort is to project the omnipotence into the parental objects, salving his helplessness by their all-powerful protection. Failing that, he has recourse to an effort to recapture his own omnipotence by the formation of an ego ideal. The ego-ideal was in Freud's view the heir of the original infantile self-love that the child's ego enjoyed. The success of the struggle for identity depends in part on the successful transfer of this original narcissism into a self-sufficient ego and its ideal (Murray 1964).

The residues of infantile narcissism are therefore distilled into the ideal, which thus comes to possess every perfection that is of value. Freud (1914) wrote:

This ideal ego is now the target of the self-love which was enjoyed in childhood by the actual ego. The subject's narcissism makes its appearance displaced on to this new ideal ego, which, like the infantile ego, finds itself possessed of every perfection that is of value. As always where the libido is concerned, man has here again shown himself incapable of giving up a satisfaction he had once enjoyed. He is not willing to forgo the narcissistic perfection of his childhood; and when, as he grows up, he is disturbed by the admonitions of others and by the awakening of his own critical judgment, so that he can no longer retain that perfection, he seeks to recover it in the new form of an ego-ideal. What he projects before him as his ideal is the substitute for the lost narcissism of his childhood in which he was his own ideal. (p. 94)

This formulation was one of Freud's most fundamental contributions to the understanding of the development and functioning of the human personality. The importance of this transformation cannot be overestimated. Murray has commented, "This transformation and socialization of narcissism would then consist in directing it toward an aim other than the egoistic pregenital one, in deflecting its expression and satisfaction to the area of idealistic, personal, and social values, and in striving to create realistically a world appropriate and suitable for such a highly regarded ego to live in." (p. 501) The mature ego-ideal is thus a highly significant factor in the maintenance of the psychic integrity and mature balance between the expression of libidinal impulses and legitimate restraints, which is fundamental to the sense of identity. The implications of the deployment of narcissistic libido in the organization of many aspects of the mature psychic structure is not settled even today.

The recovery of lost infantile narcissism serves as the basis for the constitution of an ego-ideal in adult life. The loss of infantile narcissism, when in a sense the child is his own ideal, results from disruption of the sense of primary fusion between the child and the mother. The result of this disruption is that the child is forced to begin to recognize the existence of the "not-me" world. But the desire to reexperience and regain the sense of fusion with the mother, with its implications of omnipotence and total satisfaction, continues to have its inevitable residues.

Chasseguet-Smirgel (1985) has linked this desire for fusion between the ego and ego-ideal, for recapturing the lost infantile omnipotence, with the fantasy of reunion with the lost mother of infancy. This desire takes the most regressive means, governed by the pleasure principle, and often the shortest route to this goal, many times in the process obliterating all the gains of development and maturity. Her comments are very much to the point:

> It is as if the group formation represented of itself the hallucinatory realization of the wish to take possession of the mother by the sibship, through a very regressive mode, that of primary fusion. It is the case, however, that there may be a leader (one has only to think of the Nazi groups). But he cannot, to my mind, be equated with the father. In this instance the leader is the person who activates the primitive wish for the union of ego and ideal. He is the promote of Illusion, he who makes it shimmer before men's dazzled eyes, he who will bring it to fruition. Times will be changed, the Great Day (or the Great Eve) will arrive, a heavenly Jerusalem will offer itself to our astonished gaze, our needs will be met, the Aryans will conquer the world, the day will dawn, the future yield its promise, etc. The group thirsts less for a leader than for illusions. And it will choose as leader whomsoever promises it the union of ego and ego ideal. The leader is Cagliostro. There is no absolute ruler who is not the bearer of an ideology. He is in fact the intermediary between the masses and the ideological illusion, and behind the ideology there is always a phantasy of narcissistic assumption. (p. 82)

Along this same line, Mann (1992) has offered an interpretive speculation connecting the apocalyptic myth with birth-related fantasies. The mythic account in the Apocalypse echoes mythological themes of death and rebirth in the final destruction of the world and history in the cataclysm of the final days and its restoration to eternal bliss.[1] Womb-like fantasies are reflected, he argues, in expressions like, "They shall hunger no more, neither thirst any more; neither shall the sun light on them, nor any heat" (Apoc 9: 16). The cataclysmic struggle between the forces of good and the forces of evil results in the victory of the good and the establishment of the New Jerusalem. The evils of the world and the misery of life are brought to an end and replaced by the new order of hope and paradise. The paradise that was lost is regained. References abound to the disturbances to the earth/mother's body: earthquakes (Apoc 6: 12; 8: 3, 5, 11; 11: 13, 19; 12: 16; 16: 18-19), bottomless pits (Apoc 9: 1-2; 17: 8; 19: 20; 20: 3), moving mountains (Apoc 6: 14; 16: 20), monsters emerging from and entering the earth/sea/mother's body (Apoc 12: 9; 13: 1, 11; 17: 8; 19:

---

1. The connection with mythological themes of cyclic destruction and creation are apparent. See Eliade (1954, 1958).

20; 20: 12-15), the sea is defiled and poisoned (Apoc 8: 8, 10-11; 16: 3-4), and even the sky is filled with chaos and turmoil (Apoc 4: 1, 5; 6: 1; 7: 2; 8: 5, 13; 10: 3, 8; 11: 12, 19; 12: 10; 14: 2, 13; 16: 17-18; 18: 4; 21: 3). These images of birth-related labor and traumatic destruction give way to other images of peace and tranquillity: the New Jerusalem descends (Apoc 21: 10) and the period of peace and paradise is inaugurated. The blood-stained lamb (Apoc 5: 6) as a figure of Christ suggests the birth imagery, but this lamb is far from meek and mild; unlike the innocent victim, this lamb is omnipotently hostile and destructive — the rageful infant of a traumatic birth. Mann (1992) concludes that:

> The apocalypse myth can be said to be rooted in the neonatal experience of birth trauma. In this respect we might make the following hypothesis: the adult myth maker is sublimating and finding form to an otherwise deeply repressed primordial experience. The apocalypse of mythic vision would then be a recollection of an apocalypse that has already happened, the end of the world of the womb, a world destroyed but always longed for. Out of this scenario would come the cosmic description of the end and rebirth of the world. (p. 478)

Thus the underlying fantasy and infantile wish for a return to the idyllic and idealized conditions that existed before the loss of the infantile paradise lie at the root of all millennial and apocalyptic mythic systems.

Paranoid Potential

The underlying narcissistic dynamic can take a destructive and paranoid turn. In certain cases, the narcissistic injury is so profound that the need to turn the tables and redress the hurt can turn against the world as such, resulting in end-of-the-world fantasies, as though only destruction of the world and all one's enemies with it could compensate for the shame and deprivation that has been suffered (Grunberger 1989). The same dynamic can find expression in clinical paranoia as well. The well-known case of Judge Schreber (Freud 1911) was a clear-cut example. Freud interpreted Schreber's paranoid fantasy and conviction of the imminent destruction of the world as based on total withdrawal of cathexis from the environment. The anticipated destruction of the world becomes a psychotic projection that mirrors the internal catastrophe — the collapse of the patient's inner subjective world and the fragmentation and loss of cohesion in his sense of self (Meissner 1976; Westphal 1990). The narcissistic redressment in this process took a further turn in Schreber's delusional system. The psychotic process was elevated from the level of personal dynamics to embrace the apocalyptic vision of a cosmic divine mission in which Schreber became the designated messiah-figure. The destruction of the world opened the way to the redemption and salvation of the world in which Schreber himself was to be the chosen vessel of salvation of God. God would impregnate him and he would then bring forth a new race of superior men — the reason behind Schreber's delusion that he was being turned into a woman. This salvific and redemptive moment was to take place at some unspecified time in the future — a messianic vision of a sexualized parousia in which the delusional madman would achieve the heights of narcissistic inflation and grandiosity as the wife of God destined to save the world. Westphal (1990), reflecting on the instances of messianic fervor and apocalyptic fanaticism, poses the embarrassing question:

> For in each of these cases, many, if not all, of those willing to make others into nothing but means to their own tribal ends have justified their behavior as required by a sacred cause. In fact, they have followed the Schreber recipe to a tee. They have come to see themselves first as threatened by a demonic enemy, and then as the specially chosen vehicles of a divine purpose. The question is why, if Schreber is plainly paranoid, these other cases are not also seen as paradigms of psychosis. The Schreber case challenges us to ask hard questions about phenomena such as these, especially those that are closest to us and make us feel most uncomfortable. For when other beneficiaries of such holy causes assure us that they are not using God as a means to their own ends but are rather instruments chosen by God to carry out divine purposes, we do not take these assurances as self-authenticating. Why should our own assurances be exempted from similar suspicion? (pp. 131-132)

Utopian Visions

Such utopian visions seem to have a special place in religious belief systems. The idea of heaven and salvation embodies the idealized fantasy of a state of perfection and satisfaction — a utopian projection of an internal ideal system (Pollock 1975, 1989). Such an ideal state counters the fears of mortality and death in the vision of an idealized state of life after death. The millennial fantasy translates the same ideal to a this-worldly focus where death is banished and the state of individual bliss guaranteed. The concepts of heaven and paradise in psychoanalytic terms may represent a regressive wish for return to the earliest symbiotic union, an idealized initial state of existence. As Pollock (1989) writes:

> I believe the conception of a heaven and paradise may relate to the regressive return to the earliest symbiotic union where the fantasy is one of wholeness and intactness. Paradise, heaven, or the ideal state of the afterlife may thus refer to the idealized initial state of existence. It may be that the regression to this beginning state of symbiosis forms the basis for the immortality belief (Pollock, 1964) and, I would further suggest, the deepest basis for the secular utopian wish. Reunion or joining the dead in fantasy, action, or custom, individually or collectively, seemingly has a similar basis and explanation. Resurrection, as rebirth, is frequently associated with the spring when, after the cold and barren winter, mother earth once again gives birth to life. This eternal cycle of birth and rebirth indicates that there is no end, but an everlasting cycle of life transformations. Paradise or heaven, however. has no cyclicity; it has no ending or beginning.
>
> The regression to the union with the archaic idealized omnipotent figure in the death-transformation passage to the "new existence" may be based on symbiosis with the undifferentiated god. It is my contention that this omnipotent figure is genderless and is the representation of the first omnipotent omniscient parent — the maternal being. Symbiotic reunion with this maternal, genderless god-figure allows entry into the pregenital heaven and paradise, if life has been in harmony with the superego and ego-ideal system. (p 463)[2]

---

2. Essentially the same argument is advanced by Grunberger (1989) who describes the concept of "cosmic narcissism" that recaptures the sense of total narcissistic fulfillment and grandiosity that inhered in the early symbiotic fusion between mother and child. Heaven becomes the religiously endorsed substitute for the lost mother-child monad. Grunberger (1989) writes: "In my view — and my clinical experience confirms my view — the prenatal origin of narcissism is a fact of enormous importance whose effects tend to be ignored, even though they are constantly at work in the depths of the unconscious. The foetus experiences no conflict and no desires; its host takes care of its metabolism, and it exists in a state of perfect completeness. This coenesthesis leaves sufficient traces for it to be fantasied as a state of *perfect bliss, absolute sovereignty* or *omnipotence*. Folklore, religions and literature all confirm the existence of this fantasy, which corresponds to an ideal which man has lost and continues to seek. Indeed, he seeks it all the more eagerly in that although it is a fantasy, *the demand for that ideal state is based on the reality of a lived experience with an undeniably biological substratum*." (p. 16)

Revolutionary Eschatology

It would seem that the narcissistic fantasy takes its most extreme and pathological expression in forms of revolutionary eschatology. But in those forms, the narcissism is wedded to an unmistakable and virulent form of aggressive and destructive fantasy that includes visions of total destruction of the evil and oppressive world — especially in the premillennial and apocalyptic visions of the last days that prepare the way for millennial glories. This aspect of millennarian fantasies is described by Cohn (1970b):

> . . . here one can recognize the paradigm of what was to become and to remain the central phantasy of revolutionary eschatology. The world is dominated by an evil, tyrannous power of boundless destructiveness — a power, moreover, which is imagined not as simply human but as demonic. The tyranny of that power will become more and more outrageous, the sufferings of its victims more and more intolerable — until suddenly the hour will strike when the Saints of God are able to rise up and overthrow it. Then the Saints themselves, the chosen, holy people who hitherto have groaned under the oppressor's heel, shall in their turn inherit dominion over the whole earth. This will be the culmination of history; the Kingdom of the Saints will not only surpass in glory all previous kingdoms, it will have no successors. It was thanks to this phantasy that Jewish apocalyptic exercised, through its derivatives, such a fascination upon the discontented and frustrated of later ages — and continued to do so long after the Jews themselves had forgotten its very existence. (p. 21)

We have had occasion to note the extent to which millennarian visions seem often to lead in the direction of inhumane, vicious, sadistic, and hateful destructive behavior in defense of the millennarian ideal. In psychoanalytic terms, the phenomenon involves abdication of the superego, which would propose the values of restraint, humanity, even charity. Such values, however, seem often overridden and obliterated in the blind fervor and passion of millennarian enthusiasm. Sandler (1960), writing on the superego, observed:

> . . . situations do exist in which the ego can and will totally disregard the standards and precepts of the superego, if it can gain a sufficient quantity of narcissistic support elsewhere. We see this impressive phenomenon in the striking changes in ideals, character, and morality which may result from the donning of a uniform and the feeling of identity with a group. If narcissistic support is available in sufficient quantity from an identification with the ideals of a group, or with the ideals of a leader, then the superego

may be completely disregarded and its functions taken over by the group ideals, precepts and behaviour. If these group ideals permit a direct gratification of instinctual wishes, then a complete character transformation may occur; and the extent to which the superego can be abandoned in this way is evident in the appalling atrocities committed by the Nazis before and during the last war. (pp. 156-157)

We can also observe that the same phenomenon was at work in the fanatical and foolhardy revolt of the Zealots that led to the destruction of Jerusalem, also in the ill-advised rebellion of bar Kochba, and the Crusades, the religious revolutions of the Middle Ages — the list can easily be extended. Chasseguet-Smirgel (1985) adds her own commentary:

> . . . it seems to me that the capacity for committing atrocities (insofar as they represent an instinctual gratification) is not only the result of adopting the moral criteria of the group (which take the place of a personal superego), but the necessary consequence of the ideology of the group. Whatever stands in the way of attaining the Illusion must disappear. Now, since the goal of the Illusion is the idealization of the ego and there can be no idealization of the ego without projection, the objects receiving the projections must be hunted down and annihilated. I do not think it sufficient to say that the murder is then committed in the name of the superego and hence it becomes legitimate. I think that it is undertaken above all in the name of the ideal, as in the case of the Infidels murdered by the Crusaders on the road to Jerusalem. Any reactivation of the Illusion is thus ineluctably followed by a blood bath, provided only that the group has the means to match its violence. The principle of political machiavellianism that "the end justifies the means" is indeed an idealist principle that is applied each time the Illusion is reactivated. The end (the coming together of ego and ideal) justifies the means (annihilates the superego). "Liberty, how many crimes are committed in your name!" is a cry that still resounds. (One has only to think of substitutes for "liberty" such as Purity, Happiness, Greatness, Justice, Equality, Revolution, etc.). (p. 84)

Saints and Demons

Aligned against the saints in these eschatological conflicts are the forces of evil — opposite in every feature to the army of the saints, each the negative of the other. Opposite to the conquering messiah is the figure of the Antichrist, the embodiment of evil and destructiveness, just as the messiah carries in him all goodness and love. Just as the messiah is the good son of the heavenly father, the Antichrist is the bad and rebellious son. But to the saints he is "an atrocious father, deceitful, masking evil intentions with fair words, a cunning tyrant who when crossed becomes a cruel and murderous persecutor" (Cohn 1970b, p. 86). Moreover the Antichrist was the leader of an outgroup that served his evil purposes and whose members were steeped in ignorance, deceit, and wickedness. They were the agents of the devil who frustrated and perverted the aims of God and worked in their devious ways against the establishment of the kingdom of righteousness on this earth. To the early Christian millennarians the Jews were the stubborn, stiff-necked people who stood in the way of the establishment of the Christian millennium. It was they who clung resolutely to the Old Testament and rejected the New, along with its promises of millennial glories in the second coming of Christ. For millennial cults of the Middle Ages, it was the Church and her bishops and clergy, by and large, who stood in the place of the Antichrist and his minions. As Cohn (1970b) comments:

> To those demons in human form, the Jew and the "false cleric," was attributed every quality which belonged to the Beast from the Abyss — not only his cruelty but also his grossness, his animality, his blackness and uncleanness. Jewry and clergy together formed the foul black host of the enemy which stood opposite the clean white army of the Saints — "the children of God, that we are, poisonous worms, that you are," as a medieval rhymester put it. And the Saints knew that it was their task to wipe that foul black host off the face of the earth, for only an earth which had been so purified would be fit to carry the New Jerusalem, the shining Kingdom of the Saints. (p. 87)

This set of religious convictions and beliefs became a powerful and toxic revolutionary potion when it was presented to and imbibed by the dispossessed, poverty-stricken, downtrodden and tormented poor and oppressed. It turned into a revolutionary mythology that fanned the flames of resentment and rebellion, driven by the paranoid and fanatic intensity of unbridled narcissistic and aggressive forces.

These pathological forms of belief reflect the subversion of the illusory status of belief and its diversion into the paths of subjective fantasy or objective credulity. Symbol systems, including religious belief systems, have their validity and vitality in the sphere of illusory experience. The perversion of religious beliefs can take the form of suffusion with archaic residues from the autistic world of intrapsychic and subjective fantasy, or it can result from the misinterpretation of illusory beliefs as realities, either of the present or the future. In either case, the symbolic and authentically religious dimension of the content of the belief is lost, destroyed in the crush of psychic pressures drawing it into one or other of the polarities of human experience. The apocalyptic and millennarian beliefs that undergird forms of religiously motivated fanaticism fall victim to these dangers. The beliefs themselves are excessively invaded by unconscious, derived and infantile fantasies, and the belief carries with it the conviction that these fantasy systems are imminently about to be realized or will be realized in some future time.

What is lost, often enough, is the religious meaning of the beliefs in question — in these instances, the apocalyptic promise of the triumph of good over evil through the power and grace of God, and the hope of salvation for those who are faithful to divine purposes and truth. These eschatological hopes become contaminated by relatively unsublimated and unrefined infantile and archaic narcissistic wishes from one side. From the other side, the inherent promise of revelation is mistaken for a prediction of future events in some unmetaphorical and less than symbolic understanding. This turns the belief system from a transitional and illusory understanding into a fetishistic and fanatical conviction that serves as the motivating vision for delusional expectations and revolutionary explosions. The delusional system becomes the rationale for the worst expressions of unbridled passion and instinctual rampage — especially where unbridled and destructive aggression is unleashed in the fanatical crusade whose intent is to advance and bring to realization the expected millennarian kingdom.

The Role of Apocalyptic in Religious Thought

We come to a concluding coda. Does the preceding reflection bring us to any conclusions? Is there any meaningful evaluation we can make of the welter of religious experiences that have been shaped by the apocalyptic visions and dreams of the millennium and its promised messiah?

Certainly the persistence and power of these themes cannot fail to impress. Despite the transformations and variations in doctrine and praxis, the consistency of the underlying themes stand out clearly and persistently enough. They not only persist throughout the centuries, but continue to exercise a powerful influence over the minds and hearts of men. Mankind has always struggled and striven to find ways to improve the miserable and painful conditions of their existence. We live in a harsh and unforgiving world, where Adam's curse remains in effect —

> Accursed be the soil because of you.
> With suffering shall you get your food from it
>   every day of your life.
> It shall yield you brambles and thistles,
>   and you shall eat wild plants.
> With sweat on your brow shall you eat your bread,
>   until you return to the soil,
>   as you were taken from it.
> For dust you are and to dust you shall return. (Gn 3: 17-19)

When the harshness of existence becomes intolerable, men turn to dreams and visions to seek the fulfillment of their hopes and desires. To the extent that these visions become incorporated into a religious belief system, they offer the basis for hope in the midst of despair, for a sense of meaning and purpose in life in the midst of crushing anxiety and the seeming meaningless of existence. These are the illusions that Freud so despised and excoriated. But they are also the illusions that for Winnicott were sustaining resources for man's inner life, that were essential for the meaningful extension of human life and experience. Freud could not accept a religious orientation because he saw in it the residues of infantile needs that he could not tolerate and set himself to banish. Winnicott saw the same infantile needs, but recognized them as inherent parts of the human condition that had to be accepted and accommodated if mankind were to live at all.

At some point, it would seem meaningful, if not useful — as the theologian would insist — to draw a distinction between the hopeful illusions that sustain life and increase the measure of tolerance for human existence and those fantastical visions that exceed the bounds of meaningful hope and sow the seeds of ultimate despair and discord, between an authentic faith that confirms life and identity and the fanaticism that leads away from reality and dooms its adherents to autistic solutions that solve nothing but substitute pure fantasy for the harshness of reality. As Moltmann (1967) comments:

> In the contradiction between the word of promise and the experiential reality of suffering and death, faith takes its stand on hope and "hastens beyond this world," said Calvin. He did not mean by this that Christian faith flees the world, but he did mean that it strains after the future. To believe does in fact mean to cross and transcend bounds, to be engaged in an exodus. Yet this happens in

a way that does not suppress or skip the unpleasant realities. Death is real death, and decay is putrefying decay. Guilt remains guilt and suffering remains, even for the believer, a cry to which there is no ready-made answer. Faith does not overstep these realities into a heavenly utopia, does not dream itself into a reality of a different kind. (p. 19)

Thus, in a psychoanalytic perspective, the wish-fulfillments and unconscious fantasy systems are nonetheless joined to hope. In the Christian dispensation, eschatology is the doctrine of Christian hope — as it is in the Jewish dispensation for Jewish hope as well. It is a looking forward to a promised future that is to revolutionize and transform the present. As Moltmann (1967) observes:

The eschatological is not one element *of* Christianity, but it is the medium of Christian faith as such, the key in which everything in it is set, the glow that suffuses everything here in the dawn of an expected new day. For Christian faith lives from the raising of the crucified Christ, and strains after the promises of the universal future of Christ. Eschatology is the passionate suffering and passionate longing kindled by the Messiah. (p. 16)

My preference is to join these considerations to the dynamics of the cultic process (Meissner 1984b, 1987a, in process) and its permeation by the forces and mechanisms of the paranoid process (Meissner 1978, 1987a, in process). In this frame of reference the eschatological themes and apocalyptic visions serve as part of a doctrinal system, a system of belief, which serves as a form of paranoid construction. This cognitive belief-construction serves the purpose of drawing together and integrating the component elements of the paranoid process and providing them a dimension of unity, purpose and direction. Those elements include the introjections that act as component elements in the organization of the individual's self-system and thus contribute to the patterning of his inner self-experience, his sense of self and the attributes he associates with it. These introjective components include components of aggressive and narcissistic drive derivatives: the aggressive contributing to the sense of self as evil or destructive or in the form of defensive opposites of vulnerability and victimization. These introjective components are dealt with defensively by projections: the defensive reaction to intolerable aggressive and destructive elements leads to projection of those elements onto outside objects.

In the religious framework we have been considering, the out-group is seen as evil, destructive, and dangerous, while all goodness, truth, and security rests in the religious in-group. The in-group is on the side of God and the out-group on the side of Satan or the Anti-Christ. The introjective alignment is also cast in narcissistic terms, both superior and inferior. Again, in the defensive reaction to threatened narcissistic needs, the projections act to distribute the narcissistic cards so that strength, power, specialness and superiority, even grandiosity, remain on the side of the all-powerful God and his faithful believers, while the opposite qualities of inferiority, worthlessness, and inadequacy come to reside in the out-group of unbelievers. This constellation of introjections and correlative projections is consolidated, integrated, and given a sense of direction, purpose and meaning — often cosmic — by the paranoid construction.

The system of illusions, dreams and visions that constitute the eschatological and apocalyptic beliefs and hopes thus serves a purpose beyond the mere statement of belief. From the point of view of the psychoanalytic perspective of the inner world of the human believer, such beliefs serve a vital function of sustaining the sense of identity and meaningful existence of individual believers, buffering and responding constructively to basic psychodynamic needs and conflicts — both aggressive and narcissistic — and thus contributing to the shaping through the communal devices of group membership and cultural mutuality of the patterns of social life that modify and contain the psychological forces that might otherwise undermine and destroy human culture and civilization. If these wishes and hopes for messianic triumph and millennarian glory are subjected to the pathological distortions and fetishistic contamination of fanatical desire, they can lead men toward the path of destruction. If they can be maintained in the perspective of reasoned hope and authentic faith, they can serve the function of sustaining and strengthening resources that make human existence meaningful, if not bearable.

References

Aberle, D.F. (1970) A note on relative deprivation theory as applied to millennarian and other cult movements. In Thrupp, S.L. (ed.) *Millennial Dreams in Action: Studies in Revolutionary Religious Movements.* New York: Schocken Books, pp. 209-214.

Ahlstrom, S.E. (1972) *A Religious History of the American People.* New Haven: Yale University Press.

Bangert, S.J., W.V. (1986) *A History of the Society of Jesus.* 2nd edit. St. Louis, MO: The Institute of Jesuit Sources.

Barkun, M. (1974) *Disaster and the Millennium.* New Haven: Yale University Press.

Barratt, B.B. (1986) Psychoanalysis as critique of ideology. *Psychoanalytic Inquiry,* 5: 437-470.

Barth, K. (1972) *Protestant Theology in the Nineteenth Century.* London: SCM Press.

Bartlett, D.L. (1978) John G. Gager's "Kingdom and Community": a summary and response. *Zygon,* 13: 109-122.

Bell D. (1979) Immortal nominations. *New York Times Book Review* (June 3), 12.

Bettencourt, E. (1969) Millennialism. In Rahner, S.J., K. et al. (eds.) *Sacramentum Mundi: An Encyclopedia of Theology.* New York: Herder and Herder. Vol. 4: 43-44.

Bettis, J. (1984) Millennialism and the transformation of history. In Bettis, J., and Johannesen, S.K. (eds.) *The Return of the Millennium.* Barrytown, NY: International Religious Foundation, pp. 153-166.

Boardman, E.P. (1970) Millennary aspects of the Taiping rebellion (1851-64). In Thrupp, S.L. (ed.) *Millennial Dreams in Action: Studies in Revolutionary Religious Movements.* New York: Schocken Books, pp. 139-143.

Bonsirven, S.J., J. (1963) *Theology of the New Testament.* Westminster, MD: Newman Press.

Bord, R.J. (1975) Toward a social-psychological theory of charismatic social influence processes. *Social Forces,* 53: 485-497.

Borg, M.J. (1987) *Jesus, A New Vision: Spirit, Culture, and the Life of Discipleship.* San Francisco, CA: Harper and Row.

Boyer, L.B. (1986) On man's need to have enemies: a psychoanalytic perspective. *Journal of Psychoanalytic Anthropology,* 9: 101-120.

Breasted, J.H. (1933) *The Dawn of Conscience.* New York: Scribner's.

Brinton, C. (1965) *The Anatomy of Revolution.* New York: Vintage Books.

Brown, S.S., R.E. (1977) *The Birth of the Messiah.* Garden City, NY: Doubleday.

Brown, R.E., Fitzmyer, J.A., and Murphy, R.E. (eds.) (1968) *The Jerome Biblical Commentary.* Englewood Cliffs, NJ: Prentice-Hall.

Brown, R.E., Fitzmyer, J.A., and Murphy, R.E. (eds.) (1990) *The New Jerome Biblical Commentary.* Englewood Cliffs, NJ: Prentice-Hall.

Bruce, F.F. (1969) *New Testament History.* Garden City, NY: Doubleday.

Bultmann, R. (1952) *Theology of the New Testament.* SCM Press.

Bultmann, R. (1963) *The History of the Synoptic Tradition.* New York: Harper and Row, 1968.

Cerfaux, L. (1959) *The Church in the Theology of St. Paul.* New York: Herder and Herder.

Chamberlin, E.R. (1975) *Antichrist and the Millennium.* New York: E.P. Dutton.

Charlesworth, J.H. (1987) From Jewish messianology to Christian christology: some caveats and perspectives. In Neusner, J., Green, W.S., and Frerichs, E.S. (eds.) *Judaisms and Their Messiahs at the Turn of the Christian Era.* Cambridge: Cambridge University Press, pp. 225-264.

Chasseguet-Smirgel, J. (1985) *The Ego Ideal.* New York: Norton.

Cohn, N. (1970a) Medieval millennarism: its bearing on the comparative study of millennarian movements. In Thrupp, S.L. (ed.) *Millennial Dreams in Action: Studies in Revolutionary Religious Movements.* New York: Schocken Books, pp. 31-43.

Cohn, N. (1970b) *The Pursuit of the Millennium.* New York: Oxford University Press.

Collins, A.Y. (1990) The Apocalypse (Revelation). In Brown, S.S., R.E., Fitzmyer, S.J., J.A., and Murphy, O. Carm., R. E. (eds.) *The New Jerome Biblical Commentary.* Englewood Cliffs, NJ: Prentice Hall, 996-1016.

Collins, J.J. (1987) Messianism in the Maccabean period. In Neusner, J., Green, W.S., and Frerichs, E.S. (eds.) *Judaisms and Their Messiahs at the Turn of the Christian Era.* Cambridge: Cambridge University Press, pp. 97-109.

Committee on International Relations (GAP). (1987) *Us and Them: The Psychology of Ethnonationalism.* New York: Brunner/Mazel.

Committee on Psychiatry and Religion (GAP). (1976) *Mysticism: Spiritual Quest or Psychic Disorder?* New York: Group for the Advancement of Psychiatry (Vol. IX, Publication No. 97).

Coppens, J. (1968) *Le Messianisme Royal.* Paris: Les Editions du Cerf.

Cross, F. (ed.) (1957) *The Oxford Dictionary of the Christian Church.* London: Oxford University Press.

Cullman, O. (1964) *Christ and Time.* Philadelphia, PA: Westminster Press.

Cushman, P. (1986) The self besieged: recruitment-indoctrination processes in restrictive groups. *Journal for the Theory of Social Behaviour,* 16: 1-32.

Dalmases, S.J., C. de. (1985) *Ignatius of Loyola, Founder of the Jesuits: His Life and Work.* St. Louis, MO: The Institute of Jesuit Sources.

D'Aragon, S.J., J.-L. (1968) The Apocalypse. In Brown, R.E., Fitzmyer, J.A., and Murphy, R.E. (eds.) *The Jerome Biblical Commentary.* Englewood Cliffs, NJ: Prentice-Hall, vol. II, pp. 467-493.

Davies, W.D. (1966) *The Sermon on the Mount.* Cambridge: Cambridge University Press.

Davies, W.D. (1976) From Schweitzer to Scholem: reflections on Sabbatai Sevi. *Journal of Biblical Literature,* 95: 529-558.

de Jonge, M. (1991) *Jesus, the Servant-Messiah.* New Haven: Yale University Press.

de la Potterie, S.J., I. (1968) The anointing of Christ. In O'Donovan, S.J., L.J. (ed.) *Word and Mystery: Biblical Essays on the Person and Mission of Christ.* New York: Newman Press, pp. 155-184.

Deutsch, H. (1938) Folie-à-deux. *Psychoanalytic Quarterly,* 7: 307-318. Reprinted in *Neuroses and Character Types: Clinical Psychoanalytic Studies.* New York: International Universities Press, 237-247.

Dillon, R.J., and Fitzmyer, S.J., J.A. (1968) Acts of the Apostles. In Brown, R.E., Fitzmyer, J.A., and Murphy, R.E. (eds.) *The Jerome Biblical Commentary.* Englewood Cliffs, NJ: Prentice-Hall, vol. II, pp. 165-214.

Dodd, C.H. (1935) *The Parables of the Kingdom.* 2nd edit. New York: Scribner, 1961.

Dodd, C.H. (1968) *The Interpretation of the Fourth Gospel.* Cambridge: Cambridge University Press.

Dodds, E.R. (1965) *Pagan and Christian in an Age of Anxiety.* London: Cambridge University Press.

Dudon, S.J., P. (1949) *St. Ignatius of Loyola.* Milwaukee, WI: Bruce Publishing Co.

Dulles, S.J., A. (1974) *Models of the Church.* Garden City, NY: Doubleday.

Eby, L. (1984) Millennial and utopian religion: totalitarian or free? In Bettis, J., and Johannesen, S.K. (eds.) *The Return of the Millennium.* Barrytown, NY: International Religious Foundation, pp. 119-136.

Eliade, M. (1954) *The Myth of the Eternal Return. Or Cosmos and History.* Princeton, NJ: Princeton University Press, 1974.

Eliade, M. (1958) *Patterns in Comparative Religion.* New York: Meridian Books.

Eliade, M. (1964) *Shamanism: Archaic Techniques of Ecstasy.* Princeton, NJ: Princeton University Press, 1974.

Eliade, M. (1970) "Cargo-cults" and cosmic regeneration. In Thrupp, S.L. (ed.) *Millennial Dreams in Action: Studies in Revolutionary Religious Movements.* New York: Schocken Books, pp. 139-143.

Eliade, M. (1982) *A History of Religious Ideas.* Vol. 2: *From Gautama Buddha to the Triumph of Christianity.* Chicago: University of Chicago Press.

Eliade, M. (1985) *A History of Religious Ideas.* Vol. 3: *From Muhammad to the Age of Reforms.* Chicago: University of Chicago Press.

Elliott, J.H. (1977) *Imperial Spain: 1469-1716.* New York: New American Library.

Erikson, E.H. (1959) The problem of ego identity. In: *Identity and the Life Cycle.* New York: International Universities Press, pp. 101-164. [Psychological Issues. Monograph 1]

Erikson, E.H. (1966) Ontogeny of ritualization. In Loewenstein, R.M., Newman, L.M., Schur, M., and Solnit, A.J. (eds.) *Psychoanalysis — A General Psychology: Essays in Honor of Heinz Hartmann.* New York: International Universities Press, 601-621.

Erikson, E.H. (1975) *Life History and the Historical Moment.* New York: Norton.

Falk, A. (1982) The messiah and the qelippoth: on the mental illness of Sabbatai Sevi. *Journal of Psychology and Judaism,* 7: 5-29.

Festinger, L. (1957) *A Theory of Cognitive Dissonance.* Evanston, IL: Row, Peterson.

Festinger, L., Riecken, H.W., and Schachter, S. (1956) *When Prophecy Fails.* Minneapolis: University of Minnesota Press.

Feuillet, S.S., A. (1968) The teaching of the Apocalypse. In O'Donovan, S.J., L.J. (ed.) *Word and Mystery: Biblical Essays on the Person and Mission of Christ.* New York: Newman Press, pp. 109-119.

Fitzmyer, S.J., J.A. (1974) *Essays on the Semitic Background of the New Testament.* Missoula, MT: Society of Biblical Literature.

Flinn, F.K. (1984) Introduction: the question about the millennium. In Bettis, J., and Johannesen, S.K. (eds.) *The Return of the Millennium.* Barrytown, NY: International Religious Foundation, pp. 1-8.

Ford, J.M. (1975) *Revelation* (Anchor Bible 38). Garden City, NY: Doubleday.

Fortmann, S.J., E.J. (ed.) (1966) *The Theology of Man and Grace: Commentary.* Milwaukee, WI: Bruce.

Freud, E. (1960) *The Letters of Sigmund Freud.* New York: McGraw-Hill.

Freud, S. (1911) Psycho-analytic notes on an autobiographical account of a case of paranoia (dementia paranoides). *Standard Edition,* 12: 1-82.

Freud, S. (1914) On narcissism. *Standard Edition,* 14: 67-102.

Freud, S. (1921) Group psychology and the analysis of the ego. *Standard Edition*, 18: 65-143.

Freud, S. (1923) The ego and the id. *Standard Edition* 19: 1-66.

Freud, S. (1927) The future of an illusion. *Standard Edition*, 21: 1-56.

Freud, S. (1930) Civilization and its discontents. *Standard Edition*, 21: 57-145.

Freud, S. (1931) Libidinal types. *Standard Edition*, 21: 215-220.

Freud, S. (1936) "A disturbance of memory on the Acropolis" *Standard Edition* 22: 237-248.

Fuchs, S. (1965) *Rebellious Prophets: A Study of Messianic Movements in Indian Religions*. New York: Asia Publishing House.

Gager, J.G. (1975) *Kingdom and Community: The Social World of Early Christianity*. Englewood Cliffs, NJ: Prentice-Hall.

Goen, C.C. (1962) *Revivalism and Separatism in New England, 1740- 1800*. New Haven: Yale University Press.

Goldstein, J.A. (1987) How the authors of 1 and 2 Maccabees treated the "messianic" promises. In Neusner, J., Green, W.S., and Frerichs, E.S. (eds.) *Judaisms and Their Messiahs at the Turn of the Christian Era*. Cambridge: Cambridge University Press, 69-96.

Green, W.S. (1987) Introduction: Messianism in Judaism: rethinking the question. In Neusner, J., Green, W.S., and Frerichs, E.S. (eds.) *Judaisms and Their Messiahs at the Turn of the Christian Era*. Cambridge: Cambridge University Press, 1-13.

Greenacre, P. (1969) The fetish and the transitional object. In *Emotional Growth*, Vol. I. New York: International Universities Press, 1971, 315-334.

Greenacre, P. (1970). The transitional object and the fetish: with special reference to the role of illusion. In *Emotional Growth*, Vol. I. New York: International Universities Press, 1971, 335-352.

Grolnick, S.A., and Barkin, L. (eds.) (1978) *Between Reality and Fantasy: Transitional Objects and Transitional Phenomena*. New York: Aronson.

Grunberger, B. (1989) *New Essays on Narcissism*. London: Free Association Books.

Guiart, J. (1970) The millennarian aspect of conversion in Christianity in the South Pacific. In Thrupp, S.L. (ed.) *Millennial Dreams in Action: Studies in Revolutionary Religious Movements*. New York: Schocken Books, 122-138.

Handy, R.T. (1984) *A Christian America: Protestant Hopes and Historical Realities*. 2nd edit. New York: Oxford University Press.

Harrell, Jr., D.E. (1984) Dispensational premillennialism and the religious right. In Bettis, J., and Johannesen, S.K. (eds.) *The Return of the Millennium*. Barrytown, NY: International Religious Foundation, 9-34.

Harrington, S.J., D.J. (1982) *The Light of All Nations: Essays on the Church in New Testament Research*. Wilmington: Glazier.

Harrison, F.R. (1984) Epistemic frames and eschatological stories. In Bettis, J., and Johannesen, S.K. (eds.) *The Return of the Millennium*. Barrytown, NY: International Religious Foundation, 59-85.

Hayley, T. (1990) Charisma, suggestion, psychoanalysts, medicine-men and metaphor. *International Review of Psychoanalysis*, 17: 1-10.

Hecht, R.D. (1987) Philo and Messiah. In Neusner, J., Green, W.S., and Frerichs, E.S. (eds.) *Judaisms and Their Messiahs at the Turn of the Christian Era*. Cambridge: Cambridge University Press, 139-168.

Heimert, A. (1966) *Religion and The American Mind: From the Great Awakening to the Revolution*. Cambridge: Harvard University Press.

Hofstadter, R. (1967) *The Paranoid Style in American Politics and Other Essays*. New York: Vintage Books.

Hong, K.M. (1978) The transitional phenomena: a theoretical integration. *Psychoanalytic Study of the Child* 33: 47-79.

Horsley, R.A. (1987) *Jesus and the Spiral of Violence: Popular Jewish Resistance in Roman Palestine*. San Francisco: Harper and Row.

Hultgard, A, (1980) The ideal `Levite,' the davidic messiah, and the saviour Priest in the Testaments of the Twelve Patriarchs. In Nickelsburg, G.W.E., and Collins, J.J. (eds.) *Ideal Figures in Ancient Judaism*. Chico, CA: Scholars Press, 93-110.

Hummel, R.P. (1975) Psychology of charismatic followers. *Psychological Reports*, 37: 759-770.

Idel, M. (1988) *Kabbalah: New Perspectives*. New Haven: Yale University Press.

Isenberg, S.R. (1974) Millenarism in Greco-Roman Palestine. *Religion*, 4: 26-46.

Jackson, H. (1975) The resurrection belief of the earliest church: a response to the failure of prophecy. *Journal of Religion*, 55: 415-425.

Jacobson, T. (1976) *The Treasures of Darkness: A History of Mesopotamian Religion*. New Haven: Yale University Press.

Jamison, A.L. (1961) Religions on the Christian perimeter. In Smith, J.W., and Jamison, A.L. (eds.) *The Shaping of American Religion*. Princeton, NJ: Princeton University Press, 162-231.

Johannesen, S.K. (1984) Christianity, millennialism and civic life: the origins of the American republic. In Bettis, J., and Johannesen, S.K. (eds.) *The Return of the Millennium*. Barrytown, NY: International Religious Foundation, 207-231.

Jonas, H. (1963) *The Gnostic Religion*. 2nd edit. Boston: Beacon Press.

Kagan, R.L. (1990) *Lucrecia's Dreams: Politics and Prophecy in Sixteenth-Century Spain*. Berkeley, CA: University of California Press.

Kaminsky, H. (1970) The Free Spirit in the Hussite revolution. In Thrupp, S.L. (ed.) *Millennial Dreams in Action: Studies in Revolutionary Religious Movements*. New York: Schocken Books, 166-186.

Kaplan, H.B. (1972) Toward a general theory of psychosocial deviance: the case of aggressive behavior. *Social Science and Medicine*, 6: 593-617.

Karris, O.F.M., R.J. (1990) The Gospel According to Luke. In Brown, S.S., R.E., Fitzmyer, S.J., J.A., and Murphy, O. Carm., R. E. (eds.) *The New Jerome Biblical Commentary*. Englewood Cliffs, NJ: Prentice Hall, 675-721.

Kee, H.C. (1987) Christology in Mark's gospel. In Neusner, J., Green, W.S., and Frerichs, E.S. (eds.) *Judaisms and Their Messiahs at the Turn of the Christian Era*. Cambridge: Cambridge University Press, 187-208.

Kernberg, O. (1975) *Borderline Conditions and Pathological Narcissism*. New York: Aronson.

Kernberg, O. (1979) Regression in organizational leadership. *Psychiatry*, 42: 29-39.

Kets de Vries, M.F.R. (1977) Crisis leadership and the paranoid potential: an organizational perspective. *Bulletin of the Menninger Clinic*, 41: 349-365.

Kets de Vries, M.F.R., and Miller, D. (1985) Narcissism and leadership: an object relations perspective. *Human Relations*, 38: 583-601.

Klausner, J. (1955) *The Messianic Idea in Israel*. New York: Macmillan.

Kohut, H. (1971) *The Analysis of the Self*. New York: International Universities Press.

Kohut, H. (1973) Psychoanalysis in a troubled world. *Annual of Psychoanalysis*, 1: 3-25.

Kohut, H. (1977) *The Restoration of the Self*. New York: International Universities Press.

Küng, H. (1967) *The Church*. New York: Sheed and Ward.

LaBarre, W. (1970) *The Ghost Dance: Origins of Religion*. Garden City, NY: Doubleday.

Leavy, S.A. (1986) A Paschalian meditation on psychoanalysis and religious experience. *Cross Currents*, Summer 147-55.

Léon-Dufour, S.J., X. (1968) Jesus' testimony concerning his own person. In O'Donovan, S.J., L.J. (ed.) *Word and Mystery: Biblical Essays on the Person and Mission of Christ*. New York: Newman Press, 185-199.

Lovejoy, D.S. (ed.) (1969) *Religious Enthusiasm and the Great Awakening*. Englewood Cliffs, NJ: Prentice-Hall.

Lyonnet, S.J., S. (1968a) The return of Christ to God according to St. Paul. In O'Donovan, S.J., L.J. (ed.) *Word and Mystery: Biblical Essays on the Person and Mission of Christ*. New York: Newman Press, 201-229.

Lyonnet, S.J., S. (1968b) St. Luke's infancy narrative. In O'Donovan, S.J., L.J. (ed.) *Word and Mystery: Biblical Essays on the Person and Mission of Christ*. New York: Newman Press, 143-154.

Mack, B.L. (1987) Wisdom makes a difference: alternatives to "Messianic" configurations. In Neusner, J., Green, W.S., and Frerichs, E.S. (eds.) *Judaisms and Their Messiahs at the Turn of the Christian Era*. Cambridge: Cambridge University Press, 15-48.

Mann, D. (1992) The infantile origins of the creation and apocalyptic myths. *International Review of Psychoanalysis*, 19: 471-482.

Manuel, F.E., and Manuel, F.P. (1979) *Utopian Thought in the Western World.* Cambridge, MA: Harvard Univerisity Press.

MacRae, S.J., G. (1987) Messiah and gospel. In Neusner, J., Green, W.S., and Frerichs, E.S. (eds.) *Judaisms and Their Messiahs at the Turn of the Christian Era.* Cambridge: Cambridge University Press, 169-185.

McKenzie, S.J., J.L. (1968) Aspects of Old Testament thought. In Brown, R.E., Fitzmyer, J.A., and Murphy, R.E. (eds.) *The Jerome Biblical Commentary.* Englewood Cliffs, NJ: Prentice-Hall, vol. II, 736-767.

McNearney, C.L. (1984) George Whitefield: a literal metaphor. In Bettis, J., and Johannesen, S.K. (eds.) *The Return of the Millennium.* Barrytown, NY: International Religious Foundation, 35-57.

Meeks, W.A. (1979) `Since then you would need to go out of the world': group boundaries in Pauline Christianity. In Ryan, T.J. (ed.) *Critical History and Biblical Faith.* Villanova, PA: College Theological Society/ Horizons, 4-29.

Meissner, S.J., W.W. (1973) Notes on the psychology of hope. *Journal of Religion and Health,* 12: 7-29; 120-139.

Meissner, S.J., W.W. (1976) Schreber and the paranoid process. *Annual of Psychoanalysis,* 4: 3-40.

Meissner, S.J., W.W. (1978) *The Paranoid Process.* New York: Aronson.

Meissner, S.J., W.W. (1984a) *The Borderline Spectrum: Differential Diagnosis and Developmental Issues.* New York: Jason Aronson.

Meissner, S.J., W.W. (1984b) The cult phenomenon: psychoanalytic perspective. *Psychoanalytic Study of Society,* 10: 91-111.

Meissner, S.J., W.W. (1984c) *Psychoanalysis and Religious Experience.* New Haven: Yale University Press.

Meissner, S.J., W.W. (1986a) The oedipus complex and the paranoid process. *Annual of Psychoanalysis,* 14: 221-243.

Meissner, S.J., W.W. (1986b) *Psychotherapy and the Paranoid Process.* Northvale, NJ: Jason Aronson.

Meissner, S.J., W.W. (1987a) The cult phenomenon and the paranoid process. *Psychoanalytic Study of Society,* 12: 69-95.

Meissner, S.J., W.W. (1987b) *Life and Faith: Psychological Perspectives on Religious Experience.* Washington, DC: Georgetown University Press.

Meissner, S.J., W.W. (1988) The origins of Christianity. *Psychoanalytic Study of Society,* 13: 29-62.

Meissner, S.J., W.W. (1989) Hope. In Flach, F. (ed.) *Stress and Its Management.* New York: Norton, pp. 82-90. [Directions in Psychiatry, Monograph Series, No. 6]

Meissner, S.J., W. W. (1990a) Jewish messianism and the cultic process. *Psychoanalytic Study of Society,* 15: 347-370.

Meissner, S.J., W.W. (1990b) The role of transitional conceptualization in religious thought. In Smith, J.H., and Handelman, S.A. (eds.) *Psychoanalysis and Religion.* Baltimore: Johns Hopkins University Press, 95-116.

Meissner, S.J., W.W. (1991) The pathology of belief systems. *Psychoanalysis and Contemporary Thought,* 15: 99-128.

Meissner, S.J., W.W. (1992a) *Ignatius of Loyola: The Psychology of a Saint.* New Haven: Yale University Press.

Meissner, S.J., W.W. (1992b) Religious thinking as transitional conceptualization. *Psychoanalytic Review,* 79: 175-196.

Meissner, S.J., W.W. (in process) *The Cultic Process.*

Merton, R.K. (1957) *Social Theory and Social Structure.* Rev. ed. New York: Free Press.

Modell, A.H. (1991) A confusion of tongues or whose reality is it? *Psychoanalytic Quarterly,* 60: 227-244.

Moltmann, J. (1967) *Theology of Hope: On the Ground and the Implications of a Christian Eschatology.* London: SCM Press.

Murray, J.M. (1964) Narcissism and the ego ideal. *Journal of the American Psychoanalytic Association,* 12: 477-511.

Neusner, J. (1984) *Messiah in Context: Israel's History and Destiny in Formative Judaism.* Philadelphia, PA: Fortress Press.

Neusner, J. (1985) *Revisioning the Written Records of a Nascent Religion.* Chico, CA: Scholars Press.

Nickelsburg, G.W.E. (1987) Salvation without and with a messiah: developing beliefs in writings ascribed to Enoch. In Neusner, J., Green, W.S., and Frerichs, E.S. (eds.) *Judaisms and Their Messiahs at the Turn of the Christian Era.* Cambridge: Cambridge University Press, 49-68.

Nyang, S.S. (1984) Millennialism in African traditional thought. In Bettis, J., and Johannesen, S.K. (eds.) *The Return of the Millennium.* Barrytown, NY: International Religious Foundation, 181-206.

Olden, C. (1941) About the fascinating effect of the narcissistic personality. *American Imago,* 2: 347-355.

Osiek, C. (1989) The new handmaid: the Bible and the social sciences. *Theological Studies,* 50: 260-278.

Otto, R. (1917) *The Idea of the Holy.* New York: Oxford University Press, 1958.

Pannenberg, W. (1969) *Theology and the Kingdom of God.* Philadelphia, PA: Westminster Press.

Perkins, P. (1990) The gospel according to John. In Brown, R.E., Fitzmyer, J.A., and Murphy, R.E. (eds.) *New Jerome Biblical Commentary.* Englewood Cliffs, NJ: Prentice-Hall, 942-985.

Pinderhughes, C.A. (1970) The universal resolution of ambivalence by paranoia with an example of black and white. *American Journal of Psychotherapy,* 24: 597-610.

Pinderhughes, C.A. (1971) Somatic, psychic, and social sequelae of loss. *Journal of the American Psychoanalytic Association,* 19: 670-696.

Pinderhughes, C.A. (1979) Differential bonding: toward a psycho-physiological theory of stereotyping. *American Journal of Psychiatry,* 136: 33-37.

References / 361

Pinderhughes, C.A. (1982) Paired differential bonding in biological, psychological and social systems. *American Journal of Social Psychiatry*, 2: 5-14.

Pinderhughes, C.A. (1986) Differential bonding from infancy to international conflict. *Psychoanalytic Inquiry*, 6: 155-173.

Pollock, G.H. (1964) On symbiosis and symbiotic neurosis. *International Journal of Psychoanalysis*, 45: 1-30.

Pollock, G.H. (1975) On mourning, immortality, and utopia. *Journal of the American Psychoanalytic Association*, 23: 334-362.

Pollock, G.H. (1989) *The Mourning-Liberation Process*. 2 vols. Madison, CT: International Universities Press.

Post, J.M. (1986) Narcissism and the charismatic leader-follower relationship. *Political Psychology*, 7: 675-688.

Pruyser, P.W. (1974) *Between Belief and Unbelief*. New York: Harper and Row.

Pruyser, P.W. (1979) Psychological roots and branches of belief. In Malony, H.N., and Spilka, B. (eds.) *Religion in Psychodynamic Perspective: The Contributions of Paul W. Pruyser*. New York: Oxford University Press, 1991, 155-169.

Pruyser, P.W. (1983) *The Play of the Imagination: Toward a Psychoanalysis of Culture*. New York: International Universities Press.

Pruyser, (1985) Forms and functions of the imagination in religion. In Malony, H.N., and Spilka, B. (eds.) *Religion in Psychodynamic Perspective: The Contributions of Paul W. Pruyser*. New York: Oxford University Press, 1991, 170-188.

Rausch, D.A. (1984) Premillennialism and social concern, 1865-1940: a comparison with historical trends in Protestantism in the United States. In Bettis, J., and Johannesen, S.K. (eds.) *The Return of the Millennium*. Barrytown, NY: International Religious Foundation, 87-118.

Reich, W. (1949) *Character Analysis*. New York: Farrar, Straus and Giroux, 1972.

Ribeiro, R. (1970) Brazilian messianic movements. In Thrupp, S.L. (ed.) *Millennial Dreams in Action: Studies in Revolutionary Religious Movements*. New York: Schocken Books, 55-69.

Ricoeur, P. (1970) *Freud and Philosophy*. New Haven: Yale University Press.

Robinson, J.A.T. (1958) *Jesus and His Coming*. New York: Abingdon Press.

Rochlin, G. (1965) *Griefs and Discontents: The Forces of Change*. Boston: Little, Brown.

Ruether, R.R. (1972) An invitation to Jewish-Christian dialogue: in what sense can we say that Jesus was "the Christ"? *The Ecumenist*, 10: 17-24.

Sachs, S.J., J.R. (1991) Current eschatology: universal salvation and the problem of hell. *Theological Studies*, 52: 227-254.

Sandler, J. (1960) On the concept of superego. *Psychoanalytic Study of the Child*, 15: 128-162.

362 \ *Thy Kingdom Come*

Schnackenburg, R. (1963) *God's Rule and Kingdom*. New York: Herder and Herder.

Scholem, G. (1941) *Major Trends in Jewish Mysticism*. New York: Schocken Books.

Scholem, G. (1971) *The Messianic Idea in Judaism and Other Essays on Jewish Spirituality*. New York: Schocken Books.

Scholem, G. (1973) *Sabbatai Sevi: The Mystical Messiah*. Princeton: Princeton University Press.

Scholem, G. (1974) *Kabbalah*. New York: New American Library.

Scholem, G. (1991) *On the Mystical Shape of the Godhead: Basic Concepts in the Kabbalah*. New York: Schocken Books.

Schreiber, A. (1977) *Die Gemeinde in Korinth. Versuch einer gruppendynamischen Betrachtung der Entwicklung der Gemeinde von Korinth auf der Basis der ersten Korintherbriefe*. Münster: Aschendorff.

Schweitzer, A. (1914) *The Mystery of the Kingdom of God: The Secret of Jesus' Messiahship and Passion*. Buffalo, NY: Prometheus Books, 1985.

Scroggs, R. (1975) The earliest Christian communities as sectarian movement. In: *Christianity, Judaism and Other Greco-Roman Cults — Studies for Morton Smith at Sixty*, ed. J. Neusner, volume II: 1-23. Leiden: Brill.

Segal, A.F. (1990) *Paul the Convert: The Apostolate and Apostasy of Saul the Pharisee*. New Haven, CT: Yale University Press.

Selengut, C. (1984) Eschatology and the construction of alternative realities: toward a social conflict perspective on millennialism. In Bettis, J., and Johannesen, S.K. (eds.) *The Return of the Millennium*. Barrytown, NY: International Religious Foundation, 167-179.

Shepperson, G. (1970a) The comparative study of millennarian movements. In Thrupp, S.L. (ed.) *Millennial Dreams in Action: Studies in Revolutionary Religious Movements*. New York: Schocken Books, pp. 44-52.

Shepperson, G. (1970b) Nyasaland and the millennium. In Thrupp, S.L. (ed.) *Millennial Dreams in Action: Studies in Revolutionary Religious Movements*. New York: Schocken Books, pp. 144-159.

Simpson, G.E. (1970) The Ras Tafari movement in Jamaica in its millennial aspect. In Thrupp, S.L. (ed.) *Millennial Dreams in Action: Studies in Revolutionary Religious Movements*. New York: Schocken Books, pp. 160-165.

Smith, J.Z. (1978) Too much kingdom, too little community. *Zygon*, 13: 123-130.

Smith, M. (1959) What is implied by the variety of messianic figures? *Journal of Biblical Literature*, 78: 66-72.

Stanley, S.J., D.M. (1968a) Christ as savior in the primitive Christian preaching. In O'Donovan, S.J., L.J. (ed.) *Word and Mystery: Biblical Essays on the Person and Mission of Christ*. New York: Newman Press, 21-46.

Stanley, S.J., D.M. (1968b) Christ as savior in the synoptic gospels. In O'Donovan, S.J., L.J. (ed.) *Word and Mystery: Biblical Essays on the Person and Mission of Christ*. New York: Newman Press, 47-67.

Stanley, S.J., D.M., and Brown, S.S., R.E. (1968) Aspects of New Testament thought. In Brown, R.E., Fitzmyer, J.A., and Murphy, R.E. (eds.) (1968) *The Jerome Biblical Commentary*. Englewood Cliffs, NJ: Prentice-Hall, 768-799.

Stein, H.F. (1986) The influence of psychogeography upon the conduct of international relations: clinical and metapsychological considerations. *Psychoanalytic Inquiry*, 6: 193-222.

Stone, D. (1982) The charismatic authority of Werner Erhard. In Wallis, R. (ed.) *Millennialism and Charisma*. Belfast, Northern Ireland: Queen's University Press, 141-175.

Strout, C. (1974) *The New Heaven and New Earth*. New York: Harper and Row.

Stuhlmueller, C.P., C. (1968) Post-exilic period: spirit, apocalyptic. In Brown, R.E., Fitzmyer, J.A., and Murphy, R.E. (eds.) (1968) *The Jerome Biblical Commentary*. Englewood Cliffs, NJ: Prentice-Hall, 337-343.

Sweet, L.I. (1979 Millennialism in America: recent studies. *Theological Studies*, 40: 510-531.

Talmon, S. (1987) Waiting for the messiah: the spiritual universe of the Qumran covenanters. In Neusner, J., Green, W.S., and Frerichs, E.S. (eds.) *Judaisms and Their Messiahs at the Turn of the Christian Era*. Cambridge: Cambridge University Press, 111-137.

Talmon, Y. (1962) Pursuit of the millennium: the relation between religion and social change. *Archives Europiénnes de Sociologie*, 3: 149-164.

Theissen, G. (1982) *The Social Setting of Pauline Christianity: Essays on Corinth*. Philadelphia: Fortress.

Thrupp, S.L. (1970) Millennial dreams in action: a report on the conference discussion. In Thrupp, S.L. (ed.) *Millennial Dreams in Action: Studies in Revolutionary Religious Movements*. New York: Schocken Books, 11-27.

Townsend, J.B. (1984) Anthropological perspectives on new religious movements. In Bettis, J., and Johannesen, S.K. (eds.) *The Return of the Millennium*. Barrytown, NY: International Religious Foundation, 137-151.

Tracy, D. (1978) A theological response to 'Kingdom and Community.' *Zygon*, 13: 131-135.

Trevor-Roper, H.R. (1969) *The European Witch-craze of the Sixteenth and Seventeenth Centuries and Other Essays*. New York: Harper Torchbooks.

Van der Kroef, J.M. (1970) Messianic movements in the Celebes, Sumatra, and Borneo. In Thrupp, S.L. (ed.) *Millennial Dreams in Action: Studies in Revolutionary Religious Movements*. New York: Schocken Books, 80-121.

Vawter, C.M., B. (1968) The gospel according to John. In Brown, R.E., Fitzmyer, J.A., and Murphy, R.E. (eds.) *The Jerome Biblical Commentary*. Englewood Cliffs, NJ: Prentice-Hall, vol. II, 414-466.

Viviano, O.P., B.T. (1990) The Gospel According to Matthew. In Brown, S.S., R.E., Fitzmyer, S.J., J.A., and Murphy, O. Carm., R. E. (eds.) *The New Jerome Biblical Commentary.* Englewood Cliffs, NJ: Prentice Hall, 630-674.

Volkan, V.D. (1985) The need to have enemies and allies: a developmental approach. *Political Psychology*, 6: 219-247.

Volkan, V.D. (1986) The narcissism of minor differences in the psychological gap between opposing nations. *Psychoanalytic Inquiry*, 6: 175-191.

Volkan, V.D. (1987) Psychological concepts useful in building of political foundations between nations: track II diplomacy. *Journal of the American Psychoanalytic Association*, 35: 903-935.

Volkan, V.D. (1988) *The Need to Have Enemies and Allies: From Clinical Practice to International Relationships.* Northvale, NJ: Jason Aronson.

Wallace, A.F.C. (1956) Revitalization movements. *American Anthropologist*, 58: 264-281.

Wallace, A.F.C. (1966) *Religion: An Anthropological View.* New York: Random House.

Wallis, R. (1982a) Introduction: millennialism and charisma. In Wallis, R. (ed.) *Millennialism and Charisma.* Belfast, Northern Ireland: Queen's University Press, 1-11.

Wallis, R. (ed.) (1982b) *Millennialism and Charisma.* Belfast, Northern Ireland: Queen's University Press.

Weber, M. (1920) *Gesammelte Aufsätze zur Religionssociologie.* 2 vols. Tübingen.

Weber, M. (1922) *The Sociology of Religion.* Boston: Beacon Press.

Weber, M. (1947) *The Theory of Social and Economic Organization.* (ed. by T. Parsons) New York: Oxford University Press.

Weiss, J. (1892) *Die Predigt Jesu vom Reiche Gottes.* Göttingen: Vondenhoeck & Ruprecht, 1964.

Wernik, U. (1975) Frustrated beliefs and early Christianity: a psychological enquiry into the gospels of the New Testament. *Numen*, 22: 96-130.

Westphal, M. (1990) Paranoia and piety: reflections on the Schreber case. In Smith, J.H., and Handelman, S.A. (eds.) *Psychoanalysis and Religion.* Baltimore, MD: Johns Hopkins University Press. 117-135.

Wilner, A.R. (1984) *The Spellbinders.* New Haven: Yale University Press.

Winnicott, D.W. (1953) Transitional objects and transitional phenomena. *International Journal of Psychoanalysis* 34: 89-97.

Winnicott, D.W. (1971) *Playing and Reality.* New York: Basic Books.

Worsley, P. (1968) *The Trumpet Shall Sound.* New York: Schocken Books.

Yinger, J.M. (1957) *Religion, Society and the Individual.* New York: Macmillan.

Zaleznik, A. (1974) Charismatic and consensus leaders: a psychological comparison. *Bulletin of the Menninger Clinic*, 38: 222-238.

Index